6/94

THE REBEL EMPEROR

THE REBEL EMPEROR

THE ANCIENT SECRET:
in search of the Holy Grail

JEZEBEL AND THE DAYSPRING
(a novel)

By FLAVIA ANDERSON

The
Rebel
Emperor

By FLAVIA ANDERSON

Doubleday & Company, Inc., Garden City, N. Y., 1959

No dialogue has been used except that which was authentically recorded by contemporaries.

Library of Congress Catalog Card Number 59-7900
Copyright © 1958 by Flavia Anderson
All Rights Reserved
Printed in the United States of America

ACKNOWLEDGEMENTS

I WISH TO ACKNOWLEDGE with sincerest thanks the kindness of Doctor John Foster, Professor of Ecclesiastical History, Dean of the Faculty of Divinity at Glasgow University, for his advice on what books to read, and for general guidance and constructive criticism of the manuscript. Thanks are due also to the London Missionary Society for permission to publish letters from its archives, and to Miss Irene Fletcher, the archivist, who helped me to find them.

I am particularly grateful to the Reverend Father J. Dehergne, S.J., archivist at Les Fontaines, Chantilly, Oise, for his patience in copying out for me various reports and letters, and for advice on what books to read regarding the Roman Catholic missions in China.

And finally I owe a great debt of gratitude to the staff of Glasgow University Library, and especially to Miss Enid Armstrong for her unfailing help and patience with any and every problem which can arise in research.

MAPS

A map showing The March of the Taipings in on page 162.
A map showing the land over which the Faithful Prince and Gordon waged war is on page 266.

FOREWORD

THE APPALLING NUMBER of casualties on the western front in the First World War made a deep impression on the conscious mind of nearly everyone in Europe, because nearly everyone was concerned. Death, and the multiplication of it into astronomical figures, means very little to the individual unless it touches his own way of life. Between the years 1851 and 1865 it has been calculated that twenty million human beings were destroyed in China in a civil war known as the Taiping Rebellion.

Sun Yat-sen was the first to turn back the attention of the modern world, and to point to the Taiping movement as the earliest expression of Chinese nationalism; for it was a rebellion aimed at upsetting the dynasty of Manchu Emperors and the rule of the Manchus, who had conquered and battened upon China since 1644. The Communists have also shown interest in the history of a movement which they claim was aimed at the "Haves" by the "Have-nots". Both Nationalists and Communists, writing either for the Chinese or for the Russians, have chosen to ignore the religious character of what was in fact a Holy War, a Crusade, and in Europe it has been forgotten that the issue at stake was whether China was to become, at least officially, a Christian country. For the leader of the rebellion claimed to be a Christian, and one, moreover, not merely instructed by a western missionary, not merely taught by man, but called by God, given a special revelation, caught up to heaven as had been St. Paul, to speak directly with the Almighty as had Moses. There in heaven he received the command to rule China and to preach the gospel, and in that cause twenty million souls perished violently. Had he succeeded, and had he preserved his own soul from the furious counter-attacks of the Devil, China would today in all probability be nominally a Christian country ruled by a dynasty of Christian Emperors.

This is the story of the man and of the movement known as the Taiping Rebellion.

1

HE WAS BORN ON the first day of January in the year 1814 in a little village in the district of Hua-hsien, which lay thirty miles north of Canton. His family name was Hung. So, for that matter, was the name of all the other people in the village, of whom there were about five hundred, for they were all of one clan and they were all Hak-kas.

The Hak-ka folk were strange, said their Cantonese neighbours, who lived in the villages nearby; and they would have cheerfully asked, in their Chinese fashion, "Can any good thing come out of Nazareth?" had they been consulted about the child's destiny, for they held the Hak-kas in contempt and called them "foreigners", even as the Saxons called the Welsh "foreigners", when they had reduced the original possessors of the land to subjection and poverty. The Hak-kas claimed, on the contrary, that, far from being newcomers, they had come from Shan-tung in the third century B.C. They had been a mountain people, and now their villages were dotted all over this province of Kwang-tung and in the mountains of Kwang-si to the west, and they could afford to disregard the slights and jibes of the Cantonese, for they were taller and stronger, if a little darker, than these small southern Chinese, who had also migrated into that part of the world, but at a later period. So the Hak-kas kept themselves to themselves, preserved their own language, and had all the pride of a race which studies to maintain its identity. To maintain life itself was not easy, however, for the great enemy was poverty and the hunger that is never far from it.

The village consisted of only three rows of houses, all built from the mud of the fields. There were six in each row and between each row ran a narrow lane. The house in which the child had been born, and to which the members of the clan were even now going to pay their congratulations, was in the backmost row on the west side, and, as people would afterwards point out, it was a sorry birthplace for a future Emperor.

Within the door the open space of a courtyard barely twelve feet square was already crowded with those who had come to say and do the proper thing, so that the female cousins who had been attending the mother could hardly have access to the cooking and bathing rooms which led off the yard, or to the one large room which gave on to the court and was open to light and air save for a paper screen. Here sat the father, Ching-yang. It was important to know how to address him and how to offer felicitations with propriety, for, though he was as poor as any man in the village, he, or rather the old grandfather, was nevertheless the hereditary chief of this branch of the clan, and he himself was the elected headman of the village, and stood between the villagers and oppression in the shape of the district magistrate. Fortunately the newly arrived child was a boy, for another mouth to feed, if it had been that of a female, would have made the congratulations sound forced. Ching-yang had only taken a second wife because his first, of the family of Li, had died a year or two ago, leaving him with two young sons and a daughter, and no one save the venerable grandmother to care for them. Now this woman of the Chu family had promptly added to his responsibilities, while she herself lay helpless. Such was life! the chattering villagers agreed.

Therefore amidst the bustle there was no one to supervise the doings of the children, so that the two boys, Yen-fa and Yen-ta, could raid the tiny cook-house and sample the cakes and sweetmeats, and only their two-year-old sister, Hsiu-ying, could point a chubby but accusing finger at their smeared mouths, as she balanced herself unsteadily on the floor of beaten sand and lime. Stupid and lazy boys both, thought the neighbours, but dutiful and obedient for the most part, for Ching-yang would never have countenanced unfilial behaviour. They were good enough to herd the geese and to carry night-soil. The elder of the two could already bestride a buffalo and take it to the hill pastures. But neither boy, they felt, would ever be elected in his father's place, for the duties of a headman were not light. Several of the men who had just paid their respects glanced back at him now before they took their leave. He was already venerable and bearded, though he was only about thirty-nine years of age. He it was who acted as arbitrator in their small disputes, and saved them from the dire expense of a lawsuit and the even worse necessity of entering the yamen of the district magistrate, where the "squeeze" of the under-clerks exacting bribes could reduce a man to penury in no time at all. It was the headman's duty to collect the taxes for the magistrate and also to help with the census report. Well, now he would have another name to inscribe on his list, his own third son's. The child was to be called Huo-hsiu, "Fire-flash".

Within little more than a year the lame kinsman who acted as doorman had yet another duty, and that was to dandle the new little Hung, and presently to guide his first tottering steps down the village lane and back to the inner chambers of his mother and grandmother. Sometimes, when she could spare the time from the house and the kitchen, the mother took the boy's hand herself, and went to show the neighbours the new infant cap she had bought him, embroidered with a lucky text and gilt images to decorate the frontlet, the eight genie of the Taoists. She could walk with ease, for none of the Hak-kas ever bound their feet, and, moreover, she was a poor woman, accustomed to help on the land. The headman had a few rice fields, some pigs and poultry, and two buffaloes for ploughing. Now the older boys were doing man's work to cultivate the rice and grow sweet potatoes.

At six years old Fire-flash was the friend of everyone in the village. Afterwards they would recount that he was open and straightforward and always laughing, but already he was so quick-witted that he found the company of some even of the older boys irksome, and he teased them for their slowness and stupidity.

As a concession to his precocity, on a certain night in that year he was allowed to stay up late and listen to his father making the formal account of the ancestors and the history of the clan to the second son, Yen-ta, who had attained the necessary age of ten years. Fire-flash could successfully argue that, although four years younger, he could pick out and distinguish more characters than either of his elder brothers. Secretly and to himself the father acknowledged that his third son showed promise of being a scholar, and Ching-yang was saving money so that the child might be able to go to school in the following year. Perhaps Fire-flash would advance them all by attaining office. If so, he would not be the first of the clan to acquire honours and dignity. So much the father was at pains to point out that very evening.

Any clan book which might have existed had not survived warfare and extreme poverty, but memory was long, and the names of ancestors were cherished. With a few pages of characters spread upon his knees to aid memory, he gave as clear an account of his clan as his father before him had given—the venerable old grandfather of eighty years who sat nodding a little sleepily in the only other chair in the common room.

Since mankind is fruitful and multiplies at an astounding rate, it is evident that nearly every man on earth could claim a noble ancestor somewhere at some time if all the facts were known. Because in China genealogies were kept with the care accorded to sacred things, they often went back two thousand years; and it was not surprising, therefore, that the poorest of men could often claim a noble ancestor. From the twelfth century onwards, eighty members of the Hung family had held office at the Imperial court. Some of the family had been allied by marriage to the Ming dynasty, and had remained faithful to them even when the Mings had been ousted, betrayed by the very Tartars from Manchuria whose help they had called in to quell a rebellion. Thus the Mings, unwitting and trusting their allies, had brought about their own downfall, and forever after China had been ruled by those same Manchus who had driven the true Son of Heaven from the Dragon Throne in 1644. The Ming heir had fled from the Forbidden City in Peking, and had set up his court at Nanking, and it was from this city that Ching-yang's ancestor, the Generalissimo Hung Cheng-chou, had fought the last battle in defence of his Imperial master. Even after the last remaining scions of the Mings had fled beyond the southernmost borders of China, so that no one really knew if any descendants still survived amongst the mountains of Tong-king or in the Chinese border province of Kwang-si, even then the Generalissimo Hung had continued to devise schemes for the overthrow of the Tartar conquerors; but of this Ching-yang said nothing. His sons were too young, and the times too dangerous, to make them party to the feelings of discontent which had persisted for two hundred years.

He paused, thinking of how his ancestor the Generalissimo had, with calculated cunning, taken office under the new dynasty, and had instituted a policy for enervating the sturdy Tartars, who had been garrisoned in all the great cities of China. Divided into eight regiments, known as the Eight Banners, the bannermen, ostensibly to flatter them, had been forbidden to trade or to work in any way, and had been accorded hereditary pensions. The pensions drained the Imperial treasury and on them the idle bannermen grew fat and lazy, begetting numerous children who grew more idle still. They were no longer a race of fierce soldiers, though as spies they were to be feared. The north had accepted the Manchu dynasty, but not so the south and this province of Kwang-tung. Here resistance had continued from time to time for another hundred years, and indeed might still break out, would perhaps have broken out if the attempt upon the Emperor's life seven years ago had proved successful.

Another twelve months passed before young Hung went to school, and he was busy at boy's work, carrying human excrement in wooden buckets hung from a pole across his shoulders, to dump the precious stuff in the cesspit beside the muddy pool in front of the village. From there he could hear the pupils chanting their lessons in the school-house. Only about twenty boys attended, for it was useless to pay good money if a child showed no talent. His elder brothers had attended only long enough to learn a few characters. Secretly Hung was hoping that he would do better.

At last, in the year 1821, when he was seven years old, the moment came. Now he was a sturdy little boy. He could wash himself and rinse his mouth and put on his own blue cotton jacket, but he still needed help from his mother to braid his hair into a queue. His father held him by the hand, and between them there was much to carry, for they took with them the payment to the school teacher—lamp oil, salt and tea. The fifty pounds of rice had already been trundled in the wheelbarrow on the previous day, and there was besides to be a monthly payment of half a silver dollar. It was a terrible drain upon the family resources. No wonder all the pupils worked hard, but they did not all have Hung's talents nor his grim determination.

The hours in school were from six in the morning until five in the evening, but long before the break of day the children could be heard chanting the Classics in their village homes, and Hung's shrill young voice rivalled that of the cock proclaiming the dawn, as he started to learn, as all children did begin by learning, the Three Character Classic. It was in rhyme, and there were three

characters in each line, which made it easy to memorise, and it
started with the announcement, "Men at their birth are by nature
pure!" Thus at the first Hung was taught a doctrine utterly
opposed to the Christian belief that man is born in original sin.

Amongst all his new experiences in the school-house the most
pleasant, as every small boy finds, was the acquisition of the first
real friend. Feng Yun-shan was several years older than himself.
A distant cousin on the distaff side, he lived in a village only a
mile and a half away. Already Hung was finding it difficult to
accommodate himself to the level of the other little boys, to contain his irritation when he found them stupid, not to tease them
unduly, nor order them about in too lordly a fashion. He reached
for the companionship of an older and more intelligent comrade,
and the gentle-natured, scholarly Feng, who found his own
contemporaries rough and overbearing, was glad to discover
peace with the younger boy. Although at first he helped him
with his lessons, he soon found that, despite more than five years'
disparity in age, Hung bade fair to equal him in class.

That year of 1821, the first in school, was the year when the
Emperor Tao Kuang peacefully succeeded to the Dragon Throne,
and men began to hope that perhaps a new era of prosperity
would attend his reign, for hopes at the beginning are always high,
just as they always were at the New Year Feast. Therefore on that
1st of February, 1822, the day of the Feast, Hung could feel a
special atmosphere of gaiety throughout the village, or perhaps
it was only that he had begun to observe and question the doings
of men more closely. He could remember how in the previous
year he had heard the gongs and the drums and the fire-crackers:
a most satisfying cacophony. Then all the villagers had carried
lanterns, and there had been a bonfire, and everyone had visited
everyone else, and there had been plenty of good things to eat.
But he had not hitherto taken sufficient note of the exciting preparations on the eve of the Feast. His mother was cleaning the
image of the kitchen god before restoring it to its niche above
the stove. His father had placed the table in the very centre of the
living room and behind it the high-backed chair, and now over
the back of the chair he was hanging three scrolls with paintings
upon them. Hung knew that the paintings represented the most
celestial and superb Shang-ti, the chief deity of the Taoist priests.
On the table, as upon an altar, his mother had placed three cups

of tea and three of rice-wine, and he learnt on the next day how
to kow-tow to this same Shang-ti and to burn the cheap paper
scrolls, inscribed with prayers, outside the door in the yard, in
order that those same prayers might ascend to heaven and be
heard.

That year they shared the New Year's cake served in syrup-
wine with a Taoist priest, who haunted the neighbourhood of
the villages and was the authority to be consulted for funeral rites
and the choosing of auspicious burial places, which he selected
by the art of geomancy. He wore a scarlet robe decorated with
the black dashes, both long and short, which represent the male
and female principle inherent in all things, and his hair was
dressed high in a bun and fixed with metal pins.

The boy Hung was too young to know that of the three approaches to life (for Confucianism could hardly be termed a religion) which peacefully co-existed in China—so that a man could
happily and placidly avail himself at births, marriages or death of
the services of Taoist or Buddhist priest or Confucian scholar, or
of all three together—Taoism was by far the oldest. It was the
original and universal religion of all the peoples of the world. It
held out to man the hope that, by means of an ecstatic sense of
union with all nature, he would rid himself of his self-conscious-
ness and the terrible isolation and loneliness that this brought him,
and thus eventually achieve reunion with the Godhead. Meditation, mysticism, trances, even Bacchic orgies were the means to
this end: the "Way". But it was possible for charlatans to abuse the
"Way" and to batten upon the credulous: like the priests of Baal,
whom the Taoist priests much resembled, they could tread fire,
pierce themselves with knives, chant incantations over amulets,
and forecast the future, all for a few cash coins. And if, as they
claimed, they held the secret of making alchemical gold, it did
not lessen their need for the silver which was currency. They
could, however, hold the fancy of a child more firmly than the
Buddhist priests, who were forever muttering their mantras in an
incomprehensible Sanskrit, hopelessly desiring to achieve a state
of no desire, and whose grey robes and heads entirely shaved
proclaimed them vowed to celibacy. Celibacy was odious to a
Confucian scholar, whose first duty was to beget a family, the
right behaviour and relationships of which should provide a pat-

tern whereby the very pattern of the universe could be reinspired and harmonised.

The tales of gods and heroes which the Taoist priests could tell went back to the dawn of time, and were so many and so various that the Taoists were of all folk the very best story-tellers. In return for the syrup-cake, the priest now told such a tale to the young Hung.

It concerned one Chang Tao-ling; and if Lao Tzu was the founder, or more rightly finder, of the "Way", the Tao, this Chang so ably marked out the path for those who followed that he had become the first Taoist to be venerated as a kind of pope. He had been born in the remote days of the Han dynasty, and had devoted himself to study and meditation in the mountains of western China, and there he had pursued in quietness of spirit the study of alchemy. Lao Tzu had himself reappeared on earth in supernatural shape to bestow upon him a mystic treatise, by perusing which Chang was able to distil the Elixir of Life.

One day, when he was experimenting with the precious tincture, a spirit appeared to him and bade him seek the hiding place of certain antique writings, promising that if he would but study these works, and undergo the discipline enjoined therein, he would be able to ascend to heaven. Chang Tao-ling did all that he was bid, and thus obtained the power of flying, of hearing that which is beyond hearing, and of leaving his body. After a thousand days of discipline he learnt to walk among the stars, and he fought with the king of the demons and divided the mountains and the seas, and could command the wind and the thunder. All the demons fled before him, and in nine years he gained the power to ascend to heaven. The mark of this great sage's seal was a powerful talisman against any form of illness, for he had held the secret of the Elixir of Life. It was the custom to paste up a portrait of this protector on the fifth day of the fifth moon to forfend calamity and sickness, and now the priest offered such a cheap paper scroll to Hung's father for a few cash, for it was evident to him that Hung's mother would within a few months give birth to another child.

The boy Hung glanced at the picture, which was already familiar to him, for it was the standard representation of the Taoist sage, who was richly dressed and brandished in one hand his magic sword, while in the other he held the cup containing the draught of immortality. Chang Tao-ling was riding a tiger, and in one paw the tiger grasped the master's magic seal, and with the others trampled upon loathsome and venomous creatures.

The portrait of the sage brought no very good luck, however, for the child born to the headman's wife was a female. If Hung's sister, Hsuan-chiao, caused little joy by her arrival, at any rate she caused little harm, for within a month the mother was strong enough to walk with her son the few miles to one of the neighbouring villages and there show him yet another newly born baby. The parents she had come to felicitate were her husband's third cousins. Hung, now a sturdily made peasant boy of eight years old, gazed with the usual embarrassment of his age, mixed with a sense of patronage, upon the crumpled infant face of Hung Jen-kan, and thus for the first time the future Emperor beheld his future Prime Minister.

2

BEFORE HE WAS thirteen years old Hung had mastered and committed to memory the whole of the Four Books and the Five Classics. When the neighbours spoke of the boy's talents, his father's face would brighten, and, though it was only polite to deprecate the possession of an unworthy and stupid son, Ching-yang could hardly bring himself to exercise such politeness. It was plain to all what a pride he took in the young Hung's accomplishments. Half the village was contributing to provide the provisions and clothing and school fees, because the investment would pay a handsome dividend when the boy should win to office.

Hung had in the last few years begun to realise the onus lying upon him. His friend Feng had a natural stoop, but it was the fashion for scholars to stoop as an indication of a studious disposition. At first Hung had tried to hold his own well-developed chest and shoulders in the required position, to emulate his gentle-natured comrade. But, in this last year, in truth he found his

shoulders sometimes weighed down with a new sense of responsibility. He knew now the import of the smiles that he met with
in the village, the enquiries as to his progress. He knew that
others sometimes went short of rice, content to wait for the
day when he could repay their trust. When he was questioned
about his school work, his mouth would twist wryly, and his heart
would suddenly beat faster. Supposing, supposing that he should
fail! Then he would turn to his books again, for he must not fail.
It was a heavy weight to carry for a boy not quite thirteen.

A series of examinations, open to anyone in the land, in theory
led up to the highest offices of state at Peking, though it was
common knowledge that graft and bribery had in the last hundred
years made ineffectual the original right of equal opportunity for
all. But it was not to be thought of that such evil practices could
block his own career, for surely talent and diligence would be
accorded recognition even in this degenerate age, he comforted
himself. He could, then, with confidence continue to contemplate
how he would exercise benevolence and reimburse his neighbours.

Once he had been granted the metropolitan degree at Peking,
he would be installed in office in the ninth rank of officials, the
lowest, and after a year or two's waiting he would with certainty
be given a district magistracy at the least. But never, never would
he be the magistrate of his own district of Hua-hsien, and that
was because the Manchu Emperor was afraid lest a man should
gain a following in his own birthplace and become a leader of
a territorial army. To obviate such a threat to the throne, not
only must one hold office in a distant province, but one could
hold it for three years only, before reporting back to Peking and
being automatically switched to yet another appointment, lest too
much influence had been gained with the people in the previous
one. And in each city of importance there would be a Tartar
general with a garrison of bannermen to spy upon the Chinese
official and thus reduce to almost nil any chances of rebellion.

Not that Hung wanted to rebel. All he desired was the means
to pay the debt to his neighbours, of which he felt so conscious.
If, however, he would never have the opportunity to benefit the
people of Hua district direct by keeping a benevolent eye upon
their welfare, there was an indirect and established way of showing them his gratitude. The money which he made while in office
would be his own, to do with whatever he wished, and he could

send it home here to the village. Such silver would not of course
be taken from his salary, which would be ridiculously small and
would not even cover the expense of keeping up the official residence, the yamen, or of paying his assistants and underclerks. It
would be the silver exacted by "squeeze": all the manifold bribes
which the people were forced to pay out to the officials before
any business could be conducted at all.

Hung was too young as yet to consider questions of equity. He
was thinking so far only about how he could help and repay all
his cousins. Moreover, as a scholar, he was coming more and
more under the influence of Confucius, for it was the fashion
amongst scholars to deride the Taoists and Buddhists, whose
priests had brought discredit upon religion by pandering to the
supersititions of the credulous. The one great weakness of Confucianism was the sage's failure to define the duties of a man to
the stranger without his gates. Nevertheless the sage had many
times pointed out that the test of a princely man's virtue and
ability to govern was whether or not he could keep the people
contented. Therefore when it came to the practice of "squeeze",
questions of equity or charity did not trouble the Confucian
scholar, but if the official could not keep the people contented
then there would be a rebellion, so it was a question of degree.
One must not "squeeze" too much or too hard.

In 1827, at the age of thirteen, Hung sat for his first examination.
He was the only candidate from his village, and his father went
with him to see him safely to the district city of Hua. Out of
five hundred candidates only fifteen passes would be granted, and
the tests would last for seven days. In the final result the very
first name in the very highest place was that of young Hung.
Feng's name was also included amongst the fifteen who were
fortunate. Four hundred and eighty-five candidates went to their
homes disappointed, but Hung and Feng returned jubilant to
their villages.

There began then for Hung what was to be perhaps the
happiest year of his life. He was now what was technically known
as a Qualified Student. He became a "long-gown wearer", and
though it was not of silk it added to his dignity. With happiness
and success his body decided to do some powerful growing,
giving promise of the tall, broad frame that was to be worthy of
an emperor. A Qualified Student was always accepted as a mem-

ber of the gentry (who knew to what place he might yet climb?) and was admitted to the discussion of local affairs. While his father must still prostrate himself before the district magistrate, the son must prostrate himself to no one but the Son of Heaven. A polite bow was sufficient to all other men, however great. No one could inflict upon him corporal punishment, and, because the Qualified Students were sometimes unruly, this presented a problem to the district magistrate. For that reason they might not enter any yamen, nor criticise the government, nor print any writings privately, lest any student movement cause a dissension. But they had the entry to any public library, and though the college of which Hung was now a member was in fact only the small bureau of education at the yamen in Hua, where names were listed, he could learn privately, and there were teachers who would instruct him without payment.

At first he took advantage of his new privileges and his sense of relief to walk abroad in his new long gown, to visit other villages and to speak with persons of education and enjoy cultivated conversation; and while for these few weeks he allowed himself to be at ease, his mind would dwell pleasantly upon the future. A number of districts went to make up a prefecture. His next examination would be at prefectural level. The successful candidates would then go to the capital of the province, the city of Canton, to sit for the provincial examination, which was held every three years, to compete for the title of "Talented". It was not exactly a degree, but those who acquired even this minor distinction could generally find gainful employment, such as assisting the provincial Commissioner of Education in conducting examinations. Hung set his teeth, his chin jutting forward, when he remembered that even to acquire the title of "Talented" he would have to compete for only about seventy places with nearly ten thousand candidates from all over the province. But, touching the folds of his long gown, he drew courage, remembering how he had feared the first examination, and, as it proved, his name had appeared first upon the board.

Immediately after the reception of the title of "Talented", always supposing that he was successful, he would be granted money by the authorities to travel to Peking, for he would then be eligible to compete for a metropolitan degree. With that degree gained he would be certain of office, and, while he waited in

Peking for such a place to fall vacant, he could sit for a Doctorate. If he gained honours in the examination for the Doctorate, he would automatically be appointed to the Academy of Letters, the Han-lin College, and would by way of celebrating his success be invited with his fellows to dine with the Emperor himself, for from such young men of distinction the Son of Heaven would eventually draw the members of his Secretariat and his Council of State and the Viceroys of the eighteen provinces.

The picture was rosy, but the few weeks of idleness in which to enjoy it came quickly to an end, and then the milling process began, the discipline that reduced the minds of all the literati to a pattern of pedagogic precision, and left them drained of the mental virility which could produce initiative or inspired genius: two hundred more books of history, literature and poetry to learn by heart before the next examination. As well as this he had to find teachers who could instruct him in the performance of cere-mony and a whole new branch of calligraphy—how to do honour to the names of the Emperor, Heaven, the Government, the Court, the Palace and Confucius by elevating the particular character one, two or three places higher on the paper according to the degree of honour to be accorded.

Growing apace and working hard, he had no time to become conscious of the needs of his body, and before he was aware of any necessity to restrain physical desire his father arranged a marriage for him. Because there had been no period of conscious restraint, he had gathered no impetus to make him desire a woman with his mind, or dwell secretly on what female beauty could mean in terms of voluptuous enjoyment. Moreover, the peasant girl chosen for him was not beautiful, for it was not to be supposed that after all the money spent upon his schooling his father would afford him such a luxury. But his young strong body was per-fectly ready in his fifteenth year to find quick and easy release. He came to his marriage bed without much thought, and the only real difference to his life was that the house was now over-full of women, what with his mother and his grandmother, the wives of his two brothers, and his two sisters; but the elder of the sisters was shortly to be wed, and then perhaps he might find a quiet corner in which to work at his books.

The quiet corner became available sooner than was expected, for his grandfather, failing to rival the longevity of the ancestors, succumbed to death. The family bereavement could not have come at a more awkward time, for Hung was working night and day to be ready for the prefectural examination due to be held shortly, and now here was the house completely disorganised, first by an incessant stream of visitors calling to condole, and then by unending conferences as to the conduct of the funeral rites. The Taoist priest was much in evidence, for upon him fell the duties of freeing the soul from the body and closing the coffin, and, more important still, choosing an auspicious date and place for the interment.

Perhaps the general turmoil was responsible for the disaster which now overtook Hung, but a more probable explanation is the fact that, since it was now 1830 and three years had passed since the last test, the magistrate and prefect had been newly appointed from Peking, and had had no time to take note of the fact that, even though Hung had no silver with which to buy his way into favour, his father was at least the headman of a village, whose son should in all prudence have been accorded a fair contest and not held to ransom for the sake of the "squeeze".

A thousand candidates, all of them Qualified Students, were competing for only thirty places. Day after day Hung's name appeared at the head of the list on the board. It was head of the final list of about forty. He had now only to pass one short re-examination, the purpose of which was to exclude any candidates who had happened to pass by good luck rather than sound knowledge. He could hardly believe it when he saw that this time his name was nowhere upon the board. Stricken, silent, aghast, he could not at first summon himself to collect his belongings. As in a dream he found himself at last walking alone on the road home to the village with his basket in his hand, and there began from that day a sad period of heart-searching for Hung. Success would have made him a Salaried Student with a grant of two taels of silver a year. Now there was no more money to pay for his education, for the expense of his grandfather's funeral had taken all the family resources, and he could not continue indefinitely to levy help from the villagers. He must return to work in the fields.

In a day or two, after the first shock, Hung began to review the reasons for his failure. It was well known that the first paragraph of an eight-legged essay, consisting as it did of two sentences of a classical quotation, could be the signal between the candidate and the examiner that a bribe had been duly paid and accepted. Now that Hung's ears were open, he began to hear all sorts of stories of how success could be bought, at the expense of throwing out from the limited number of places those whose merits deserved to be rewarded.

Feng, who had passed the prefectural examination the year before, and who now moved in a circle of Salaried Students which was quick to criticise the government—though in secret—comforted his young friend with the many current tales of such abuses. Hung was only just sixteen. There was plenty of time. He would be able to re-sit the examination at a later date, and by that time perhaps influence could be brought to bear. Meanwhile it was as well to take stock of the difficulties which would lie ahead, and to realise that success did not entirely depend upon his own merits, but that his career could be blocked at any moment by the greed and wickedness of the officials. Hung listened quietly to all that was said. He was grateful that at this moment he was not deprived of Feng's company, for his cousin's village lay near the hills to which Hung now took the buffaloes to pasture. His long gown had been put away. Now he was nothing but a herd-boy, vaulting each morning on to the back of his father's buffalo and riding it to the hills to browse.

Presently he began to recover his sense of proportion, and to take a more cheerful view of the future. He remembered the well-known tale of the poor lad who suspended his book from the horns of his buffalo while following the plough. That must indeed have been a difficult feat, but there was nothing to prevent his sitting quietly here on the hillside working. Next day he carried his books slung in a bag on his back, and whenever their subject matter seemed too hard to grasp without the benefit of personal instruction, he would remind himself of that other well-known moral story: of how a young scholar, fearing that the work assigned him was too hard, gave up in despair, and was returning to manual employment when he saw an old woman rubbing a crow-bar on a stone. The boy asked the reason for her action, and she replied that she was just in want of a needle, and thought she would rub down the crow-bar until she got it small enough. The patience of the aged female provoked him to make another attempt at passing his examination, and he succeeded in attaining to the rank of the first three in the Empire.

Curled up in the grass beneath a tree on the hillside, one eye upon the buffaloes, and with a book in his hand, Hung would chuckle as he thought of this tale. He was young, and he would fight back, for he had many days before him. He thought for a moment of Yen-lo, the sovereign of the underworld, he who determined the length of men's days. Had he not often seen his image clothed in a black robe, his face dark and very terrible to behold? It was said that when a man died the three assistants of the god read out a list of accusations against the departed, and Yen-lo then gave sentence, and the evil man was taken away in chains to suffer terrible tortures. Hung hoped that whichever individual it was who had accepted a bribe to prefer another name to his own at the examination might one day suffer those same tortures.

The reward of his determination to continue working at his books was not slow in coming. Before the year was out a rich man's son with whom he was acquainted invited him to associate himself in joint study, for he hoped to benefit from Hung's talent. The contract, entailing his keep and a small fee, was to date from the New Year Feast of 1831, and it gave him the chance of freedom from manual labour to work hard for twelve months. Fortune favoured him, for within that period the post of schoolteacher in his own native village fell vacant, and the villagers naturally chose him to succeed to the position. He had between ten and twenty pupils to teach. Less than ten could not support the salary of a teacher, and more than twenty made the class unteachable, for he had to hear each one repeat the lesson by heart. He would receive three hundred cash per year, his lamp oil, salt, lard, tea, and four weeks' holiday at the New Year, in return for exercising patience with the young and stupid, a form of patience which had never come easily to him.

In the very same month that Hung began to teach in the school at Hua, rebellion broke out in the neighbouring province of Kwang-si, the province lying to the west and piled up against that central Asian mountain barrier which is continuous from the Himalayas through Tibet to the borders of China. There in the foothills the aborigines, known as the Miau, were not of Chinese stock. They resembled more closely their neighbours, the Malays, and, though for a thousand years they had been subjects of the Son of Heaven, they were regarded as a primitive folk. Into their mountain fastnesses had disappeared some of the scions of the Ming dynasty more than two hundred years ago, and these Miau had always been ready to join any venture aimed against the present Manchu dynasty, not because they entertained much sentiment about the matter—there was not a scholar amongst them—but because they were a race of sturdy hill-men ever ready for the joys of battle, who found too protracted a period of peace irksome.

On the fifth of February in that year of 1832 they rose lustily from their boredom and apathy under the leadership of a cheerful and bloodthirsty bandit, who, meeting with initial success in his first forays, had himself proclaimed "The Golden Dragon King", assumed the Imperial Yellow robes, and announced his intention to overthrow the Manchu dynasty. The Imperial troops woke to action with difficulty, for the reason that half the men listed upon the military strength had been made rotten with opium. At least, that was the excuse which the officials preferred to the Emperor. It drew attention from their own incompetence and fastened it upon the evil machinations of those Western Barbarians, the British, who were responsible for importing the drug. So serious were the reverses of the Imperial troops that on July 24th the Emperor, who alone had the right to do so, memorialised Heaven: that is to say, he went in conformance with ceremony to the altar of Heaven in Peking and there publicly made his report, together with his plea for help, to whatever power might be thought to exist in the regions above.

That the Imperial troops were so weak as to be unable to resist the onslaught of a primitive hill-people was a matter that could not be hidden from the mass of folk in the neighbouring provinces, and it gave them food for thought. In particular it gave much food for thought to Hung, as he sat alone after school hours in the school-house, burning his precious lamp oil and studying for his next attempt at the examination.

Everywhere it was being whispered that the Heavenly Mandate was about to be withdrawn. The Heavenly Mandate was the divine commission to the Emperor and the Imperial dynasty to rule China. The claim to the succession was the reception at the death-bed of nomination by the departing sovereign, and to that extent the succession was hereditary. But good government and the will of Heaven alone established the right to rule: disaster was Heaven's way of manifesting that the divine commission had been withdrawn, as a penalty for violating the "Way" of Heaven. Floods, plagues, famines were the signs.

The Five Relationships, for which Confucius had laid down the principles of right behaviour, were those between sovereign and subject, father and son, brothers, husband and wife, and friends. Loyalty to the Emperor was as essential to the virtuous life as filial piety. Treachery to him was considered to be par-ricide—at least, it was so considered for as long as he could be shown to hold the Heavenly Mandate, but only for so long. A father, no matter how lacking in virtue, could not be removed, though you could remove yourself from him; but an Emperor could be removed if he ceased to hold the divine commission. Had not the sage Mencius said, "Whoever protects the people is their prince, and whoever tyrannises over them is their enemy"? At the last the officials were not responsible. Final responsibility lay always with the Emperor, and he alone could be called by the people to account.

If, as many men believed, mind could mould matter and give it form, then the conception of a pattern, the focussing of thought upon an ideal, could result in the clothing of an idea in flesh; and thus the Emperor as the father of his people must present that pattern of virtue which would repeat itself in the family of every peasant and inspire every man to filial piety, so that in every cottage the same pattern took shape, echoing from the throne downwards and re-echoing back and up again in a harmony that gave man both the power to command the universe and the humility to defer to an aged parent. If, then, the Emperor failed to play his part in this presentation of a pattern, the harmony of the universe would be disturbed, and the pattern in danger of being damaged in the humblest home and between every father and every son. Then Heaven could, in the face of such danger, with-draw its mandate.

Hung, as he sat alone by lamplight in the school-house, was only reviewing in his mind the common knowledge with which any student of Chinese history was expected to be acquainted. But recent events now turned his thoughts from the general to the particular. For a hundred years after the fall of the Mings this province of Kwang-tung had kept up spasmodic efforts to overthrow the invading Tartars and the foreign Manchu dynasty, and even in the last century the feeling that the Manchus ruled, not by divine commission, but by force, had been preserved in the lodges of the secret societies. The society of Heaven-and-Earth was the most powerful, and its lodges were spread secretly throughout China. Now these men, who called themselves "brothers" because together they had taken their vows of initiation, were in open arms in the province of Kwang-si, and had sworn allegiance to this bandit who called himself the Golden Dragon.

The word "bandit" held no deprecatory meaning, for in the Chinese there was only the one word which served for both bandit and rebel, and rebellion was the only means whereby Heaven could manifest its withdrawal of the mandate. Had Hung been able to compare his own land with that of the Western Barbarians, he could have said that rebellion was the only equivalent of the democratic vote. Revolution was against principles and traditions, rebellion against rulers. As history showed, of all nations the Chinese were the least revolutionary and the most rebellious. But the only opportunity for a successful rebellion was a combination of a bad emperor, weak ministers, and an unusually strong leader for the rebellion. It seemed doubtful whether this Golden Dragon was the man for the moment. Yet men were everywhere whispering that the moment was ripe, for Heaven was beginning to manifest its will in a series of natural disasters.

It would, however, equally need to manifest certain signs to the man of its choice before Hung could feel convinced. He remembered how in his studies of history he had read the letter of the generalissimo who had made the last stand at Nanking, in answer to the Manchu usurper's demand to deliver the city. The generalissimo had pointed out that the brother of the late Ming Emperor, in whose defence he fought, "has the right to the throne, the Mandate of Heaven and the backing of popular opinion. On the first day of May when he arrived at Nanking he was received by myriads of people, who thronged the streets, and their cheers reverberated far and wide. Prior to his coronation phoenix gathered in the city; the river stream appeared clear.

On the day of coronation purple clouds surrounded the city like a fan, and lumber floated out from the Great River for the reconstruction of the palaces. Are these not the signs of the Heavenly Mandate?"

Well, so far no such signs had been accorded to the Golden Dragon, so Hung would reserve his opinion. He closed his books and extinguished the lamp, and took his short way home by moonlight. After all, who was he to be concerned? He had enough to think about in studying for the next examination, though if a new emperor would bring to an end the graft and bribery of the officials he might stand a better chance of success. Things had not been thus in the Golden Age, and in the reign of the Mings his family had held high office. He was beginning to feel that the grinding poverty of the people and the abuses practised by the officials might perhaps be due to the fact that the rulers of the land were after all foreigners, even though they had adopted Chinese ways and had held the Dragon Throne for the last two hundred years and more.

Throughout the next year of 1833 Heaven continued to manifest its displeasure with the Manchu dynasty. In Kiang-si there were earthquakes followed by general destitution, and in Ho-nan and Ho-peh a famine was beginning which was to attain terrifying proportions. Further hardship was being caused by the Imperial government's first attempts to grapple with the problem of international exchange. The British East India Company was in the process of reorganisation and their monopoly of the China trade was about to come to an end. One-sixth of the whole Indian revenue was at that date dependent upon opium sales to China, and unless Britain could sell the opium grown in India she could not buy tea from China. As it was, the Imperial Board of Revenue was fearful that silver was being drained out of the country by the Western Barbarians, and to combat the danger it raised the exchange value of silver ingots in relation to copper cash.

To Hung, who had been desperately saving his strings of cash against the need of bribing the officials to mark his next examination papers fairly, this came as a blow, for the land-tax had to be paid in silver, and it would need all the family's resources now, his own included, to raise the necessary taels of the precious metal. Gone was any hope of buying favour. But there was still the hope of enlisting influence. After all, Ching-yang had for decades been the headman of the village, and in the course of years he had met with many influential persons, albeit on his knees in the attitude of prostration.

The Tao-t'ai, the official who had control over a subdivision of a province, had it in his power to nominate to the Commissioner of Education one or two promising students who had failed the examination at prefectural level. Such persons then became automatically "Presented Students", and could by-pass the prefectural test and enter for the provincial examination. As this was held triennially and was due to take place the following year, there was little time to be lost in gaining the ear of the Tao-t'ai. Then—and perhaps here lay the most hopeful chance—there was the district magistrate, a new man since Hung's set-back of three years ago, and one with whom the headman was accustomed to transact business.

Ching-yang could brush aside the parasites, the underclerks and police-runners, for he came to the yamen on an official matter. It was his duty to deliver the land-tax of the village, and those who brought silver could not be gainsaid. He entered the yamen by the southern gate of the courtyard, a huge triple gateway, whose fantastic ornamentation and paintwork were in bad repair, as was the paintwork of the rampant dragons, red and white on the blank wall opposite. The magistrate, like all his predecessors, evidently did not intend to waste good money on a residence which he was not allowed to occupy for more than three years. Hardly had the gateman admitted the bearded and venerable headman before the magistrate himself entered the street in procession, returning from the performance of some ceremony. Four lictors in tall black felt hats cleared the crowded street with their whips, and they were followed by a group of boys holding on high the red boards on which were inscribed the titles of the official. Behind was borne a scarlet umbrella, inscribed with ten thousand names, a proof of the popularity of the benevolent man, and gifted by the grateful people of the district where he had previously held office. Then, surrounded by soldiers on horses and mules, came his sedan chair, carried by four bearers, and following came his secretaries, some of the more important in sedans and the rest on foot.

Thus could a contact, the only one, be made between the Imperial administration and the people: the meeting of the village headman and the Father-and-Mother Officer, as a district magistrate was often called.

3

IT WAS ACCOMPLISHED! Hung was a Presented Student, but exactly by whose good graces was never to be clear. One did not ask such questions. One accepted gratefully the intimation of the authorities that one might present oneself for examination at the triennial test.

Hung was twenty when in the month of August 1834 he came for the first time to the city of Canton. It was pleasant to have the company of Feng upon the journey. Both young men were once again at the same level in their scholastic careers, and bent upon the same purpose: to gain the title of "Talented".

The province of Kwang-tung, comparable in size to the whole of Italy, had a capital city which housed a million and a half people. Hung had been amazed at the hugeness of the wall, twenty-five feet high by twenty broad, through whose gate he had lately passed. The two friends were now making for the main street which ran east and west, the Avenue of Benevolence and Love. The shop signs, gilded boards hanging downwards, colourfully inscribed with characters, proclaimed such auspicious trade names as "Celestial Affluence" and "Perpetual Success", and there were myriads of advertisements in scarlet paper. What diverse goods! Here was nothing but embroidered boots, and there nothing but musical instruments. The next shop was that of a chandler, and beyond it a hereditary leech. Here was a pipe-maker, and beside it a window with a card displaying the legend "Foreign Mud". One could peer in and see amongst the darkness and filth the sallow and sickly faces of those who lay couched and asleep enjoying their opium dreams. Hung made a wry mouth. What a waste of silver and strength!

They went next to the harbour to admire the two-masted war-junks and the river boats and coastal traders, so thick upon the water that you could almost have stepped across the estuary as upon a bridge, if you could have threaded your way through the forest of masts.

They left the quays and went back to take a look at the cook-shops in the Avenue of Benevolence and Love—not that a poor man could afford to eat in such a quarter. The sight and smell of sea-slugs in vermicelli, or of sharks' fin soup, vied with forcemeat puffs; and outside the teahouses croupiers were jerking reeds in a box, or spinning a ball within a revolving wheel. Gambling! Hung pursed his lips in contempt. Not so would he waste his silver, he who had seen his brothers sweat and toil in the fields to gain it.

Before they grew too hungry, they visited the handsomest part of the city in the neighbourhood of the Confucian Hall near the South Gate. Here there were trees and courtyards, yamens and temples, and many young men of their age were to be seen glancing first here and then there, for close by at the south-east angle of the city wall was the examination hall, and the city was full of young students anxious to view from outside the place of their coming ordeal. The so-called hall consisted of rows of buildings between broad paved walks, each row separately tiled and divided into a quantity of cells: eight thousand, to be precise, and each would presently be filled. Eight thousand candidates was not so enormous a number, having regard to the size of the province, but the number of passes to the examination was limited to two hundred, and some even of these were reserved for the Tartars, who were so stupid that they had to be accorded the privilege of a special examination.

At the sight of all those cells and at the thought of the ordeal before him and the slenderness of his chance of success, Hung's heart sank and he went suddenly pale. The month of August was the hottest in the year, and at any moment now the monsoon might break. There was a heaviness in the atmosphere which brought the sweat to his brow. Perhaps his pallor was what caused him to be particularly noticed, amongst the passing to and fro of so many students, by the man who now grasped his arm.

From his wide-sleeved gown, and the hair caught in a knot on the top of his head, it was evident that he was a Taoist priest, and Hung was brought to a halt by the man's accosting him just outside the entrance to the yamen of the provincial Commissioner of Finance. At this point of vantage the Taoist had been plying his trade as soothsayer, but now, strangely enough, he made no demand for cash, but volunteered a prediction before Hung, who had decided to risk a few coins to enquire concerning the results of the examination, could strike a bargain.

The eyes of the Taoist looked into his and there was a searching, a moment's stripping of the soul, which Hung found embarrassing. "You will attain the highest rank," the seer then told him, "but do not be grieved, for grief will make you sick. I congratulate your virtuous father."

Secretly delighted, though fearful of admitting to superstitious beliefs in front of Feng, with whom as a fellow Confucian scholar he had often discussed such soothsayers to their detriment, Hung fumbled for his string of cash. But the man would take no reward, which was all the more heartening as it encouraged belief in the genuineness of his powers. In a decidedly more cheerful frame of mind, and now so hungry that appetite could no longer be denied, the young men made their way back to their lodging.

As the Hung clan numbered twenty thousand, who claimed descent from the original ancestor, it was not to be supposed that they had need to lodge with strangers. His grandmother of the Wang family had seen to that. It so happened that there had always been much coming and going between Hung's village and the district city of Kwei, for although the latter lay three hundred and fifty miles away in the mountainous province of Kwang-si, you could get there with comparative speed and ease by the river traffic. You went straight up the West River from Canton, and boats were frequent, for it was the main traffic route for bringing goods from the interior to trade with the Foreign Devils, and along that line nearly everyone had a hand in the trade. Cousin Wang, a cousin on the distaff side, had settled at Kwei on the river bank. There he had a small interest in tea, for which the Foreign Devils in Canton would pay much silver, and he employed a porter to handle the chests in Canton. This man, Yang Hsiu-ch'ing, shared a house and courtyard in the city with other porters of the foreign trade. He was a Kwang-si man, and had once been an orphan

and homeless, but now he was earning good money for carrying the tea chests off the river boats. Through the Wang cousins,
the clan of Hung's grandmother, a marriage had been arranged
a year or two ago between Yang and Hung's elder sister, his
half-sister, Hsiu-ying.

Yang was short and square and pitted with smallpox, but what
he lacked in looks he made up for in personality. His welcome
was warm. He was vociferous, a fluent speaker, easily able to
express his feelings in words which flowed from a mouth decorated by a scanty but bristling moustache. He was above all
volatile, and, as they sat over their evening rice conversing, his
quickly changing expressions and vivid interest in every subject
mentioned made a complete contrast to the demeanour of the
clean-shaven, retiring, pedagogic Feng. Yet these two men were
to be in the future united in their determination to seat the
youngest of the three upon the Dragon Throne.

Yang was holding forth now upon the subject of an elder sister
of his, who was married to a rich old man in far-away Kwang-si.
Their son, Yang's nephew, was already a gilded youth of nearly
fifteen, Cheng Yin-chen by name, and if the boy could be brought
to see that there was much money to be made in planting tea . . .

The conversation turned to trade, and from trade to the scarcity
of silver, and from silver to what a man would spend it upon if
he had it; and when Feng went to fetch his bundle, and Yang's
wife was occupied at cleaning the rice bowls, somehow Hung
found that he and Yang had said a word here and a word there
which did not entirely accord with propriety. Hung became
aware that had Yang had the necessary silver he would have
availed himself of it to contract a marriage with a more person-
able female.

Instead of feeling any anger that his half-sister gave Yang insufficient pleasure, Hung was conscious of a curious sense of relief
at hearing another man at last put into words the very feelings of
which he himself was beginning to be conscious. He was not
alone, then, in supposing that there might exist pleasures to which
he was a stranger! But poor men had no silver with which to take
a second wife, and he himself would always be a poor man, unless
he could pass the examinations. He had better follow Feng's example and fetch his books from the bundle for a last and desperate
survey. The hungry wails of Yang's infant son would make study

difficult. At least, thought Hung, his brother-in-law had a child by the woman he had wed, whereas his own plain-faced wife appeared to be barren, so that, for all the contract had appeared to be cheap, it had turned out a bad bargain.

A couple of days later, on August 8th, the signal gun fired at dawn gave notice to the city that the Triennial Examinations were about to commence. Close to the examination hall stood the temple of Confucius, in a large open space dotted with trees and ornamental pools. Here towards evening the opening ceremonies were to take place. Here were gathered the Commissioner of Education, who was the final judge, and the Proctor who was responsible for organising the conduct of the examinations, together with the Censors who held the privilege—and it was sacrosanct—of being able to criticise the administration and even the Emperor himself. Their duty was in this case to act as spies and report any suspicion that graft or bribery had interfered with the strict fairness of the competitive means to advancement. As office was being openly sold for silver by the Emperor's authority, their appearance made Hung's smile disdainful.

Above the now open doorway of the temple were inscribed the words "The Teacher and example for ten thousand generations", a tribute to Confucius, and within the body of the temple was the sage's image, flanked on either side by the images of the seventy-two persons worthy of association with him. Here sticks of incense were offered by the Commissioner and all the due and proper rites were performed, and at last the great man came out within the view of the thousands of students, his sapphire button glowing in the evening sunshine, and in his hands the paper inscribed with the usual prayer: that if any revenge were desired by the habitants of the underworld, it should be carried out now, forthwith, within the examination halls. The recitation of the prayer before the paper was burnt was somewhat depressing to the young men who had to listen to it. As the fire caught the paper and the smoke took it to heaven, Hung remembered the tales he had heard of how men had been known to die of exhaustion and strain and perhaps despair in the close imprisonment of the cells.

The entry of his name and the particulars of his ancestors and habitat was a business already accomplished, and now he went to the entrance of the cell for which he held the number, to undergo the close inspection of his belongings, an inspection for which he was well prepared. He could show that his cap and clothing had no linings in which the minutely printed cribs which were known to be manufactured could be hidden. The paper soles of his shoes were thin and equally innocent. His ink-stand was of thin transparent stone, and his charcoal candlesticks and brush-holder, together with his food, his mattress and his blankets, were all in a basket of the regulation pattern. He had seen that the cake which his sister had baked for him was properly cut into small pieces, so that no paper could be concealed in its soft heart. By sundown he was alone, locked into a cell only four foot square in which he could not properly lie down.

All next day he would have to write upon "The Doctrine of the Mean" and the works of Mencius. The cells would be unlocked on the morning of the tenth. On the evening of the eleventh he would be again incarcerated and the next day's work would be based upon the Five Classics. Another day's freedom, and then once again imprisonment while he composed essays upon the art of government. Though the forms of the essays, their length and the number of characters in a line of verse must conform to strict pattern, yet there might be no erasure, least of all a blot. Such would lead to instant disqualification. His heart was beating fast, as on the first morning he read the opening question. Carefully he prepared his brush.

A knowledge of the Classics, some of them two thousand years old, had little relation to the knowledge required in an efficient nineteenth-century civil service, but one of the questions on the second day of his ordeal related closely to his future interests in the world of the spirit.

"Ssu Ma-ch'ien, in making history, took the Sacred Books and ancient records and arranged the facts they detailed. Some have accused him of unduly exalting Taoists, and thinking too highly of wealth and power. Can you give examples and proofs of this statement?"

Hung might have been tempted to write at length, but the stereotyped form of the "eight-legged" essay forbade it, and in-dependent thought was not encouraged, so he took no risks. But as he lay sleepless after completing his essay, he gave himself to thought. He was no longer quite the same brash young boy who had dismissed Taoism because of the malpractices of the ignorant

country priests, and because of his first intellectual pride at being
numbered amongst the literati, who were for the most part followers of the principles of Confucius. Under the tuition of the
various scholars of repute to whom he had had approach in the
last years, he had begun to realise that there were more things in
heaven and earth than were dreamt of in the philosophy of the
commentaries upon Confucius, and that indeed the sage had been
sufficiently humble himself to admit that there were powers in
heaven beyond his ken. There was a distinction to be drawn between the Tao, the "Way", and those who merely pretended to
pursue it. In particular he had become interested in the Taoist
studies of alchemy.

He would have been even more interested to know that the
Western Barbarians had also pursued the art, and that their writings confirmed his own surmise: namely, that the goal of the
alchemists was to change the dross of human nature to a spiritual
excellence which would survive death, and that the alchemical
recipes were merely cabalistic and secret terms for concealing
the directions for a discipline of the spirit which would achieve
this desired result. In far away Europe the alchemists, who ostensibly had sought to find the philosopher's stone, whereby metals
could be transmuted to gold, had often in their writings declared
that their search was not for "vulgar gold". In China, since time
immemorial, the search had been not for the stone but for that
fabulous substance known as the Elixir of Life, which was reputed
only incidentally to have in addition the power of transmuting
metals. In China also the recipes gave one to suppose that the
Elixir concerned not merely the prolongation of man's life on
earth, but his survival after death. For the change of copper and
mercury into gold must be preceded by the death and corruption
of the first two substances; by the loss of the metallic lustre and
life of the copper as it passed into inert black earth; by the loss
of the silvery mobility and life of the mercury as the flame changed
it into a red powder, as if its very blood had been shed and passed
into the body of its death. Only after that death came the Elixir,
the eternal life, the resurrection, the sunrise—yellow gold; the life
of the mercury of copper restored, but in refined and transmuted
form.

On the morning of the sixteenth of August Hung's cell was
unlocked for the last time, and after he had seen to the cleansing

of it he was free to go. His hands cluttered with his belongings, his basket and his blankets, he stood blinking in the sunshine, conscious that other students were everywhere hurrying around him to greet their friends or pursue their separate ways to their lodgings. Most, like himself, would remain in the city to await the results. Sometimes it took the examiners as long as forty days to read the eight thousand papers. There were as many as sixty-five "Talented" graduates to help the two members of the Academy of Letters, who always travelled specially from Peking to assist the Commissioner in judging the final leet. Meanwhile, very few students would dream of tamely going home. Besides, it was advisable to be on the spot to hear of any possible graft that might prevent a fair marking of the papers. Yang would no doubt find him some remunerative work as a tea-porter, and then, Hung reflected, he must arrange for a professional runner to report the Viceroy's announcement of the results.

There was a new Viceroy, one Lu, who had been appointed on the dismissal of his predecessor for failing to quell the rebellion in the interior, a rebellion which was still dragging on amongst the mountains. It was the custom for the Viceroy to announce the results at his levee, which, following the pattern set by the Emperor, was held at sunrise, when the sovereign appeared in his character of Brother of the Sun to face southwards to the favoured subjects kow-towing in the inmost courtyard of the Forbidden City. Since it was impossible for all eight thousand of the candidates to press into the courtyard of the Viceroy's yamen, professional runners were employed to carry the news and the names throughout the streets.

Meanwhile a little rice-wine would not come amiss as a restorative. Hung set off to dump his belongings at his sister's quarters before seeking consolation for his exhaustion. Thus began the days of waiting, and while he gained a little money here and there, enough to pay for his rice, like every other student he could not for very long keep away from the vicinity of the examination halls in which his fate was being decided.

On one such day Hung observed that outside the entrance to the halls stood two men, who seemed to be distributing something to the crowd who were gathering round. Could some new regulation have been printed regarding the examination? To reassure himself, Hung drew nearer. One of the men was addressing the passers-by. He was bearded, though his age was not venerable, and the manner of his speaking was forceful and held an appeal. He was begging his hearers to accept as a gift the slim printed books which his assistant carried in a basket. It seemed that he was attempting to acquire merit by bestowing upon others the fruits of his own hard-won knowledge and labour as comprised in these volumes. No doubt he was a Buddhist, thought Hung, for they made a practice of acquiring merit by works of charity, that they might reap the benefit in a next incarnation.

Catching sight of Hung's handsome face and expression of alert intelligence, the man now turned to him and proffered a little bundle of paper books, and almost automatically Hung's hand went out to receive it. After all, it was only good manners to accept a gift gracefully and to make adequate thanks, which he did. He moved away, and had no more time than to glance at the title of the series of publications, and to observe that it was called "Good Works for Admonishing the Age". Then Feng grasped him by the hand, and pointed out that they were already late for the midday meal.

Back in their lodgings, somehow the books were mislaid for a day or two, and by the time Hung found them again he had no appetite for book-learning. He had had his fill of it since the age of seven, and this was his only opportunity to see the sights of a great city. But reverence for paper and the written word was the sign of a civilised people. It must never be destroyed or thrown away, so he packed away the books amongst his bundle of belongings.

At last the day came. The signal gun at dawn proclaimed it. There was shouting in the direction of the yamen. Nearer now someone was cheering. Hung and Feng waited at the doorway. Would the professional runner abide by his contract and bring them the news, or would he bilk, pocket the deposit of cash, and abscond? He came at last panting, making a great show of wiping the sweat from his brow, the better to plead for an increase of fee.

The result was but another heartbreak. Hung and Feng had both failed. Their names were not among the list of the two hundred successful candidates. Sorrowfully Hung turned away into the house to see to the packing of his bundle, but on this occasion he suffered no sense of shock. He knew now that men

of three times his age still went up for this same examination
every third year after every third year. Had he not seen the grey
heads of such candidates at the inaugural ceremonies? He would try
again, if necessary he would go on trying all his life, for his
humble employment as a village school-teacher at least ensured
him sufficient rice and the opportunity to study in the evenings.

When he arrived home at his village, he unpacked his bundle
and put the little pile of booklets with which he had been presented on his bookshelf; and there, pushed to the back and hidden
by the forever multiplying volumes which his studies necessitated,
they remained unread and unheeded for more than eight years.
They were, had he known it, a set of Christian Protestant tracts,
which might have set him upon the path for which he was now
to seek so passionately and in so lonely a fashion in the intervening years.

Until 1807 China had been the field of Catholic missions only,
but in that year the Reverend Robert Morrison had arrived at
the little port of Macao, on the estuary opposite the city of
Canton—the place from which all Europeans were forced to conduct their trade, save for the small strip outside the city walls
of Canton itself, known as the Factories. Morrison, who worked
under the auspices of the London Missionary Society, was the
first Protestant missionary to come to China.

The position was very different with regard to the Catholics,
for from the days of Matteo Ricci they had held appointments at
Peking as astronomers to the Imperial court. Since the early part
of the nineteenth century, however, they had been subjected to
growing persecution. In the very year of Hung's birth, 1814, the
unauthorised Catholic training school for priests in west China
had been discovered, and Dufresse, the Vicar Apostolic, had been
beheaded. There were martyrdoms again in 1815 and 1820. The
penalty, as ordained by the Emperor, for spreading the gospel
was death, and the priests went in fear of their lives. In 1822
they once more fell under the Imperial displeasure, and were
banished to Macao. But, so great was their desire to share with
their brother men the pearl of great price which they believed
more precious than life itself, that within a year or two they were
attempting once again to make an organised, if secret, effort to
win souls for Christ. Moreover, the Napoleonic wars being

happily a thing of the past, France was ready to finance the missions.

In one respect the Roman Catholic priests, in their missionary work, had an immense advantage: with more than two centuries of experience behind them, they possessed a thorough knowledge of the language. Morrison, realising that for half a century Protestant missionaries would be unfit, by reason of their ignorance of Chinese, to penetrate the country, hoped meanwhile to spread the written word, for he had begun to realise, as no one else before him had, the tremendous power which lay in the use of ideographs.

There was no one Chinese language: there were several, not to mention the hundreds of dialects, and they ranged from the Cantonese tongue to the elegant Mandarin of the Peking officials. In alphabetical writing a man would have had to learn to write and spell each separate language, in both their ancient and modern versions. But a Chinese character, an ideograph, once learnt, even though there were thousands to learn, could be read by any scholar in China, whether it had been written yesterday or two millenniums previously.

Morrison completed his translation of the New Testament in 1814. There was much to be said for his view that its distribution would greatly speed the spreading of Christianity, but there were dangers ahead, of which the Catholics could have given warning. Without commentaries and historical and geographical notes, the Scriptures might easily be misunderstood.

In 1813 Morrison was joined by the Reverend William Milne. Not being allowed to stay in China, he went to Malacca to realise Morrison's alternative plan for a mission, taking with him one of the latter's type-cutters, Liang Fa.

It was while working on the complete Bible, which Milne had helped Morrison translate, that Liang became an earnest seeker after truth, and turned to the Buddhist priest nearby for help. Buddhism failed to convince him, and after a sermon by Milne on the Atonement he asked for Christian guidance. He was baptised, and later ordained the first Chinese evangelist, and when Milne died in 1822, Liang returned to Canton. His spiritual house had been well and firmly built upon the rock of Milne's and Morrison's teaching, and in character he was humble, loving, and very conscious of his need for a Saviour.

From time to time Liang was challenged by members of the Chinese literati on the need for commentaries to Morrison's printing of the New Testament, and so he himself began to write sermons, and to print them in volumes, together with passages from the New Testament taken from Morrison's translation.

Already Morrison was revising his first translation of the Gospels, and now he had help from one Karl Friedrich Gützlaff, who had been sent out to Macao in 1827 by the Netherlands Missionary Society. Gützlaff was working upon the first translation of the Old Testament, and so greatly did he need money for the printing of it that he had managed, with considerable dexterity, to square his conscience while he undertook the work of interpreter upon the opium-smuggling ships. Between the years 1831 and 1833 he made voyages up the coast of China to distribute with an equal efficiency medicines, opium and Bibles.

Dr. Morrison, on the other hand, had the kind of conscience which no specious arguments could easily lull to sleep, and the money which was also a necessity to his work he gained by acting as interpreter to the British authorities.

Just exactly what the British authorities consisted of, and what was to be their status vis-à-vis the Imperial government, became the burning question of 1834, as Liang Fa found to his cost when he returned to Canton in the month of August from his journeys inland. Liang, in a moment of inspiration, had realised that the best way to distribute his printed tracts, so that they might reach the widest and least conservative circle of the literati, was to trail the Commissioner of Education to all the prefectural examinations in the province, and there distribute them to the candidates thronging in and out of the examination halls. In 1830, he and his assistant had travelled a hundred and fifty miles into the interior and had given away as many as seven thousand tracts.

His return to Canton in 1834 from his various journeys was carefully timed to coincide with the date of the triennial examination, the very examination for which Hung was to enter. There Liang found his teacher-missionary, Dr. Morrison, so worried and preoccupied with his duties as interpreter to the British authorities that there was fear for his health.

The problem was this: the Imperial government had made plain that it would only accept a merchant to replace the Select Committee of the East India Company (whose monopoly of the trade

had now come to an end), for it was against the law for foreign
government officials to reside in China. Nor did China intend to
change the law, for it was based on the confirmed policy of
keeping all Barbarians at arm's length, lest they pervert the people,
while at the same time enjoying the benefits of a trade which
was lucrative. A merchant could be kept in his place and
"squeezed", whereas a foreign envoy might cause the kind of
trouble which would necessitate the Imperial troops having to
be sent on a punitive expedition to deal with those primitive folk,
the British.

Exactly because the merchants were heartily sick of being
"squeezed" and treated as primitive Barbarians, Lord Palmerston,
the Foreign Secretary, had set Lord Napier the impossible task
of at once both taking up residence at Canton and thus breaking the law, and of fostering trade relations. Arrived at Macao,
he was bidden by the Viceroy to wait there while further directions from Peking were sought. But Napier had had his orders to
brook no nonsense, and he insisted on immediately sailing up the
estuary and disembarking at the Factories, the strip of land outside the walls of Canton city to which foreigners were confined.
The Viceroy answered this challenge by promptly stopping the
trade. The quarrel proceeded by moves and countermoves, until
on August 26th Napier had notices printed and posted at the
street corners of the city. The notices, posted by spies, since
Europeans were not allowed to enter the city, had the purpose
of making an appeal, over the head of the Viceroy, to democratic
feeling in a land which was not a democracy.

It was an incitement to rebellion, and the Viceroy was speechless with rage. He issued a proclamation against Napier, denounced
as traitors any who entered the Factories, ordered all servants
of the Foreign Devils to withdraw, and set himself to find out
who had been so bold as to do the actual printing and posting
of the placards.

According to Liang's own account, he first took up his station
in front of the examination halls, where Hung met with him, on
August 20th, and that day distributed five thousand booklets.
On the 21st he gave away another five thousand, and on the 22nd
he and his assistant were questioned by the yamen police and
hauled before the city magistrate, for it was against the law to
disseminate "heresies opposed to orthodox learning". But the

magistrate could find nothing subversive in the volumes, nor anything to destroy virtue in the readers of them. Liang and his
assistant were therefore set free, and all would have been well
but for Lord Napier's placards. In reply to them the divisional
magistrate of the city gave orders to seize all "persons who
fraudulently make depraved and obscene books of the Outer
Barbarians, and, falsely assuming the pretence of admonishing
to virtue, print and distribute them."

Liang, innocent of any implication in the affair of Napier's
placards, knew that he would nevertheless be suspected, for he
did now possess a printing press, and he did print the Bible of the
foreigners; so on the same day he moved into hiding in the city,
and sure enough on the next his house was searched and his
assistants seized. One was beaten with forty blows upon the face,
but remained silent. The other disclosed Liang's whereabouts before being put to death.

On September 7th Lord Napier, determined not to be beaten
in the battle of wills, brought British men-of-war from Macao
and sailed up the estuary, firing upon the Chinese forts which
protected the approach to the city. Hung could have heard the
reverberation of the gunfire as he set out to travel back to his
village. The confusion certainly gave cover for Liang to escape
to the little island of Lin-tin in the estuary, and here, protected
by the British, he lived for a time before finally emigrating to
Singapore to continue his work as a missionary.

Lin-tin was the great and only depot of the British opium trade.
The voyages to and from India of the opium clippers, a magnificent fleet of full sailed ships, each with twenty guns, were regu-
lated by the seasons of the monsoons; and since it was not possible so openly to flout the law as to discharge and store the
precious cargoes on the mainland, and since the cargoes, coming
only twice yearly, were large, they were transferred to receiving
ships which lay permanently off the island of Lin-tin and were as
permanently guarded by British guns. These man-made islands
were massive and mastless hulks of ships no longer seaworthy,
and their decks were walled and roofed to form floating warehouses. Such a receiving ship, although a safe refuge for Liang,
was not by any means a quiet place, for the smugglers came here
from day to day to ship the opium chests and smuggle them
through the customs patrol to the mainland. It was not a work as

dangerous as it sounded, for the mandarins and the authorities were all in the game, and even the Viceroy got his rake-off from the profits, but face had to be preserved, so it was necessary to employ men of discretion.

On one such receiving ship worked a certain Lo Ta-kang; and whether or not he had discretion he certainly had a very lively intelligence, as well as brawny muscles with which to handle the opium chests over the side. A Kwang-tung man and a sailor, he knew every pirate and smuggler up the coast, and with them he would discuss all the knowledge of the waterways of China: a practical knowledge with which he was one day to supply Hung, who had learned of the Great River and the canals only from books.

And so, at this point in time and space—Lin-tin in the year 1834—Liang wrote a report of his adventures to his missionary teachers before moving out of the story to make way for Lo Ta-kang, who was presently to play such an important rôle in the Taiping rebellion.

4

HUNG WAS BACK AT his books again, was back once more in the village from which it seemed that nothing was ever to deliver him. Was his horizon never to include any more than the schoolhouse with the pool and the midden beside it?

Fighting the depression brought on by the monotony and the frustration of his hopes, the scholarly stoop, which he had at first affected, became a habit. But there was one compensation which could make him straighten up, a new-found happiness in the company of Jen-kan. This cousin, whose face Hung had first beheld as that of a wrinkled new-born infant, was now a lad of thirteen and one of his pupils. Teaching him, Hung was experiencing in reverse the relationship which he himself had once enjoyed with Feng. The boy was extremely intelligent, and repaid tuition, and was moreover so good-natured as to be a general favourite with everyone in the village and at the home of Hung, where he boarded.

For his part Jen-kan entertained a hero-worship for his teacher. As he was in future to record, he found his older cousin unusually handsome. To him Hung's oval face showed a friendly and open expression. His fair skin belied the assertion that the Hak-kas were a swarthy race, who had intermarried with the peoples of the southern border, and on the contrary bore witness to the purity of his descent from the settlers from northern Shan-tung. The bridge of his nose was high and his ears small, his well braided queue was black and glossy, and his eyes were large and bright and gleaming with intelligence. He was tall and beautifully made in proportion. Thus Jen-kan saw him, and thought the world of him. Nor did the boy always need to restrain his liking for Hung to the reverential behaviour expected between pupil and teacher or between the younger and older generations, for they shared many jokes and often teased one another, and when Hung laughed the whole house used to resound to the cheerful noise, or so it seemed to Jen-kan.

Such laughter had to be subdued for a time when Hung's wife died. She had proved barren, but no one could say that he had not shown patience and benevolence towards this woman who had cooked his rice. He wore the white clothes of mourning, but he did not grieve unduly.

In the province of Kwang-si the rebellion of the Golden Dragon had fizzled out and the leader had been executed, as Hung had foreseen would happen. Had there been a worthy heir to the Ming dynasty, Hung might have risked a good deal in his cause, for he was growing every year more conscious that the Manchus were responsible for the miseries of the people. But the descendants of the Mings—the few who had survived the downfall of their house—had been compelled to join the Tartar regiments, the Banners, and had been deliberately vitiated, so that if any now existed they would be but degenerate scions of their mighty ancestors.

In Kwang-tung province, after the rumpus caused by Lord Napier's mission, the Viceroy had been forced to patch up peace and reopen the trade, for the profits of it were the perquisite of the Emperor personally, and the Son of Heaven had no intention of allowing his private pocket to suffer for long. But the persecution of Christians had continued, and the missionaries had more than ever to work in secret, so that Hung had no knowledge of them.

This was the state of affairs when in 1837 he once again visited Canton for the provincial examinations. For a reason not easily understood, they seem to have been held that year in the spring, or perhaps Hung had been summoned to an examination at prefectural level, which he had never actually passed, though the grant of the status of Presented Student had enabled him to circumvent it. His resolution to remain patient, and if necessary to go on submitting himself to such tests, was becoming more and more difficult to keep. He was only twenty-three, but every day he grew more conscious of the needs of the people, of the abject poverty around him, and of the maladministration and malpractices of the officials. Unless he could soon gain a foot upon the ladder of advancement, he might be so stuck in the rut of village schoolteaching that, when the moment came for the Heavenly Mandate to be withdrawn from the Manchu dynasty and bestowed elsewhere, he would be unable to play his part in the glorious reconstitution of the Empire and the return of men to the virtues of the Golden Age.

For this reason he had been working harder than was wise, studying late into the night, month after month. Now he was once again shut into the cells, and he remembered all too vividly the stories of candidates who had died in such imprisonment, for he was feeling far from well, and was afflicted by an unstrung feeling which caused his hand to shake and his brow to sweat. When the last day of the examination was over, and once again he found his way into the light and air, and stood there blinking, he felt that there was only one thing to do to throw off this sensation of trembling, of remoteness, and, yes, of fear. He must occupy his mind during the month of waiting with all the sights that poverty had denied him on the previous occasion.

He walked first to the quays, and, coming by chance to that part of the river where the ladies of pleasure had their floating abodes, he allowed himself, in order to distract his attention from the ills of his body, to gaze at them directly. The floating brothels were gay with flowers, lanterns and music, even at this early hour. From their ships' verandahs the heavily powdered

faces of the courtesans smiled at him, and one or two of the girls
advanced across the decks, swaying as gently on their bound
"lily" feet as willow branches in the wind. He was intrigued to
be able to gaze overtly at such fragile beauties, but after a minute or two he turned away, for the principles of Confucius in-
culcated virtue, and to go whoring had never been acclaimed a
virtue. His period of mourning was at an end. No doubt his father
would soon arrange another marriage for him, and perhaps this
time the girl would not be without charms.

He re-entered the city, and went to the gate which gave on to
the Factories, for he was anxious to have a glimpse of the
Foreign Devils, whose guns he had heard when last he had
travelled back from Canton. It was said that despite their general uncouthness they were expert handicraftsmen. They could
manufacture fine cotton and woollen cloth and watches and clocks
such as any man would wish to possess, and furthermore they
could make the terrible fire-ships which had wrought havoc
amongst the estuary forts. For half an hour he peered through
the gate, and managed to catch sight of several of the "red-
haired" Barbarians, the British, whose fair complexions and profuse
bristling moustaches or side whiskers really did, he thought, present a most uncanny appearance. No wonder the Viceroy confined them as outcasts to this desolate strip of land beyond the
wall!

For the next thirty or more days Hung haunted the city,
walking, always walking in an attempt to disregard utterly the
unhinging that seemed to affect not only his joints but something
deeper still. Once he paid for Yang and himself to visit the
theatre, because the play-bill of the tea-house of the Olea caught
his eye. This particular performance, as described by Mr. Lay
a few years later, was one calculated to delight Hung. The
characters were dressed as personifications of the upper regions.
The Sun was crowned with his disc and the Moon with her
crescent. The Thunderer, as he wielded his axe, somersaulted
with a skill and a noise which brought the heart to the mouth.
The story of the play concerned a monarch who had found his
way into the upper regions through the partiality of a mountain
nymph. A wicked courtier, disguised as a tiger, rushed at one
moment into the nymph's quarters, and threw the heir apparent
into the moat. The monarch finally renounced the world and

nominated the Great Fool, the innocent and naïve peasant, to take his place. It went on for hours and hours, and so did the cacophony of the musical instruments.

Hung was delighted to have so good a return for his money. In the intervals between the acts he almost forgot the shaking of his fingers, so interested was he to consider all that this play was bringing to his mind. Was there, he wondered, such a place as paradise? The Buddhists said that those good souls as yet incapable of achieving Nirvana, the goal of a loss of identity, went between incarnations upon earth to the Paradise of the West, ruled by Amitabha Buddha. But the Taoists located paradise amongst the stars. It was a palace of pure pearl with a golden door.

The Sun-king and the Moon-queen had recalled to his mind references to the secrets of alchemy; for the metals were each attuned to the planets, and when the mercury of the waning moon was bedded with the vulgar gold of the sun they sank into corruption and the grave, turned black, and stank, before the final purification of a new Sun and a new Moon, united as a hermaphrodite, from whom issued in turn the true Elixir of Life. Hung had learned to understand the symbology, though the people of China had too much delicacy of taste to portray the marriage of Sun and Moon in pictures bordering upon the pornographic, as the medieval alchemists of Europe had once done.

What most struck him was the graceful and becoming method of dressing the long hair of the men in Ming costume. The present fashion of shaving the pate and appearing bald, except for the braided queue which hung like the tail of a monkey behind, was a custom imposed upon the Chinese by their Manchu conquerors as a mark of subjection, and not to conform with the order was tantamount to open rebellion. Hung reflected that his countrymen had grown so used to their slavery that now their own native fashions had become merely the antiquated and curious stage properties of the theatre. He felt suddenly sickened as well as wrathful, and grasping Yang's arm he sought resuscitation in the fresh air outside.

The days dragged on, and when at last the signal gun was fired and the professional runner came hot-foot to Yang's quarters, it was already plain that Hung's pallor and sweating brow and shaking hands were those of a man on the verge of some strange collapse. When he learnt that once again he had failed to pass the examination, he glanced wildly round, as though it was the world about him which was disintegrating, and then he fell.

How long he lay unconscious he did not know, but returning from oblivion he knew that he felt very ill. His father and mother would be distracted if they heard that he had fallen sick, and they were not present to care for him. He must get home.

He arrived back in his village on the first day of April, carried the full thirty miles in a sedan chair by two stout porters. It was a nightmare journey. Hung, hunched within the confined space, strove to keep both balance and consciousness when the chair swayed or jolted, and would from time to time cant forward or slouch back as he lost both. The family raised cries of anxiety when they first saw the state that he was in. He was carried to his bed, where he promptly sank once again into oblivion, or so they thought, for he lay very still, hardly breathing. He was not, however, unconscious of existence, but the faces he could see were not those of his kin.

There were a great number of people and they were welcoming him amongst them. Faces, faces and more faces. What were these words of welcome? It seemed that he was being congratulated on the accomplishment of a dangerous journey. To what place, then, had he arrived? In the midst of his bewilderment the voice of his mother, beseeching him to come to himself, penetrated his mind, and his love for her and the habit of filial duty brought him slowly to open his eyes, and to see her bending over him here in his cottage home. But the memory of all those other faces and the utter weakness of his body gave him to think that in truth he was about to die and go into the presence of Yen-lo, the god of the underworld. In a whisper he bade his mother summon his father and all his relatives closer to his bedside.

When he saw that they were near enough to hang upon his words, "My days are counted," he told them, and his gasping breath gave them cause to fear he spoke the truth. "O my parents!" his voice caught in a sob. "How badly have I returned the favour of your love to me! I shall never attain a name that may reflect its lustre upon you." He seemed to be struggling to say more and to lift himself. His two elder brothers raised and supported him in a sitting posture, but before he could speak again he collapsed. They laid him gently down. For many long minutes it seemed that he was dead. But even as the physician arrived, together with the Taoist priest, Hung gave out a great sigh and began to moan.

He appeared to be in great distress of mind. But the delirium, if it was that, was accompanied by no fever. He was murmuring something about a dragon, and presently it was a tiger of which he spoke. Perhaps it was the priest rather than the physician who was most needed.

The Taoist began to recite prayers. These constant ejaculations of the delirious man concerning a tiger gave cause for hope. To ride the tiger was perhaps symbolic of the soul riding the body, as Chang Tao-ling, the founder of the Taoist priesthood, had ridden it, treading beneath him what was loathsome and venomous. So long as the young man continued to grapple with or bestride the tiger, his soul might continue linked to his body, and it was a fine body, as fine as that of the tiger, whose head stripes formed the character "Wang" and proclaimed him king of beasts. Yes, this Hung's body was worthy of an emperor, and when an emperor died he was borne to heaven upon a dragon. To say that an emperor had mounted the dragon was to declare him dead. Perhaps the sufferer's mutterings concerning a dragon had not been so auspicious as his ejaculations about the tiger. Now, however, he was calling out something about a cock. Truly this young man was weaving his way through the tortuous paths, the maze of mental images which lie ever between the finite and the infinite, for the cock was a well-known symbol of the five merits of state. By his cap he was known as a civil official, and by his spurs as a warrior. He had both the courage to face his adversary and the benevolence to call others to share the corn, and he was faithful to his duties as a herald. It might be, therefore, that to dream of a cock would lead to official advancement. The priest surveyed young Hung doubtfully, and was able after a minute or two to observe that at last the patient lay quietly, albeit in a deep coma from which there was no rousing him.

Hung kept very still, in perfect possession of his faculties, waiting for the light to spread, the light which the cock had heralded. It was spreading, not from the east, but from above. Now once again he could see the faces of those who had first welcomed him, and from whom he had been so unwillingly separated. Now he could see a great number of men advancing towards him, and

he beheld them so clearly and distinctly that he knew he had
never before seen men as they truly were. If this was the abode
of Yen-lo, then here was no place of shadows, no lack of what was
concrete, for these men were playing upon musical instruments,
and even the make of the instruments was more real, the glimmer
of brass and the polished wood said more to the eye, than any
cymbals, pipes or drums that he had ever before beheld.

He was being bidden by these people to take his place in a
sedan chair that they might bear him with all honour on their
shoulders. He was confused and astonished at such honour being
done to him, but on a sudden he knew that to demur would be
impossible, for here in this place there could be no false politeness,
and to question judgment and authority now would constitute
the grossest discourtesy. Humbly he did what he was bidden, and
was carried shoulder high between multitudes of men and women,
who all saluted him joyfully, as they stood before the beautiful
and luminous palaces where they dwelt.

He was, however, not taken to any of these, but down through
the greenest of grasses to the brink of a river, whose water ran
clear as crystal. Here he was told to dismount, and was delivered
to the care of one who sat upon the river's bank. From her stillness she might have been sitting there forever upon the rock, her
grey robes part of it: a woman so old, a face so wrinkled and so
worn with patience, that his heart smote him lest he had kept
her waiting.

"Thou dirty man," she addressed him, but the eyes which
peered from the wrinkled lids were kind, the eyes of a woman
who had nursed many children, "why hast thou defiled thyself?
I must now wash thee clean." Once again Hung was conscious
that here in this place one submitted, whether to honour or dis-
honour, without demur. He gave himself into her hands, and in
the river she washed him, supporting him in her arms as a midwife with a newly born child.

Perhaps he even slept in her arms, for next it seemed that he was
entering a large building, though he could not remember his
approach to it. He was in the company of many virtuous and
venerable men, and he was made aware that amongst them were
the ancient sages: one, at whose side he stood, was that very
Wan who was the originator of the Chou dynasty in the Golden
Age. In the presence of such persons he must show no fear, for he

knew that they meant to act with all benevolence towards him, though what they were about to do was passing strange. It seemed that an operation must be performed upon him. They were discussing the rites and ceremonies that should accompany it, and now he was bidden to lie down upon a couch. With the utmost skill and no accompanying pain they opened his body with a knife and drew forth his sore, sad heart. He was conscious of an enormous relief, and that his troubles had been lifted from him. Then they put in its place a fine new heart, red and glowing with life and light, and they closed the wound so that it was as though it had never been, and his flesh was whole and no scar to be seen. He rose to his feet and gave them thanks, and then, while he waited with them, he examined the tablets upon the walls. These all carried inscriptions exhorting men to be virtuous. For what were they waiting? There had been this preparation, for he knew now that it was but a preparation. But for what? Even as he turned to ask Wan the answer, he became conscious, not that he was rising, but that the world and all it held was sinking beneath him, while he was held aloft. He was being borne upon wings not his own, carried in the bosom of some power, while space fell away beneath him.

"Up to the Thirty-Third Heaven!" Had he heard those words, or were they but his own affirmation of the certain knowledge? He found himself at last in a luminous place. Dimly he knew that it was a hall of much beauty and splendour, but all his attention was fixed upon the source of the light. It came, surely, not from the throne set in the highest place, nor from the figure seated therein, wearing a robe that appeared black in contrast to the face above it. It was the face which was the source of the light, the face of one so ancient of days that he must from the beginning of time have sat upon the throne. And from the face of the Venerable-in-Years flowed light, and he was bearded, and the light and the beard and his flowing hair were one, and they were golden. His eyes, gazing upon Hung, filled with tears, but they were tears of compassion and not of weakness. And then he spoke, and Hung cast himself with his face on the ground, because the voice was at once both so terrible and yet so comforting: a voice that could create, or preserve, or destroy at will.

"All human beings in the world are produced and sustained by me," he heard. "They eat my food and wear my clothing, but

not a single one among them has a heart to remember and venerate
me. A greater evil yet: they take my gifts and therewith worship
demons. They purposely rebel against me, and arouse my anger.
Do not thou imitate them."

Hung was bidden to rise. By what agency he was set upon his
feet, whether it was that which had borne him hither upon wings,
or by what powers and principalities he was now attended, he
could not afterwards say. At the bidding of the Venerable-in-
Years he was girded with a sword, and given the command to
exterminate demons, but to spare his brothers and sisters. Into
one of his hands was put a seal that by the name upon it he might
overcome all evil spirits, and into the other a yellow fruit, which
he was bidden to eat. Was it from the tree in Paradise where grew
the peaches of immortality? Obediently he bit into it, and the
sweetness and the flavour of it were beyond what the taste of
mortal man can assess.

He was required then to withdraw. The audience, if such it
could be called, was for the moment ended, but he would be
recalled. He found his way into an outer hall, and in it were
collected many men. Their faces were not at peace but were full
of anxiety and a contentious spirit, and Hung knew that they
were some of the rebels of whom the Venerable-in-Years had
spoken. True to his charge, he instantly began to exhort them to
return to their duties to the Ancient-of-Days, whereat some began
to moan and declare, "We have indeed forgotten our duties to
the Ancient and Venerable," and others grew defiant and swore,
"Why should we venerate him? Let us only be merry, and drink
together with our friends."

Then Hung began to weep because of the hardness of their
hearts, and because he saw now the magnitude of the task thrust
upon him. He turned about, and, caring nothing for protocol,
fled back into the hall of the Presence and cast himself upon the
ground. No anger was evinced at his intrusion. The voice of the
majesty upon the throne was infinitely patient. "Take courage,"
he heard, "and do the work. I myself will assist thee in everything."

The Venerable-in-Years continued to speak. It seemed that
Hung was to receive a new name. He, who had been named by his
parents "Fire-flash", was now to be called "The Accomplished
and the Perfected". The unsteady flame was to be blown upon,

the light made constant, the work of creation finally accomplished, whereof the pledge was to be this new name—Hsiu-ch'uan. Therefore as Hung Hsiu-ch'uan he rose from his knees, and the Presence came out with him from the hall to an assemblage of the old and virtuous, and declared before them all, "Hsiu-ch'uan is competent to this charge."

The Venerable-in-Years then led him out to the balustrade of the verandah and bade him look down, and Hung, expecting to see the garden in which the yellow fruit had grown, clung giddily to the balustrade and peered into immeasurable space.

"Behold," came the voice, "behold the people upon the earth! Hundredfold is the perverseness of their hearts."

Now it was that either his sight grew more powerful, or earth rose up more closely and was spread out below him, and Hung was able to see all the sins of men, as they went to and fro about their business, and the sight of that sin and its totality and weight were beyond his endurance. He turned to the Ancient-of-Days in despair. But the Presence accepted no despair, and held out to him a book, enjoining him to read it well and regard it as proof of his mission. Hung took the gift into his hands, and faced about once again to peer over the balustrade. The earth below began to drag him towards it, and he grew heavy with a heaviness which no winged power could any longer uplift. He sank into oblivion still clutching to his breast the precious book.

He woke from his trance, with hands grasping at the coverlet, and came to himself at a moment when his mother and younger sister had left him for an instant unattended. His first emotion was one of violent anger at the ingratitude of men to their Maker, and his next impatience that here he lay in his bed, when he should be immediately about the business entrusted to him. Forgetting the feeble state of his body, he rose at once, and began to put on his clothes. Though he was exhausted, his fingers no longer shook as he buttoned his blue cotton jacket. Then he left his bedchamber, and, with still uncertain feet, walked into the living-room where his father was sitting, alone and anxious. The womenfolk came running from their tasks, astonished at seeing him upright and walking.

He made a low bow to his father, and, before the old man could rise from his chair to help steady his son, straightway began to speak. "The Venerable One above has commanded that all men

shall turn to me, and all treasures shall flow to me." Perhaps Hung
meant to continue by saying that the work would take him from
home, and that filial piety demanded his father's permission and
blessing. But the effort of walking from his chamber had proved
after all too great.

Filled with both joy and fear Ching-yang managed to support
his son only just in time. The young man was again on the verge
of collapse. Between them the family got him once again to bed,
and once again he fell into a trance, while Ching-yang bent over
him fondly and pondered with pride and awe what the strange
words which his son had uttered might mean. If only his spirit
might return, prayed the fond parents.

But Hung's spirit was once again far away. He stood upon the
battlements of a celestial city whose every stone gave forth light,
and the frontier of the land which that city defended was space
itself, falling away into the abysmal deep whence rose the stench
of evil. The darkness was thick with demonic powers, the brush
of the wings of corrupting spirits. One after another the gates of
all highest heaven's city had been besieged, and now he, Hung,
must defend this gate on whose tower he stood. In his hand was
the sword so lately bestowed upon him, but he knew nothing of
sword-play, and the demons, which were even now rising to en-
velop him in the darkness of furred wings and scaly coils, were
more than any mortal man could withstand. He turned to fly, to
cast away his sword, and even as he relaxed his hold upon it the
hand of another man come down over his own and showed him
how to grasp the sword more firmly.

The man who had come to his aid he now saw to be neither
young nor old, and of such a noble countenance and withal so
friendly that Hung took heart and asked him who he was. He
learnt that he was the son of the Ancient-of-Days, and from his
position of authority Hung judged him to be the firstborn son,
next in dominion to his father, and the heir. He promised to
instruct Hung in the reading of the book which the father had
bestowed, and to accompany him to the uttermost regions in
search of the evil spirits that must be slain. Nor did he fail to keep
his promise. Out into space they launched together, Hung brandishing his sword. . . .

In the small confined bedchamber Hung's brothers attempted

to hold him down, while Ching-yang wrung his hands in bitter grief to see the delirium into which his son had fallen. The young man had leapt from his bed, and he appeared to be not so much shadow boxing as brandishing an invisible sword, while he cried out, "Slay the demons, slay, slay! There is one and there is another! Many, many cannot withstand one single blow of my sword."

From the Thirty-Third Heaven Hung, by virtue of the Elder Brother's help, drove all the demons; two-thirds of them fell to his sword, and the rest fled from the sight of his seal and were driven down below, down under. . . .

Once again he stood before the Venerable-in-Years and waited to abase himself, waited because there was another servant ahead of him who hung upon the judgment of the imperial glance. Hung recognised the face and form of that greatest of sages, Confucius, and to his astonishment heard the sage reproved, rebuked because he had omitted in his books clearly to expound the true doctrine. The teacher and example for ten thousand generations confessed his guilt and withdrew in shame and sorrow.

Now it was Hung's turn, and his heart smote him with fear and terror and love, as he sank to his knees, only to hear the benevolent injunction; "Return to earth, set your heart at rest, be not alarmed. You are my son."

In all, the trance had lasted on and off for forty days. When at last he came truly to himself, Hung could not believe that so long a time had elapsed. At first his father, in a dreadful anxiety, had ascribed what he deemed a misfortune to the fault of the geomancer in selecting the wrong spot for the burial of Hung's grandfather. All the resources of the physician had already been tried: cupping and acupuncture; stag's horn, mercury, sulphur and myrrh; musk and ginseng and the blood of an eel. A remedy against seeing spectres was to wrap a man's tooth in paper and burn it to ashes, and then mix the ashes with wine as a draught, but it had been impossible to approach Hung for the purpose of extracting a tooth, for he was strong in his delirium and would call out, "How could these imps and demons dare to oppose me? I must slay them. I must slay them. Many, many cannot resist me." The priests performed fumigations to drive the evil spirits away from him. Sometimes he broke into a song. "The virtuous swain he travels over rivers and seas; he saves many friends, and

he kills his enemies." Then again he would burst into tears and
proclaim, "You have no hearts to venerate the Ancient Father,
but you are on good terms with the impish fiends. Indeed, indeed,
you have no hearts, no conscience more."

Hung's brothers kept his door barred, and watched to prevent
him from running out of the house in his moments of semi-
lucidity. When he was known to be in deepest coma, the neighbours would come to steal a glimpse at him, for he was thought
now to be a madman and that was a matter for awe. For what
after all *was* madness? Shaking their heads they would creep
quietly away to ask themselves this. There were days when he
appeared to be fully in possession of his faculties. Then he would
speak of how he had been duly appointed Emperor of China. To
humour him some of his relatives so addressed him, whereat he
was plainly gratified, not because of any self-conceit but because
belief in his sanity brought him reassurance. But some, more
cruelly, called him mad to his face. Then he would laugh and
reply, "You are indeed mad yourself, and do you call me mad?"

While he was still deemed to be sick he began to compose
verses:

"My hand now holds both in heaven and earth the power to punish and
    kill—
To slay the depraved, and spare the upright; to relieve the people's
    distress.
My eyes survey from the North to the South beyond the rivers and
    mountains;
My voice is heard from the East to the West to the tracts of the sun
    and the moon.
The Dragon expands his claws, as if the road in the clouds were too
    narrow.
And when he ascends, why should he fear the bent of the Milky Way?
Then tempest and thunder as music attend, and the foaming waves are
    excited,
The flying Dragon, which the Yi-king describes, dwells surely in
    Heaven above."

Hung was describing the powers he had enjoyed in heaven, and
affirming his faith that his prayers were still heard there. He was
not so mad as to suppose that he already held temporal power,
but his spirit had mounted the dragon, and of his appointment

as Emperor he held no doubt. A change was taking place in his
personal appearance and demeanour. The scholar's stoop was
gone, and he seemed to his neighbours on a sudden to have grown
taller and to have an extraordinary power of body and understanding. They found his look piercing and difficult to endure. He
carried himself with dignity, sat erect with hands on his knees
and never crossed his feet. He spoke less than he had been used to
do, and laughed seldom. Many of the neighbours ridiculed him,
but there was a calmness and nobility in his expression which
made the laughter die on their lips. His new quiet confidence was
impressive. Anxiety had been lifted from his shoulders. Relieved
of the milling process that enslaved the mind and enervated the
body of China's scholars, both his body and his mind began to
thrive.

Andrew Wilson, a contemporary and editor of *The China Mail*,
was to write in his account of Gordon's campaign that the symbology in which Hung had received his visions was no more
than "the ordinary stock-in-trade of the village geomancers of
Kwang-tung", but he went on to add that "looking at the verses
he soon began to ejaculate, there is something about him—that
which Goethe used to call dæmonic—which defies analysis, and
even description". Wilson, a product of his generation, had never
considered that some symbols are archetypal and common to all
mankind, preserved in the folk-tales of Europe as much as by the
Taoist priests or the Christian clergy, just because they are the
common language of psychic experience: the need for rebirth
and the washing administered by ancient crone, midwife, or
Mother Church; the cock which heralds the light of Mithras, or
the dawn of the day of the Crucifixion; and finally the father-
image. That Hung was acquainted with such symbolism, that
Taoist legends, performances at the theatre, or the initiatory rites
of the secret societies had given him the subject matter for his
visions could not destroy their validity, for these very legends,
performances and rites were equally based on the psychic experience of mankind.

It was to be argued with more reason that Hung, at some time
prior to his visions, despite his solemn assurance to the contrary,
must have read at least a few pages of the Protestant tracts, before
he put them away on his bookshelf, there to lie forgotten, and that
his worries over his examinations and his subsequent illness caused

him to forget that he had done so. The present day knowledge of the process of "brain-washing" makes it perfectly feasible to suppose both that he did read the tracts and that afterwards he had no memory of having done so. But once again such a possibility could have no real bearing upon the validity of the visions. St. Paul on the way to Damascus was perfectly aware that Jesus of Nazareth had existed. He may even have seen him in life. Joan of Arc was equally familiar with the stories of the saints before she heard their voices. The genuineness of a vision seems to consist not in the revelation of a new sight or subject matter but in the quality of the seeing. Thus St. Paul's eyes were opened to see Christ in a light in which he, whether dreaming or awake, had never seen anyone before, and this quality of seeing touched and changed his whole life, as it was to touch and change Hung's, for to the gift of increased sight was added a new gift of increased hearing. Certain commands were given to St. Paul and St. Joan, and both were held in ridicule for their obedience to them. Hung also was at first to be held in ridicule.

Even his father was at a loss what to think on the day when he found the paper in the door. He had helped to set a chair outside the gate, that his son might sit out in the air and enjoy the pleasant evening sunshine. As he came back Ching-yang noticed a slip of paper that had been inserted in the crack of the doorpost. He pulled it out. Upon it was written in red characters (and it was the privilege of the Emperor alone to sign decrees with the Vermilion Brush), "The Noble Principles of the Heavenly King, the Sovereign King, Hsiu-ch'uan". The old man shook his head. Perhaps, if he provided a wife for his son, it might distract the young man's mind from these dangerous thoughts. He would consider the matter.

5

IT IS SAID THAT in the Buddhist paradise of Tushita one day is equivalent to four hundred years on earth, and in that of Shiva sixteen hundred of earth's years constitute only one day. A thousand years in God's sight are but as yesterday. All religions concur that time is only relative to the state of being, and that being itself transcends space. But to change rapidly from one state of being to another brings confusion and terror, for if a man cannot immediately and correctly judge the point in time and space where he stands, he is thought to be mad, and the fear of being so lost and outcast can truly send him out of his mind. Thus a mystic, descending from exaltation, needs the sharp and if necessary painful response of nerves to stimuli to reassure himself that he is where he is, and that he is what he is. A simple fellow could pinch himself to prove that he was awake. A priest could practise self-flagellation. But there is also the way of pleasurable stimuli. Hung's father had common sense, and he had guessed something of this, and that a woman might bring his son back to normality more quickly than any argument. Besides, Hung was nearly twenty-four, and it was high time that he in his turn should have a son, and cease to sit brooding over the meaning of his visions. No matter how poor they were, this time a girl must be found sufficiently beautiful to distract the young man.

In the village of Chiu-kuan, eight miles away, Ching-yang at last found such a girl as he had in mind in the family of a man called Lai. Her name was Lai-shi. Feng, who had failed in the September examinations at Canton, was most helpful in making the necessary arrangements. The sedan chair, trimmed with sham gold, which was kept in the locality ready for hire among the villages, had to be booked for the required date, and when the day came Feng went with it to fetch the bride. The procession, when it came back, made little impression upon the neighbours, for the bride's dowry was small, the livestock few, and the furniture carried in procession was negligible. The dowry she brought was her beauty, but that, under the red veil of her bridal crown, they could not see.

When Hung saw it, when at last the ceremonies and feasting were at an end, when at last he was alone with her, he drew a deep breath, and straightway began with the utmost willingness to experience those delights which were to give him the name of a voluptuary. As the taste of the peaches of paradise upon the tongue in the celestial sphere, so was she the fruit of life for which his hands stretched out on this terrestial plain. Her hair was like a cloud, her face a flower. He had not dreamt that breasts could be as white as nard. She was so small and fragile, that with his two hands beneath her rounded buttocks he could lift her easily and carry her hither and thither about his bedchamber as though she were a child. He could not have enough of her, and would gladly have turned day into night that he might lie with her the more often, but presently he had to restrain himself. For all that Lai-shi was as light and delicately built as the mountain nymphs of legend, she was to be no barren woman, and presently her jade-white belly began to swell.

When Hung knew that she was to bear his child, he felt a great pride and contentment. One day, he determined, she should be his empress, the mother of his heir. Her heart-shaped face and the dark pools of her tender eyes would look well beneath an ornament of jade and pearls.

Hung was not only proud and contented, but his months of lovemaking had given him back both bodily health and normality of mind, or so his father thought. What had actually happened was that Hung was able to review calmly and with his intellect the experiences which had so shaken his soul, to analyse these experiences and to seek the meaning of them; but he no more doubted that his soul had experienced another state of being than he doubted the reality of the rice he ate, the rice which was, incidentally, becoming increasingly scarce. Kwang-tung was on the verge of a famine, which was already afflicting the neighbouring provinces. That was an added reason for turning his mind to the problem of how he was to fulfil Heaven's command and succour the people.

Hung had learned not to talk of the divine commission freely save only to his cousin Jen-kan. With his own brothers he could not hope for intelligent appreciation of his problem. They were kind, not unready to believe, but stupid. To Jen-kan, now a boy of sixteen, he had recounted all his experiences, and how in his visions he had often met and as often been helped by the son of the Ancient-of-Days, and of how the Venerable-in-Years had told him that he, Hung, was also his son. Jen-kan, with his trained ability to learn by heart, committed every word of what Hung told him to memory, so that he could at any time have repeated with accuracy the description of Heaven and Hung's experiences there.

The problem they would discuss was this. Hung knew now what it meant to receive the Heavenly Mandate, and that it was no loose term for the will of the people or blind chance. The divine commission to rule China could not have been more definite, but how, with no power or the silver to buy power, was he to accomplish Heaven's will? The only way to power lay through taking office, and that very year of 1838 the Emperor Tao Kuang brought out a list to make public the scale of the sums for which office could be bought: 1,000 taels of silver for the eighth rank, 2,000 for the seventh, and so on. At first he strove to keep the ninth, the lowest rank, the reward of merit only, at least on paper, so that the civil servants should have at any rate some pretensions to efficiency before buying their way further up the ladder. It was the Opium War which forced him to change this policy.

On December 31st of that year, 1838, the Emperor appointed one Lin as special and Imperial Commissioner, with powers overriding those of the Viceroy, to go to Canton and there put an end to the opium traffic which was undermining the health of the people throughout China. The Viceroy, when he read the posting in the Imperial Gazette, straightway fell into a swoon, for he himself was implicated in the traffic, and had good cause to fear the arrival of Commissioner Lin. Presently the situation would lead to war with the British, and it was the need of money to wage it, and later to pay the indemnities for it, which would force Tao Kuang to revise his price list for the sale of office.

At the moment, however, the lowest degree of "Talented" could not be bought openly, though it was known to be purchasable privately, but in any case Hung had not enough silver. Yet he had received the Mandate of Heaven to rule China. From whom though, he wondered, had he received it? He did not know who was the Lord of Heaven, nor by what name to call Him.

Neither, alas, did the missionaries, who were at that time disputing in committee in Canton how to translate the name of Jehovah. The cosmogony accepted by the Confucians was couched in philosophic rather than anthropomorphic terms. The Ultimate Principle had created by first dividing itself into the masculine and feminine principles known as Yang and Yin. Yang and Yin transcended the merely biological sexes of male and female, and were as far removed and above them as the stars from the earth. All that was creative, dynamic, hot, fiery or dry was masculine, from the solar orb to the sand of the desert. All that was receptive, gentle, cool and moist was feminine, from the lunar disc to the rich soil of the river valleys. Only the Ultimate Principle had existed before this division whereby the creation had taken place.

For the Taoists Shang-ti was the supreme deity, yet above any deity was the Tao, the "Way", which again is a principle rather than a person. It had the meaning inherent in Christ's words "I am the way", but lacked that very "I am", the ineffable name of Jehovah, which gave authority to follow it.

For the Buddhists the state of Nirvana, that fusion of all personalities to achieve a blissful loss of identity, was a goal for which the gods themselves strove, showing in their struggle that they were mere demi-gods.

In the Classics of the third century B.C. it was written, "Heaven is the origin of truth", and from Confucius himself came the saying, "The will of Heaven is called nature". In this sense the will of Heaven meant not swimming against the current. Again no personality was involved.

The Roman Catholic term for God had come to be T'ien-chu (Lord of Heaven), a created term without Chinese antecedents. The majority of the Protestant denominations now adopted Shang-ti (Supreme Ruler), and thus forever after Protestants and Catholics were to preach in the name of a God on whose very appelation they could not agree.

It was hardly to be wondered at that Hung, with nothing to instruct him but his visions, should be at a loss to put a name to the Ancient-of-Days. He could distinguish that Yen-lo, demon-

king of the underworld, was the chief rebel against the Lord of
Heaven, but who that Lord was he did not know. He had, however, to moderate his search of the Classics, for now he was
sufficiently well to work again, and he had a living to gain both
for himself and for his wife and the child that was to come.

He was offered the post of teacher at his wife's village. They
were to live with her cousin, Lai Wen-kuang. It would mean a
change of scenery, if not of occupation. Once again he must listen
to the shrill interminable chanting of the beginners, as they recited
the "Three Character Classic". Appointments were always made
as from the New Year, so in the last half of February 1839 he
moved to take up his new post. There was plague about, and the
famine-stricken people had no strength to withstand it. So when
his child was born safely, he forgot his disappointment that it was
a daughter in gratitude that Lai-shi was restored to him sound in
health and as beautiful as ever.

For intellectual companionship he had her cousin, Wen-kuang,
a sturdy fellow given to shadow boxing and sword play, and ever
ready to talk over with Hung the news of what was going on in the
world, of which the chief was the doings of the Red Barbarians.
They had been thought to be only a small sect of the little colony
of primitives who were confined in isolation to the Factories at
Canton. Now it appeared that these British were sufficiently hardy
and numerous to dare to try their strength with the Viceroy.
Armed strife might at any moment break out. Wen-kuang's eyes
lit up, for he was by nature a fighting man and might long ago
have entered himself as a soldier on the quota of the district
magistrate, if the magistrate's militia had not borne such an evil
repute, as a band of idle vagabonds and flunkeys, that no honest
man with a family would endanger his good name by joining it.
Wen-kuang would sigh as he put away his practice-sword after a
bout with Hung, little dreaming that one day he would command
one of Hung's armies.

The trouble with the British had begun in April of that year.
Commissioner Lin had insisted on an immediate stoppage of the
opium traffic, and in May the British had perforce delivered to
him for destruction twenty thousand chests of opium, valued at
somewhere between two and five million sterling. Captain Elliot,
nephew of the first Earl of Minto and Superintendent of the China
trade, had directed the merchants to accede to the order. In return

Elliot had given the merchants a bond on the British government. Lin had next demanded that henceforward all vessels engaged in the trade should be confiscated, and all traders should suffer death. Naturally Elliot had refused to comply with the murder of his countrymen. He had bidden the merchants evacuate Canton, had withdrawn his ships to anchorage, and had called on the Governor General of India, Lord Auckland, for armed assistance. The Opium War had in fact begun.

"A war more unjust in its origin, a war more calculated in its progress to cover this country with disgrace, I do not know and I have not read of," was the uncompromising opinion of young Mr. Gladstone. In defence of Whig policy, it was said that opium killed no more people in China than did excessive drinking in England, but none dared use this argument who had ever come face to face with the effects of the drug: the shrivelled and tottering limbs, the sallow and sickly face, and the feeble voice.

Hung had seen these symptoms often enough, and in his opinion no penalty was too great for those who either distributed the poison or smoked it. But he had no violent hatred for the Red Barbarians in particular, for he knew that his own people, especially the officials, were as deeply involved in the iniquitous peddling of the drug as anyone. Of the cultivation of the opium in India, and the monstrous and meticulously organised method of its arrival in China, he knew as yet little, and could not therefore judge. What was of paramount interest to him was that these Red Barbarians were now waging a successful war with the Imperial administration, from which two facts were to be deduced. First, that these British were not the primitive folk which the lying officials would have had the people of China believe. Their terrible fire-ships and irresistible engines of war and guns might show them to be depraved, but certainly not primitive. They were a power to be reckoned with, and one to whom the Imperial government would have been wise, therefore, to show greater courtesy. His second deduction was that, despite their fire-ships and guns, their force was so small that for the Imperial armies to be withdrawing in confusion only showed how utterly rotten was the administration, and that any small united force could cut through the heart of China as easily as a knife through lentil-curd.

All the weaknesses which he had suspected, when the rebellion of the Golden Dragon had proved difficult to quell, were now so evident that talk of them was on every man's lips: the under-manning of quotas in the militia, that the officials might draw pay for non-existent troops; the last minute recruitment of undrilled and undisciplined men; the division of what strength there was into the Banners of the Tartars and the Chinese regiments, with no united control of either. If the Red Barbarians could cause such disarray, what might not the Elect of Heaven effect, he who had received the divine commission to sit upon the Dragon Throne?

The small British force was everywhere triumphant, and the people began to be afraid. The excesses of their own Imperial troops were not the least of their fears. Trade was at a standstill, particularly the opium traffic. At Lin-tin there was no longer any immediate hope of gaining a livelihood. Lo Ta-kang slipped over the side of the receiving ship, where he had worked so long, into a small boat which had come alongside, and pulled for the pirate junk anchored nearby. He was subsequently to pursue a career in piracy, until he gained the dubious rank of captain of a whole fleet of marauders upon the high seas, before throwing in his lot with the Taiping forces.

No tea was being bought by the Foreign Devils, and all the tea-porters became suddenly jobless. Hung's brother-in-law, Yang, had been a tea-porter in Kwang-tung, and now found himself without money or work. He and his wife decided, like thousands of others, to go back to the interior, to the province of Kwang-si, whence he had originally come, where there was no war, and where Cousin Wang grew tea. Because virgins were in constant danger of rape from the Imperial troops, Yang's wife offered to take her young half-sister. Cousin Wang could be trusted to ar-range a marriage for her. She was approaching the age of eighteen, and it was high time she was wed.

On August 21st 1841, Sir Henry Pottinger, who had been sent to replace Elliot, started out with an armed force to continue the war, and before January 1842 he had taken two important cities and had possessed himself of the island of Hong Kong. The Man-chus were beaten, and the Emperor gave to his uncle, Prince Kiying, the Imperial commission to sign a treaty of peace at Nan-king.

This Treaty of Nanking made big changes. Though the Chinese refused to legalise the opium trade, they agreed to pay six million sterling as indemnity for the expense of the war. Hong Kong was

ceded as an island, where the British Chief Superintendent of
Trade and Plenipotentiary would in future reside, and be in control of the Consuls to be appointed to the five ports now "opened".
Gone were the days when the Europeans might venture no further
than Macao and the Canton Factories. Now they might also reside
in concessions on the coast at Amoy, Shanghai, Ning-po and Fu-
chou, though nowhere else, and the interior was still forbidden.
There was to be toleration for the missionaries to preach in these
places, and they might now construct churches. Though the interior was forbidden equally to the missionaries, there was now a
large field for their work and few to cover it. Within the next
ten years missionary societies represented in China rose from
twenty to one hundred and sixty-five, and were of nearly every
known denomination.

In order to pay for the indemnity to the British, the Emperor
increased both the prices and advertisements of the sale of posts
in the civil services. With characteristic euphemism such sales
were called "Contribution for appointment to public office", but
nobody was deceived. If Hung had had the silver, he could now
have purchased his degree for only 200 taels, or the fourth rank
and the post of Tao-t'ai for 30,000 taels.

Famine, plague, then war, and always grinding poverty, and
finally the land-tax to pay with depreciated "cash"—no wonder
the people groaned. In two hundred years the Cantonese had
never entirely given up hope of unseating the Manchu dynasty.
The last resistance of the Mings had been in Kwang-tung province, and here subversive activities had been carried on by various
secret societies. The most powerful of them, the Heaven-and-
Earth society, which had backed the recent rebellion of the
Golden Dragon, was said to have been founded as early as 1683
with the express purpose of overthrowing the Ch'ing (the dynastic
name of the Manchu Emperors) and restoring the Ming. In fact
the society was very, very much older than that. It had existed
since the fourth century A.D., and its initiation ceremonies were
contemporary with the Greek mysteries. The word "Ch'ing"
meant "vital force", or the matter in which the soul was immersed.
"Ming", on the contrary, was the word for "light" and the perfected spirit in man. The esoteric meaning, therefore, of the
initiatory oath to overthrow the Ch'ing and restore the Ming was
to oust darkness from the soul and substitute spiritual light.

The society was not confined to Kwang-tung. Its lodges were spread all over China, but, exactly as with the Freemasons in Europe, while the ritual of an ancient mystery religion was preserved, the purpose of the society had, since the seventeenth century, become political and subversive: a weapon in the hands of a man who could learn to use it, for there was hardly a city in the Empire without its lodge.

To Lo Ta-kang, ever since he had left the opium receiving-ships at Lin-tin, piracy and smuggling had brought a quick return in silver and power. Now he was captain of his own vessel, with a small fleet of pirate ships willing to follow him in raiding along the coast, or to cover up his appearance whenever he chose to step ashore at Canton from some apparently innocent trading junk. He was bound this night upon a secret errand: his initiation into the Heaven-and-Earth society.

He, like so many others, had seen the weakness of the Tartar forces in the late war, and like many others he had suffered at the hands of the corrupt officials. Any change of régime would be for the better. But what to do? Men must band together, but how? He had seen the Red Barbarians fighting at Canton, and he knew their strength, but now there was no way of using it, for the Foreign Devils had made a treaty with the Tartars. Nor would he have wished to change one set of masters for the other, for both were foreigners.

It had been in a tea-house that he had first come across the stranger who was responsible for having drawn him into the present venture. He had wondered why the man had made such a prominent use of three fingers only to lift his tea-cup, and why other men he had saluted had raised their cups in similar fashion. It was the secret sign of recognition amongst the members of the society, the "brethren". He knew now why the society had been named as it was, for his instructor had told him, "When Heaven, Earth and Man combine to favour us, we shall succeed in subverting the Tartar dynasty. Therefore we are called the society of the Three United or Triads, or the Heaven-and-Earth Society. Only the man is missing; the Golden Dragon was not the man."

From Formosa to Hu-nan, and from the Yang-tze to Kwang-si, the same thing was being whispered in all the Triad lodges, as Lo Ta-kang knew very well from his association with the pirates and smugglers, who carried news down the coast and up the waterways. Nor did you have to be a "brother" to know that there was a prophecy more than a hundred years old that the Manchu dynasty would be overthrown in the year beginning on the first day of February 1851. Even the Foreign Devils had heard of this prophecy, and there was a rumour that a scion of the Mings still existed and would be revealed at the proper time. Lo Ta-kang, as he swung down the dark alley-way in a Canton suburb to halt opposite the corn chandler's warehouse, whose stores disguised the entry to the hall of the lodge beyond, wondered if this might be true.

The ritual which followed was to make some few Europeans, when they came to have knowledge of it, suspect that Hung had himself at one time or another undergone initiation, and that his visions were spurious and a mere recapitulation of his experiences in a similar lodge. Yet Hung denied this, and his whole future policy of antipathy to the society endorsed the truth of his denial. The truth itself lay deeper, for those prepared to search. The ancient ritual was based on a symbolism common to all men's psychic experience, and was of an archetypal pattern.

Lo Ta-kang's admission and reception into the small room of paper screens caused him no alarm. He had been as far before, and was already familiar with the small idol of the god of war, the tutelary deity of the brothers, before whom he must burn incense. This place, he knew, was approximate to the world wherein he had been born and with which he was all too well acquainted. He put down before the idol the purse containing his subscription, and remembered to say the required words, "All purses in the world are the same". Then, bending nearly double, he passed for the first time between two ranks of the brethren, who held crossed swords above him, and who brought the flat of them from time to time down upon his neck. At the end of his passage he paid three "cash" to use stepping-stones, which existed in the imagination only, and thus, crossing the river at the "Bridge-towards-the-Mount", for the first time he entered the lodge proper. Here he was greeted ceremoniously by the "Big Brother", the Master himself, and his two attendant incense-masters, and was delivered over to the "White Fan Instructor" for the ritual divestment.

"Wash clean your traitorous heart," began the White Fan. "Divest yourself of the garment of Ch'ing, the emblem of servitude, and in place thereof don the raiment of Ming."

Lo Ta-kang, though he was accustomed to swagger in his sea-faring piratical finery, was as naturally modest as most Chinese, and as he doffed his clothing, unplaited his queue, and shook his hair loose, he felt in truth almost as naked as though he had put off body and bared his soul. His usual bravado was so much sub-dued that, although he began to cleanse himself in the bowl of water held out to him, he nearly forgot to recite his response, and remembered only just in time to say, "My hair is not yet dry and I am only recently born."

Then he put on the grass sandals and the white garments of mourning and of the dead, and someone helped him to comb his hair, and to bare his right arm and breast and his right knee.

Next he was brought before the Red Guard, whose business it was to scrutinise the heart of the candidate for initiation, and to weigh it. He stood by a fiery furnace with a pair of scales, and went through a series of ritual gestures to indicate his office, be-fore requiring from Lo Ta-kang the oaths of secrecy. There were thirty-six of these, and here Lo Ta-kang did not need to tax his memory, for they were inscribed on paper, and were burnt in the furnace one after another as soon as he had recited them. At last he came to the end. "This night I pledge myself that the brethren in the whole universe shall be mine as from one womb, begotten as from one father, and nourished by one mother, and that together with them I will obey Heaven and act righteously."

The Red Guard thereupon struck the head from a white cock —it had made an unpleasant screeching noise as he seized it—and, dipping his hand in the blood, Lo Ta-kang swore, "So may my head be struck off if I should prove a traitor."

He was glad to have done with the divestment and the ordeals. Now there remained only to give an account of the long journey he was supposed to have undertaken. He had managed to under-stand from previous instruction that his journey concerned the progress of the soul and its arrival in paradise, but, as both his instructor and himself had been more interested in present day politics, neither had sought very deeply into the meaning of the antiquated ritual which he must now recite. It was the Grand Master, the "Big Brother", who began the questions, and he barred the way to beyond, as he stood flanked by his two assistants.

"Whence come you?"

"From the east," answered Lo Ta-kang correctly.

"At what time?"

"At sunrise, when the east was light."

"How came you?" asked the Master.

"On a ship. On the bow was the image of the God of Fire. On the left was the clear-perceiving Ear and on the right the thousand-mile-seeing Eye."

The Big Brother bowed his head in confirmation, and continued, "What thing was most precious in the ship?"

"A pure white pearl."

"To what place did you sail?"

"To the City of Willows." This Lo Ta-kang knew to be the name of paradise amongst the brethren.

"How came you to it?"

"By the Cloud-Bridge." He was remembering his answers well. Almost he felt that it was the journey itself that he was recalling and not the mere words.

"Who stood at the end of the Bridge?"

"A man selling fruit, who told me, 'I am the old man of the Southern Mountains, searching for heroes on the Bridge-of-Two-Planks. My name is Shi-pang, and I sell peaches. If I turn myself round I am again the old grey-head.'"

Once more the Master nodded. "What is held highest in the City of Willows?"

"The lamp—the light."

Lo Ta-kang had passed all the tests: the divestment, the judgment, the reiteration and assessment of the knowledge acquired on his journey. Now came the investment, the endowing. The Master of the Lodge drew back to disclose a table on which were displayed the ritual ornaments of the lodge: the scissors for birth, the scales for judgment, the model of the peach tree. The new initiate was made to take one after another into his hands. Next the mirror. "This precious mirror handed down to us from of old," intoned the Master, as he proffered it to Lo Ta-kang. "This precious sword, which lies in the City of Willows and with lustre is resplendent." The pirate Lo Ta-kang was a little taken aback to find that the resplendent sword was made of nothing more deadly than peach-wood; and when last of all he was handed the lamp he lit it with the usual flint and tinder, for much of the secret significance of the ritual had been lost, and not even the Master of the Lodge could have taught him that the mirror was for conjuring fire from the sun, the "sword" but the universal poetic and esoteric epithet for the burning brand it ignited, and the lamp a symbol for the body in which the light of light must be begotten in man from above.[1]

As to the final oath and the sealing of the covenant between Lo Ta-kang and his Triad brethren, that also was a mysterious and secret ceremony of which more must be said hereafter.

The Imperial government was well aware of the unrest fermenting underground all over China, and particularly in the proscribed secret societies to which Lo Ta-kang now belonged. To avoid trouble on two fronts, the administration was at last seeking friendship with the Foreign Devils. It was better to submit to the terms of the Treaty of Nanking with a good grace, and thus gain time for the Emperor to strengthen himself against both menaces. The advocate of at least outwardly turning over a new leaf and treating the Barbarians with courtesy was Prince Kiying, the Emperor's uncle, who had signed the treaty. His seat was now in Kwang-tung as both Governor General and Imperial Commissioner, specially commissioned to deal with the affairs of the Foreign Devils.

The Europeans had hopes that the days of their being despised as lepers were over for good and all. They did not know that orders between the court and the officials spoke of "soothing the uncontrollably fierce Barbarians", and that the soothing process held no genuine desire for friendship, but was purely a temporary expedience, though Kiying himself was more genuinely attracted to his new acquaintances than was altogether wise for his future safety at the hands of his sovereign. But the "soothing" did have one lasting effect. The people of Kwang-tung began to notice that a prince of the Imperial family was on visiting terms with the Foreign Devils. The Barbarians could not therefore be the moral outcasts which the officials had led them to believe. There began to be a fashion for taking interest in the foreigners, and particularly in such of their books as were translated, and Hung's cousin Li now came across some of these translations. Perhaps he had been hoping to understand the secrets of how the foreigners made such excellent clocks and guns and steamships. If so he was

[1]For further explanations of this symbolism see *The Ancient Secret* by the same author (Gollancz, 1953).

disappointed. But all the same, the books were very curious, he thought, and worth reading.

It came about in this way. Hung had been offered more lucrative employment in a new school at Water Lily village, ten miles from his home, where lived the family of his father's first wife, the deceased mother of his two half-brothers. The Li family had got him the appointment, which as usual began after the New Year in that February of 1843, but at first there was no house for him and he boarded with his cousins. In the month of June sufficient rooms became available for him to fetch his wife and child and the furniture from home. Cousin Li, a blacksmith by trade, came to help him with the packing up and the transport, and now for the first time in nine years Liang Fa's tracts came to light from the back of the bookshelf. At home again in Water Lily village Cousin Li settled down to read them for himself, for Hung was too busy working for the next provincial examination to have time to attend to Li's smothered ejaculations and obvious interest in the little books which he had found.

In August Hung went up to Canton for his third attempt at the provincial degree. The weather was unbearably hot, and the monsoon wind brought no rain. That would mean a terrible drought. There would be more hardship, more famine. In Heaven's name how, just how, he wondered, would it ever be possible for a struggling and impoverished schoolmaster to obey the divine command which had been laid upon him, and seize the Empire? He failed his examination for the third and last time.

Never again would he try for it, he decided. The whole system was a Tartar plot: a plot to enslave the mind and enervate the body. Did he really want to become an official? Certainly not the kind of official which the system produced. They could not govern and they could not fight, and they could not even tell a man who ruled Heaven, which was the one question all men desired to have answered. Why should he force himself into such a groove?

Back again from Canton he flung down his books upon the table in front of the astonished Li and said, "Wait until I myself open the examinations and choose the Empire's scholars!" To choose men from those holding the metropolitan degree was an Emperor's prerogative. Li was startled, though he knew that

Hung believed himself to have received the Mandate of Heaven in vision, but of late Hung had ceased to talk openly of such wild ideas.

The way, thought Hung, who had never relinquished his faith, must lie not through peaceful advancement but through war and an uprising of the people. He had for years been studying military history. He knew now in theory how an army should be organised. But who would follow him? Where should he find the troops? Should he perhaps after all have remained in Canton, as he had been tempted to do, and have joined the society of Heaven-and-Earth, the Triads, and thus have had a weapon ready to his hand? Such suggestions had been made to him, as frequently happened to men nowadays, for the lodges were pulling in recruits, and there was no doubt that sooner or later the secret societies would rise against the government. Should he go back to Canton even at this moment, he asked himself, and overcome his distaste for dark alleys and bloody sacrifices? He stood there doubtful, hardly seeing Li, on whose face was an expression of enquiry.

Then he became conscious that Li was offering him something —those books, which he had been given so long ago on his first visit to the provincial capital. What was his cousin saying? That really he should read them, for they would distract his mind from his present worries, and Li had found them so curious and strange that he wished to have a scholar's opinion on them, for he himself was but a simple and almost uneducated man.

So Hung acceded with a smile, as was only courteous, and took the books to his room.

6

THE TRACTS, ENTITLED "Good Works for Admonishing the Age", consisted of nine volumes. Alone in his room Hung began to read the first, and the opening passage was a translation of the first chapter of Genesis, the story of the Creation but not the Fall. Liang had used for God the name of Jehovah, and had rendered it in phonetic fashion syllable by syllable into Chinese. Thus, by the dispensation of providence, the very first words which Hung read were, "Shen ye huo hua", for which the Chinese meaning syllable by syllable was "Spirit old-man fire bright".

His interest quickened. In his mind he saw again the brilliant countenance of the Ancient-of-Days. Daniel had described the bright light round Jehovah's head as hair, white like pure wool, but Hung had seen the light as golden, and the dominion and rulership and power had been made manifest in masculine qualities, for he had seen the Ancient-of-Days as bearded.

A house indicates a builder, argued Liang Fa in the adjoining discourse. It could not have built itself. "How much less could heaven, earth, all creatures and kinds, so great a work, just happen of itself? There must be a creator. And if a creator, there must be a governor to keep it from disorder. This is the true God, without form or image." Not without form, Hung privately commented, for had he not himself seen this governor? "Existent of Himself from everlasting to everlasting, called Shen-T'ien Shang-ti (spirit-heaven ruler-above). He is enthroned forever in heaven," Liang had written. "Men in every country of the world should daily reverence Him and worship Him alone. He needs no temple made by men's hands, nor image set up for worship. A clean place in the open air, or a clean audience-hall, or a clean small house will do."

Hung read on, breathless, transfixed. At last, at last he was to learn more of that Lord of Heaven from whom he had received the mandate to rule China. He seemed to hear again the words which he had heard in his vision, "All human beings in the world are produced and sustained by me." It must then be this same Shang-ti, creator of all things, who had spoken to him. Had not the Ancient-of-Days given him a book, and enjoined him to read it well, and regard it as a proof that his experience had been a true one? But when he had come to himself, there had been nothing in his hands save the coverlet of his bed. Was this the promised proof? If so, it was a direct gift from Heaven, intended specially for him. Trembling with reverence and fear, almost afraid to touch the paper, he turned the page and began to read the first chapter of Isaiah, which Liang had chosen to follow the story of the Creation.

"The Lord hath spoken, I have nourished and brought up children, and they have rebelled against me . . . the whole head is sick, and the whole heart faint. Wounds and bruises and putrefying sores, they have not been closed. Your country is desolate. Your land, strangers devour it in your presence. Bring no more vain oblations. Incense is an abomination unto me. Your new moons and your appointed feasts my soul hateth. Wash you, make you clean . . . relieve the oppressed, judge the fatherless, plead for the widow. . . . Thy silver is become as dross. Thy princes are rebellious and companions of thieves, every man loveth gifts, and followeth after rewards. Therefore, saith the Lord . . . I will restore thy judges as at the first and thy counsellors as at the beginning."

It was plain to Hung that if the people of China knew nothing of the Supreme Ruler, He knew all about them. He was aware, then, how the land had been taken by the Tartars, and how they oppressed the poor, and how the officials would give judgment only in return for bribes. He even knew that men could no longer get silver at the old value. But the return of the Golden Age was promised. He heard again the ancient woman at the river's edge say, "I must now wash thee clean", and he felt the cold blade of the knife as his heart was removed. But his wound had closed. He felt his ribs. The sentence which struck him most, however, was, "They have rebelled against me", for this was almost word for word what the Ancient-of-Days had said to Hung.

Again he turned the page, and there, for his soul's sake, Liang
had translated the fifth, sixth and seventh chapters of the Gospel
according to St. Matthew. He read the Beatitudes. Who, he
wondered, was this individual who had apparently all the virtues
of Confucius, but who could speak with authority and knowledge
concerning "your Father which is in Heaven"? It was true that
the Ancient and Venerable had called Hung "son", and had bidden him spare his brothers and sisters. Thus Hung knew that
all men and women were children of Shang-ti, all, that is, save
those who had rebelled and forfeited their position in their
Father's house, all, that is, excepting the Tartars. It seemed that
this virtuous man who had spoken the Beatitudes must indeed be
that very one who had held the position of eldest son in his Father's
house. If so, it was Hung's Elder Brother, his Heavenly Elder
Brother who was speaking to him now from the printed page.
And what a message he was sending to his humble younger
brother!

Presently Hung came to the Lord's Prayer, and in that small
clean room he sank to his knees.

"Consider the lilies of the field . . ." While Hung in school
listened to the interminable drone of the boys reciting the Three
Character Classic—"Men at their birth are by nature pure"—
his trained Chinese memory was recording what he had learned
in the three chapters of Matthew. He did not know who Solomon
might be, but supposed that as an example of glorious array he
must have been an emperor. Well, when he, Hung, was raised
to the Dragon Throne, he would re-institute the costume of the
Ming dynasty, such as he had seen in the Canton theatre. No
more of this bald head and monkey tail! He would grow his hair,
and the Heavenly Father would provide the silks and satins and
crowns befitting the ruler of the Celestial Empire. He could
hardly wait until the boys left school to seize the second volume
of Liang Fa's tracts.

The second volume was harder reading. It began with a sermon
on the text, "For God sent not his Son into the world to condemn the world, but that through him the world might be saved."
It was never to occur to Hung that his Heavenly Elder Brother
was other than the first of God's creatures. Already he felt the
need for a new heart, the new heart promised in vision. Already

he was conscious of his faults and of the need for pardon. At
once he accepted with childlike faith the need for atonement
and that his Heavenly Elder Brother was the Redeemer. But the
difficulty which had rent apart theologians from the days of
Athanasius and Arius—namely, that if Jesus was merely a man,
albeit the first of men, his death could no more atone for the sins
of mankind than the death of the many righteous and innocent
men who had died, and were presently to die in millions at the
hands of the Tartars—altogether passed him by.

The sun was beginning to set. He took the book nearer to the
light. He was nearly thirty years old, and already his eyes were
beginning to give trouble. He was reading the first twenty-one
verses of the third chapter of the Gospel according to St. John:
Christ's words to Nicodemus. Liang's commentary ran thus, "To
be righteous is hard, unless one repents sin, receives water of
baptism washing clean body and soul, moreover receives the
virtue of the Holy Spirit, bringing to life again the good nature of
heart and soul, leaves the evil and perverse, and runs the good
way. Then one can enter the kingdom of God and enjoy the
blessing of everlasting joy. Otherwise one cannot enter the kingdom of God, but will go down to hell to suffer everlasting woe."

Hung had need for expansion, the expansion of a heart overflowing. He rose from his seat in the school-house window, and
began to pace the room. Here was the exact description of what
had happened to him in vision: the need for washing, the need
for bringing to life again of the heart, and, from what he had
read, it seemed that this was a rite which could be performed not
in vision only but in the flesh.

Once again he sat down to read. It was the nineteenth psalm
which Liang had chosen to print next, and inscrutable providence
had ordained that the word for "wholeness, altogether, entire",
which in the Chinese is "ch'uan", should be read by Hung as
referring to his own name, the name by which he had insisted
upon being called ever since the Heavenly Father had bestowed
it upon him in vision: "Ch'uan", the perfected or complete.
Beginning with the sonorous and rhapsodic, "The heavens declare
the glory of God," it went on, therefore, "Their voice is gone out
to the country of Ch'uan . . . the judgments of the Lord show
Ch'uan righteous, more to be desired than fine gold." What
could any man feel but humility towards a Father who, despite

all Hung's failings, so acclaimed him? Humility at first, but afterwards a flush of pride to the cheek when he began to consider that, if God so acclaimed him, then men must do likewise.

The seeming cruelty of nature's limitations, which tie men helpless in the bonds of language, was offset somewhat by that which Hung read on the following page. It was the thirty-third psalm, and was from henceforth to become his favourite. In the Chinese it ran, "Jehovah God from heaven looks down. He sees on earth all the sons of men. From the place of his habitation He sees all the inhabitants of earth. He made alike the hearts of them all. He considers all their works."

For a moment the tears stung his eyes. So close a description was this of that moment outside time when he had stood beside the Heavenly Father, and peered down over the balustrade of the celestial realm to the earth below, that the present exile from the Father's presence was almost unbearable. But there was no time to weep, for here were his Father's very words, and not one of them must he miss.

Liang had given next a translation of the central part of the forty-fifth chapter of Isaiah. "I am the Lord, and there is none else, there is no God beside me. I girded thee, though thou hast not known me." Indeed Hung remembered how he had been girded with the sword wherewith to fight the demons! "Thus saith the Lord," he read on, "my hands have stretched out the heavens and Ch'uan's host have I commanded." Once again Hung had fallen into the trap of language. "He shall build my city," he went on reading. "And he shall let go my captives, not for price or reward, saith the Lord of hosts." Hung did not know who the Egyptians, Ethiopians and Sabeans might be. They must, he thought, refer to the Outer Barbarians, or perhaps even to those very Foreign Devils whom he had seen fighting in the late war. According to this scripture they were to come presently and do him homage, not because he had fire-ships and guns, but because the Heavenly Father had chosen him. "In chains shall they come over and they shall fall down unto thee. They shall make supplication unto thee, saying surely God is in thee."

Cousin Li arrived then to see what had become of Hung. The evening meal was ready. He picked up the volume to see how far Hung had read. The next page was Liang's account of the Flood. On the way to the house they conned it, and discussed it over supper. There had been no rain, and the fields were dry. It was September and there should have been rain in the monsoon of August. Lai-shi, as she cleared away the rice bowls, asked about this flood of which her husband was speaking. Had the Yellow River in the far north burst its banks yet again? Hung and Li were uncertain whether the Flood had already happened or was about to happen, but the women of the family were sure that it was a thing of the past, for they had already heard such a story from the Taoist priests. There had been a great inundation in ancient times. The Mother of the Gods had repaired the rents in heaven with stones of five colours, the rainbow. Lai-shi was quite certain about it.

Hung fell silent when he heard mention of the Mother of the Gods, but began to ponder in his heart and to search in his memory to distinguish between the powers and principalities who had welcomed him in heaven. Had there indeed been a mother in that jewelled city of vision?

Despite the extravagance, he lit the lamp after supper, and began to read Liang's discourse upon the twenty-fourth verse of the seventh chapter of the Acts of the Apostles. "God dwelleth not in temples made with hands. . . . He hath made of one blood all the nations of men to dwell on all the face of the earth." Thus the Outer Barbarians were his brothers. It could not be correct, therefore, to call them Foreign Devils. He pondered on this conception of universality.

The next of Liang's sermons had as its text, "If ye endure chastening, God dealeth with you as with sons; for what son is he whom the father chasteneth not?" All men, then, were God's sons. He glanced at Cousin Li. Nevertheless, Li had not received the Heavenly Mandate to rule China. There were sons and sons, and a different degree of responsibility was accorded to each. Thus, when Hung turned to read next a paraphrase of the twelfth and thirteenth chapters of St. Paul's Epistle to the Romans, he read it as a ruler might read a report concerning his subjects, and not as closely concerning himself. "Live peaceably with all men. . . . Avenge not yourselves for it is written, vengeance is mine. . . . If thine enemy hunger, feed him. . . . The powers that be are ordained of God. Whosoever, therefore, resisteth the power, resisteth the ordinance of God; and they that resist shall receive to themselves damnation. . . . He beareth not the sword in vain for he is the minister of God, a revenger to execute wrath upon him that doeth evil." This last sentence did, or so he thought, concern him closely. Had not the Heavenly Father given him the sword of office? He, Hung, was therefore appointed to be the minister of God, his viceroy to rule China, and any who resisted his rule would receive damnation.

He turned to a paraphrase of the fifth chapter of James, and it was followed by a translation of the fifty-eighth chapter of Isaiah. Loose the bands of wickedness, undo the heavy burdens. Let the oppressed go free. Break every yoke, said the prophet. Feed the hungry, clothe the naked, keep the Sabbath. Hung was puzzled, for he did not know how to keep the Sabbath, nor indeed how the rite of washing should be performed.

Liang had next given an account of his own conversion and into this Hung now plunged. "I not only did not myself go to worship any images of gods, or Buddhas or Boddhisattvas, but seeing others do so, I pitied their folly. I wanted to take the holy precepts of the true scriptures to admonish and change their foolish hearts." Liang was showing Hung the way. First he must learn, then he must teach. He must teach his younger brothers and sisters, of whom the Heavenly Father had spoken to him, saying, "Spare them". Then, when he had carried out the will of the Heavenly Father, the Father would give him dominion.

At last he saw the way clear. At last he was relieved of the pangs of conscience and the fear of failing to fulfil the mission entrusted to him. It was a question of faith and of doing his part and of leaving God to do God's. He gave a great sigh of thankfulness, knowing that there was no more cause for anxiety, that at last his orders were clear, and that he was capable of carrying them out. For to learn, to examine, to comment and to teach had become to him second nature. He was, after all, a schoolmaster. He put out the lamp and went to bed. All he had to do now was to rise an hour earlier, nothing unusual for a scholar and study these writings every day before school met.

He began at 4 A.M. next morning, and it was an easy passage: the fifth chapter of Ephesians. The exhortations therein were such as any Confucian would have approved. St. Paul inveighed against whoremongers, fornication, foolish talking and drunkenness. All right-thinking men agreed that such things were matters for shame. Who was this Paul, Hung wondered, who spoke with the virtue of a Confucius, but who knew that practical help from heavenly persons was needed if men were to remain virtuous? Once again Liang gave him the answer with an account of Paul's vision of the way to Damascus, and he followed it with the second and third chapters of the First Epistle to Timothy, wherein it is shown how this practical help may be received. "For there is one God, and one mediator between God and men, the man Jesus Christ, who gave himself a ransom for all." From these words it seemed clear to Hung that the Heavenly Elder Brother was a man, like himself, but oh indeed what a man!

Now what was this concerning the correct behaviour of bishops and deacons? Teachers of some kind, he supposed, holding the metropolitan degree, or even members of the Han-lin College, perhaps. Certainly not Viceroys or members of the Imperial family, for they were allowed apparently only one wife. They must, therefore, be poverty-stricken scholars like himself.

He had reached almost the end of the sixth volume of the tracts. The last pages of the volume gave a translation of the twenty-first chapter of the Revelation of St. John.

The boys were tripping into school, but Hung was not there. They paused, uncertain, for there was no one to whom they could make their customary bows.

Hung, uplifted by the words he was reading in his bedchamber, felt almost as though he were once again exalted to that realm beyond time and space. "And I saw a new heaven and a new earth. . . . He that overcometh shall inherit all things; and I will be his God, and he shall be my son." Even so had the Heavenly Father declared to Hung, "You are my son". Once again he seemed to stand in the Heavenly City, and now he learned its very name, the holy Jerusalem. The city was of stone most precious, even like jasper stone, clear as crystal, and it lay four-square surrounded by a high wall with twelve gates. And the city was of pure gold, like unto clear glass. The walls were made of precious jewels, and the gates were of pearl, and the streets were of gold. "And I saw no temple therein, for the Lord God Almighty and the Lamb are the temple of it . . . and the kings of the earth do bring their glory and honour unto it." And in the Chinese the last words ran, "Blessed are they that hold fast sincerely. They have the right to take the tree of life." Even so had he tasted of the yellow fruit given him by the Heavenly Father.

There was some grumbling by the parents of the boys that the
school-teacher was late in the mornings. If he must study for his
degree, then he should light a lamp at night. Did they not pay
for his oil?

The days went by. Hung had completed his reading of the
first and second chapters of the First Epistle to the Corinthians.
Now Liang gave him an account of how virtuous men from the
west had travelled myriads of miles to Kwang-tung, and spent
myriads of cash to study the language and translate the scriptures.
"It is therefore highly desirable," he read, "that the men of the
great and glorious Middle Kingdom who see these books should
not vainly boast of their own country being the land of true
principles, of propriety and fine literature, but with a humble
mind put aside their own prejudices, and the thought of what
country they are derived from."

It was hard to suppose, reflected Hung, that the Outer Barbarians had received a knowledge denied to the people of the
Celestial Empire of China. He began to search the classics for
references to the worship of Shang-ti in the Golden Age. Just as
he had suspected! In the ancient times the Supreme Lord had
indeed received due and proper worship. Presently he would
write an essay to show that this was so.

"Perhaps," wrote Liang, "one will say, God is the Lord of
heaven and earth, of man and of all creation, most holy and
revered. Men and people are things slight and mean, dirty and
defiled, and dare not worship him. He is for princes and great
mandarins and the like to reverence and worship, not for the
common people. What an idea! For the great Lord of heaven and
earth, men and all creation, is the great Father and Mother of all
lands, all kinds of men. From prince to commoner all should
revere and worship him."

For more than two thousand years only the Emperor, the Son
of Heaven, had been entitled to worship at the Altar of Heaven;
for though philosophers might dispute as to whether Heaven was
an Ultimate Principle, or a Way of Life, or nature, and though
they were more or less agreed that it was not a person, yet it was
the highest power of which men could conceive, and it was held
that only the highest in the microcosm might address petitions
and reports to the highest in the macrocosm. Hung there and
then resolved that, when the Heavenly Mandate was made

manifest in himself, he would decree that all men might share
with him the right to memorialise the throne of the Heavenly
Father.

So intent were his thoughts upon this new conception of the
Father's relation to his sons that the next translation—"Though
I speak with the tongues of men and of angels, and have not
charity, I am become as a sounding brass"—did not sink into his
soul. It would be untrue to say that Liang's tracts were drawn
predominantly from the Old Testament, for there was a fair
proportion of texts and translations, as rendered by Dr. Morrison,
from both the New and the Old. That Hung sometimes failed to
catch the spirit of the New, in particular the exhortations to
forgive his enemies, was not entirely his fault. To expect of him
so much would be tantamount to expecting that Moses could
immediately have seized not only the significance of the Burning
Bush, but the whole new dispensation of Christ's incarnation in
his one short lifetime.

Hung stood now at the door of his little mud-and-wattle house
with the tracts in his hands, gazing out upon the wide sky, and he
was as dumbfounded and astonished as Moses had been when he
had first heard the voice of Jehovah. A revelation of the unity,
the person and the Fatherhood of God was quite enough to fill a
man's soul, unprepared as Hung was. The person of Christ had
not yet touched him, was never indeed to touch him in the
deepest places of his soul. For his Heavenly Elder Brother was,
in his estimation, his fellow man only, and the beneficence of
God's incarnation could not therefore pluck at his heart-strings.
Yet that this Jesus had carried out the will of the Father as a
filial son should, and had thereby saved the world, he did not
doubt.

He had just read the translation of the fourth chapter of John's
First Epistle, "God sent his only begotten Son into the world . . .
to be the propitiation of our sins". The word "begotten" in the
Chinese is the same as that for "produced" or "made", and it had
no special significance for Hung. As a follower of the teachings
of Confucius, he knew that propriety demanded submission and
reverence to elder brothers. He thought of his own fat, lazy and
stupid half-brothers, and how, even to them, he had succeeded in
showing always the outward courtesy and submission that was
demanded in the order of the Five Relationships. But now he

could say with all sincerity to the Man of his vision, to the
Eldest Son of the Heavenly Father, to the friend who had shown
him how to fight the demons, "Your humble, stupid, younger
brother bows his head and pays his respects".

He went on to read the twenty-third chapter of Jeremiah,
wherein he was warned against those that prophesy false dreams,
"saying, I have dreamed, I have dreamed". He took this to be a
criticism of those Taoist soothsayers who were forever muttering
of their dreams and omens. Without knowing it, Hung ejaculated
his contempt aloud, and Li, who sat beside him in the shade of
the courtyard on that particular evening, leaned from his mat,
on which he sat, to see what his cousin was reading, and questioned him upon his contempt.

Hung closed the book and was pleased to expound. "The
scholars of these days do not distinguish between the true and
the false, between the correct and the corrupt. Fortune-telling,
physiognomy, geomancy and other secret arts are considered as
true, though they are indeed only so many different means to
support those who practise them." He shifted in his chair. Was
he purposely forgetting the account he had given to Jen-kan of
how the soothsayer in Canton had foretold that he would fall
sick? How did one distinguish between true dreams and false?
Only the dreamer could know, and know beyond doubt, as he
did himself. "The more intelligent scholars dare not confess the
truth, although they know it," he went on after a minute. "The
less informed are unable to discern it. Themselves blind and
perverted, they teach a corrupt doctrine. The whole world lies
entangled in the net of the devil." He sighed. "They cannot rid
themselves of vain desire after riches and honours. They seek a
short happiness, as if it were everlasting. They desire bliss but
attain no bliss."

Li was amazed at the flow of words and at the majestic figure
his cousin made, seated now in the bamboo chair, with hands
upon his knees, his tall bronzed body lit by the red sunset, his
eyes beholding something which Li could not see.

Hung had no doubts as to the validity of his own dreams and
visions. He took up the book again, and, as though to testify to
the genuineness of the revelation made to him, Liang's next
written discourse was upon the text, "Quench not the spirit.
Despise not prophesyings." The story of Cain and Abel followed,

and there was a sermon upon the last judgment, but Hung was uncertain if this was to come or if it had already been held in the days of Cain and Abel.

The whole of the nineteenth chapter of Acts was given: the account of Paul and the riot of the silversmiths at Ephesus. Within a few years Hung was to have cause to study more deeply Paul's miraculous healing of the sick and the coming of the Holy Ghost in that same chapter, but just now his mind was absorbed with the problem which he foresaw would arise. There was no doubt that the idol and amulet makers of China would object as furiously to his taking away their livelihood as had Demetrius. To throw down the idols would be a revolutionary measure needing courage.

As though to comfort him, Liang now gave Hung translations of Colossians, chapter three, and Ephesians, chapter six, wherein the exhortations to virtue were very similar to those of Confucius, but the final verses had a special message for Hung. "Put on the whole armour of God, that ye may be able to stand against the wiles of the devil. For we wrestle not against flesh and blood, but against principalities, against powers, against the rulers of the darkness of this world, against spiritual wickedness in high places." He was immediately carried back in memory to a sight of those loathsome demons, who had fought their way even to the gates of the Thirty-Third Heaven, and whom he had withstood only with the help of the Heavenly Elder Brother, who had shown him how to wield a—yes! Here it was! "Above all . . . taking the sword of the spirit, which is the word of God."

Hung was alone, for long ago Cousin Li had gone into the room for the evening meal. Lai-shi had given up her attempts to call her husband to the bowl of rice and lentil-curd, which she had prepared so well. He was free of this world. He stood up. Almost he could feel the grasp of that sword hilt in his hand: the sword of the spirit. There was only a page or two unread. His heart was overflowing. He wanted to be alone. He took the book down to the rivulet and there, screened by a grove of bamboos, he finished the last of Liang's discourses. It was a sermon upon the text, "This is a faithful saying and worthy of all acceptation, that Christ Jesus came into the world to save sinners."

All through his life, Hung had failed the expectations men had had of him, and he was aware of it. It can therefore be believed that, alone in the dusk among the grey shadows of the bamboos, he knew at that moment as much as any Christian regarding the burden of sin, which is pain and shame; and that his heart was for that hour at least filled with gratitude and love for the Saviour who would take the load from him.

7

WITHIN A MATTER of days Hung had converted Li, and almost as soon had come to the conclusion that the rite of baptism could be administered by one to the other. They went one evening, therefore, to the gate of his little courtyard, carrying between them a basin of water. In turn each submitted himself to the sprinkling while the other pronounced the words which Hung, lacking any precedent, had chosen as best he could. "Purification from all former sin, putting off the old, and regeneration." No sooner had they received this form of baptism than the heavens suddenly opened, and a torrential rain descended, drenching them to the skin. Hung took it as a sign that the Heavenly Father had himself performed the ceremony. The rain was much needed, and its long-delayed appearance seemed a kind of miracle. Full of joy, he re-entered the house and sat down to compose his first Christian hymn. It was in the form of an ode.

"When our transgressions high as heaven rise,
  How well to trust in Jesus' full atonement!
  We follow not the Demons, we obey
  The holy precepts, worshipping alone
  One God, and thus we cultivate our hearts.
  The heavenly glories open to our view,
  And every being ought to seek thereafter.
  I much deplore the miseries of Hell.
  O turn ye to the fruits of true repentance!
  Let not your hearts be led by worldly customs."

Hung's next step was to cast away the idols of the small household gods. At first Lai-shi argued strongly against the destruction of the kitchen-god. As for the rain, she said, everyone knew that the Dragon of the Eastern Sea brought it, for all that her husband now held that it came at the will of this new Lord of Heaven. Hung saw that he would need patience if he was to convert his wife. She was expecting another child, and for the moment must be humoured.

To avoid the sight of her tears shed over the fragments of the kitchen god, Hung and Li withdrew to the school-house. There they began to cast away similar idols, and, what was of greater significance, removed the commemorative tablet of Confucius, which was displayed in every school throughout the land. While they worked, they discussed Hung's visions, in the prophetic meaning of which Li was now a firm believer. Hung was explaining that the demons which he had fought in heaven would be represented on earth by these very same idols which they were now intent on destroying, and by the Tartars. In future he was invariably to speak of both idols and the Imperial soldiery of the Tartar régime as demons, imps, fiends; so that it was not always easy to know, when he issued his Imperial decrees, which of them he meant, or even whether he was alluding to the Prince of Darkness himself and his disembodied minions.

Hung's brothers and sisters, whom the Heavenly Father had bidden him spare, were the men and women who would receive the gospel. The kingdom of Heaven referred to in the scriptures was, as Hung pointed out to Li, obviously the Celestial Empire of China, and Li agreed that the matter was too plain to admit of any argument. The promise to the chosen people that they should inherit the kingdom was a direct promise to the Chinese, and in the person of Hung the prophecy would be fulfilled. The word "heavenly", on the other hand, did not refer to China but to the highest sphere of all, the realm of God the Father.

When between them they had staggered out of the schoolhouse with the heavy stone tablet commemorating Confucius, Hung put in its stead a large piece of paper on which he had written the name of Shang-ti.

There was considerable trouble when the pupils arrived next morning. It was customary on entering school to bow to the tablet of Confucius. They stood before the paper nonplussed, and

when Hung showed them by example that in future they were to
burn incense sticks to the name of Shang-ti, some few went home
to their parents to complain. The schoolmaster had a reputation
for being rather severe with his pupils, and a few of the older
boys were delighted at the opportunity of a little revenge, though
they had not meant his punishment to be as hard as it was. They
miscalculated the seriousness with which their parents would regard any tampering with tradition. He lost his job. He would
not give way, and the villagers had the power of the purse strings.

There was nothing for it but to take his pregnant wife, his
daughter and his furniture back to his birthplace, and there seek
shelter and sustenance from his father until he could find other
means to support himself. He went first alone to ask his parents'
permission thus to cast himself upon their resources, and in the
few days of his visit succeeded in converting the two friends most
dear to him. Jen-kan was now the schoolmaster in the home
village, being by this time a young man of twenty-one. Feng,
who taught in a hamlet only a few miles away, came to hear this
great news of which Hung was so full.

When they had accepted the truth of his message, he took
them to a nearby stream and there in the clear water he baptised
them. Afterwards they sat together on the river bank, and it was
there, as he read aloud to them passages from the scriptures, that
he spoke those words whose poignancy made them historic, for
they expressed so exactly the truth about how he had come to
adopt his new belief and to act on it.

"These books," he explained to his friends, indicating the pages
spread upon his knee, on which flecks of light and shadow from
the cool ferns and banyan leaves were falling, "are certainly sent
purposely by Heaven to me, to confirm the truth of my former
experiences. If I had received the books without having gone
through the sickness, I should not have dared to believe in them,
and on my own account to oppose the customs of the whole
world." He paused, pulling a piece of grass through his fingers.
"And if," he went on, "I had merely been sick but had not also
received the books, I should have had no further evidence as to
the truth of my visions, which might have been considered as
mere productions of a diseased imagination." Once again he
hesitated, and then he raised his voice and spoke in a bold
manner. "I have received the immediate command from God in

His presence. The will of Heaven rests with me. Although thereby I should meet with calamity, difficulties, and suffering, yet I am resolved to act. By disobeying the heavenly command, I would only rouse the anger of God. And are not these books the foundation of all the true doctrines contained in other books?"

Jen-kan never forgot those words. Both he and Feng were so impressed that, with an almost frightening precipitancy of events, they went straight back to their respective school-houses and removed the idols and the tablets. This time the villagers rather than the children were nonplussed. Word had got about, and if all the schoolmasters were to take the same attitude, then what could parents do about it? And perhaps after all these learned scholars really had discovered something new and worthy of replacing the old traditions. Hung, in celebration of Jen-kan's action, began another ode and, to show Jen-kan courtesy and honour, asked him to finish it.

"Beside the God of Heaven there is no other God;
  Why do foolish men take falsehood to be truth?
  Since their primeval heart is altogether lost,
  How can they now escape defilement from the dust?"

Jen-kan promptly took up the rhythm and continued with—

"The mighty heavenly Father, He is the one true God,
  Idols are made of wood, or moulded from the clod.
  We trust that Jesus came, to save us who are lost,
  That we may soon escape defilement from the dust."

Within a day or two Hung made the short journey to Water Lily village to fetch his wife and their baby daughter, and all that they could immediately carry.

He returned to find strife in the village. His father, the headman, was ageing, and, with no one to advise him but his two eldest and rather stupid sons, matters had got out of hand. A certain individual by the name of Mo had persuaded the villagers of ten different villages to appoint him as their inspector of ground for assessing taxes. He flattered the rich and oppressed the poor, but had so worked upon first one person and then another that there was hardly a man in the neighbourhood over whom he did not have some hold, either a debt or a secret knowledge of some small misdemeanour; so that none of them dared make the first move to dislodge the creature from the position to which they had originally elected him.

When Hung heard of the misery and scandal that this fellow was causing, he was filled with indignation. "Yesterday I yielded to the wishes of men, but today I follow the rule of heaven," he vowed to his astonished father. He left the old man trembling with both hope and fear, and went straight out and gave orders for the gong to be struck throughout the villages for an assembly. Ninety families obeyed the summons, and, to their surprise and delight, found that Hung, imbued with some strange new power and confidence, was able to level accusations against the offender with such fire, such acumen and such a commanding manner that their persecutor crumpled. He even confessed his guilt and asked forgiveness.

Whence, wondered the villagers, had Hung this strange power of command, and this confidence which made him fearless of the opinions of men? His family began to listen to him, to reverence his words and even to obey him. He removed the small idols, all save the kitchen god, to which Lai-shi and his mother still clung.

A certain provincial graduate, one Wan, was an influence in the neighbourhood by reason of his title of "Talented" and also because he was a man of some means. After studying the scriptures, he had the temerity to suggest that there were certain errors in them which his brush could correct neatly with ink in marginal notes. Hung's reply was indignant and wrathful, and he was able to quote from the psalms, "It is written therein Jehovah's word is correct." So angry was he that he did not even stay to eat the good fowl which his host had prepared for dinner, but straightway left the house.

His family asked him how he had dared to be so highhanded. In reply he broke into an almost boisterous song, one of the hymns he had been composing.

"Brethren, be of good cheer. God has the rule of all.
With faithful hearts and deeds in proof you rise to heaven's hall."

Then he went out for a little walk in the good air, leaving them, as was usual nowadays, somewhat perplexed. But if they understood only a little of what he was trying to teach them, they did recognise that Hung had a new sense of purpose. It was plain that he was drawing great strength from an unknown source, and they were intrigued.

He came home to find his wife in labour and his old mother praying in front of the kitchen god. Gently he removed it, and managed to convey to her all his feeling of tenderness and filial duty together with his uncompromising determination to save her soul from the demon hordes.

"Believe in God," he told her, "and in the end be blessed. Trust not in God and be at last distressed."

It was yet another line from one of the hymns he was writing. Lai-shi's labour was much easier with this her second child. When at last Hung's mother and sisters-in-law brought him the news that he was the father of yet another daughter, they were ready to commiserate with what they regarded as a calamity. Another mouth to feed and presently a dowry to find, all to the advantage of the baby's future husband, and no profit to the family which must rear her!

Hung smiled and was apparently perfectly contented with his lot. "Those who believe in God," he replied to their apologies for his wife, "are the sons and daughters of God. Wheresoever they come, they come from heaven. Wheresoever they go, they go to heaven." He was very pleased to welcome this little daughter of God into his home.

Hung's father, his age now come upon him, had picked on Hung's last saying. This talk of coming and going concerned him also, for whither should he go when he died? He sat with his wrinkled old hands plucking at the cotton of his blue trousers, and the lip above his straggling beard trembled a little, as he dared to ask his son whither indeed he should go.

"Keep the holy commandments," Hung tenderly encouraged him, "worship the true God, and then at the hour of departing heaven will be easily ascended."

Presently he was able to preach to all the villagers, and his fame began to go throughout the countryside. Cousin Li asked him to return to Water Lily village and address the people, and he went, first enjoining Jen-kan and Feng to continue to preach the word in his absence.

Only to cousin Li and to Feng and to Jen-kan did Hung ever

now speak openly of what God would do when the moment was ripe, of how, when the word had been preached and the people converted, the Lord of Heaven would raise him to the Dragon Throne, whence he would rule the chosen people in peace, and set up the kingdom of heaven on earth, as had been promised. But the Supreme Lord had forewarned him that first the demons must be exterminated, and were not the demons the Tartars? The kingdom of heaven could not be established without the shedding of blood. Therefore Hung must be ready for the valorous adventure that was before him, and cousin Li was helping him to forge a sword. They worked secretly by night in the smithy, and the weapon when it was finished was an artifact of great beauty, one of which to be proud, even though it was but a terrestrial thing and not the celestial brand of Hung's vision. On the blade were inscribed the characters, "Sword for beheading demons", and when it was finished Hung wrapped it carefully away in a piece of silk to await the day when the Supreme Lord, Shang-ti, should command him to use it.

It was while he was thus wrapping it that he heard in the outer room cousin Li's loud cries of indignation and the lamentations of his wife. Jen-kan had arrived, and in such a state of distress that they were appalled. It turned out, as they found on questioning him, that, in his determination to spread the word, he had removed the tablet of Confucius from the school. The pupils had promptly been withdrawn, whereat his elder brother had struck and beaten him beyond bearing. His clothes were torn and his head was bloody. "I answered him," Jen-kan said, his breath uneven for he was almost in tears, "how is Confucius able to teach after being dead so long? Why do you force me to worship him?"

They comforted Jen-kan, but his experience was but the prelude to a period of persecution. For two of the Hung cousins, both newly baptised converts, life at home became so impossible that they decided to leave the district. Grandmother Wang, now so old that she was but skin and bone and more frail than a dried leaf, suggested that they should carry and preach the word to her own folk, to Cousin Wang who had settled on the river in mountainous Kwang-si. So to Cousin Wang the two refugees from persecution duly set out, sure at least of a welcome from their grandmother's kin.

Hung himself remained, but he was grieved that here, in his

own village, the very people to whom he owed most and to whom he most wanted to present the pearl of great price would not accept it. Some of course did, but many did not, and Hung, as he dressed the stillraw stripes on Jen-kan's back, voiced his complaint.

"Those who believe not in the true doctrine of God and Jesus, though they be old acquaintances, are still no friends of mine, but they are demons." He was applying a healing ointment and Jen-kan was wincing. "On the other hand, all who believe in the doctrine of God and Jesus are true brethren of heaven, and true friends. If they do not believe my words, everyone must go his own way. I cannot bring him into heaven, and they shall not draw me to hell. If my own parents, my wife, and children, do not believe, I cannot feel united with them, how much less with other friends!"

Hung was deeply hurt that Lai-shi had not immediately acclaimed him and his message, and was still proving obstinate. There was for the first time a certain estrangement between them. Of his mother he had greater hopes. It was not to be expected that a parent should immediately acclaim a son, and he was prepared to exercise more patience in her case. "Only the heavenly friendship is true," he went on, as he applied Jen-kan's bandage. "All other is false. A short happiness is not a real one. Only eternal happiness can be called real. What others gain, they cannot impart to me, and what I gain I cannot share with them. I only desire that very many may enter into heaven, and grieve that they should go to hell. Therefore I cannot withhold preaching to them the true doctrines."

Not only could he not refrain from preaching, but he was determined that his own homestead, however divided it might be within, should show an outward example of unity and obedience to God's word. The New Year festivities were approaching. The womenfolk were already cleaning the house and polishing everything within sight that would bear polish. Presently they began to stick up the strips of red paper on which were printed characters implying wishes for happiness, wealth, or good fortune. These he strictly censored, and when it came to pasting up fresh paper prints of the door-gods over the entrance to the courtyard or the main living-room, he forbade it. There should have been new clothes and visiting and idleness and frivolity for the fourteen days of the Feast, and here they were, complained Lai-shi, poor and out of work and hardly able to pay their debts, as must certainly be done before New Year's day if they were not to lose face forever with the neighbours, and now Hsiu-ch'uan must deprive them of even this small consolation of the door-gods!

It was, he supposed, typical of a woman that what she would not concede to his superior knowledge of things both celestial and terrestrial she yielded to him only when he was faced with persecution from outside. It began with a demand from the elders of the village that he should, as usual, use his talents to write odes for the idols, so that the inscribed paper should be ready in time for the Feast of Lanterns, which was the grand culmination of the New Year festivities and lasted for the final three days of the two weeks' holiday period. Hung politely but firmly refused, and explained at length why he was no longer able to use his humble talents to honour false gods. Not content with refusal, the deputation returned, or at least those few of it who bore Hung a grudge, and wished to provoke him into a fit of temper from which he might lose face. But it was Lai-shi who took upon herself the onus of replying, and a woman in a rage does not lose face, or not very much. Hung, coming from his inner chamber, saw her receive the villagers and waited, fascinated, as he heard her reprove their ignorance and idolatry, and prophesy their eternal perdition.

Thus their estrangement came to an end. Hung did not know whether it was more absurd or delightful to discover that this female of his, who was so beautiful, now presumed to demand reasons and to attempt to discuss, albeit in childish terms, the abstract. The sudden appreciation that she was not only his female, but also a daughter of God, added a new zest to his love-making. It was as though she was a territory that he was invading all afresh.

The more friendly of the elders, dissociating themselves from the few who had tried to bait Lai-shi, now wrote an ode themselves in an attempt to persuade Hung to change his mind, and the paper was duly delivered at the house. Hung read it with some amusement, for he was in great heart after his reconciliation with his wife. He straightway called her to bring him his brushes and ink and composed a reply, also in verse.

"Not because of evil saying,
  Did we disobey your orders,
  We but honour God's commandments—
  Act according to his precepts.
  Heaven's and perdition's way
  Must be rigidly distinguished.
  We dare not in thoughtless manner
  Hurry through the present life."

The matter ended in a friendly way. The elders were obliged
to acknowledge that Hung had acted with courtesy and propriety.
In secret they even admitted to him that he had convinced them
as to the truth of his message, but that they were afraid to avow
their conviction in public.

Hung smiled a little sadly as he listened to the fire-crackers
and the drums, the horn-blowing and the gongs, and saw the glare
of the bonfire and round it candles set in the earth to represent
the constellations. Through which of those constellations, he
wondered, had his soul once travelled to heaven? The village was
gay with the people carrying lanterns, and to such a display of
light he had no objection, nor on the next day to the fiercesome
paper dragon many yards long, which to the delight of his four-
year-old daughter was wending its way through the lanes of the
village, supported on the heads of men whose legs only were
visible.

To the people of China the dragon, far from being associated
with Yen-lo, the demon-king of the underworld and the powers
of darkness, was on the contrary the celestial servant of the
Emperor, his guardian, his heraldic beast, and its image decorated everything in the palace from the doors to the Imperial
robes. Hung's daughter grasped her father firmly by the hand,
and demanded to be taken where she could see more closely, and
Hung, remembering how in vision he had mounted the celestial
counterpart of the paper monster, allowed himself to be led by
the child. But when he met with a procession on its way to burn
incense and odes in a nearby temple, he turned back. Not,
however, before his ears had caught some jibes from those taking
part, concerning the mad schoolmaster and his new and crazy
ideas.

Biting his lip, he found himself repeating the words of scripture,

"A prophet is not without honour save in his own country". He was brought to a sudden halt as a new idea was borne in upon him. Why, then, should he not leave his own country, and go, for a time at least, further afield? To the unknown cousin Wang, perhaps?

He went almost immediately to visit Feng, and found his friend only too willing to accede to the plan and to accompany him. Jen-kan was under contract to take up a new appointment as schoolmaster at the village of Clear-Far several miles away, yet another nest of the Li clan, and therefore there was good hope of many converts there. It was upon Hung's road, and so he and Feng went with their younger cousin so far, and there left him, but not before Hung's eloquence had drawn several candidates to the baptismal water administered by Jen-kan.

8

IN APRIL OF THE YEAR 1844, therefore, Hung and Feng left Clear-Far and set out upon their journey, carrying each a pack of writing brushes and ink to peddle, and thus pay their way. They went first to Canton, and there bargained for a passage on one of the many river boats which plied its trade up the West River. The journey would take more than a month, for it was all of three hundred miles to Kwei, where cousin Wang lived.

When they had travelled almost halfway and were approaching the borders of Kwang-si province, Hung began to realise that the hills on which he had once pastured the buffaloes were only gentle swellings on the coastal plain, where he had lived all his life amongst the flat ricefields. A week later he knew that what he had taken to be the mountains of Kwang-si were only in fact small foothills, and, as the gigantic barriers began to tower round him, the sight of the precipices and gorges gave him a new appreciation of the magnificence of nature and of its Creator. When the boatman told him that all that he saw was again only the beginning of that immense Central Asian barrier which divides China from India, Tibet, Burma and Tong-king, the plainsman was filled with awe.

All along the valley of the river and its tributaries lived those Chinese who spoke Cantonese, and who had made themselves comparatively rich by their industry and trade. Interspersed with them were colonies of Hak-kas, of whom cousin Wang was one and Hung himself another. They were not so well-to-do, and there was great rivalry in the valleys between the supplanters and the supplanted, but both were valley folk. In the foothills and on the mountain ridges lived yet a third people, the aboriginals, the Miau, who were akin to the men of Tong-king on the other side of the watershed.

When Hung heard that there was a great loop ahead in the river, the inexperienced plainsman thought that he could breast the hills on foot and find the pass, and thus save paying further passage money.

In the trackless wilds he and Feng lost their way, and might have perished on the towering desolate mountains, but for the hospitality of the Miau. At first these aboriginals had peered doubtfully from below their conical wide-brimmed hats. They were squat, large-bellied men and shock-headed. They stood confronting Hung on the mountain path, armed with cross-bows and fingering the swords which they carried always slung round their necks. The Chinese believed that these people had tails. If so, they concealed them beneath clothes of woven grass and felt; warm felt, thought Hung and Feng enviously, as they shivered in their cotton garments so unsuited to the mountain air. Cold and starving, they were taken to the village, to the houses built on piles in Malay fashion, and as they tasted mountain rice for the first time they tried to express their gratitude. But the language of the Miau was incomprehensible. Hung was deeply disappointed. He had hoped to repay highland hospitality with the words of eternal life. All he could do was to smile his appreciation, particularly of the women, who in their striped skirts and turbans and their long earrings came at first to peer at the strangers and at last to honour them by performing a little dance in which there was much snapping of castanets, and a good deal of smothered giggling.

Next day several of the men accompanied him and Feng to within sight of a tea-house, from which it was apparent that they were approaching a valley and a village. Here they found shelter with a certain Kiang, a schoolmaster, and were able to convert and baptise their host, and to leave him as a gift one of the precious tracts. In return he gave them sufficient silver to continue their journey, and in the month of June they at last arrived at cousin Wang's home, coming down on to the West River opposite the district city of Kwei to find the valley ablaze with a summer heat which was almost unbearable after the cold of the heights. Hung had learned his lesson. His determination to familiarise himself with mountain lore was to stand him in good stead when he came to conduct armies in that country.

Cousin Wang Shen-chun lived in a village called Valley Home —Tz'u-ku—in the district of Kwei, which in turn was part of the prefecture of Kwei-p'ing. He gave Hung a great welcome, for the fame of the young prophet had gone before him, carried by the two Hung cousins whom Wang was already sheltering. Now cousin Wang raised his voice aloud to give thanks to God before all his family that here was Hung Hsiu-ch'uan himself come to instruct and administer the cleansing water of baptism to them all. To all, that is, save his most dear and only son, as he explained with tears in his eyes. A disaster had befallen the family, and as Hung was bidden to sit at the table on which the food dishes were being arrayed, and to take the most comfortable of the chairs, the host interspersed his hospitable enjoinders with lamentations for his son's misfortune. Wang the younger, it appeared, had refused to pay "squeeze" money to one of those parasites of the district ya-men, the underclerks, and the clerk had had him falsely accused and cast into prison. In Kwei gaol he had been languishing since a month ago.

All through the evening Hung and Feng talked with their host about his anxiety, and tried to bring him comfort.

"Heaven often bestows riches and prosperity upon the wicked," Hung sought to give him courage, "but holy ones are perfected by much sorrow and tribulation." There was nothing he could do that very night in the way of an appeal to the authorities, but he could help to strengthen the old man's faith. Presently the cousins from the village crowded in, and such an impression did Hung and his gospel message make that Jen-kan afterwards recorded that the people in Valley Home thought he had come down from heaven.

On the next day he wrote a petition to the magistrate, and took it himself to the yamen in Kwei city. There were at least some advantages in being a Presented Student. He was of the minor gentry, and if fear of students' riots forbade him access to the magistrate's judgment hall, at least he had the right of direct approach to the educational secretary, into whose side office he was presently shown. As a result, within that same day Wang the younger was set at liberty, and on the next the people of Valley Home village gathered both to celebrate his return and to listen to Hung's preaching of the gospel.

From the verandah of cousin Wang's house, he spoke to the villagers gathered in the shade of the pine and maple trees with which the slopes of the hillside were dotted. He told them how he, Hung, could bear personal witness, for he had himself been caught up to heaven and had with his own eyes seen the Father and the Heavenly Elder Brother. He spoke to them of the demons and of the wickedness of idolatry, and gave them a warning. "Cleave to worldly customs, believe in devils, and ultimately Hell cannot be avoided. Those who worship demons are the slaves of demons; at the time of their birth by the devil led astray, at the time of their death by him *carried away*."

His listeners shuddered. This young man had such a forceful way of expressing himself, that truly it made a fellow pause to consider whether or not he had been upon a dangerous road, or indeed on any road at all. You could see that he was sincere, full of fire, and with a most kingly countenance and form. Now he was speaking poetry. What a deep mellow voice! What sonorous periods! With their lips, but silently, they formed the words after him, in a sudden and spontaneous desire to join in whatever angelic chorus he had heard and was echoing.

"Heavenly Father, high and supreme, the God of all nations,
Who sustains the whole human race with infinite bounty:
In six days thou createst the world with mountains and waters.
Spendest thy gifts upon men to enjoy in brotherly union.
Father, thou art near related to us; thou expellest the demons,

Gavest thy holy commands to instruct an ignorant people.
After thou Jesus hadst sent to give his life as a ransom,
Thou didst command Hsiu-ch'uan to proclaim the truth of His doc-
   trines."

Within a matter of weeks Hung had baptised a hundred converts, including his own young sister and the brother-in-law
whom he now met for the first time. Cousin Wang had not failed
to do his duty by the Hung family, and though the young girl had
lived at first with her half-sister and Yang, who had brought her
safely out of Kwang-tung at the time of the Opium War, it was
cousin Wang himself who had arranged for her a marriage with a
certain Hsiao. Hsiao Chou-kwei was his full name, a farmer and
planter who had made enough in timber and tea to support a wife
in reasonable comfort. He lived at Wu-hsuan just north of Kwei-
p'ing, and had come to invite Hung thither that he might for a day
or two be reunited with his sister. Hung glanced at the tall, clean-
shaven and graceful young man, a few years his junior. There was
something about him which made Hung remember stories and
heroes of the Golden Age. Of his valour and courage Hung was
presently to have proof, for Hsaio, though he had no great intellect, was to become the idol of Hung's armies on account of his
grace and dashing qualities.

Four extra mouths were too many to expect the Wangs to feed
forever. Besides, there were Lai-shi and the children, whom Hung
did not wish to desert any longer. In November, therefore, he felt
that he had sown in Kwang-si sufficient of the gospel seed for that
year. He sent Feng and the two Hung cousins ahead of him, and,
at cousin Wang's special request, remained himself for a further
week or two before setting out alone for home in December.

All this time Hung's other brother-in-law, Yang, had been away
from the district. He had been employed by his rich nephew,
Cheng, to supervise the building of the nephew's new house some
distance away in a place called Thistle Mount—Tzu-ching-shan
—about eighteen miles north of Kwei-p'ing city. He was proposing to move there himself, build a smaller house, and act as steward
for his relative. He had come down to the river to trade for timber
with the raftsmen, and he had with him ten of his nephew's work-
men to transport it. Thus Feng, waiting to bargain for a passage
home, by chance met with him. The opportunity was too good to

be missed. The gospel must be carried to Yang. Disobeying
Hung's instructions to go straight home, Feng therefore left his
other two kinsmen to proceed down river, and himself accompanied Yang back to Thistle Mount. Almost before they reached
it, Feng's gentle voice had converted not only Yang but the work-
men. The rich young nephew fell almost as quickly under his
sway. He offered Feng the post of school-teacher in the village,
and Feng, seeing that with a wealthy patron and many pupils there
was a great opportunity for preaching the word, decided to remain.

Thus when Hung arrived back at Hua in January of 1845, he
was astonished and perturbed to find that Feng had never turned
up there. Even more distressing was the fact that Feng's wife and
Feng's mother, a formidable kinswoman whom he addressed as
aunt, held him responsible, and berated him. It was all his fault for
taking Feng on such a wild and harum-scarum adventure. It was
dangerous country, and for all anyone knew he might even now
be lying murdered by bandits on some lonely mountain path, and
no one to bury him! There was no government postal service save
for official despatches. There was nothing to do but wait, and have
faith that Shang-ti would protect his own, but they had to wait
for nearly three years before there was news of Feng.

Despite the wrath of his aunt, however, Hung's reputation was
now high in the district. The two kinsmen had brought back news
of how in Kwang-si Hung had been acclaimed as a messenger
from heaven. In the villages of Hua district men began to feel that
they ought to be proud of their own local celebrity. He was given
another post as school-teacher within reach of his home, and began
to preach and baptise without fear of persecution.

Now he took a new step forward in his fight against idolatry.
After further study of Liang's tracts—so far his only source of
reference—he had come to the conclusion that he had been wrong
to write up the name of Shang-ti in the school house and to bow
before it, so he removed it.

About this time, because his father was ageing, Hung was
forced to take upon himself the duties of a headman. In practice if
not in name he was acting for the village, and because of this his
uncle was jealous, and spread reports about his severity. He had
the opportunity for criticism when scandal flared up in the village,
and not one but two adulterers were caught where they should not

have been. The small community was torn between outraged propriety and ribald comment. One wag expressed himself so lewdly that Hung was irritated to fury. "This man," he said to the elders gathered to ask counsel of the headman, "has lost his conscience. He forgets the great mercies of God, transgresses the holy commandments, and despises the merits of Christ. I really exert myself to teach and instruct you carefully," he addressed the man who had lately received baptism at his hands, "and you treat the matter frivolously."

His sincerity so fired the elders that they submitted to his directions. Public whipping was to be instituted against those whose depravity threatened the morality of the people. On his instructions wooden rods were cut on which were inscribed different characters, such as "Beat all vagabonds plotting evil", "Beat thieves, robbers and gamblers", "Beat the female seducers".

In front of the school-house the adulterers duly received their punishment, and though they were not driven away, they lost so much face that of their own will they left the village. To his uncle's objections to such strict measures, Hung replied, "Too much patience and humility do not suit our present times, for therewith it would be impossible to manage this perverted generation."

His fury and loathing of adulterers was as much Confucian as Christian. To steal another man's wife or to seduce another man's daughter was to strike at the foundations of family life. It was theft. And if women were the daughters of God they must be cherished, instructed and fed. Seduction of virgins led always to their being abandoned to hunger and further promiscuity. Adultery left husband and wife divided and robbed of happiness. To rob, to steal was the great crime. For that reason he disapproved of gambling, for it led to poverty, and that in turn to theft. As to how many women a man might lawfully possess, that was a question of how many he could afford to feed and cherish, and Hung, being a poor man, had not yet given the matter a thought.

He often at this time would meet with Jen-kan, who was teaching at the nearby village of Clear-Far. He had been delighted to find on his return from Kwang-si that Jen-kan had already instructed and baptised over fifty converts in that one small village where he worked. Jen-kan was one of the very few to whom Hung could dare to speak openly of his hatred of the Tartars.

"God has divided the kingdoms of the world," he said to him once, "and made the ocean to be a boundary for them, just as a father divides his estates among his sons; every one of whom ought to reverence the will of his father, and quietly manage his own property. Why should these Manchus forcibly enter China, and rob their brothers of their estate?"

The political situation was still in a ferment in this year of 1845. The crops had failed in Kwang-si, and that would mean famine; and the bands of starving marauders which famine always brought would threaten the already harassed administration. The officials were getting worried, and to distract attention from their own shortcomings they began once again to stir up the people against the Foreign Devils. The European Consuls made complaints to the mandarins, and enquiries were instituted regarding certain cases of insult which had been offered to the Europeans by the country folk.

Hung at this time, speaking to Jen-kan, said, "If God will help me to recover our estate, I ought to teach all nations to hold every one its own possessions, without injuring and robbing one another. We will have intercourse in communicating true principles and wisdom to each other, and receive each other with propriety and politeness. We will serve together one common Heavenly Father, and honour together the doctrines of one common Heavenly Brother, the Saviour of the world. This has been the wish of my heart since the time when my soul was taken up to heaven."

Nevertheless, foreigners were not popular after the Opium War. So much Hung had to admit to himself, and if Christianity was a foreign import, it would make the spreading of the gospel doubly difficult. He was convinced from further study of the question that the worship of Shang-ti was not a foreign innovation, but that Shang-ti had been the original supreme deity of China. He now began, therefore, the essay that was to prove his point. Its historical references, going back more than two thousand years, could be appreciated only by his fellow Chinese scholars, but his opening sentences had a universal appeal.

"Who has lived in the world without offending against the commands of Heaven? But until this time no one has known how to obtain deliverance from sin: now, however, the great God has made a gracious communication to man, and from henceforth whoever repents of his sins in the presence of the great God, and avoids worshipping depraved spirits, practising perverse things, or transgressing the divine commands, may ascend to heaven and enjoy happiness for thousands and myriads of years, in pleasure and delight, with dignity and honour, world without end."

He had spoken to Jen-kan of the thirty-three heavens through which his soul had risen to the highest sphere. Now in this essay he wrote of the eighteen hells wherein the souls of the wicked were tortured. The multiplicities of heaven and hell were both borrowings from Buddhism, but Dante had received from Christendom more sympathy for his writings about the heights and depths than Hung was to receive from the missionaries, who criticised him harshly for borrowing from such a pagan source.

The most important pronouncement in this essay, which was at a later date to be incorporated in an Imperial edict and distributed to all his people, was his clear affirmation that *all* men were God's children. "The great God is the universal Father of all men throughout the world. Sovereigns are those of his children whom he clothes with power, but the good are those of his children who most resemble him; while the common mass are still his children, though steeped in ignorance; and the violent and oppressive are his disobedient children." When the missionaries came to criticise Hung for his own blasphemous claim to be a Son of God, they tended to ignore this part of his edict, which he had sent them for their perusal.

He was still sitting writing this, his first Christian essay, alone in the school-house after hours, when one of his converts, a certain Mo, asked leave to enter. This young man had just returned from an expedition to Canton on family business. He put down the paper and ink which he had been asked to purchase there for his preceptor, and then, instead of withdrawing, he seemed to hesitate, unwilling to take his leave. Was his honourable teacher too busy perhaps to listen to his humble younger brother?

Hung glanced up from his work, smiled, and bade him proceed. It appeared that Mo, while in Canton, had by purest chance met with a missionary's assistant, a Chinese, and had taken it upon himself to speak of Hung's spreading the gospel, and had been astonished to find that the missionary's assistant knew all the gospel story. Now it appeared that this man was very desirous of meeting with the honourable teacher, and might even be sending him a letter. Had Mo done wrong? Had he presumed? Was Hung pleased?

Hung was very pleased indeed, in fact he was filled with excitement, and could hardly wait for the letter. Why, he asked himself, had he never before thought of tracing the source of the tracts? It would have been difficult for him to have done so, because from the days of Liang's flight to the signing of the Treaty the Christians had been greatly persecuted, and had been working very much underground.

To meet these wonderful men, who had brought the knowledge of Jesus so far from the west, now became Hung's one desire, and when the promised letter duly arrived he read it avidly.

"Having heard from Mo Li-pan that you, honoured brother, about ten years ago received a book, the contents of which agree with the doctrine preached in our chapel here, we the missionary, Lo-han, and the brethren will rejoice if you will come hither and assist us by preaching in the chapel."

The invitation to preach was merely a Chinese expression of courtesy, and Hung recognised the euphemism as concealing a real invitation to receive instruction. He was more than willing to receive it, but, alas, he could not absent himself from school now in December. He would have to wait until his contract terminated at the New Year. He replied to this effect, and when he realised that he had two whole months to wait, it seemed unbearably long.

Disappointed and frustrated, he went to bed, and there lay tossing and awake long after Lai-shi was asleep. Surely the promised kingdom of heaven must soon be established? The progress of spreading the gospel was so slow when carried forward merely by a poor school-teacher, who was bound to his contracts. From the Dragon Throne he could have taught and saved the people of half the Empire by now. It was time the present dynasty was removed. The ancient sage, Mencius, had said, "In the course of five hundred years a king will arise, a man of universal fame." There had been no such man for the last five-hundred-year period. It was time that such a one arose again. Had the Heavenly Father really decreed that he, Hung, should have the dominion, he wondered?

Tormented with doubt, Hung at last fell into a sleep, and straightway dreamt one of those dreams which only the mystic can recognise by its essence as being of a significant nature. He dreamed that he saw the sun, and that, as it sank towards the horizon, it grew red, and became a copper sun, a sun dying in the quick-silver of the dusk in the great alchemical crucible of the sky. And he knew that from the mortifying sun there would presently be discovered the true gold, the Elixir of Immortal Life. He put out his hand, because he desired this Elixir more than anything in the world. As he did so, behold the great red fiery orb that dwarfed the hilltops on which it had begun to rest became suddenly small, so small that the Great Alchemist, invisible save for the suggestion of a hand, reached down and put the glowing ball into Hung's hand, where it filled the hollow of his palm as neatly as the red jade ornament carried by an Emperor—only it was not of red jade now, but of the true gold, the Elixir, emitting light like a crystal.

The sun was the symbol of the Imperial power. One of the Emperor's titles was "Brother of the Sun". On this Hung reflected when he woke, and he was greatly comforted by the dream, for now he knew that the Heavenly Father had not forgotten his promise. He straightway celebrated this confirmation of his divine commission by writing a poem.

> "Now that five hundred years have passed,
>   The true sun moves in sight,
> And as it shines, demons and imps
>   Are cowering from its light.
> The North and South, the East and West
>   To it their homage pay
> And hosts of the Barbarian Tribes
>   Are yielding to its sway."

There were further verses. This sun was to illuminate the whole world. It was a eulogy not of himself alone, but of the kingdom of heaven, the triumph of light over darkness, the gift of the Elixir of Eternal Life, with all of which he was identified by the Heavenly Mandate and the promise that he should establish, spread and distribute them.

In February of 1847, directly after the holiday period of the Feast of Lanterns, he went to Canton to the address which Lo-han had given in the letter. As to who this Lo-han was, fate could hardly have delivered Hung into more unsuitable hands. The Reverend Issachar Roberts—such was his real name—who was to figure so largely but on the whole so sorrily in Hung's life, was an uneducated American missionary from Sumner County, Tennessee. Fired by Gützlaff's world-wide propaganda as to the need of labourers for the spiritual harvest, he had come out to China ten years ago, sponsored by no greater authority than the Roberts Fund Society, in other words the zealots in Sumner County who had raised a special subscription to pay his passage. He then worked under the ægis of the American Baptist Board, but, finding his association with it uneasy, was later to transfer to the Southern Baptist Convention. Finally he left that also, to end up in an independent state which owed no allegiance to any authority. Under the tuition of Gützlaff he had, however, become an excellent speaker of the Cantonese tongue. He was the first Baptist missionary to reside in Canton rather than Macao, and had since the war negotiated for a piece of ground on the banks of the river a mile or two below the Factories. There he had erected a house both for a dwelling and a chapel. He wore Chinese dress, which the other missionaries thought rather odd, since even the Catholic priests seldom went so attired in Canton, but only in the interior when in danger of their lives. He was a bachelor, now about forty-four years old, and rumour had it that he was not an easy man, but was given to sudden tempers.

Nevertheless, at first all went well. Hung was ready to see only the best in Lo-han, for the honourable missionary teacher had given into his hands to be his very own the first complete copy of the Bible which he had ever seen. It was according to the translation of Gützlaff. Now at last he could study the full list of the Ten Commandments and read the Gospels not merely from extracts. His gratitude was tremendous and was to last all his life.

As to what else he learnt, Mr. Roberts never bothered to keep any record, but from usual Baptist practice it can be deduced that for the initial period Hung's instruction would have consisted of bringing him to a sense of his sins, to repentance, and to an understanding that a sacrifice had been needed to appease God for the sins of mankind, and that Christ had taken upon himself to be that sacrifice. Not much more instruction than this was ever attempted in the first three months, and as Hung, through a strange blow of fate, was to stay no longer, this is probably all that he ever ab-

sorbed of doctrine, dogma, and theology from a western missionary, though he was presently to invent a weird and tangled version
of them for himself.

As for ritual, in the little chapel there was no crucifix or image
of any kind, nor any pictures, least of all any image of the Virgin.
At service Mr. Roberts sat behind a communion table with a Chinese deacon on either side of him, and conducted prayers without
any prayer book, in the expectation that he would be guided by
the spirit. Every Sunday there was a service known as the "breaking of bread", and then communion was handed in two kinds by
the deacons to the seated communicants, but not of course to the
unbaptised, of whom Hung was considered one, for he now learnt
that his self-administration of the cleansing water had had no
validity to purify him from sin. He could see the cup upon the
communion table, and he had read the account of the Last Supper
in the Gospels, but without further instruction it could have only
one significance for him, and that was a Chinese reading of the
mystery of which more hereafter.

More easily comprehensible was the homely rite of saying grace
before and after meals in the mission house, and this custom he
never lost. He learnt besides to call his fellow Christians
"brethren", and not to refer to Europeans as Foreign Devils.

The reason why Roberts took no trouble to record his methods
of instructing Hung in those few months was that, while he immediately recognised Hung's scholastic ability and general efficiency, and even had his eye upon him as a possible future
assistant, he had not the slightest idea that he was dealing with a
man of outstanding spiritual insight. And this for the simple reason
that it was beyond Issachar's conception that any "Chinaman", so-
called, could be the chosen recipient of such insight.

Soon after his arrival Hung, overcome with gratitude for the gift
of the Bible, confronted Mr. Roberts one evening when they were
alone together in the chapel, and tried to tell him of his visions.
Issachar was really not interested. These Chinamen did have the
strangest fancies, and the importance they attributed to dreams
was the inheritance of a heathenish upbringing. He pocketed the
carefully written account of Hung's visions which the young convert was offering him, and promptly mislaid it, for which lapse of
memory he was afterwards, when the wheels of history began to
turn, to feel some embarrassment.

To do Roberts justice, he was but a child of his era, and not alone in his distrust of what seemed to him fanciful. No contemporary Protestant, and perhaps even no Catholic, really believed that direct revelation was accorded in the present age, least of all to a heathen. The visions of Bernadette at Lourdes lay in the future. The Catholics were still prone to fight the goddess of the French Revolution, the goddess of Reason, with her own weapons. As for the Protestants, they pinned all their faith to the Book, the Holy Scriptures. Furthermore, if God were in his beneficence to accord some direct revelation of Himself, surely it would be to a missionary, to one who had given up all to follow the Master, to Mr. Roberts himself, for instance, and not, oh certainly not, to a heathen "Chinaman"!

Unfortunately for Hung the missionary's paid assistants, all of them Chinese, were not so blind to Hung's qualities. They realised that his intellect and scholarship constituted a grave threat to their own positions. It was plain that he could easily rival them and rise over their heads to the position of deacon. So great was their jealousy and fear of losing their own advancement and pay that into the hearts of two of them Satan entered, and they conspired to undo Hung.

He was eagerly awaiting the moment when Issachar should consider him sufficiently prepared to receive baptism, a moment which he had been assured would not now be long delayed. In Canton he had been living from hand to mouth as best he could, feeding sometimes at the mission, more often at the cheap eating-houses, and sometimes not at all; and sleeping nearby in the house of strangers to whom he must pay silver. Aware that his resources were nearly at an end, his two jealous rivals saw a way in which to be rid of him. They knew that their employer Lo-han, like all the missionaries, feared lest any of his converts might be "rice-Christians", a term for those who accepted the gospel teaching merely in order to eat free rice at the missionary's expense. They therefore persuaded Hung to ask for financial assistance. Mr. Roberts, they promised, would be only too ready to pay him a monthly allowance while he was undergoing instruction. Hung, hungry and anxious, fell into the trap, and frankly disclosed to Issachar that he could no longer support himself in Canton without employment, and that, if he was to continue to study, he would need help. Would Lo-han allow him a small sum monthly?

The result was all that his rivals could have wished. Roberts refused peremptorily, and, what was infinitely worse, put off the date of Hung's baptism indefinitely, on the ground that he must have further proof of the man's genuine desire to follow Christ.

Hung went back to his poor lodging desolate, and sat alone with his head in his hands for long and anxious hours. He could not continue indefinitely in Canton without funds. Even if he could live himself without eating, he had a wife and two children to support. He saw now that against such intriguers he would always be powerless. There seemed nothing for it but to return home. Perhaps later, when he had earned some more silver by teaching, he would be in a position to come back to Lo-han, for of the missionary's integrity he had no doubt, and he continued to have for him a warm regard.

His decision made, he went to take his leave of Roberts, and thus the missionary allowed the future Taiping Emperor to pass from his care, unbaptised and almost uninstructed. Perhaps some last-minute misgiving caused him to be extra generous in the bestowing of Bibles, for Hung left Canton carrying a whole stock of them. But that, apart from his bundle of clothing, was all he did carry, for he had only a hundred cash in the world. It would have been enough to take him back to his family, for the distance was only thirty miles on foot, but now fate stepped in again, and political events prevented him from heading for home.

One of the terms of the Treaty of Nanking was that foreigners should be allowed entrance into the walled city of Canton, and no longer be kept as lepers without the gates. There was no real advantage in entry save that of prestige; equally, the Chinese policy of exclusion had no real aim except to lower it. Because of the "soothing" policy adopted by the mandarins, the British had never insisted on implementing this clause of the treaty, but, when the mandarins had become less amicable, Palmerston had written to Sir John Davis on January 9th of that year 1847 to tell him to adopt a firmer attitude.

On receipt of Palmerston's letter, Davis decided to take action, and in April, without warning, he sailed from Hong Kong with a small naval and military force. He entered the river, and, descending like a thunder-bolt, seized the estuary forts, occupied the foreign settlements, and insisted on the immediate possession of land promised by the treaty as a site for warehouses and never handed over. Since entry into the walled city was purely a matter of prestige, he felt that he had read the Chinese a sufficient lesson, and did not insist upon it.

Nevertheless, "entrance to Canton was the key to the whole difficulty", as Consul Parkes was to write to Palmerston three years later, meaning that entry into the city had become, absurdly perhaps but in hard fact, the test case as to whether the mandarins should or should not be able for always to enjoy the benefits of British trade while "squeezing" and cheating and insulting the British traders. The forcing of this ridiculous but crucial issue, as to whether an Englishman might walk peacefully down the Avenue of Benevolence and Love to do a little shopping and see the sights, was in the future to prove catastrophic to Hung's throne and Empire.

His immediate undoing on leaving Mr. Roberts, however, was the sudden descent of Davis's expedition in April. Hardly had he left the mission beside the foreign concession when the guns began to fire. Men were taking refuge, not only from the guns but from the far greater danger of being impressed into the provincial militia. Hurrying down a dark alleyway Hung found shelter, and mysterious hands reached out to help him. Was it for a day, or a week, or longer that he disappeared amongst the shadows? In dismal tea-houses and back courts he lay low, and he learnt during that time the significance attached to lifting a cup with three fingers prominently displayed. For such help as he received from the secret society of the Triads he was grateful, but he would not undergo initiation or take the oath. He became sufficiently acquainted with members of the organisation, however, to know both the strength and the weakness of it, and it was because of its weakness that he refused to join. The weakness, he realised at once, was that the Triads had no new message with which to revivify the people of China. They were merely subversive and reactionary, and, whatever eternal good their ritual might once have embodied, it had degenerated into an unmeaning pantomime, a cover for banditry and bloody oaths.

Yet he dared not go home, for now all over the countryside the officials were levying troops to meet the threat of attack from the British. The last thing on earth he wanted was to be impressed into the militia to fight for the Tartars, for it was to fight against them that he had received the Heavenly Mandate. Amongst the

Triads men spoke of little else but of how the Mandate was about
to be withdrawn by Heaven from the present ruling dynasty.
Natural catastrophes in the province of Hu-nan that year made it
all the more plain that Heaven was about to remove the present
occupant of the Dragon Throne. Little did the Triad brethren
know that he himself was appointed to mount it. Unwilling to
commit himself to joining the secret societies, fearful of returning
home lest he be impressed, whither, he wondered, should he go?
Presently the answer came—to Kwang-si of course, to the mountains, where he had sown the gospel seed! Would there be any
harvest?

He left Canton in June of 1847 with only the hundred cash
which he had had upon him when he quitted the mission, and
there was before him a journey of more than three hundred miles.
Having insufficient money to purchase a passage by boat, he set
out to walk. He had gone about fifty miles when he was set upon
by bandits, who took his bundle and his cash but left him with
his life, and fortunately his Bibles. In extreme distress he wrote a
petition to the prefect of the nearby city. The prefect disclaimed
all responsibility for the outrage, but out of pity gave the destitute
man four hundred cash.

It would hardly be enough to replace the padded quilt in which
to wrap himself at night. Hung stood by the landing wharf, pon-
dering what to do: whether to buy food and a quilt, or to spend
the money to get to his destination. A chance passer-by, observing
his downcast face, encouraged him with a cheerful proverb.

"A broken cord is mended with a line. And when the boat comes
to the bank, the way opens again."

Hung thanked him, and did indeed find his courage renewed.
"These words are correct," he replied to the good Samaritan, "and
they correspond with the true doctrine."

So he left the future to take care of itself, trusted to the Heavenly Father that he would not starve, and duly bargained for his
passage on a boat, the money to be paid on his disembarkation. It
was hard to watch his fellow passengers eating the usual three
meals a day. Hung took only one meal at the cost of about two-
pence. There were three travellers who were obviously members
of the literati, and he was a little ashamed that they should see the
straits to which he had been reduced, for his own speech betrayed
him as being one of their number.

The innate courtesy of their race enabled them, however, to address him after a day or two without wounding his feelings. "Sir," said the elder of the three, "by your noble countenance, it is easy to perceive that you are a man of talent. But as you, without being sick, still abstain from eating, we must conclude that you are in distress."

Hung confessed this to be the case, and told them how he had fallen among thieves. They asked him to share their food, and in return Hung offered them the benefit of his learning, always a thing of value and to be prized by a Chinese scholar, and acquired whenever possible. So for the next seven days Hung preached to them the words of eternal life.

He gave them an account of the Creation, the Flood, the Exodus, the plagues, the crossing of the Red Sea, the manna, the pillars of cloud and fire, and the giving of the Law. He spoke to them of the ancient worship of Shang-ti in China, and expounded his theory that idolatry had set in only in the third century B.C., when the custom had first been instituted of hiring men to represent the ghosts of the departed at funerals. Then he began to tell them about the Heavenly Elder Brother, and the need for the redemption of mankind, and at last he came to quoting from his own recent composition. He had been writing an "Ode for Youth" in which were detailed the duties of man both to God and to his fellow men. On the obligation to reverence Jesus he had written:

"Jesus, his firstborn Son,
Was in former times sent by God;
He willingly gave his life
To redeem us from sin.
Of a truth his merits are pre-eminent.
His cross was hard to bear.
The sorrowing clouds obscured the sun;
The adorable Son, the honoured of Heaven,
Died for you the children of men.
After his resurrection he ascended to heaven;
Resplendent in glory, he wields supreme authority.
In him we know that we may trust,
To secure salvation and ascend to Heaven."

If Issachar Roberts chose to consider Hung not yet fit to receive baptism, Hung's own countrymen were quick to acclaim his spiritual maturity. The three men to whom he had been preaching were so impressed that, when they disembarked at the next stopping place on the borders of Kwang-si, the elder of them bowed as he bade farewell to Hung, who had many days of travel before him, and said, "You ought not to be discouraged in travelling. You must be prepared for everything, even to be robbed." He took out a string of six hundred cash, worth about two shillings in the English currency of those days. "We have told the Captain not to demand any passage money from you," he went on, "and here we have collected a small sum for you, to enable you to proceed on your journey." With the utmost delicacy he proffered the string of copper coins, and Hung, with tears of gratitude in his eyes, was persuaded to accept the gift.

He would be able to go all the way by boat to Kwei, and to eat every day sufficient. Perhaps it was on that very occasion, as he sat down in the bows of the river-junk to eat a good full meal of rice, that he composed the words of the grace which he was later to teach all his future subjects to repeat.

"We thank thee, O God, our Heavenly Father, and pray that thou wouldst bless us with daily food and raiment, exempt us from calamity and affliction, and grant that our souls may go up to heaven."

Thus in the hottest month of the year, in July of 1847, Hung came safely to the city of Kwei and to the village home of cousin Wang.

9

WHEN COUSIN WANG first gave Hung the good news, he could hardly credit it. Feng was not only safe, it seemed, and preaching at Thistle Mount seventy miles up the river, but was the acknowledged teacher of more than two thousand converts. Thus had the gospel seed taken root and multiplied in the last two and a half years.

Hung wanted to set out at once for Thistle Mount, and there express his love and thanks to his quiet, unassuming friend who had proved himself so good a servant of Shang-ti. How to get there? He was uncertain of the way. Cousin Wang would provide a guide, a recent convert from Kwei and a fellow Hak-ka. Thus Hung first made the acquaintance of Shih Ta-kai. He was a young man of about twenty-six years old, a rich farmer, well-educated and of a good family, with knowledge of both civil and military affairs, and a minor degree. But Shang-ti in his wisdom, thought Hung as they strode over the hills together, gives not too many gifts to any one man, lest he grow proud, and his companion had certainly not been endowed with any good looks. His ugliness was really of an extreme character: his complexion dark to the point of sootiness and his shaven skull rising to such a peak that it was ghoulish. He was tall, and his spindle-legs could cover the hills more swiftly even than Hung's, and his face was full of gentleness and benevolence as they spoke together of the Bibles which Hung was carrying. Shih Ta-kai was promising that he would have more copies printed in Kwei at his own expense, for he had much silver. He seemed embarrassed at Hung's thanks, and his manner was more full of awe than was demanded merely by Hung's seven years' seniority. He had heard from Feng, he explained, that the honourable teacher had been caught up to heaven and was the Elect of the Ancient-of-Days.

Hung was deeply touched by his old friend, Feng's, loyalty. Here was a man with more than two thousand followers, who could very well have set up for himself as a prophet and even as a king, instead of which, when they met, he fell upon Hung's neck, and proclaimed to all around that the chosen instrument of Shang-ti was at last arrived. There, also at Thistle Mount and anxious to welcome him, was Yang, his own brother-in-law, pock-marked and squat and volatile as ever. He presented his rich nephew Cheng, who would also help with the printing of the Bibles. He also was a convert, a member of the congregation for which Feng had chosen the name of the God-worshippers.

Word of Hung's arrival spread like wildfire. On every man's lips it was whispered, "He has been in heaven. He comes from heaven. Therefore he must have the Heavenly Mandate." The whispers spread up and down the West River and its tributaries, and from the valleys it was carried up to the hillfolk, the Miau.

There were prayer-meetings everywhere, so many that there were not enough preachers unless further Bibles could be printed. More silver began to be needed than Shih Ta-kai or Yang's rich nephew could immediately supply. Yang suggested that yet another new convert might be approached, and he brought him to see Hung.

Wei Cheng lived in Chin-t'ien village below Thistle Mount. He was only about eighteen years old, but he had inherited from his deceased father a rich pawnbroking business, and owned besides considerable property in the town of P'ing-nan. He was hereditary chief of a clan numbering more than a thousand persons, all of whom would follow whatever faith or politics their young representative chose to adopt. His father had purchased for him a provincial degree, and he was therefore counted at the yamen of the district city as a petty official. Such a convert could be of the utmost help to the God-worshippers, not only with silver, but in keeping the magistrate quiet if he should show any desire to censor "unorthodox learning".

Hung, therefore, felt blameworthy that he could not immediately bring himself to like or trust Wei. He was tall, dark as a Malay, and had already a black moustache: good-looking in his way. Why, Hung asked himself, did he on a sudden call to mind Issachar's warnings against the Prince of Darkness? Although the lad had rather a proud and overbearing manner, he showed a real desire to fight God's enemies, the Tartars, and Shang-ti would need such warriors, Hung reflected, when the hour for the Holy War at last came.

Within a few months the ritual at the prayer-meetings became stereotyped. There was to be a big congregation of the God-worshippers at the rich nephew's mansion in Thistle Mount on the next Sabbath, and the Sabbath, due to a faulty reading of the calendar, was always a Saturday. Down from the hills had come the Miau, hundreds of them, all dressed in their winter felts and turbans. And up from the river traffic had come the Hak-kas, again in their hundreds, and there were many of the Cantonese-speaking people also.

The vast gathering was as though some Chinese painter had sought to depict the scene of the Sermon upon the Mount in oriental fashion, as the people knelt, facing the verandah of the mansion on which the honourable teacher and his assistants would presently come out. Below the verandah was placed a table, and on it two silver lamps, and between them three cups of tea in honour of the deity whom the congregation had been taught to praise as "three persons, who united constitute one true Lord". The cups of tea were a borrowing from Taoist ritual, and Hung was later to declare that God was one and indivisible, so that this praise of the Trinity had been copied from something he had picked up parrot fashion from Mr. Roberts.

The leaders of the movement, all of them long-gown wearers, were coming out on to the verandah now: first the two rich men, Shih Ta-kai, so ugly with his pointed skull, but smiling pleasantly, and young Wei, dark of skin and with a proud look, fingering his moustache.

Then came Hung's two brothers-in-law, first the squat, pock-marked Yang, laughing and bluff, and beside him the handsome and golden-skinned Hsiao, carrying himself as might a soldier or an ancient hero, but with unselfconscious ease.

All so far had been hillmen from Kwang-si. Now came the plainsmen from Kwang-tung: first Feng, the oldest of all, slight and diffident, with a scholarly stoop and something of a saint's face. The hair of his queue was already greying.

And last of all there came out Hung Hsiu-ch'uan himself, his skin as light a gold as that of Hsiao, but his breadth and height greater, and his carriage that of an emperor.

From behind him stepped his two sisters, and modestly and without ostentation they slipped away from the steps of the verandah and went to sit amongst the women. There was a strict segregation of the sexes at worship, and the people spread over the grass pasture were divided into two large groups, the men on one side, and the women on the other.

The service was beginning. Sinking to his knees, Feng began the usual daily morning prayer, and the congregation, also kneel-ing, echoed his words.

"I thine unworthy son, kneeling down on the ground, pray to thee, the Great God, our Heavenly Father . . ."

Hung had been for weeks teaching them the Lord's prayer as he knew it. Now, at Feng's request, his deep voice proclaimed the words, and once again the congregation murmured in repetition.

"Supreme Lord, our Heavenly Father, forgive all our sins that we have committed in ignorance, rebelling against thee. Bless us, brethren and sisters, thy little children. Give us our daily food and raiment; keep us from all calamities and afflictions, that in this world we may have peace, and finally ascend to heaven and enjoy eternal happiness. We pray thee to bless the brethren and sisters of all nations. We ask these things for the redeeming merits of one Lord and Saviour, our Heavenly Brother Jesus' sake. We also pray, Heavenly Father, that thy holy will may be done on earth as it is in heaven; for thine are all the kingdoms, glory and power. Amen."

In thus rendering the Lord's prayer, there had been a very significant omission. There had been no mention of forgiving others, as they hoped to be forgiven.

When the people had sat down again upon the ground, Hung began to teach them the new Three Character Classic which he had composed. He had written it for the benefit of the young, ready for the day when throughout China children should learn from their earliest years, not that "Men at their birth are by nature pure", but the story of man's redemption from his impurity. As with the old classic, it was in rhyme and had but three characters to every line, so that already the young people could repeat a good deal of it.

> "The great God
> Made heaven and earth;
> Both land and sea,
> And all things therein.
> In six days,
> He made the whole;
> Man the lord of all,
> Was endowed with glory and honour.
> Every seventh day worship,
> In acknowledgement of Heaven's favour:
> Let all under heaven
> Keep their hearts in reverence.
> It is said that in former times,
> A foreign nation was commanded
> To honour God;
> The nation's name was Israel."

The verses continued with the history of the Exodus and the giving of the Law. You could see that the children were delighted

with the account of the plagues in Egypt. Then the honourable
teacher from heaven began to speak more slowly.

"The celestial law
Cannot be altered.
In after ages,
It was sometimes disobeyed,
Through the devil's temptations,
When men fell into misery.
But the great God,
Out of pity to mankind,
Sent his firstborn Son
To come down into the world.
His name is Jesus,
The Lord and Saviour of men,
Who redeems them from sin,
By the endurance of extreme misery.
Upon the cross,
They nailed his body;
Where he shed his precious blood,
To save all mankind.
Three days after his death
He rose from the dead:
And during forty days,
He discoursed on heavenly things.
When he was about to ascend,
He commanded his disciples
To communicate his Gospel,
And proclaim his revealed will.
Those who believe will be saved,
And ascend up to heaven;
But those who do not believe,
Will be the first to be condemned.
Throughout the whole world,
There is only one God
The great Lord and Ruler."

The verses went on to explain how originally Shang-ti had
been worshipped in China, but how with the coming of idolatry
God became displeased.

"And has sent his son
With orders to come down into the world."

The people hung now upon his every word, for they knew that
Hsiu-ch'uan was speaking of himself.

> "Having first studied the classics,
> In the Ting-yew year
> He was received up to heaven,
> Where the affairs of heaven
> Were clearly pointed out to him."

Hung proceeded to give in verse an account of his visions.
Then he paused, and at last bowed to show that the recitation
was for the moment ended. He had not yet finished the final
composition, nor was it yet wise to speak too freely of the authority
committed to him by his Heavenly Father. Let it be thought for
the moment that it was a spiritual authority only.

He now invited Yang to take a part in conducting the service
and Yang read aloud the Ten Commandments, and after each
he read Hung's commentary. The people replied with hymns of
Hung's composition, accompanied by the weird strains of Chinese
music from yet more weird instruments. Hung's rendering of the
Commandments preserved the spirit of the Mosaic Law, but to
the Commandment against adultery he had adjoined a prohibition
against opium.

He was in fact prepared from henceforth to do his own thinking. He had given much thought and heart-searching to the
question of the validity of his baptism, and had come to the
conclusion that any water which Issachar Roberts had power to
give or withhold could not be more efficacious than that which,
at the bidding of the Heavenly Elder Brother, he and Li had
poured over each other's heads. Nor, apparently, had Issachar
bothered to instruct him that a man must be baptised in the
names of the Father, the Son, and the Holy Ghost.

One after another the several new candidates for baptism approached the table below the verandah, on which a large bowl
of water had now been placed. The first man to kneel before
it was a simple fellow, one of the Miau. He gave a slight shiver
as he removed his felt coat and bared his breast, and when he
took off his turban his shock of shoulder-length hair sprang out
round his head. He had first to take vows not to worship corrupt
spirits, and to observe the Ten Commandments. Then from his

trembling and not very clean hands he produced a piece of paper. On it was inscribed a confession of his personal sins. The paper was set alight, and his confession sent aloft to Shang-ti unproclaimed to men, but to the Heavenly Father all was now confessed, and he would be forgiven. He felt the cold douche of the water Feng poured over him, and heard the words, "Purification from all former sins, putting off the old, and regeneration". Then, obeying Feng, he dipped his hand in what was left of the water in the basin and anointed his breast, that his heart might be renewed, and began to recite the words which he had learned beforehand. "My previous sin is washed away. I have put aside the old, and am made new." His face was shining as he walked away, so that the rest of the congregation could see that this baptism was a thing to give men fresh courage.

It was a fitting time to celebrate and to eat, for it was close on midday. Rice, fruit and wine were offered before the table, together with a slain ox, not as a sacrifice or burnt offering, but in thanks and as a preparation for the grace which every God-worshipper now said before sitting down to meat. After the feast, and as the afternoon drew on, Hung once again addressed them.

"That Shang-ti can only be worshipped by the Emperor is a delusion of the Devil." Only to think, they whispered, we also may approach the Altar of Heaven! What was he saying now? "To follow the customs of the world complies with the Devil's wishes." That was harder to understand. There had always been certain customs. "To accuse us of following foreigners is the Devil's dupe." He himself had met foreigners, and said they were not all lacking in virtue. "A false rumour attributes to Yen-lo the determining of the length of man's days." Now this did concern each one of them very deeply. Not a word must be missed. "This king of the underworld," he continued, "is none other than the old serpent, the Devil, who transforms himself in a variety of ways to deceive and entrap the souls of men." He went on to tell them of how, when his soul had been wandering in heaven, he had slain the demons.

Heaven! Everyone knew he had been there, and therefore he had come from Heaven on a special mission. Therefore he must hold the Heavenly Mandate. But let not the whisper go beyond these hidden places in the hills, or the officials would strike first, and the time was not yet ripe for armed rebellion, though they waited only for him to give the word.

Hung never gave it. He waited always for God's command, God's hour. He gave instead, forced thereto by destiny, the order to destroy certain images; and, since that was contrary to law and order, the God-worshippers found themselves overnight in conflict with the existing authorities.

It happened in this way. Soon after that very Sabbath's meeting, one or two of the congregation were seized with an infectious dysentery, and the infection spread. The attacks were slight but inconvenient, and when people began to consider the cause, they remembered that in the department of Siang there was a god of great renown, who had a particular reputation for thus afflicting men's bowels, if any should dare to speak against him. It was plain, said some, that this monarch of the spirit world, whose name was Kan, must have heard Hung Hsiu-ch'uan inveighing against all images, including his own. There was a small falling off from the congregation, because some were now afraid of the power of this renowned spirit to do them harm.

They sent spokesmen to Hung to tell him of their danger. Did the honourable teacher from Heaven know how powerful was the spirit of this Kan? Men said that he had once been a man, living in Siang, who had asked a geomancer to select him an auspicious place of interment in the usual way. The geomancer had prophesied that by a bloody burial great prosperity would result to Kan's family. Whereupon the wretch had killed his own mother, and buried her as the first person on the indicated spot. Another story ran that he had forced his elder sister to have intercourse with a profligate, and it was this very same Kan who was responsible for the obscene songs which the honourable teacher so disliked, and had taught the God-worshippers not to sing.

Hung frowned, for the Kwang-si songs were very obscene, and he had been trying to wean the people from their love of these old songs.

Another spokesman was now holding forth. Had the honourable teacher not heard how only recently the spirit of Kan had possessed a young lad in Siang? The boy had been frantic, and had pushed his way through the ranks of lictors and run right up to the sedan chair of the district magistrate, and in the name of

Kan had demanded a Dragon robe for Kan's image, which the magistrate had not dared refuse. It was well known that the temple wardens were afraid to sleep in Kan's shrine. Morning and evening, when they entered to light the lamps and burn incense, they beat a great gong to prevent the god from appearing to them.

Hung's face had set in a look of grim determination. Was he to lose his converts because of the fear they had of this renowned image? He turned to the spokesmen and said, "This kind of demon I used to exterminate when my soul was wandering in heaven."

Straightway he took with him Feng and cousin Wang's son, and started on the two days' journey up river to Siang.

Who was he, this terrible sovereign, the aspect of whose image was reputed to be so dreadful that men shook with fear? Was the shrine but the place of some four-thousand-year-old nature cult, at which at least one sacrifice of human blood had been thought necessary to establish its "mana", and where men and women had coupled and sung obscene songs to encourage procreation in nature? Had the doings of all the wicked men of Siang who had lived since then been credited to this god of the crops? Or was there indeed an earth-bound spirit attached to the temple, something that had once been a man, but was now turned malevolent in its desire to rend and destroy? Or was the idol the focus of some more puissant and demonic power? Hung had no doubts but that the idol of Kan was inhabited by a demon. Probably no one believed that the Supreme Deity, if such existed, would inhabit an image, but it may be very true that for those who are telepathic an image, whether it be the bone of a Christian saint or the golden face of a Buddha, can act as a catalyst between individual minds, fusing them in realms beyond time and space, so that the holy thoughts of all the holy men who have contemplated the object powerfully affect the present beholder of it. A communion of evil minds could just as easily find a focus in some chosen idol. However it was, something which stank of evil had come out of the darkness to challenge Shang-ti.

Feng and Wang the younger took possession of the temple doors, thrusting the startled wardens aside and making way for Hung, while the people, who had gathered in the train of the iconoclasts, stood open-mouthed, aghast yet hopeful, to see what the young prophet would do, and what terrible vengeance the sovereign Kan was about to wreak.

Hung, armed only with a stout stick, walked straight up to the lewd and leering image, raised his arm and began to lay about that idol and to castigate it with all the force of his powerful body. Blow after blow rained down, and between each Hung straightened himself and flung at the image's battered face accusation after accusation, the list of the crimes for which Kan was receiving punishment: matricide; contempt of God; frightening the people; procuration; obscenity; pride; the extortion of silver.

He tore off the Dragon robe, broke the censors and the vessels, and finally overturned the image, dashing it to pieces and crumbling the fragments in his hands. He stood then to face the people, as they crowded in to see what he had done. Never had he appeared more kingly or more like some prophet of old, the sunlight falling on his golden skin, his countenance as noble in wrath as it was in repose. It seemed that St. John's words were being fulfilled, that the sons of God should be like Him, the Heavenly Elder Brother, and that here stood Christ expelling the thieves from the temple. Yang might yet become another St. Peter. In the end Feng would perhaps prove the truest to his prototype, a St. John to bring comfort, love and loyalty and the greatest understanding to his master. He urged him now to make all haste, to have done, and to withdraw from the vicinity, for the reaction of the civil administration to such a breach of the peace would be swift. Indeed it was. Almost immediately a hundred silver dollars were offered for the apprehension of the iconoclasts.

When Hung returned unscathed to Thistle Mount, the story of his prowess went through all the countryside and his fame became greater than ever before. Not only was he the chosen recipient of the Heavenly Mandate, but the Heavenly Elder Brother was holding him safe and invulnerable from the powers of evil. The images had no more power to hurt him or any man. The Godworshippers, free of anxiety and fear, fell upon the objects of their old dread, the images to which they had paid much silver and whose yoke had been hard. Idol after idol was overturned, dashed to pieces or burnt. Only the Confucian temples and the ancestral shrines with the tablets of ancestors were respected, and this by Hung's express command. Moreover, in the years to come these always escaped desecration, so long as there were responsible officers in charge of the insurgent troops. But for the rest of the images, the God-worshippers exulted in their destruction.

It was plain that matters could not proceed thus without the movement coming into conflict with civil authority. A rich graduate named Wang—the written character means "king", and there were more Mr. Kings in China than in the English-speaking world—was the first to lodge a complaint about the general destruction at the office of the district magistrate, where he gave a plain warning that the present craze for iconoclasm was tantamount to, and but a pretext for, open rebellion. The district magistrate of Kwei-p'ing promptly clapped the nearest leaders of this sect of fanatics, the God-worshippers, into gaol, and it happened that they were Feng and Feng's young assistant.

Hung was distraught when he learnt that calamity had fallen upon his friend rather than on himself. "If we," he groaned to the messenger who had brought the ill-tidings, "because of the true doctrine suffer such persecution, what may be the design of God in this?" But Hung did not waste time lamenting. He was a man of action. He could think of only one way in which to free Feng. He had remembered that the Viceroy, old Prince Kiying, the Emperor's uncle, was on very good terms with the foreigners, had even dined and wined with them; and that it was this very prince who had signed the treaty whereby the Chinese were permitted to profess Christianity. He would go straight to Canton and there make a personal appeal to the prince. Somehow he would find means of approaching him, and then he would explain that Feng's only fault was his profession of Christianity, and that he was therefore wrongfully imprisoned. He set off at once.

Meanwhile Feng resigned himself to his imprisonment, nursed his assistant who was ill with gaol fever, and, not content with writing odes and petitions for his release, settled down to work out a new calendar for the God-worshippers.

In Canton Hung went first to the mission house. Roberts was away on a trip to Macao, and as for Prince Kiying, he had left only two days ago for Peking. Hung was desperate. He spoke to his acquaintances amongst the secret society of the Triads, but they were too concerned with their own affairs to listen much to his.

The brethren of the Heaven-and-Earth society had at last found their man, so they said; the three—Heaven, Earth and Man—were at last united. The individual in whom they thus put their hopes was a certain Chu from Hu-nan. He had been a Buddhist monk and had left his monastery. In Kwang-tung province the Triads had received him on their knees with much sacrifice of oxen at a secret meeting. They could rely on Hung's known views not to betray the cause. Would not Hung come and see this scion of the Mings? His name of Chu, the family name as distinct from the throne name of the Ming dynasty, was a fairly common one, but this man, they said, was truly of the Imperial blood. Would not Hung come and meet him, for it was known that Hung had a following in Kwang-si?

Hung went: not a long journey, but only so far as one of the secret lodges in the back streets of Canton. He saw a man of about twenty-six years old, an obvious weakling, full of conceit, a failed scholar and a lapsed monk; mincing a little, and probably one of those natural eunuchs from the womb of which the gospel spoke so enigmatically.

Hung's smile was a mixture of scorn and compassion for the degenerate offspring of a once great house. It was plain that the Triads could give help neither to his immediate problem of releasing Feng nor to the Empire. It was true that the Ming dynasty had been originally founded by a Buddhist monk, a beggar and illiterate. There was nothing to prevent Heaven from bestowing its mandate upon a poor man, but certainly not upon this brittle-boned creature, who still affected the entirely shaven skull and grey robes of his late monastic life.

Hung fingered the hair on his own forehead, which he was already allowing to grow against the day when the Heavenly Father should place upon it a coronet of gold and pearls and jade, but he was thinking not so much now of any personal grandeur in the future, as of the desperate need of Feng, who might at this moment be dying of gaol fever or torture.

That night Hung committed his despair to paper in the form of an ode.

"When shall I meet again with faithful brethren,
 And preach the word along the river's strand?
 When find again true sympathy and virtue

And joyful tones mingle without restraint?
Alas! for noble courage and for honest hearts,
With whom I would restore to peace the universe!
Alas! for all the quarters of the earth
What men shall stand by me?
The Dragon clouds and Tiger winds assemble;
When shall the hour of congregation come?
The heavenly law is not to blame.
Has God no more compassion?
Oh for one mind from first to last!
What day shall we triumphantly ascend?"

On the next morning Hung rose from his poor bed in a mean
lodging-house; putting aside his despair, and remembering all
the enjoinders in the holy scriptures, he began to tramp the streets
of Canton, and, as he did so, to pray and to pray and to pray, for
there seemed no help in any man now, but only in God alone, if
Feng were to be rescued from prison, as St. Peter had been.
Afterwards, in his Imperial decrees, Hung was to record how,
alone and disconsolate in Canton, "We besought the Father to
come down and manifest his terrors".

10

HUNG'S PRAYER WAS answered in a very curious manner.
More than three hundred miles away, in Thistle Mount, Yang
was sitting in his little house and with him was Shih Ta-kai,
who was teaching him to read, for Yang was almost illiterate,
and yet he desired to be able to read the scriptures for himself.
They were together studying those very tracts of Liang Fa which
Hung believed to have been placed in his hands by the special
intention of providence, and which, therefore, of all holy writ
was held holiest by the God-worshippers, and influenced them
most deeply. They were reading the nineteenth chapter of the

Acts of the Apostles, and Yang's voice was slow and hesitating but determined, as he stumbled with the difficult ideographs. "Have ye received the Holy Ghost since ye believed?" Shih Ta-kai helped him with the next few characters, and read on, "and when Paul had laid his hands upon them, the Holy Ghost came on them, and they spake with tongues and prophesied."

Shih Ta-kai bade Yang continue, but when there came no answer from his companion he glanced up, and was astonished to find that Yang's eyes were glazed, and his mouth open. When at last he did speak the syllables tumbled over each other and were slurred. All at once he was on his feet, and those feet were planted firmly upon the ground, and Yang stood as stalwart and square as a foundation stone, while words poured from his lips. The only phrase Shih Ta-kai could catch perfectly clearly, which was often repeated and later incorporated in the Imperial records, was, "The Heavenly Father has come to direct affairs. The Heavenly Father has come to direct affairs." What followed Shih Ta-kai managed to put together from disjointed sentences. Money was to be collected, an apologia for Christian doctrine was to be written, together with a copy of the Ten Commandments, and the silver and the writings were both to be sent to the district magistrate in Kwei-p'ing, together with a petition for Feng's release. Yang seemed to be giving himself orders. But was it Yang who was giving the orders? Or was he merely the recipient of them? It turned out that he was not even the direct recipient, for afterwards he had no knowledge of what had transpired, and needed to be told by Shih Ta-kai what words had just passed his lips. It therefore became apparent to the God-worshippers that it was the Heavenly Father who had spoken through Yang. And now Yang could not find his own voice, was reduced to speechlessness, and, like Zacharias before him, was stricken slowly dumb as his tongue clove to his mouth.

That Yang should be the chosen instrument through which Shang-ti would take personal direction of affairs was not to be wondered at, for, like Peter, he was a practical man. He was of the earth, earthy. He was also extremely volatile, easily set alight, laid open as it were to be easily dominated by spiritual powers, what a future century would call highly suggestible to ideas, and therefore dangerously vulnerable, if the spiritual power should come not from above but from below. For once the idea, or the prompting of angel or devil, was entered firmly into his mind, no mere circumstances would from henceforth deter him, and all his practical powers—and they were great—would be directed as his angel or devil chose to command.

It seems fair to suppose that at this moment Yang was being directed by some good influence, for the result resounded to the credit of the gospel-preaching. The district magistrate was softened by the exposition of the Christian doctrine, and released Feng on the condition of banishment from the province back to his home in Kwang-tung.

Feng's assistant had died of the terrible conditions then existing in Chinese prisons, but two yamen police were ordered to escort Feng to the border of Kwang-si. There was no fear of his escaping, for his neck was fastened in a cangue, a kind of large wooden grid which prisoners in transit were forced to wear: it was somewhat similar in purpose to the scold's collar or the stocks of medieval Europe. Feng had no need to escape, for, as he walked between his guards, he began to preach to them the gospel; promptly converted them; was freed of his encumbrance; and was escorted by them back to Thistle Mount with all honour.

The God-worshippers gave them a tremendous welcome, and celebrated Feng's triumphant return by much slaying of oxen for a feast calculated to fatten his half-starved body. As soon as he was able, Feng set out for Kwang-tung and Hua district to put Hung's mind at rest, and also to find out what had become of him, but they missed each other.

Hung arrived back at Thistle Mount in mid-June to hear the glad news that Feng was at liberty, but was on his way to Hua. He found Yang only beginning to recover from the dumbness with which he had been stricken. Hung tried to take in the import of the strange tale. What could such a manifestation portend, he wondered? He stayed for a month or two in Kwangsi to strengthen the organisation, and committed certain authority to Yang, as the apparently chosen vessel of the Heavenly Father, before setting off back to Hua, for word had come that his father was ill and failing.

But on the very day that he was to embark on a river-boat, the strange phenomenon of Yang's directed speech was repeated, this time through the mouth of Hsiao, his brother-in-law. The leaders of the movement had assembled at Thistle Mount to bid Hung a temporary farewell. They were all gathered in the reception room of the rich nephew's mansion, and Hsiao, with his usual easy long-limbed grace, had just come up to him to wish him well. Hung began by congratulating him on the birth of his first son, and then they went on to speak of how the disciples of the Heavenly Elder Brother had been sent to preach throughout Galilee. The handsome face of Hsiao was full of animation, and his pale golden skin caught the light of the morning sun, when all at once he fell silent, his expression abstracted. Then in a voice deeper and more powerful than his own he began to utter, and there fell a sudden hush amongst those present as they listened.

What exactly were the words which came from Hsiao's mouth on the first occasion of his speaking with tongues was never recorded, but the God-worshippers accepted without question that this time it was the Heavenly Elder Brother who wished to address mankind, and that Hsiao was to be from henceforth His chosen mouthpiece. The Imperial records say that it was in this month of October 1848 that Hsiao was first "commissioned by the Redeemer to manifest divine powers", and in a further record Hung claimed that from this date "The Father and Elder Brother led us to sit on the throne of the Heavenly Kingdom". It seems therefore that for the first time open witness was borne that Heaven had bestowed its mandate to rule the Empire upon Hung Hsiu-ch'uan. Up to that time anything that had been said had been voiced in whispers behind closed doors.

Hung went back to Kwang-tung, therefore, as an individual consecrated for the throne, of whom the Redeemer himself had borne open witness, and to whom men had paid in private the homage fitting a new emperor. As to why he left his still perilously small empire in Kwang-si at such a moment, none of his countrymen would have questioned such a decision. His father was dying, and not to be present at his obsequies would set such an example of unfilial behaviour as in an ordinary man would elicit only contempt, but in an emperor could have wrecked the harmony of the universe. Furthermore, custom demanded at least a year's mourning for the death of a male parent, and a complete retiring from office, public affairs, entertainment or travel. It was plain, therefore, that for the next twelve months the Heavenly Elder

Brother, that pattern of filial conduct and virtue, would give no further commands for action to his humble younger brother.

Hung duly arrived back at Hua in November 1848 to find Feng in good health and spirits, but his father already dead. The old headman had for a long time past professed Christianity. Weeping quietly, Hung's mother now told him of his father's last words on his death bed.

"I am now ascending to Heaven," he had said. "After my decease you must not call any Buddhist priests, or perform any heathen ceremonies, but merely worship God and pray to him."

Hung put on the long white garments of mourning, and the grass sandals, but he had no need to grow his hair, as was customary in such times of bereavement, for it was already long and he could twist it into a knot beneath his white turban.

He sent for no geomancer to decide on an auspicious day for the funeral. Instead he was for long hours closeted with Feng, while he gave himself and his powerful intellect time to appreciate the scholarly precision and patience with which Feng was working out a new calendar. The one employed by the present dynasty was based on the moon and was inclined to be inaccurate. To change the times and seasons had been throughout the entire world and in all ages the prerogative of a consecrated monarch only, and one for which gods and men had held him responsible at the cost of his life, if he tampered wrongly with what could affect the dates of sowing and reaping. The institution of Feng's solar calendar was to be one of the first of Hung's Imperial decrees, and it was to have the purpose not only of greater accuracy, but of breaking down superstition regarding auspicious days. Of it Hung was to write, "Thus every year is lucky and favourable, every month and every day is lucky and favourable. Whoever truly venerates our Heavenly Father and Celestial Brother is under the protection of Heaven, and can engage in his duties whenever he thinks proper."

Within a few days, therefore, the funeral procession, with the women in hired sedan chairs, wound its way to the family burial place on the hillside. Hung had himself closed the coffin. He stood now within the small circular wall, dotted with trees, and watched as the coffin was placed near the tomb of brickwork, beside which the roof-tiles were piled ready for laying over it. The women were placing the usual wine, tea, rice, and a dish of savoury meat before the tomb, as an offering to Shang-ti for any hunger that old Ching-yang's soul might feel upon the journey. Then Hung began to pray aloud, and it was a prayer which was later to be incorporated in the liturgy of his realm for use at all funerals.

"I thine unworthy son, kneeling down upon the ground, present my supplications to thee, the great God our Heavenly Father. There is here present the soul of thine unworthy servant Hung Ching-yang, who seven days ago departed this life; having placed the body in a coffin, put on mourning, and conducted the funeral to the place of burial, I reverently prepare animals, wine, tea and rice, offering them up to thee, the great God our Heavenly Father, earnestly beseeching thee, of thy favour to admit the soul of thine unworthy servant, Hung Ching-yang, up into heaven, to enjoy abundant happiness with thee."

The prayer continued with a request that fear, dread and demoniacal influences might be banished "through the merits of our Saviour and Elder Brother, the Lord Jesus, who redeemed us from sin". There was the usual wailing as the coffin was then lowered into its little house of brick, but amongst the cries there was frequent mention of "Our Saviour, the Lord Jesus".

Thus old Ching-yang went to his rest: a good man, and a fond father. Hung's grief at parting from him was genuine and deep, as real as his love for and pleasure at seeing again his beautiful Lai-shi. Since, however, he could not co-habit with his wife in the first period of mourning, he turned his thoughts to other things. Presently, he knew, ceremony and protocol would wrap him round more firmly than a cocoon of silk wraps a pupa. While he was yet free, he would enjoy the simple pleasures of his boyhood, and at the same time render them more poignant by offering them to Shang-ti.

Each morning now he would vault on to the back of the largest of the family buffaloes, while Feng scrambled less elegantly on to another, and together they would ride up to the hill pastures, there to preach the word of God to the herd-boys of all the surrounding villages. He laughed to think that he had ever considered herding an irksome duty. Now the days seemed too short in which to enjoy such a sweet pastoral life. He would see, as he stood in the shade of the trees, the single files of beasts winding

up towards him from the various valleys, and on the back of each
a lad in his red or green or blue cotton jacket and trousers, and
they would be yodelling their shrill pasture-songs. When they
had slid from the backs of the beasts, and the blackbirds and
magpies had taken their places, perching on the shoulders of the
browsing buffaloes, they would gather round him in a circle. He
would tell them then the gospel story, and often they heard him
say, "My own soul has ascended to heaven, and my words are
true".

When the sun sank low he would lead them all, riding buffaloes,
down to the valley, and together they would sing one of the
hymns he had written and set to music.

"All happiness in the world comes from Heaven,
It is therefore reasonable that men should give thanks and sing."

Nevertheless, life at Hua was not always so peaceful. There was
work to be done. The Redeemer's voice had proclaimed him
and the time was nearly ripe.

If the province of Kwang-si was to rise in favour of Hung,
while Kwang-tung rose in favour of some degenerate scion of the
Mings, there would be confusion and disaster. The situation must
be assessed. Feng therefore went to Canton, mixed with the
members of the Triads, and duly became a "brother" and initiate
of the secret society. Then he persuaded the scion of the Mings,
who had adopted the title of "Celestial Virtue", to accompany
him back to Hua, ostensibly to hide him from the authorities,
but in fact so that Hung might have the opportunity of both
sizing him up and keeping a certain hold upon his person. If
for the moment Hung was forced by circumstances to appear as
the humble liegeman of Celestial Virtue and to defer to him, it
was a small deception, which he had no doubt Shang-ti would
pardon.

Chu's company had both advantages and disadvantages. By
temperament the lapsed monk was proud and jealous and took
offence easily, but he was incongruously enough an expert in that
part of the classics known as the Rites of Chou, wherein was set
forth the art of military organisation and strategy. Hung picked
his brains, and became equally as adept at knowing how many

regiments had gone to make a division and how many divisions to an army in the Golden Age.

Less pleasant was Chu's jealousy of Hung's relations with his wife. When spring came, Hung could no longer keep himself from Lai-shi, whatever the customs of mourning might dictate, and Chu, a guest in the house, seemed to recognise with some hypersensitive perception that Hung was enjoying to the full what he, Chu, could never enjoy. Although Chu was no longer a monk and therefore free to take a wife, and moreover was twenty-six years old, he remained celibate, which suggested that he was unable rather than unwilling. But while his sudden fits of spleen indicated that he grudged Hung his pleasures, he found an outlet, and a means of tantalising Hung, by endless talk of the famous courtesans and concubines which his Imperial ancestors had enjoyed, and with a smile here and a subtle innuendo there would make plain that the simple pleasures of one wife only were as nothing to what he, Chu, would presently be called upon to enjoy as emperor.

Hung was all the more irritated because, after a little more than a month of making love to his wife, Lai-shi became unusually and prematurely sick with a new pregnancy, and he, who had been for too long without a woman, had yet again to restrain himself. Chu's conversation inflamed him, for those things of which Celestial Virtue spoke concerned not Chu's future but his own. It was perfectly true that as an emperor he would be expected to insure the continuance of the dynasty by means of a harem of carefully chosen concubines. Surely the Lord had drawn the lines of his destiny in pleasant places: a goodly heritage wherein pleasure and duty would presently be combined! But that heritage lay in the future. Meanwhile he must keep his thoughts from lusting after other men's women. He remembered his own rendering into Chinese of the last Commandment, "Thou shalt not conceive a covetous desire". And to it he had added for the benefit of the God-worshippers his written commentary, "When involved in the sea of lust, the consequences are very serious". Lust meant to Hung the desiring of women not his own, the seduction and theft of females from their rightful owner. Never would he be guilty of it, and, until such time as Imperial protocol presented him with his own harem, he would contain himself.

Nevertheless his thoughts were turned to woman and the mystery she presented to the universe. He remembered how in heaven he had seen many beautiful sisters as well as brothers amongst the children of the Heavenly Father. Then one night he dreamed one of his strange dreams. When he woke he could remember nothing clearly, no shapes, no forms, but an experience of a state of being only, and the vivid apprehension that there existed in the source of all being the Yin Principle as well as the Yang Principle, the feminine as well as the masculine. He straightway petitioned the Heavenly Father on his knees, pleading that, since he had no books to tell him whether or not the Ultimate Principle had indeed divided itself into Yin and Yang in order to create, he was at a loss to understand the import of his dream. Once again he slept, and this time he heard the Heavenly Father's voice clearly.

"Search in the neighbourhood, and you will find books which contain all my doctrine. For the rest, be at peace. I am with you to protect you, and nothing will be able to resist you."

On the next day Feng was going to Canton for one of the Triad meetings. Hung told him of his dream, and neither was entirely surprised that Feng found in an old bookshop in the back streets of the city a parcel of books which plainly had something to do with Christian teaching. The ways of God, they thought, were very wonderful.

The account of the incident from a Jesuit Father many years later makes plain that what had fallen into Hung's hands were books more than two hundred years old, mostly in manuscript. They had been inscribed by those Jesuits who had converted the last Ming Empress Dowager, and the Emperor's wife and heir, when they had all been refugees in Canton in the seventeenth century.

Hung fell upon this literature greedily. According to the Catholics all men, as brothers of Jesus, could be children also of Mary. The Protestants, when they came to read his later edicts, were dumbfounded at his blasphemy in calling himself a son of God, a uterine brother of Jesus, brought forth by the same mother. They failed to recognise his doctrine as a Catholic one, because it was clumsily expressed, and the Catholics failed to recognise the harvest of their own sowing because Hung, once launched upon a quest for the Yin Principle, did not stop there.

Who was the Bride of the Lamb? At first it seemed that this was a poetic description of the Holy Jerusalem, and for the moment Hung was content to leave the question unanswered. However, the proximity of Chu, the lapsed Buddhist monk, was having its effect. That men had lived many times on earth before, and would return to it again after death, unless they attained Nirvana, was the central tenet of Buddhist belief. From this very wheel of ceaseless reincarnation the Buddhists sought to free themselves. To suppose that the soul was only created by God at the moment of physical birth was inconceivable to an Asiatic. Even one of the early Christian Fathers, Origen, had held that souls must have had some existence in another sphere before they were called to birth in this world, though he had been reproved by the Church for such a suggestion. To Hung it was plain, had always been plain and would always remain so, that men died and returned and died and returned. If Christ, then, was the firstborn of God's sons, he had existed in heaven before his incarnation at Bethlehem. Not as the Logos, for of the Logos Hung knew nothing, but as the firstborn of God's sons. And if he had so existed, then there must exist also his other half—the Yin Principle.

In his dreams Hung began to see a face . . . the face perhaps of the Bride of the Lamb? But as yet he was uncertain. Only he knew this: that in the first chapter of Genesis it was clearly stated "God created man in his own image, in the image of God created he him, male and female created he them". The scholar who had written this had, it seemed to Hung, perfectly understood that God had divided himself into the Yang and Yin Principle, and had created man in his own image, also divided into Yang and Yin.

As the summer drew on, it became apparent that Hung would have to return to Kwang-si before the full completion of his year's mourning. There was famine there, and bandits were rising, as they always did in times of hunger. The situation must not be allowed to get out of hand, for the timing of concerted action was vital. The signs that the Heavenly Mandate of the Manchu dynasty was outrun were increasing. There was a plague in Canton and Hong Kong. There was never-ending rain in the Ning-po and Shanghai districts, where the images of the gods were put out in the downpour, "to see how they liked it".

There were natural catastrophes in Hu-nan and along the middle reaches of the Yang-tze. The officials were everywhere being forced at last to organise soup kitchens for the destitute. The people would presently rise in protest against their miseries. Hung must be about his Heavenly Father's business, and let the dead bury their dead, and even take his leave of Lai-shi before his child was born. She gazed at him now as they parted, and there was fear and mute appeal in her eyes. She knew now that her husband would one day wear the Imperial Yellow, and that there would be many beautiful women placed at his disposal. If only, if only this time she might bear him a son! Then he would continue to love her as the mother of his heir.

Hung could not bear the expression of hope, fear and unspoken prayer on her face, and left her quickly to give certain last instructions to his brothers regarding the safe-keeping of Celestial Virtue. Then he left Hua and his old home for the last time in July of 1849.

II

HUNG ARRIVED BACK among the God-worshippers in Kwang-si to find them in the throes of an extraordinary psychic experience. Missionaries have had frequent occasion to remark that the results of conversion to Christianity do quite often produce the same signs which puzzled the onlookers on that day of Pentecost when the apostles were first filled with the Holy Ghost. On that very occasion in Jerusalem there had been those ready to mock and say, "These men are full of new wine", and sceptics have continued ever since to suggest that the symptoms shown by those professing to have received the gift of tongues are due to hysteria. As against this, it can be argued that a man possesses only one set of nerves through which to express different emotions, strings, as it were, of a violin, which certainly vibrate whatever touches them, yet the player may be a great maestro or a mischievous child.

Hung found the God-worshippers experiencing all the known symptoms: ecstasies, perspirations, exhortings, reprovings, prophesying, and words delivered in apparently spontaneous rhythm. Yang had been chosen, it seemed, as the mouthpiece of the Heavenly Father, and through Hsiao's lips came the voice of the Heavenly Elder Brother. But there was hardly a man or a woman who had not manifested some disturbance of the spirit. Yang, who despite his own experiences was a practical fellow and no fool, had given out that some of these manifestations bore true witness and others false.

Hung remembered Christ's words, "By their fruits ye shall know them", and immediately confirmed Yang's pronouncement that some "voices" came from God and some from the Devil. He not only quoted Paul, "Quench not the spirit. Every spirit is of God that confesseth that Jesus Christ is come in the flesh", but straightway put Paul's dictum to the test. Those who next fell into ecstasy and prophesied in trance were severely questioned, and at least one man was expelled from the congregation for refusing to confess Christ.

In a modified form the manifestations continued. Yang, perhaps inspired by the story of how handkerchiefs and aprons from the body of Paul had cured disease, was effecting cures of the sick by intercession and by vicarious suffering. He called himself the Honai teacher, whatever that might mean—in years to come no European could translate the word—and when he asked the Heavenly Father's permission to take upon himself the pains and aches of the sick, his face became drawn with suffering and the patient improved in health. He was perhaps of too simple a mind to consider that such experiments might be dangerous, particularly if the patient were delirious. For his own soul's sake, the exorcising of an evil spirit might need far greater protection than Yang knew how to call down round himself.

It was not to be supposed that, if Hung was indeed the Elect of the Heavenly Father, Satan would not also choose him as a special target for attack. Those missionaries who later doubted the validity of Hung's visions, because of the personal failings of both him and his followers, perhaps ignored the obvious truth that God's choice of a messenger must always be followed by the Devil's special interest in the chosen individual, and that the issue always does hang in the balance. This was for all time demonstrated in Palestine on the Mount of Temptation. Things had been going too well for the God-worshippers. Satan had been challenged, and now the counter-attack was about to begin. The first victory of the powers of darkness was, however, so small, and fought over territory of such strategic unimportance to the major campaign, that Yen-lo would need to use considerably more cunning if the spreading of the gospel message was to be finally prevented.

The small victory to which he might lay claim was in leading Hung to enjoy what was the prerogative of every emperor, a harem of women. Unlike Yang and Hsiao, Hung never experienced any of the psychic phenomena of ecstasies or prophesyings in public. Any revelation he received was by means of dreams and visions, when he was quiet and alone, or even asleep, except for that first occasion in 1837, when he was reputed to have leapt from his sick bed to fight invisible demons. Now and for the future his behaviour was remarkably quiet and essentially sane, and he left to Yang and Hsiao the exercise of their curious gifts, while he busied himself with the organisation of more mundane matters. Perhaps in his heart he felt it was indecorous for the future Emperor to perspire, cry out or be shaken with emotion like some gyrating Taoist soothsayer; and on every lip now, albeit in secret, was the word that Hung Hsiu-ch'uan was chosen for the Dragon Throne.

It soon became plain, therefore, to those men clever enough to think of the future, and of how to advance their status under the new rule, that, if they could forge a link between their own families and the future Emperor by contracting marriages for their daughters, the rosier would their chances of promotion be. The quicker the better, for Hung had as yet no male heir, and the first woman to give him one would be able to establish herself over her rivals. Thus the competition to supply him with concubines, that is to say secondary wives held in honourable esteem, grew apace. The leaders of the movement made discreet offers of their sisters through a middleman, and after that many men of consequence bethought themselves to do the same. The necessary silver, and a house of several courts, was easily provided by the several parents anxious to have a foot upon the ladder to advancement. Even the chiefs of the Miau had daughters to offer, and Hung could not afford to wound their parental pride. Besides, it was his duty, following Imperial custom, to beget many sons and thus establish an Imperial clan.

He found the duty most pleasant. He was thirty-five and at the height of his physical powers, and the piquancy of distinguishing the beauties of one woman from those of another was at first intoxicating. This one had hands so small and apparently boneless that he could crumple the two of them like flowers in his one great fist! That one's eyebrows were as delicately drawn as the wings of a moth, and the eyes below were of the shape of almonds! The hips of this one were pear-shaped, and the buttocks of that little creature as round as one apple!

Hung would have been intensely surprised to know how deeply the missionaries would be shocked by the number of his women. Had not that paragon of virtue, Solomon, had seven hundred wives and three hundred concubines? He would have argued that his own harem of scarcely two dozen was modest in comparison. Nor would he ever be guilty of David's sin in stealing another man's wife. Hung's own women would always be virgins, for whom he paid the parents a fair price, and whom he would feed and clothe and cherish as the daughters of God should be cherished; and if he enjoyed their beauty and freshness, that was only a proper appreciation of God's bounty to him.

Nevertheless, when word reached him that on the 9th of November Lai-shi had borne him his first son, he was heartily glad that she would be his Empress, the mother of his heir. Jen-kan had sent word of a phenomenal manifestation of Heaven's goodwill at the time of the birth. Crow cries were considered unlucky, but the sight of several magpies near a house was said to indicate that a son would presently be born. The old house at Hua had been visited for days before the birth of Hung's son not only by magpies but by hordes of starlings and blackbirds perched in the surrounding trees. Never had the village seen such a sight.

So full was Hung of joyful thoughts of Lai-shi and his child that for several days he withheld himself from his women. Then he remembered the new concubine recently pressed upon him by an ambitious family, and he visited her court. Once again his fires were kindled when he held a new little virgin upon his knees, while his hand sought within the robe of embroidered silk which the wealth of a flattered parent had provided, to find breasts that were of finer satin still.

He was inflamed and infuriated when he remembered how the Tartars, by their law forbidding honourable intermarriage, pretended to despise these beautiful Chinese females, while secretly debauching them. "Alas!" he was writing in his composition book, from which he was later to draw copy for Imperial edicts calculated to enrage the populace against the Tartars. "Alas! If all the bamboos of the southern hills were to be used for writing, they would not be enough to detail the obscenities of these Tartars. The Manchu fiends have taken to themselves the beautiful women of China to be their slaves and concubines. Thousands of our young women have been defiled by these rammish dogs, and myriads of our ruddy daughters have been ravished by these lustful foxes."

The insult to Chinese women no doubt rankled the worse, because subconsciously Hung, in the first fervour of finding himself possessed of a harem, felt capable of enlarging it to include every one of his future female subjects with any pretensions to beauty, and their ravishment by the Tartars was a direct personal loss to himself. His initial ardour was, however, only a phase, and it soon cooled. The dark Yen-lo's victory was short-lived, for he was outwitted by the fact that nature has set a limit to the number of women with whom a man, busy with world affairs, can live and be at peace. The harem, it is true, continued to exist, and would be considerably enlarged to conform with the need for Imperial grandeur, but sooner or later, in one generation or the next, monogamy would probably have followed in the wake of Christianity. Yen-lo's weapon against Shang-ti had proved a poor one. His attempt to debauch Hung with wine was even less successful. Hung drank more than his fill for a week or two, and then declared that "it is better to take rice as rice, and not as rice-wine", and straightway foreswore it for the future. As for opium, not only would he never try it, but he forbade it to his followers. "The opium pipe is like a gun," he said, "wherewith you wound yourself. How many heroes are stretched dying upon their pillows!"

In February of the year 1850 the old Manchu Emperor died. The news was kept secret for more than a month, in order that his weak and degenerate son, Hsien Feng, a young man of only nineteen, might have time to establish himself against any danger of revolt or a coup d'état. In far away Peking the Vice-President of the Board of Rites began to prepare proclamations in which the sovereign's usual titles would be listed: Celestial Ruler, Monarch of the Universe, Brother of the Sun, and of course Son of Heaven. If ever a Christian sovereign ascended the Dragon Throne, he would need to modify some of these pretensions to semi-divinity.

When the news of the old Emperor's death percolated to Kwang-si, it set the God-worshippers astir. Preparations for revolt were already going on in secret. Now in June Hung dreamed one of his significant dreams. In it he heard the voice of Shang-ti, and when he woke he straightway recorded the words, for the divine message was to the effect that the hour had struck. "I will send down calamities," Hung had heard the Heavenly Father proclaim. "Therefore call thou thine own family and relations hither." Hung at once sent for Kiang, the schoolmaster who had rescued him when he had been first lost among the mountains of Kwang-si, and who was now working for the God-worshippers as a spy, and despatched him with orders to proceed to Hua and fetch Hung's whole family to Thistle Mount.

From all over Kwang-si the families of the God-worshippers began to set out for the same rendezvous, their belongings packed in cockle-boats upon the river or swinging from their shoulders. Despite Hung's nights of love, his days had been spent working hard to prepare for this hour. Those who arrived now at Chin-t'ien had already sold and converted their land into silver, and came prepared to march. Between ten and fifteen thousand men had been sworn and now assembled.

For the most part they were Hak-ka farmers, charcoal workers, porters thrown out of employment by the late Opium War, and peasants, but amongst them were a thousand miners, who would be useful in obtaining the minerals necessary for arms. The forging of these had been going on for some time. Wei, the rich, saturnine young convert, had put his wealth and the labour of his clan of a thousand men towards their manufacture. Plough-shares had been beaten into swords, and to cover up the noise of the ringing forges, herds of cackling geese were pastured round about them. Then the arms had been submerged in the village ponds for better hiding, so that, when now they were hauled up, some of the simpler people acclaimed it as a miracle. Spears and halberds were the favourite weapons. Fixed on bamboos they were very heavy to wield, but deadly. Saltpetre was extracted from old bricks, an art with which the insurgents were familiar, and the Miau knew how to extract iron from nuggets. The charcoal from Thistle Mount was used for the smelting, and the gunpowder was made at the charcoal ovens. It seemed yet another miracle when the God-worshippers, preparing to dig the foundations of a commemorative monument in honour of Shang-ti, came upon a load of argentiferous lead. Bullets were made by hollowing a half-mould in each of two bricks, and then holding them together and pouring the molten metal down the channel, but the God-worshippers had practically no muskets from which to fire them. Cannon they would presently seize. Meanwhile they made ready shells of brass. But their most efficacious missile was the stink-pot: an earthen jar filled with a suffocating combustible. Nevertheless, it was by the sword and the spear that they were to win their victories.

The match was first put to the political gunpowder by the rising of the Triads round Canton in the first week of July. Meanwhile the God-worshippers in Kwang-si lay low. No doubt Hung had contrived that the secret societies should test the ground, before he came out into the open. On July 13th the Viceroy, Siu, issued out of the northern gate of Canton, with such troops as he could muster, to crush the rebellion. As his sedan approached the gate, there posted upon it, a flagrant insult to the viceregal eye, was a rebel proclamation.

"His Sovereign Majesty, Celestial Virtue, Chu, hereditary prince of the dynasty of Ming, having received orders from Heaven to take pity on the people and punish the crimes of its present rulers, has published this for the information of all . . ."

The placard went on to offer a reward for the capture of the Viceroy himself. Siu, infuriated, sent his lictors to tear it down. Where was this rogue Chu? Only let him lay his hands upon the rascal!

The Triad rebels would also have dearly liked to know where was their Ming pretender, in whose name they were rising, and whose proclamation they had so adroitly posted. Too late did they learn that he was even now on his way to Kwang-si to join Hung Hsiu-ch'uan. Hung's brothers had carried out their instructions perfectly. Ostensibly they were escorting Chu to honourable safe-keeping in the mountains, the better to preserve his precious Ming blood. The Triads must therefore continue to fight for him, and for his benevolent protector, Hung.

Things were going very well, far too well for the satisfaction of Hell's dark lord. So far his attacks against Hung's personal character had brought him only minor victories. Yen-lo needed to devise a more cunning scheme, aimed not at Hung's soul only, but at the whole movement. If initial success brought such a tremendous influx of recruits as would swamp the God-worshippers, then Hung would be unable to teach the gospel to so many new followers, and the rebellion would become merely another rebellion against temporal authority. To this end the Powers of Darkness had been working for some time past, and now a series of apparently disconnected events began to have all the one result, a huge increase in the number of Hung's adherents.

On the twenty-third of the previous October, a British naval force, at the express request of the Viceroy Siu, had sailed from Hong Kong to break up and destroy the pirate fleets, which were becoming a menace to peaceful coastal trade. The fleet, with two thousand pirates and fifty-eight vessels, had been duly wrecked in a particular bay on the southern border where Kwang-tung joined Cochin China. The pirates struggled ashore, and promptly formed themselves into a robber band under the leadership of their captain, Lo Ta-kang. From the bay, it was only a few days' march north through the passes to Kwei district, and since they were all members of the Triad society, as soon as it was known that the Canton Triads had risen, and that the Ming pretender was believed to be with Hung, they made straight to join him.

Meanwhile, in the province north of Kwang-si, Hu-nan, there was famine and a consequent lawless banding together of the hungry. Word came that Imperial troops were being sent north to disband them, so they promptly crossed the border and came south into Kwang-si to find that province already in rebellion.

To crown all, a blood feud broke out in Kwang-si itself between the ancient folk, the Hak-kas, and their supplanters. A very rich Hak-ka had taken as a concubine a girl already promised in marriage to a man of the incoming race. Challenged by her betrothed, he refused to give her up, for she was his by right of the bridal price he had paid to her parents. The poorer man salved the wounded pride of his clan by organising a huge cattle reiving expedition. The Hak-kas replied in kind. At the district magis-

trate's office their rivals then lodged daily accusations against the
Hak-kas. The indolent magistrate washed his hands, and advised
them to enforce their own rights. A local clan warfare broke out,
and the less numerous and on the whole less wealthy Hak-kas got
the worst of it. Their cattle were driven off and their houses
burnt, and being now homeless they sought refuge with the God-
worshippers at Thistle Mount.

The district magistrate of a certain market town then woke
sufficiently to life to remember that one of these same troublesome
Hak-kas had lately been guilty of this lamentable craze for image-
breaking. He had a note of the name, and it might now be
opportune to make an example. So he sent and cast cousin Wang's
son into prison.

So far Hung had restrained his own adherents, the God-
worshippers, from open warfare, probably because he wanted the
Imperial troops to waste themselves upon the Triad rebellion,
which was raging in Kwang-tung, while he had opportunity to
perfect his organisation and increase his arms, if not in complete
secrecy, at least not so blatantly as would force the exhausted
authorities to take note of what was going on. When therefore,
towards the end of September, he heard that cousin Wang's son
had been seized, and that action might be expected against the
God-worshippers at any moment, he himself withdrew for greater
concealment to a mountain recess in the P'ing-nan district—for
it was vital that his own person should not be seized—taking Feng
with him. The move was one of his few tactical errors, because he
was unaware that the local commander of the Imperial troops
already had orders to secure Hung's person at all costs, and the
steep walls of the mountains formed a trap from which he could
not escape unaided, when the Imperial troops suddenly took up
their position at the valley's only exit.

Then at the moment of his greatest need, when he looked from
the house where he was sheltering and saw that he was surrounded
by his enemies, though they were still at a distance, the incredible
came to pass yet once again. Truly Shang-ti fought for him!

Truly Shang-ti spoke for him! He spoke from the mouth of
Yang in trance, where he was camped in Thistle Mount with the
nucleus of the first army. Clear and distinct and not to be disobeyed came the command of Shang-ti to lead the God-
worshippers to the rescue of their leader, and Yang set out at once.

He took a thousand men, and marching with all speed he was just in time. The date was somewhere between September 28th and October 3rd when the God-worshippers first joined battle with the Imperial troops. They fell upon them in all the wrath of men launched upon the holy war for which they had so long prepared, and foremost and most furious in wielding his sword was that mouthpiece of Shang-ti, Yang Hsiu-ch'ing. Hung, entrapped and waiting for rescue, watched the sword of Yang as it whirled about his head, and from the tracts of Liang the words of Jeremiah came into his mind. "Behold a whirlwind of the Lord is gone forth in fury, even a grievous whirlwind. It shall fall heavily upon the head of the wicked."

No sooner was the battle won and the Elect of Heaven rescued, than the God-worshippers retaliated. With Hung and Yang and Feng to lead them, they turned straight upon the local head-quarters of the Imperial troops at Wu-hsuan and sacked the place. It was here that they were joined by Lo Ta-kang and his piratical Triads.

Bringing all the Imperial army stores, Hung returned in triumph to Thistle Mount, and there he found that most of his family were safely arrived: his mother, and Lai-shi, and his baby son; the Lai family; his own two brothers, bringing Celestial Virtue; and a whole host of lesser cousins. But several of both his and Feng's relatives were still detained in Hua, unable to get through the lines of the Imperial troops, who were trying to contain the advance of the Triads. Amongst those thus detained was Jen-kan. Hung was disappointed, for he could well have done with Jen-kan's support, and would as gladly have dispensed with the company of the Ming pretender, if he could have done so with safety. Nevertheless, to please the Triads and particularly Lo Ta-kang, whose qualities as a leader he had instantly recognised, he gave Chu his title of Celestial Virtue and called him "worthy brother". The man was an incumbrance, but, after all, there was that in Hung's veins which bound him to receive a Chu in amity and deal softly with him. If the God-worshippers wondered why the Elect of Heaven should bother to cushion the place of Celestial Virtue's confinement and bedizen his person with silk and satin, they would know soon enough!

Meanwhile Hung could gather from Lo Ta-kang all the gossip of the Triad lodges as to how matters were progressing in Kwang-tung, and thus assess how and when to make his own next move. Everywhere they had risen the Triads had been successful. The whole coastal plain of Kwang-tung was in arms. The difficulty which dogged the Imperial forces was this: not only had the profession of soldier become despised, so that the militia was recruited from vagabonds, but—and here lay the real danger to the Manchu dynasty—the officials dared not report the seriousness of the situation until too late. A magistrate who had bought office had probably laid out his whole capital to purchase it. He could not recoup himself from his salary, which was negligible, but only from receiving bribes: dismissal from his post, therefore, meant financial ruin. To ensure loyalty to the existing dynasty, the higher officials had to bear responsibility for the misdemeanours or inefficiency of their underlings, and could be degraded—and so lose their capital outlay—through the faults of their inferiors. Where responsibility was mutual, a mutual shielding was the only answer. Therefore day after day a magistrate would report to the prefect above him that the situation was in hand, when in fact his militia had been routed. By the time the prefect realised that his whole prefecture was in the hands of the rebels, in his turn he dared not tell the Tao-t'ai that the circuit was threatened.

So it went on until, at the highest level, the Viceroy memorialised the Throne to the effect that the Imperial troops were everywhere winning victories, when in fact he knew that town after town and city after city was falling to the Triad rebels. Since the Viceroy could only command the Green Battalions of the Chinese and not the Banner regiments of the Tartars, there was no united policy and strategy. Between the Viceroy's two provinces of Kwang-tung and Kwang-si, there was at this time a total military strength of 89,000 soldiers, of whom 55,000 were garrisoned to protect cities. The city officials, rather than let their only protection go, kept the garrisons idle where they were, and bribed the rebels to betake themselves to the next town. The Viceroy, Siu, sentenced to death by decapitation when the real state of affairs became known in Peking, had recently been pardoned and given another chance. He had his hands full coping with the situation in the coastal plains. Now was the moment for Hung to strike in mountainous Kwang-si.

Against the exhausted authorities and the undisciplined Imperial troops, Hung was about to launch the strength of the Lord's host.

"God is the father of the generals of this army," he told his men. Every man was revivified because the cause was God's and it was a holy war, a crusade of Jehad. Nor need they fear death in battle. "Believers will be saved and ascend to heaven," Hung promised them. "Seize or dissipate the demon Tartars," he exhorted the populace, "and come over to submit yourselves to our heavenly dynasty. In the present world you shall have glory and honour without compare, and in heaven enjoy happiness without end." But the army of the Lord was to be no undisciplined horde of raggle-taggle vagabonds. Hung's first edict, issued at Thistle Mount in January of 1851, made that clear. "The first requisite is to obey the commandments." Not only the commands of officers, but the Ten Commandments of Shang-ti.

In that same month of January he fell upon the market town where cousin Wang's son was imprisoned. The God-worshippers needed more stores and money and the booty of war, with which to equip the ever-growing influx of recruits. The prosperous unwalled market town could provide all these, and the suddenness of the attack made the taking of it easy. While officers were deputed to requisition all stores, Hung visited the gaol. In the dark cells many of the prisoners were strung up by their thumbs, to kneel on chains until they died of agony. Disease was rife, and the sores of castigated flesh putrid. Cousin Wang's son was dead.

Within a day the Imperial troops moved up to besiege the town. They made a sufficient show of firing off their guns, so that they might not lose face, but they kept to such a respectable distance that their fire was wasted. A small squadron of Imperial cavalry galloped about, and their officers cut a very dashing appearance in their blue uniforms with red cassocks, but they showed no desire to give battle.

The town was not fortified, and was strategically unimportant. Hung had no intention of staying there. He had merely wanted the stores. The problem was how to withdraw from it. Before doing so, he once again sent for Kiang the spy, and told him to get through the lines, dressed as a physician, proceed to Kwang-tung, and at all costs bring back Jen-kan and Feng's relatives. Now that he, Hung, was in open rebellion, his cousins would meet a sorry fate if they fell into Imperial hands.

Quietly at night Hung marched his army out of the market town. Throughout the following day women and boys beat drums in the houses close to the river opposite the besieging force, so that the Imperial commander believed the town still occupied. When he discovered his mistake, he allowed his troops to wreak a terrible vengeance upon the citizens. But this was the invariable practice of the Imperial soldiery. Murder, rape and pillage were regarded as the just rewards of their labours. Two thousand shops were burned, and most of the women assaulted. What had astonished the townsfolk was that the occupying army of the God-worshippers had not acted in the same way. Next time a town was taken by these God-worshippers, it might be better, they thought, to flee with them, even to join them, rather than fall into the hands of the Green Battalions or the Bannermen.

12

To Hung's encampment Lo Ta-kang now brought seven fellow Triad chiefs, each with a small army. Was it true that he, Hung, was himself the Ming heir, they wanted to know? In a vast pavilion gay with banners they met in conference, round a banqueting table at which Hung's chair was raised upon a dais higher than those of his guests. Hung's reply to their overtures was polite but uncompromising.

"Though I never entered the Triad Society, I have often heard it said that their object is to subvert the Ch'ing and restore the Ming dynasty."

His remark was met by guttural noises of approval.

"Such an expression," he went on, "was very proper in the time of K'ang-hsi, but now, after the lapse of two hundred years, we may still speak of subverting the Ch'ing, but we cannot properly speak of restoring the Ming."

Then he sent for Celestial Virtue, and Chu came mincing from his luxurious confinement and deferred to Hung, calling himself his humble younger brother. Hung put a necklace of gold and pearls about the neck of the fragile creature, who was ten years his junior, and then bade him withdraw, and Chu, smiling and grateful, made no demur, but bowed to the assembled chieftains and went.

Hung waited for a moment, allowing silence to reign, while the sturdy Triad chieftains had time to recover from the effect of his parading of this weakling. One or two of them appeared crestfallen, for it was plain the Celestial Virtue was not the man, even though all the powers of Heaven and Earth should unite in his favour, who could found a dynasty or fight for a throne. One or two of the rebel chiefs wore puzzled frowns, for the expression on Hung's face had shown neither love nor scorn, merely a benevolence that was enigmatic, and difficult to explain between rival claimants for supreme power. Or did he regard the claims of the Ming pretender as beneath contempt, because he was aware that there existed a scion of the old dynasty with a yet nearer claim to the succession? It was true that Hung's own mother had borne the same family name, Chu, but it would be too far-fetched to think that he was now laying claim to Imperial blood through a woman, for did not a woman always become a member of her husband's family? Nor was there anything to show that his mother had been of the Imperial stock. There were hundred and thousands of Chus. It was probable that many scions of the Ming dynasty did in fact exist, if one could trace them.

The Triad chieftains began to see how, if they insisted on putting the clock back, they would need to resort to ridiculous and impractical measures. Besides, as they knew, possession of the Dragon Throne was not the prerogative of the dynasty, for the mandate lay in the power of Heaven to bestow. Yet they were sworn by their vows of initiation to restore the Ming blood: vows which they were now beginning to regret.

They listened with increased attention as Hung began to address them again. "When our native mountains and rivers are recovered, a new dynasty must be established. How could we at present arouse the energies of men by speaking of restoring the Ming dynasty?"

Even now his smile held no slightest suspicion of scorn for the weakling he had just banished; least of all did it suggest besotted love. He sat there, magnificent, regal, healthily virile, and already well-known to enjoy his many women. They were at a loss. Hung waited just sufficiently long for their puzzled expressions to become a question that demanded answer. Then he gave it them. He simply told them that Chu was his sworn brother, and listened to their sighs of relief at this news, which absolved them from breaking their final vow of initiation, while allowing them to pledge fealty to the Elect of Heaven, Hung Hsiu-ch'uan himself, in whose veins now flowed the old Imperial ichor. The matter concerned not only the final sealing of the covenant in the lodges, and the Ming blood, but curiously enough Hung's own attitude to the Christian sacrament, for both rites were the consummation of the Covenant of Blood.

Why did the God-worshippers attempt to administer the sacrament of baptism, while apparently making no effort to institute the Lord's Supper? What had been Hung's thoughts when first he saw the chalice given from the hands of Issachar Roberts for distribution by the deacons? What had he understood from the gospel account, and from Christ's words, "This is my blood"?

Perhaps a great truth, like a rich jewel, has many facets, so that the light may be seen from many directions by many different men, and each in his pride may swear that he alone has seen the flash of the cut brilliant. In the Near East and in Europe the rites of sacrifice tended from ancient times to manifest one aspect only of the truth. The man or animal sacrificed was identified with the god, and consumed by the worshippers. This effected a communion between the deity and the recipients, whereby men became excited and exalted in spirit, knowing themselves to have partaken of the nature of the god. No such rites had ever existed in China. No attempt had ever been made to identify the sacrifice with the deity. On the contrary, the slain animals, the fruits, the rice and the wine were merely placed as a thank-offering beside the Altar of Heaven, in much the same way as the fruits of harvest thanksgiving are placed round a pulpit.

What the Chinese had preserved, and the Europeans had not, was an understanding of the rites of blood-brotherhood, and it seems that the sacrifice of a god or animal-substitute may be only a development of this far more archaic rite. Blood-brotherhood was concerned not with the dead flesh, and slain sacrifice, but with the living essence coursing in live veins. The rites foreshadowed the dim and distant day in the twentieth century when blood transfusions would save life. To primitive man blood *was* life;

and the greatest expression of faith, and of love between men, was to share life and to share blood. Thus men became brothers, and not merely brothers but two souls in *one* body, closer than twins, because the flesh was knit, making one body only, to which either soul had access. Therefore an oath sworn to a blood-brother was more binding to a man than any obligation to his own parents, wife and children; and his goods could be called upon by his brother, and his life also. Thus "Jonathan and David *made* a covenant" (in the Hebrew "*cut*"), and "the soul of Jonathan was knit with the soul of David".

Dr. Livingstone in far away Africa was beginning to understand the sacredness of the bond, and in the course of his missionary work was himself contracting such relationships with the chiefs. Since no men yet knew just how to perform an actual transfusion, the rites were merely symbolic, and they differed. Sometimes the arms of the two friends were cut, and their arms held together, so that a drop or two of the life fluid flowed from one wound to another. More often a drop or two from each wound was mixed with wine in a cup, and drunk by both parties. This had been the custom in Syria in early times, whence it is thought to have spread throughout the world, and to China. This was the rite which sealed all members of the Triad Society as brothers. And when at Lo Ta-kang's initiation the covenant was finally sealed between him and his brother Triads, it was sealed in blood by the drinking of a cup, wherein a drop from his veins was mingled with a drop from theirs, and with wine; and it was sealed by the oath of blood-brothers: "To live and die together."

If this were indeed the earliest rite known to man, the development from it becomes easier of understanding. Only five words need to be added to the oath to put the whole of St. Paul's logic into a sentence. "To live and die together, *and therefore to rise together.*" If a man could contract a blood-brotherhood with God, then not only would God protect him in this world, but the immortal ichor in his veins would defy death. Thus man began to look about for a substitute, a symbol, to represent God, from which he could draw blood; not dead blood for his stomach, but a transfusion of the essence of life for his veins. Because of his ignorance, he was forced to swallow it first, rather than have it enter his blood vessels directly; but he had faith that presently it would be coursing in all his limbs, bringing him a share in the

life of the immortal one. But this did not complete the rite. It had
to be a mutual exchange of blood to make the covenant binding.
God must also take into his veins the blood of man. Therefore,
Abraham divided the sacrifice so that the one half should represent
man's blood, and the other God's. Therefore Moses took the blood
and put it in basins; and half of the blood he sprinkled on the altar,
and half on the people. Man's blood was received by God, and
God's blood by the people. Exchange! Reciprocity! Inter-
relationship! A mutual binding to live and die together, and therefore to rise again together! The object of blood-brotherhood and
of the blood covenant is therefore a transference of life. The Chinese, however, had not gone beyond the exchange of blood between men, since, possibly owing to the caution of Confucius,
they did not recognise a supreme personal deity, and therefore
could not aspire to share his life.

Hung Hsiu-ch'uan, knowing all the implications of blood-
brotherhood, knowing that the Triads practised it, witnessing the
reception of the chalice by fully initiated Christians in the mission
chapel, and reading the gospel account of the Last Supper without personal instruction from Mr. Roberts, could only have come
to one conclusion. He would have concluded that Christ had invited the apostles to become his blood-brothers, and to take the
oath to live and die together. His interpretation may not have been
wrong, since eternal truth can mercifully include many interpre-
tations. The jewel has many facets. . . .

The significance of what Hung had just told the Triad chieftains was immediately plain to them. If Hung had sworn blood-
brotherhood with the scion of the Mings, then in Hung's veins
also flowed the blood of the Imperial dynasty. They could place
Hung upon the Dragon Throne without foreswearing their vows
to restore the Ming dynasty. Equally they could be confident that
Hung would never lift a finger against Celestial Virtue and thereby
wound the susceptibilities of the Triads, who were all blood-
brothers of Chu. Furthermore, Hung was now in some sort their
own blood-brother, through his covenant with Celestial Virtue.
Did not the oath of the lodges run, "This night we pledge our-
selves that the brethren in the whole universe shall be as from one
womb, begotten as from one father and nourished by one
mother?" No wonder the Triad chiefs sighed with relief, knowing
that they could rightfully acclaim the obviously preferable candi-

date for Imperial honours. And there would be nothing to prevent Hung from sharing these same honours with Celestial Virtue, who could remain forever in the background, a humble younger brother enjoying cushioned ease.

From Hung's point of view he could henceforth with perfect truth declare, as he was often to do, that he was not a Ming, while at the same time he could give orders to repair the Ming tombs of his ancestors. It would depend on what audience he was addressing.

By a master stroke he had penetrated the Triad lodges, becoming not only one of the Triad "brethren" but eligible as their candidate for the throne, while remaining entirely free from any obligations or oaths to the society. He had only to preserve an attitude of personal benevolence to Celestial Virtue. Apart from this tedious duty, he was therefore free to dictate his own terms to the Triads, which he proceeded to do on the next day. He would take command of only such Triads as would accept Christianity and would observe his regulations regarding discipline. He wanted no raggle-taggle horde of bandits to corrupt his army of single-minded God-worshippers.

"There are several evil practices connected with the Triad society which I detest," he told his own generals privately. "If any new member enter the society he must worship the devil, and utter thirty-six oaths. A sword is placed upon his neck, and he is forced to contribute money for the use of the society. Their real object has now turned very mean and unworthy. If we preach the true doctrine and rely upon the powerful help of God, a few of us will equal a multitude of others."

The seven Triad chiefs had decided that Hung's was a good banner under which to fight, and they therefore agreed to join him and undergo religious instruction. But presently they foreswore their allegiance, for the discipline Hung demanded, the observance of the Ten Commandments, his laws against bribery and corruption, and the penalties for breaking these were not acceptable to such robber bandits. Their defection and the subsequent news that they had joined the Imperial troops did not worry Hung, though he was pleased that Lo Ta-kang and his band had remained faithful, and were now baptised and incorporated in the army of the God-worshippers.

Henceforth the position of the Triads throughout China was to be one of doubt, not as to whether they could accept Hung as representative of the Ming dynasty, but whether they could stomach the Christianity and the discipline which he demanded as a condition of their allegiance. Time and again he was to lose allies for the sake of this condition, while his critics both amongst the Europeans and Imperialists accused him of having adopted Christianity merely as a political expedient, a disguise wherewith to wheedle guns from the British.

Nevertheless, although he would not accept or take responsibility for the Triads as his allies, they were useful to him, in that their continual rebellion harassed the Imperial administration and exhausted the Imperial troops, and many of the individual Triad brothers did come over to him and accept baptism.

In late January of 1851 the enormous camp at Thistle Mount was in preparation to acclaim Hung Emperor. It was essential that he should not be regarded as merely another bandit chief, and that the proclamation, and his assumption of the Imperial Yellow, should be made as public as possible; and the feast of the New Year would be a suitable occasion.

In his pavilion Hung sat at his writing-table, preparing the orders which would govern protocol. He was acting for the moment as his own President of the Board of Rites. There was dispute as to who should be the leader of all the armies. He could have trusted Feng, but Feng was more of a scholar than a soldier. It was obvious that his choice must fall upon Yang, who was after all his brother-in-law. Yang was a plain man and a doughty warrior. He was popular with the troops, for he was impartial and just. Furthermore, Shang-ti had spoken through him, promising to direct affairs from heaven. And finally, a Kwang-si man would know the mountains.

Feng, however, should rank next as deputy commander. Hung paused over the characters he was inscribing. Later, he decided, he would give his generals each the title of prince. Yang should be the Eastern Prince, and Hsiao the Western Prince. But for Feng he would keep the warm kindly South, to which the Emperor's throne must always face. And for the fierce Wei, the North.

As for himself, had he not dreamed that he held in his hand the red sun? The Emperor's titles would have to be revised in the light of Christian doctrine. "Son of Heaven" would perhaps encroach on the privilege of his Heavenly Elder Brother, but his own identification with the solar orb might be preserved. Under his breath he repeated to himself part of an ode which he had lately composed.

"China was once subdued, but it shall no more fall.
God ought to be adored, and ultimately shall.
The founder of the Ming in song disclosed his mind.
The Emperor of Han drank to the furious wind.
From olden times all deeds by energy were done,
Dark vapours disappear on rising of the sun."

He felt today in a mood for directing his energy, not only towards preparing the rites for his ascension of a throne, but also towards a better understanding of the philosophy on which those rites were based. He reached for his Bible, turned to the 19th psalm, and read, "In them hath he set a tabernacle for the sun, which is as a bridegroom coming out of his chamber". Then he turned to that verse in the New Testament, "Let your light so shine before men. . . ." It was becoming his custom to write marginal comments in his Bible, and against this last verse he now wrote: "God is flame, the sun is also flame, therefore God came with the sun. God is the holy spirit, and came with the Holy Ghost. After fifty days the Holy Ghost descended, and there was flame and wind. The flame and wind both proceeded from God and accorded with one another. God is flame, therefore a flaming spirit. My Brother is flame, therefore a great splendour. I am the sun."

His thoughts presently passed to Christ's promise that the Celestial Kingdom should be set up, that Kingdom of Heaven which was a direct pledge of China's renaissance. There was to be great tribulation immediately before the promise was fulfilled. He turned now to the twenty-fourth chapter of Matthew, and read Christ's prophecy that "immediately after the tribulation of those days shall the sun be darkened, and the moon shall not give her light, and the stars will fall from heaven".

Hung's interest quickened. Far from fearing his own eclipse as the symbolic sun of China, he immediately recognised the secret language of alchemy. But of course! Why had it never struck him before?

Believing, as he did, in the pre-existence of souls, to leave paradise and be born into the world could be considered a kind of death. He referred to the sixth chapter of St. John's Revelation, where it was prophesied that the sun would become black and the moon become as blood. They would therefore cease to shine in paradise in order to be born into the great alchemical crucible of the material universe, from which they could only escape in transmuted form, the true gold.

He began to write the comments on these verses of the scriptures which would lead European missionaries to suppose him mad, because these Victorian gentlemen had completely forgotten the alchemical language of their own medieval ancestors. "To turn black like blood," he wrote, "covertly signifies descent and incarnation. The stars of heaven are the celestial troops. By falling to the earth is covertly meant a descent into the world to exterminate the demons." He paused to choose a finer brush, for his marginal comments in the Bible needed to be very small. "My Elder Brother," he presently continued, "when he was in the world went about secretly because he feared the people. I am the sun. I descended into the world and became a man. When I changed I became non-luminous. My wife is the moon. She descended and was incarnate, and no longer sheds light. The heavenly captains and hosts, even the stars, became incarnate, and fell from heaven upon earth. My Elder Brother ascended into heaven on the clouds, and shall gather his people together from the four quarters."

He proceeded next to draw up a list of titles for himself and his captains, based on these alchemical symbols. He himself could follow Imperial custom, and be addressed as the Sun. Lai-shi was to be the Moon. Hsiao, the Western Prince, was to be the Master of the Rain, the gentle, beneficent, and life-giving moisture, because by Hsiao's mouth the Redeemer chose to speak. The fierce Wei was to be Master of the Thunder, and Prince of the cold dark north. Shih Ta-kai should be the Master of the Lightning, for he was quick of wit.

But what of Yang, the Eastern Prince? Without vapour the Elixir of Life could not be produced. Hung called to mind how Yang had rescued him from the trap in the mountains, and of the words that had risen then spontaneously to his mind, "Behold a whirlwind of the Lord is gone forth in fury". Of course, then, it was obvious that Yang must be given the title of the Wind.

Flame and wind must act together, for thus God's spirit would come to all men.

His ideas on the pre-existence of souls and their identification with the elements were carrying Hung away, for he had a deep love of the poetic and symbolic. Now, beside the account of Christ rebuking the wind and the sea, he wrote, "The wind employed by Heaven was the Eastern Prince, Yang, so of course he was obedient".

The confusion caused by the different words pneuma, breath, wind and spirit had always, even in Europe, been a stumbling block to those seeking the truth about man's soul. Hung had no conception of the idea of the Trinity. He would to the last swear that God was One, an indivisible person, a father. Jesus was the first of his creatures. The Holy Spirit was but another name for God the Father. The blasphemy of which he was later to be accused was unfair, and based on a misunderstanding by the missionaries, for in fact he never, as his detractors claimed, presumed to say that Yang, the Master of the Wind was identical with the third person of the Trinity, the Holy Spirit.

Hung, the poet and alchemist, sat back and surveyed his accomplished calligraphy. He probably did not believe that he was an actual incarnation of the sun, nor that Yang was an incarnation of the wind; but his own title was in tune with previous Imperial custom, and it was, moreover, the Emperor's duty to "harmonise" the universe, and bring order and rhythm out of chaos: to depict a pattern in which every man should feel himself related to the pattern in the spheres, and know his place in it.

Yen-lo, that old serpent, had cause for satisfaction, for now Hung's pride in his poetry and alchemical knowledge could be used to keep him separated from the Victorian missionaries for just so long as that pride would refuse to admit of any alterations to his flowery literary compositions. The Powers of Darkness were encroaching. Until now Hell's campaign to swamp the God-worshippers with recruits, and corrupt their faith, had met with only a modicum of success. Soldiers of the rank and file in camp or on the march have never been the best exponents of the finer points of theology, but on the whole the new recruits had come to believe in Shang-ti and the Heavenly Elder Brother, and to obey the Ten Commandments. And they were all praying, which was truly a menace to Hell's dark Lord. What Yen-lo really needed was an ally, a willing instrument. He had for some years past been working upon the soul of young Wei, and now the Master of Thunder and Prince of the North was fast becoming his servant.

All was ready before dawn on the first day of February in 1851. In order that the troops might bear witness to the elevation of their leader to the throne, a huge platform had been built in the open air. Round it ornamental arches were hung with lanterns, poles were gay with banners, and the floor was carpeted. To represent the actual Dragon Throne in faraway Peking, a dais had been richly draped in yellow satin. The platform, brilliant with its lanterns, shone out of the darkness and mountain mist like some Chinese artist's representation of a spirit world suspended in the clouds. The troops were drawn up in ranks, and on those nearest to the platform the light of the lanterns was shining. They had all, according to orders, grown their hair long, thus defying Tartar regulations and giving open proof of their intention to rebel and restore the ancient Chinese customs. Already in the last weeks the Imperialists, probing the periphery of the encampment area, and coming up against the pickets and sentries, had dubbed them "the long-haired rebels", and as such they were to be known by their enemies for always. The hair was neatly twisted into a knot at the nape of the neck and caught in a red bag over which they wore red turbans. Their tunics were yellow, and buttoned down the front rather than at the side, as was the Tartar custom, and across their chests were sewn calico plaques on which huge black characters depicted the names of their units. The officers had cassocks, bordered with yellow, and their standard bearers carried triangular pennants. Square flags indicated where the generals were waiting, those who were shortly to receive the title of prince. They were dressed entirely in yellow, not only their helmet-shaped hoods, but their padded jackets and long gowns.

They were all waiting in the semi-dark because the Emperor must always hold his levée at sunrise, but presently torches were extinguished, for the sky was paling. Only the lanterns continued to glimmer. From every direction gongs and drums and weird instruments began to be beaten and plucked. Then, as the sun topped the hill, the Imperial sedan came into sight, a huge affair borne on the shoulders of sixty-four porters, and it was brought to a halt below the platform. The generals received the new Emperor on their knees, and then, rising, led him beneath a scarlet umbrella to sit on the Throne, which faced south. To his left, in the Chinese place of honour, stood Yang, Prince of the East, who had that in him of which Shang-ti might yet make a St. Peter. To his right stood Hsiao, Prince of the West, as straight and gallant as a St. Michael. In front of him Feng, Prince of the South, was making the first ritual kow-tow—kneeling and bowing his head to the floor three times—and his heart was so full of faithful love for his Emperor and cousin that in him were some of the qualities of St. John, though he was older than his master. And in the dark north behind the throne stood Wei, so placed that he could stab the Emperor in the back when Yen-lo gave the word for him to play Judas, but sufficiently pleased with his promised title of Northern Prince to bide his time.

Hung's fifth general was Shih Ta-kai, Master of the Lightning, shortly to be entitled the Assistant Prince, and he was even now unfurling the new Imperial standard while the five armies cheered themselves hoarse. The kingdom of heaven was come, and its name on earth, which Hung himself had chosen, was T'ai-p'ing T'ien-Kuo, which meant the Heavenly Kingdom of Great Peace. From henceforth Hung's people were to be known as the Taipings, the most ironical name ever chosen, since they were to bring not peace but a sword to China.

The Emperor was even now handing the sword for slaying demons, the sword which he had long ago himself forged, to Yang, as a symbol that henceforth the Eastern Prince, mouthpiece of Shang-ti, was to command the army for the Lord of Hosts.

Hung himself had taken the title of The Heavenly King, the T'ien Wang, for he would not as a Christian presume to call himself the Son of Heaven. He sat now upon his throne in all the glory of Imperial trappings. His long hair was wound up beneath a high yellow mitre of Ming design. He wore the Dragon Robe of Imperial Yellow satin encrusted with golden dragon embroidery. His boots were of satin similarly embroidered. From his waist hung an apron heavily stitched with gold, and his yellow satin girdle was decorated with the lapis lazuli which an emperor wears

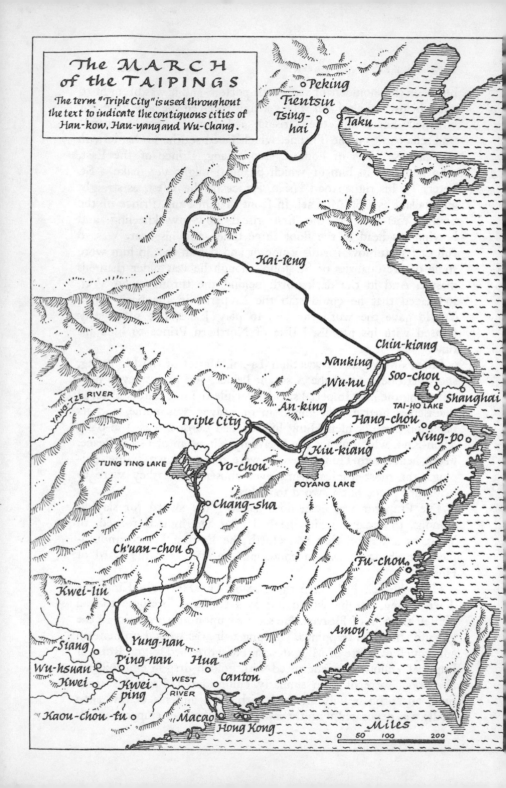

The MARCH
of the TAIPINGS

The term "Triple City" is used throughout
the text to indicate the contiguous cities of
Han-kow, Han-yang and Wu-Chang.

Peking

Tientsin
Tsing-
hai   Taku

Kai-feng

Chin-kiang

Nanking

Wu-hu   Soo-chou

YANG-TZE RIVER   An-king   Shanghai

TAI-HO LAKE

Triple City   Hang-chou

Kiu-kiang   Ning-po

TUNG TING LAKE   Yo-chou

POYANG LAKE

Chang-sha

Ch'uan-chou

Fu-chou

Kwei-lin

Amoy

Siang   Yung-nan

Wu-hsuan   Ping-nan   Hua

Kwei   Kwei-   WEST   Canton
ping   RIVER

Kaou-chou-fu   Macao

Hong Kong   Miles

0   50   100   200

when serving at the Altar of Heaven. The wealth of the market
town and the industry of thousands of women had done justice
to the occasion. For the next two years of hard fighting such
finery would have to be put away, but at least a brave show had
been made at his first levée.

Now the T'ien Wang was speaking. His words were passed
from rank to rank, from those who could hear him to those who
could not.

"We brave men, courageous as tigers, will straightway proceed
to tread down the enclosed land." There was a murmur of approval as his words were relayed. "The dragon will fly, to the
fifth nine." That meant Peking. Some classical allusion, so the
officers were explaining. "And cause the days of Yao and Chou
to revive." That meant, as every man knew, the Golden Age.

Thus he had told them that they were to march on Peking, a
distance greater than from one end of Europe to another, and
they cheered him to the echo because he was the Elect of Heaven,
and they had perfect faith that somehow he would lead them
there.

Certainly for Hung himself there could be no drawing back
now. Henceforth he was committed, for he was guilty of at least
two of the Ten Crimes for which even the Manchu Emperor in
Peking could not remit the death sentence: treason, and daring to
imitate things of Imperial style.

13

IN ORDER TO MARCH on Peking, the Taipings had first to
get out of the "enclosed land", the regions of Kwang-si, where the
mountain ramparts formed a very efficient enclosure indeed.
There were only two ways from which to choose. One was to fight
their way eastward straight down the main valley of the West
River to the coastal plains of Kwang-tung, and there join with
the Triad rebels and take the city of Canton, three hundred

miles distant from their present headquarters. The other way was to go westward up the river towards its source, take the right-hand branch where it forked at Kwei-p'ing, go north to the Siang district, and there struggle over high ground and through passes to the other side of the watershed. From this point the Taipings could descend into Hu-nan and follow the rivers and lakes. These connected with the middle reach of the Yang-tze in a waterway provided by nature in an almost continuous line from a hundred miles north of Siang, through the heart of China, to Nanking, which commanded the mouth of the Yang-tze.

The easterly route would obviously be the easiest, and this was the choice of the T'ien Wang and his generals, even though the way to the coast was heavily defended by the Imperial troops, who were at all costs anxious to keep the "long-haired rebels" from joining forces with the Triad insurgents.

There was to be no attempt at consolidating conquests. Like the children of Israel, the Taipings were on the march to a promised land—Peking. It was a march that was remarkably comparable with that of the Exodus, for a whole people was moving, between thirty and forty thousand of them; of these not more than between five and ten thousand were fully armed soldiers, and they had to protect their women, their children and such goods as they could carry. Strategy, therefore, demanded the taking of a town, a speedy requisitioning of its stores of rice and silver, and an equally quick abandoning of it. As soon as the Taipings captured a town, the Imperial troops moved up to surround and besiege it. The Taipings then broke out, and the Manchu officials hopefully reported a victory, and moreover plucked up courage enough to pursue their enemies. They were then cut to pieces in the open and routed. This was to be the pattern of warfare for the next two years, while the Taipings journeyed through the wilderness.

To march a whole people through enemy country needed not only organisation, but a strictly enforced discipline, and also at times encouragement from Heaven above. Just as Jehovah had spoken by the mouth of his prophets in Israel, and just as Moses had alternately rebuked or encouraged the Israelites on the march with repetitions of Jehovah's words, so now Yang and Hsiao urged the Taipings forward in the name of Shang-ti and the Redeemer. They appeared to speak in trance, and that the words delivered were truly those of the Heavenly Father and the Heavenly Elder Brother the people never doubted. Such words were faithfully recorded in the T'ien Wang's Imperial decrees, and were termed "descents" of the Heavenly Father or of the Heavenly Elder Brother. When the missionaries later read that God the Father or God the Son had descended upon earth on such a day at such a time at such a place to speak to the people, they were at first horrified at such blasphemous nonsense, until eventually they came to realise that the T'ien Wang was referring in his decrees to this phenomenon of inspired speech.

It began in April, just after the Taipings had lost their flag, which, spattered with blood, had become to them a symbol of victory. They were much downcast, and on the nineteenth of that month, in the village of Tung-heang, Yang, the Commander-in-Chief, gathered the troops round him, and, looking up to heaven, appeared suddenly to be filled with a higher power than his own. He began to speak to them in a voice which they knew now to be that of the Heavenly Father.

"Oh, my children! Do you know your Heavenly Father and your Celestial Elder Brother?"

The murmur of assent was heard from every man within hearing.

"Do you know your Lord, and truly?"

Their Lord was the Heavenly King, the T'ien Wang, and cheers rang out, "We know our Lord right well!"

"I have sent your Lord down," from Yang's mouth issued the words, "into this world to become the Heavenly King. Every word he utters is a celestial command. You must be obedient. Assist your Lord and regard your King." Yang pointed to where the T'ien Wang stood beside him, regal, in his battle dress, a short padded jacket of scarlet over the yellow sash from which hung a great sword.

After that it was comparatively easy for the sovereign to bid the people forget the loss of their flag, their fetish, and to command that once again the Taipings, like the Israelites before them, should "go forward".

Again on April 23rd in the same district Hsiao was inspired to speak in the name of Jesus.

"Oh, my younger brethren! You must keep the celestial commands, and obey the orders that are given you, and be at peace among yourselves".

The soldiers were silent, hanging on the words of this gallant young general who was their idol, and whose vital beauty and strength made a fitting vessel, they thought, for the indwelling of the Heavenly Elder Brother.

"You should not go into the villages to seize people's goods," Hsiao went on. "When you go into battle you must not retreat. When you have money, you must make it public and not consider it as belonging to one or another. If, after being instructed, you should still break Heaven's commands," he paused, "do not be surprised if I, your exalted Elder Brother, issue orders to have you put to death."

It was natural that a close examination by the missionaries of the record of this "descent" of the Saviour should cause them to deplore it. To suppose that here was gentle Jesus issuing orders for the death penalty was offensive and contrary to their conception of the Good Shepherd. It might be credible that the words had been spoken by Jehovah. In fact Jehovah had thundered his wrath to the Israelities in terms very similar. The Taipings had reached a stage of spiritual evolution very like that of the Israelites in the desert. They could understand and accept the commands of Jehovah, of Shang-ti, and recognise the One God, of whom no image must be made. They could comprehend that he was a father both loving and stern. They had not yet grasped the spirit of Christ's new dispensation of love. Yet Jehovah had shown patience with the Jews for more than a thousand years between the giving of the Law and the sending of the Messiah. The missionaries were to show less patience than Jehovah.

The Taipings were spreading out over the main valley—an inadequate term for so vast an area—and were gradually moving eastward.

"The whole country swarms with the rebels," reported the Governor of Kwang-si in April of 1851 in a letter to the Governor of Ho-peh province. "Our funds are nearly at an end, and our troops are few; our officers disagree, and the power is not concentrated. The Commander of the Forces wants to extinguish a burning waggon-load of faggots with a cup full of water. Further, he keeps up an endless moving and despatching of the troops, who are wearied with marching along the roads."

The Governor must have deduced that Hung's new religion was akin to that of the Roman Catholic priest whom he had just had tortured to death, for he jumped to the conclusion that the rebel chief was not a Chinese at all, but some kind of European. "Hung Hsiu-ch'uan," he went on in his letter, "is a barbarian of some sort. He practices the ancient military arts. At first he conceals his strength, then he puts it forth a little, then in a greater degree, and lastly comes on in force. He constantly has two victories for one defeat. The other day I obtained a rebel book, describing the organisation of one army. It is the system of the Chou dynasty. A division has its general of division; a regiment has its colonel; an army consists of 13,125 men, that being the strength of an ancient army. Our troops, the more they fight, the more they fear. The rebels generally are powerful and fierce; and they cannot by any means be likened to a disorderly crowd, their regulations and laws being rigorous and clear. Our troops have not a tincture of discipline; retreating is easy to them, advancing difficult, and though again and again exhorted, they always remain as weak and as timorous as before. . . . All proceeds from the mistakes of the Imperial Commissioner, who employs himself on nothing but talking!"

So might some city governor of ancient Canaan have written when Joshua's forces fell upon the land.

Nevertheless, despite the inefficiency of the Imperial troops, the sheer weight of their numbers prevented the Taipings from moving across the border into the province of Kwang-tung, for the gateway between the mountains and the coastal plain was comparatively narrow at the provincial border, and easily held.

Meanwhile Siu, the Viceroy, offered 90,000 taels of silver to anyone who could bring him the head of Celestial Virtue, since not unnaturally there was still confusion in the minds of the Imperialists as to who exactly was the leader of the rebels. He also offered the Triads 300,000 taels to raise the siege of Kaouchou-fu, in which city he was himself shut up. The Triads pretended that they might be so persuaded if the silver could be shown to exist. Siu levied the sum in taxes from Canton, and had it brought in chests by porters. En route somehow the chests fell into a river which the porters were fording. The heavy coffers were fished out and delivered to the Viceroy, who opened them to find only stones from the river bed, and himself the victim of a skilful act of substitution. He swore by his moustaches to have his revenge.

Some of the silver found its way to the beleaguering force of the Taipings round Yung-nan, and went to pay for the printing and distribution of a portrait of Hung Hsiu-ch'uan, the Heavenly King, printed on a leaflet. Some of the ingots were changed into copper cash and reminted, for the T'ien Wang was making a tentative effort to produce his own coinage.

One of the cheap leaflets fell into the hands of the Viceroy, and Siu conned the portrait of the rebel chief, uncertain whether it represented Celestial Virtue or Hung Hsiu-ch'uan, but he was impressed by the intelligent face and the Ming headdress. This was no common bandit. He decided to send an embassy to negotiate, and demand the chief's surrender.

The embassy returned to Siu much bewildered. The man before whom they had made their bows had replied, "Masters, you misunderstand me completely. How can a prince submit to his own subjects? I am the eleventh descendant of the Emperor Tsoung-tching, of the great dynasty of the Mings, and I now rightfully levy troops in hope of recovering my ancient territory." Then he had pointed to the Taiping standard flying outside his pavilion, and had said, "I have appointed a great general." And next he had told them that he intended to march on Peking and take the Imperial Palace. But the envoys had brought a copy of a proclamation in which the rebel chief had written, "My ancestors were subjects of the Mings, and during the two hundred years which have elapsed since their fall, they have had nothing to do with the Tartar dynasty."

Siu was at a loss to know exactly who was this man with whom he had to deal. Was he indeed a scion of the Mings and identical with that rogue Celestial Virtue, who had dared to pin his placards on the very gates of Canton? Or was he the man who called himself the T'ien Wang, the Heavenly King, and was believed to be a certain Hung Hsiu-ch'uan from the district of Hua? When he tortured his Triad prisoners they said one thing, and when he tortured his Taiping prisoners they said another. The only matter of which he could be certain was that the rebel chief was a man of considerable education, for his replies had included many classical allusions. Well, if the rebel chief could search the classics to acquire military skill, so could Siu!

Unfortunately Siu had not Hung's gift for distinguishing in ancient history what was and what was not relevant to modern conditions of warfare. Simulating the deed of some archaic hero, Siu gave orders for four thousand buffaloes to be herded together. Fire brands were then tied to their tails, and they were driven at night into the enemy camp in the hope of setting fire to it. Taipings and Triads together easily traced the light of the fire-brands in the dark, headed off the maddened beasts, and feasted for the next few weeks on the carcasses. If Siu chose to revictual the camp of his enemies, so much the better!

Siu was at last replaced, and in July 1851 the new Viceroy arrived in Canton, one Yeh who was shortly to be known in both Kwang-tung and Britain as the infamous Yeh. So far as the immediate surroundings of Canton were concerned, he quickly got the situation under control. The Triads began to lose heart, as Hung had foreseen they would, and Yeh was able to bring in thousands of Triad prisoners. Then the executions began.

The Europeans in the Canton Factories were horrified at the barbarous means of dealing out punishment and the appalling numbers of prisoners done to death, half of them innocent of any crime other than being distant relatives of a rebel. Most of them were Triads, and the Europeans had as yet no idea that the Taipings claimed to be co-religionists, for the mandarins were most anxious to keep this fact secret, lest the British should be persuaded to help their fellow Christians. Nevertheless, stories began to leak through. Monsieur Callery, interpreter at the French Consulate, had heard one or two things. He believed the leader of the insurrection to have the title of Celestial Virtue, and to be a scion of those last Mings who had been converted to Christianity by the Jesuits two hundred years ago.

Thomas Meadows of the consular service had been very busy collecting reports and sending them to Sir John Bowring, whom Palmerston had lately appointed to be Consul at Canton. Meadows had been down to the suburbs of the city to the execution yard, a small walled enclosure, and had seen the rack of de-composing heads. The ground was saturated and rank with steaming blood, and pigs rooted there when it was not immediately in use. From a pottery works opposite a woman tending her child stared at him with eyes so accustomed to brutality that she found the Foreign Devil's interest extraordinary. Because he must report to Bowring, Meadows steeled himself to witness the execution of the next batch of prisoners. Thirty-four were to be slain on that twenty-ninth day of July 1851, a small amount compared with the numbers in the following weeks. Police runners cleared the lane with rattan canes, and the presiding mandarin arrived with a flunkey to carry incense and keep the stench from his master's nostrils. The prisoners were carried in, caged in bamboo baskets borne on poles by two men, like beasts trapped for slaughter. One after another they were unpacked, and made to kneel with hands bound behind them, while the executioner's assistant held up their pigtails. There were no blocks. With a quick jerk to the arms the assistant forced the head forward, and the curved three-foot sword of the executioner flashed downward. He prided himself on his skill, and, by means of changing his sword for a new razor-blade edge once or twice, he managed in exactly three minutes to decapitate thirty-three men. While the features moved in ghastly contortions, the figures remained kneeling and motionless for what seemed a long minute before they fell. The last prisoner was to be fastened to a rough cross for the worst of all punishments, known as "cutting into a thousand pieces". His flesh was to be sliced from him morsel by morsel like ham. Meadows did not stay to witness this last horror.

For the next twelve years the Taiping Christians in their millions were to suffer death in this manner, but it was a cruel age, and the Taipings would themselves inflict exactly the same barbarous death upon their enemies.

In the face of such dangers, why, it might be asked, were the Taiping units swollen with a daily intake of recruits? The young man who was now for the first time marching with the Taipings was already beginning to know the answer.

It had all begun for him on the day when a platoon of the T'ien Wang's soldiers had bivouacked in his native village, which lay by the river leading up to the city of Yung-nan. He and his brother and his cousins had read the proclamation which the lieutenant had posted up on the school-house door. It had been signed by the Western Prince Hsiao.

"Those worshipping Shang-ti need not be afraid or run away," the proclamation had told them, and it had gone on to urge them to join the army, and had warned them that their village homes would presently be burned down to avoid their giving cover or supplies to the Imperial troops, who would shortly be following up the Taiping advance.

Li Siu-cheng, for that was the young man's name, had read the proclamation with consternation, for although he was only twenty-six years old he was responsible for his mother and his sisters, and also for his brother. If the family fell into the hands of the Imperial soldiery, all the women would be immediately raped. That was well known. Whereas these Taipings were under the strict control of their lieutenant, and had not so much as dared to look upon a woman. If Li had led his family down to the main valley of the West River, they might have been able to hide amongst the tall sugar cane, but then, if they had been discovered by the Imperial soldiers, it would have been presumed that they were vagabonds and therefore rebels, and not only would his mothers and sisters have been raped, but he and his brother and cousins would have been decapitated, after the soldiers had violated the younger boys.

And so Li had decided that, of two evils, it was better to join the Taipings. He had hoped that perhaps a chance would come later for escape, but he saw now that this would be impossible, because his mother and sisters had been taken from him, and were marching in a separate unit under the most vigilant protection, lest any insult should be offered to matron or virgin. He had seen female officers riding ponies, shepherding the women, and he was thankful to know that his mother and sisters would be safe from any indecent assaults. But now he must follow wherever the Taiping army went, if he was ever to rejoin his family.

He glanced back down the valley towards his old cottage home and the school-house, where he had spent two years of his youth learning to read. They were going up in flames. He could see the smoke beyond the trees. If he could have, he would have gone back. But there was no way back. The Imperial troops were only thirty miles behind this, his new unit. There was never to be any way back for Li, and perhaps he guessed as much. Therefore, being a young man of determination, he set his face to climb the hill, and not only that hill but all the steep places which might lie ahead in this new life. If he must be a Taiping soldier, then he would be a good one and an efficient one, a lieutenant perhaps.

He was in fact to reach the rank of Commander-in-Chief of all the T'ien Wang's armies. But meanwhile it was difficult not to be downcast, and he was glad, when a new platoon of recruits came up, to recognise his neighbour and friend Ch'en. They had already been in a skirmish, and Ch'en had a nasty sword cut over one eye. His fellow privates, when that night they helped him redress the wound, immediately bestowed on him in cheerful barrack language the nickname of "Cockeye", and as Cockeye he was to be known for all time.

Li was being issued with his bright yellow jerkin by the sergeant. The sergeants all had names such as "Powerful", "Daring", "Martial". The privates took names such as "Van-guard-repelling", "Enemy-breaking", "Rush-on-foe", and "Report-success". The sergeant was waiting with a pot of black paint to inscribe Li's huge identification plaque of calico with giant characters, and thus depict his name and the number of his unit. Perhaps Li chose the name of Faithful, the character which would one day be incorporated in his princely title.

By the time he joined the main camp of the army besieging Yung-nan, he had already learned a thing or two about how it was organised. In all there were now about thirty thousand fully armed men, and the same number of young boys, whose duties were to act as loaders, squires and runners. Each of the nine armies was divided into five divisions under generals of division, and these again into five regiments under captains. Faithful was immediately placed under a sergeant for training in the use of sword and spear. He had to box daily to keep fit, and to handle the wretched matchlocks which were no use against muskets, but there were few of these last to be had. He was growing his hair, and already his forehead had a short crop below his red turban.

When his daily hours of training under the sergeant were finished, he could not relax, for then began the religious teaching. The instructors wore long black robes and black hats decorated with silver. Under pain of death he had been given three weeks to memorise the Ten Commandments and the Lord's prayer, but that was a simple matter if one had learned to recite the Classics at school, as he had. On the first day of instruction the black-robed teacher had told him, "God is the father of the generals of this army. He is also your father. Moreover, he is the father of all men in every nation under heaven."

Faithful was by now beginning to know quite a lot about Shang-ti and the Heavenly Elder Brother. There was something

about this new learning which greatly pleased him. He could
already repeat one of the hymns which the Heavenly King, the
T'ien Wang, had composed for his people. Faithful already
thought of himself now as one of the T'ien Wang's people, his
subjects.

"Our Heavenly Father, of his great mercy and unbounded goodness,
Spared not his firstborn Son, but sent him down into the world,
To give his life for the redemption of all our transgressions.
The knowledge of which, coupled with repentance, saves the souls of
    men."

Faithful liked the Sabbath, too, when there was public preaching, sermons, and hymns; and now that he was baptised he had
really no longer any desire to escape, though he would have liked
to see his mother and sisters. As soon as he was able, he had gone
to the house in a nearby village where he had learnt that they
were quartered. But a large notice over the doorway forbade
entry to any male on pain of death. It had been sad not to be able
to talk with them; on the other hand he was glad that no lustful
brutes could by any means approach his women, and from a
distance his mother had shouted to him that one day they would
be together again, and that meanwhile he must pray to Shang-ti
and the Heavenly Elder Brother; so she also was receiving instruction in this new religion.

Several times he had seen the fate of those who had dared to
disobey the T'ien Wang. Rape, prostitution, the smoking of
opium and desertion from the army were punishable by death;
but for the breaking of Shang-ti's commandment against adultery
—that is, for taking another man's wife—the most horrible of
punishments was reserved. It was known as "Lighting the Lamp
of Heaven", and the offender was wrapped like a cocoon in
coarse cloth dipped in oil, and fire was set to it, so that the
wretched being became a human torch. The alternative penalty
for breaking the seventh commandment was to be torn to pieces
between five horses.

Faithful shuddered at the thought. He had no temptations
towards wife-stealing, knowing, as every man did, what the
penalty would be. It was not so easy to remember all the other
regulations and to avoid lesser punishments. Drinking, smoking
and gambling were forbidden on pain of a stiff bambooing. All

stores taken from the enemy, particularly rice and silver, must immediately be turned over to the common treasury. "For sharing the property together" was the slogan he had been taught, which would usher in the Golden Age, it was said.

As Faithful stood reading the latest posting of army regulations, he was all at once conscious of a bustle in the camp, and drew back just in time to avoid the clattering of hooves of a small escort of cavalry. He could see from their blue coats, red cassocks and the pigtails fastened inside their leather belts that they were of the Imperial army. Men were saying everywhere that these envoys were under safe conduct, and were bringing the T'ien Wang a summons from the Tartar General, Shaishanga, to surrender. The Taiping soldiers were laughing in scorn, for the investment of Yung-nan was complete, and the chance of taking their first walled city was good.

The T'ien Wang's reply to the Tartar Prince was duly carried back.

"The Manchus who for two centuries have been in hereditary possession of the throne of China, are descended from an insignificant nation of foreigners." Shaishanga's oblique eyes narrowed in fury as he read the opening insult. "Such a thing has never been known," the epistle ended, "as one dynasty being able to trace a line of a hundred generations of emperors. The right to govern consists in possession." To the Tartar prince Hung was able to dispense with any nonsense about being heir to the Mings. He claimed the Heavenly Mandate, which was much more important.

Yung-nan was built four-square, surrounded by a great wall with four gates between gate-towers. The force detailed for the assault on September 28th 1851, numbered 16,000 against 30,000 of the Imperial troops. Fire crackers began the panic amongst the besieged. Then from both land and river the Taipings came on; up went scaling ladders. The yellow and red of their uniforms were like flares suddenly springing to light everywhere over the old brickwork. Gaudy pennants were leading on the scaling parties. Sometimes they were obscured by the smoke of the cannon of both Taiping and Imperial gunners. The forests of Taiping spears and halberds at the foot of the wall were as thick as bamboo groves. Now the scaling parties had got a foothold above, and drove the defenders off the ramparts with their stinkpots. Men

were choking in the suffocating fumes. Up and over—they were
in! The Imperial forces ran for it, and for the most part escaped
by one of the gates, leaving the city empty, save for civilians and
the district magistrate and lieutenant-colonel. These two were
promptly decapitated for having dared to resist the army of the
Lord of Hosts.

There was a triumphal entry of the T'ien Wang in his sedan,
and behind him was borne the sedan of Celestial Virtue, prince
and scion of the Mings, of whose company Hung must have been
very tired. But he had promised him the empty trappings of
glory, and to a blood-brother he could not break his word.

So furious was the Emperor Hsien Feng to hear of Yung-nan's
fall that he threatened his three generals with death unless they
retook it within a fortnight. Shaishanga moved up to invest the
city almost at once, but it was to be many months before the
Taipings broke out, and left him once again with an empty lair.

Meanwhile, for the first time in a year the troops could enjoy
the comfort of good quarters, and for a while the rules against
co-habiting with wives were relaxed. As for Hung Hsiu-ch'uan,
for the first occasion in his life he could hold court, if not in a
palace, at least in the very spacious yamen of the city magistrate.
His harem moved in also, and now at last the Sun King could look
upon his Moon Queen, and find satisfaction and pride in adorn-
ing Lai-shi's head with pearls and white jade ornaments, as he
had long ago promised himself he would do. Now again he could
wear his Dragon robes for audience, but the pride he had in his
own grandeur was nothing to the voluptuous pleasure he felt in
bedecking Lai-shi, as though she were his thing, his creation,
whom his own powers had raised from mere womanhood to
Imperial rank, almost to divinity. He instituted the custom that
womenfolk might attend the latter half of banquets, for he could
not altogether resist the temptation to look into the eyes of that
poor fragile degenerate, Celestial Virtue, and see there the envy
and malice and frustration, as Chu beheld the latest pearl coronet
or jade hairpin which he, Hung, had ordered to be placed on the
head of his beautiful queen, the mother of his heir.

Not an image nor an idol survived the first few hours of the
Taipings' seizure of the city. Special squads of iconoclasts were
detailed to smash the abominations, but not a woman of the
civilian population was offered insult.

The T'ien Wang published several proclamations and rescripts while at Yung-nan. One of these stated, "We sincerely announce to you that, since we have all had the happiness to become sons and daughters of our Heavenly Father, and brothers and sisters of our Celestial Elder Brother, we shall enjoy incomparable dignity in this present world, and interminable felicity in the next." He did not, therefore, as some of his later European critics supposed, regard his position as a son of God as singular, but believed only that his responsibilities were specially important. Nor did he claim to be on the same level as his Heavenly Elder Brother, for, in the particular Chinese technique of honouring names by elevating them so many spaces in the line of calligraphy, he elevated the name of God by four spaces, the name of Jesus by three, and himself only by two. Moreover, so anxious was he not to encroach upon honours only to be accorded to the divine, that on November 30th 1851, at Yung-nan, he published a proclamation to his officers and soldiers.

"The great God our heavenly Father and supreme Lord is omniscient, omnipotent, and omnipresent, the Supreme over all. There is not an individual who is not produced and nourished by him. He is *Shang*, Supreme, he is the *Ti*, ruler. Besides the great God, our heavenly Father, and supreme Lord, there is no one who can be called *Shang*, and no one who can be called *Ti*. Therefore, from henceforth, all you soldiers and officers must not call me Supreme, lest you should encroach upon the designation of our heavenly Father. . . . Our heavenly Father and celestial Elder Brother alone are holy; and from henceforth all you soldiers and officers may designate us as your Lord and that is all, but you must not call me holy."

As he sat in the late magistrate's private bureau quietly composing this proclamation, he was rudely interrupted by the discovery of a group of conspirators who had plotted to hand over the city to the enemy within the next forty-eight hours. The T'ien Wang was immediately summoned to cope with the situation.

It was a vile and treacherous plot, but it would not have found its way into the sacred records of the Taiping dynasty had not men acclaimed that its discovery was by the direct intervention of God, and therefore a miracle.

As to the source of the intervention, it must be remembered that if Shang-ti could speak in the camp, so could Yen-lo! If

Heaven could direct a man's speech, why, so could Hell! Yang in his pride, had thought that he could lay his feeble soul open and vulnerable to unearthly powers, trusting to be used by Shang-ti only, whereas his very pride in the simple psychic phenomenon had laid open an entrance for Yen-lo also. But the Prince of Darkness would be too subtle to enter himself, lest he be recognised by the black power of words and obscenities which always betrayed him. There was a far more cunning means to direct the speech of Yang, and that was through the mind of Wei. Wei's complete surrender to Yen-lo had been effected because his pride was hurt by an insufficient recognition of his powers as a general, on an occasion when his prowess had rescued the Taiping army from a perilous situation amongst the Purple Thorn Hills.

The plot to surrender the city, as Hung was learning, had been devised in this way. Jen-kan had not yet managed to get from Hua through the enemy lines and join the Taiping forces. Nor had Feng's relatives. But it was not only the T'ien Wang and the princes who were anxious for their kin. Many officers and men were also hoping daily for the arrival of their loved ones in Yung-nan, where they would be safe. A certain officer named Chou had made repeated applications to Hung and the generals that he might be allowed to return to the town of Po-pih and there assemble nearly two hundred "brethren and sisters" and bring them safely to Yung-nan. Instead of bringing them to Yung-nan, he had taken them to the Tartar general's camp, and had there delivered them to Shaishanga to be put to death. The incentive for this treachery had been Shaishanga's offer of a mandarin button of the sixth rank, on the condition that Chou would return to Yung-nan and co-operate in an attack to be delivered simultaneously within and without the city on December 6th.

Chou had arrived back on November 26th in company with his brother officers and some of his friends, who were, except for one, ignorant of his intentions to betray the city. He had been met by anxious enquiries from every direction as to what had happened to the "brethren and sisters", for there was hardly a Taiping who had not hoped to be reunited with some lost kindred. Chou gave out that it had been impossible to get through the enemy lines with such a large company, and that he had safely hidden the refugees en route in a cache to which he would presently return. It was remarked by those made perspicacious by anxiety that Chou did not immediately report his arrival to his superior officers. On the next day he was seen to be examining the turrets over the four city gateways in consultation with his fellow conspirator, and certain words were overheard by the sentries on duty. His lack of discretion was complete, for he then hastened to his wife, and secretly enjoined her to be ready for what was afoot. She in her turn was heard by a neighbour saying to her little son, "You won't wear these cotton clothes long. In three days' time you will be dressed in silks." She was then observed to be packing her boxes and sharpening a dagger.

Meanwhile the anxious relatives of the slaughtered flock had, it seems, reported their suspicions. Wei straightway had Chou arrested, and himself conducted in private the examination of the manacled prisoner. Although he was convinced that Chou was guilty, he did not exact a confession or put the man to torture, for almost certainly he had seen that his conspiracy might be used to his own advantage. He had no desire to betray the Taiping army, for he hoped in the distant future to command not only that army but every other power, and in the end himself to occupy the Dragon Throne. But if he could use this conspiracy to lower the prestige of Hung Hsiu-ch'uan, and make him subject to the directions of inspired speech; and if at the same time he could break down Yang's psychic defences, so as himself to direct Yang's speech—then he would weaken the position of the sovereign and his Commander-in-Chief to such an extent that presently (and he was prepared to be very patient) he would be able to reap the benefit and step into supreme power.

He therefore straightway called for his sedan that evening and visited the Eastern Prince. What passed between them remains a mystery. It is very possible that Wei had hypnotic powers. By the time Feng and Shih Ta-kai were summoned, they could recognise that Yang was speaking under the direction of an alien influence, and, having no cause to suspect his good faith, they presumed that he was under the influence of the Heavenly Father. The T'ien Wang was therefore immediately sent for, because when Shang-ti himself held audience, it was for earthly monarchs to quit their palaces and obey the summons, and now it was demanded that the T'ien Wang should even kow-tow, which Hung therefore did, reverently enquiring, "Is the Heavenly Father come down?"

The exact words of the examination that followed were recorded by a scribe, detailed for the purpose and kneeling there in a corner of the room.

Through the lips of the Eastern Prince an indication was given that it was indeed the Heavenly Father speaking, and the voice proceeded, "I am going to take this matter in hand today. A mere mortal would find it a hard task. Are you aware Chou is in communication with the enemy?"

Hung had already learned so much from the urgent messages brought to his yamen, so now he answered, "Yang has already informed me of this."

From the next room the traitor was brought in chains and flung at the feet of the Eastern Prince.

"Who is it now speaking?" came the words from Yang's lips.

The prisoner, recognising that his inquisitor was in a state of trance, and knowing that the Eastern Prince was believed to be the mouthpiece of Shang-ti, answered trembling, "The Heavenly Father".

The inquisition went on for some time, conducted supposedly by Shang-ti himself, while Chou again and again swore that he was no traitor, and was as constantly exhorted to confess. In the end, either from superstitious terror or from fear that physical torture would soon follow, and that in any event his case was hopeless, for Wei's spies probably had too much evidence against him, he broke down and made full confession, pleading for mercy.

Wei then went out to harangue the troops who were gathered in a mob in the huge courtyard of the official's stately dwelling. News had got round of the conspiracy, and the soldiers were yelling for the traitor's blood, for it was their own helpless relatives and womenfolk whom Chou had delivered to death.

From the steps of the audience chamber giving on to the courtyard Wei spoke to the people, and he knew how to work upon their feelings. "Soldiers! We are indebted to the power and ability of the Heavenly Father and great God in having laid open and confounded the schemes of the demons and in having exposed the treacherous designs of Chou." He went on to explain to them all that had taken place. Somehow, in the subtlest way, it became evident that it was not the so-called Elect of Heaven, Hung Hsiu-ch'uan, who had saved the situation. It might have been inferred that the T'ien Wang had been lax in not making it his business to know more of the dangers around them all. It was Shang-ti who had discovered the conspiracy. Wei was quite content that for the moment Shang-ti should have all the credit. In fact he would need the people to have a superstitious belief in Shang-ti, when the moment came for Wei himself to become the recipient of the Heavenly Mandate.

The mob shouted their acclamations of the divine intervention. "The Heavenly Father, the great God, he is omniscient! He is omnipresent!"

Back once more in the bureau of inquisition, Wei heard sentence passed upon the traitor—death by cutting into a thousand pieces. The T'ien Wang had risen from his knees. He was shaken and disturbed by what had taken place. He needed to be alone to think. He was about to withdraw, when once again Yang had a fleeting moment of the trance-like state. Yang now addressed the T'ien Wang. "Ponder what has passed . . . fear not! I hold the superintendence of affairs."

Certainly Hung needed to ponder very deeply. As he was carried back in his sedan to his Imperial yamen, the people—it was nearly dawn—were already beginning to prepare pigs and oxen for a great thanksgiving feast to celebrate the miracle of Shang-ti's intervention, and throughout the city it was being said, "Who would have thought that God was directing all affairs, and that he would so suddenly appear and discover what was really about to take place!"

Hung sat in his private writing bureau with his head in his hands, and he was filled with a sense of guilt. Had not men once doubted his own visions? Yet how wonderfully Shang-ti was fulfilling his promise to place a poor and unknown schoolmaster upon the Dragon Throne! Why then had he suddenly doubted the mouthpiece of Shang-ti? When he had been trapped in the mountains, the Heavenly Father had spoken from Yang's lips, and issued orders to rescue him from a peril of which Yang could not possibly have known. It was wrong, therefore, to doubt, for though he knew there were demons as well as angels, yet by their fruits should they be known, and the city had just been saved from treachery within. Perhaps his suspicions had merely been a cloak for his Imperial pride, which had suffered at having to kow-tow to another man, even though that man was the mouthpiece of Shang-ti. In future he must school himself to be more humble, as some of the more virtuous kings of Israel had been, when rebuked by prophets speaking in the name of the Lord. Meanwhile he must prepare to meet Shaishanga's planned assault on December 6th.

Shaishanga's assault failed dismally, for he had counted on inside help which was not forthcoming. He was degraded in rank by the Emperor Hsien Feng, but continued to command the besieging force.

The investment was now so complete that the plight of the Taipings began to grow desperate. After much hardship in the wilderness, and a near-defeat in the Purple Thorn Hills, it had been a strategic necessity to take a large walled city, in order that the troops might recuperate and the wounded be able to recover in peace for a while. But now they were growing alarmingly short of food and salt and gunpowder. The Taipings were acquiring their first experience of the fact that it is sometimes easier to break into a walled city than to break out. Twice in February there were sorties, both times unsuccessful. At the end of March, when they had been six months shut up in Yung-nan, the risk of a general break-out had to be taken if they were not to starve.

In preparation for this, Hung sent once again for Kiang, the spy, and ordered him to make a last attempt to rescue Jen-kan. Word had come that five or six hundred innocent men in the Hua district had been slaughtered by the Imperial troops. The mystery of Jen-kan's whereabouts and fate, and also that of Feng's sons, gave the T'ien Wang and the Southern Prince many sleepless nights.

On April 5th the T'ien Wang issued a proclamation giving directions for the break-out. It began by encouraging the troops to have firmness, patience, courage and ardour, and to believe in God's help. "If he could make the land and sea in six days, you may easily believe that our ghostly Father is a hero. High Heaven has commissioned you to kill the hellish fiends. Our Heavenly Father and Celestial Elder Brother have their eyes upon you. Let the male and female officers all grasp the sword."

Then the proclamation continued, like some Mosaic injunction, to give orders that baggage and precious goods must all be left behind except for one change of clothing, and ended, "Divest yourselves of worldly motives and look to heaven, where there are golden tiles and golden houses all glorious to behold. In heaven above you may enjoy happiness and dignity in the extreme. The very meanest will be clothed in silks and satins. The males will be adorned with dragon-embroidered robes, and females with flowers."

The break-out began on the evening of April 7th 1852, and it was to be touch and go whether or not the army was annihilated. At 8 P.M. Wei sallied out first with 6,000 men to cut a passage through the enemy lines. At 10 P.M. he was followed by Yang and Feng with the main army surrounding and guarding the terrified women, amongst whom were the sedan chairs of the T'ien Wang's harem, the wives of the princes, and Hung himself on horseback.

At 2 A.M. Hsiao, acting as rearguard, fired the east gate of the city to facilitate his sortie and came out with the remaining thousand men. He had under his charge the sedan chair of Celestial Virtue. They were already a league distant from the main force, and heavy rain had begun to fall, when the Imperial cavalry fell upon them. In the hard fighting and confusion of the dark Celestial Virtue was captured, and Hsiao was only himself able to rejoin the main force after a stiff fight in which he lost many men.

The break-out had been successfully accomplished at the total loss of 2,000 men. However, it was impossible for the Taipings to continue their march to the east, since the way was barred by the Imperial forces. So they turned back towards Siang, for now they had cut behind Shaishanga's force, and there was little opposition between them and the westerly escape route.

Meanwhile what of Celestial Virtue? He was sent to Peking for decapitation, and on the way wrote the confession which it was usual to extract from political prisoners. His exact history was always to remain a mystery. The Europeans had been under the impression that Celestial Virtue was the title of the leader of the insurrection, and now for the first time it appeared they were mistaken. Thomas Meadows thought the error was due to a wrong reading of Chinese characters, and that such a man had never in fact existed. But then, whom had the Imperialists captured? For they certainly had possession of a prisoner. Meadows believed that the confession was merely extracted under torture, in order that the Imperial generals, who were in disgrace, might restore their reputation at Peking by pretending to deliver a prisoner of more importance than he really was.

But the actual word-for-word confession of Celestial Virtue gave the clue to his position vis-à-vis the T'ien Wang. He gave his name as Hung, not Chu—"But it is only since I contracted a brotherhood relation with Hung Hsiu-ch'uan that I changed it." The significance of the blood covenant had been insufficiently understood by those Europeans seeking to disentangle the mystery. To protect any relations he might have, the prisoner disclaimed any wife and children and said that his parents were dead: thus he gave no details of his Ming ancestry, though even the Europeans in Canton had heard that he was a scion of the old dynasty. He spoke of his life as a monk, boasted of his book-knowledge of military arts, and inveighed against the Christian superstitions of the T'ien Wang, by whom, he claimed, he was considered co-sovereign. He also bitterly inveighed against Hung's love of women, of whom there were already thirty-six in the harem, according to his calculation. And he ended, "I wished to hear of his destruction and defeat, for then I could succeed in obtaining dominion." His head was hung upon one of the gates of Peking as a warning to rebels.

As for the T'ien Wang, he was no doubt somewhat relieved to be free of such a pensioner. In Israel David had pensioned off Jonathan's lame heir, and Hung's situation may have been very similar: he also had received the Heavenly Mandate over the head of a scion of the previous dynasty, and if he breathed a little sigh of relief when Hsiao brought news of the man's capture, he cannot be more greatly blamed than David.

Now, however, he had other things to think of—the westerly advance to the district of Siang, the backdoor of China. They came to it in mid-April. For more than a year they had been in the "enclosed land", and their battles had ranged over an area rather larger than Switzerland and comparable in its mountainous character. At last they were to get out! Up they went and over the watershed. They were in the heart of China, with the city of Kwei-lin before them in the valley. No more mountain barriers to contend with! Nature's waterways lay almost continuous from the river below them right up through the great lakes to the Yang-tze.

14

THE TAIPINGS, USING siege towers, invested Kwei-lin, a city with 400,000 inhabitants, for thirty-one days. They raised the siege on May 19th, and marched on to cross the provincial border into Hu-nan, where from all sides the Triads rose and joined them, swearing allegiance to the T'ien Wang, and accepting Christianity at least for the meantime.

Several miles north-east of Ch'uan-chou, they commandeered all the small boats and took to the river. From now on they could go by water almost all the way to the middle reach of the Yang-tze; and Lo Ta-kang's skill and knowledge became invaluable, a native skill in seamanship and piracy joined to whatever training he had acquired from the British sailors at Lin-tin.

Nevertheless there was a disaster on this first occasion of taking to the water, for the Imperial general ambushed them at the So-i ford. The boats were wrecked, and there were many casualties. Feng, already seriously wounded, was transferred from his stretcher to the shore, while for two days and nights the battle raged and the enemy burned all the rivercraft. Alas, Feng died, and thus the T'ien Wang lost the most Christian and the most trustworthy of his five princes.

From the So-i ford the Taipings marched overland to Yung-chou, where the tributary joined the main river. They took four more cities, and now the whole district and river and the main way to the capital of Hu-nan province was laid open.

Chang-sha, the capital, and equivalent to the capital of a small European country, lay on the river, its battlements reflected in the limpid water, and behind it rose black basalt mountains covered with forests. But they were not so high as the Kwang-si mountains, and they formed no barrier, because the river from Chang-sha led into the great lake of Tung Ting, an inland sea easily crossed by boat.

On September 11th Hsiao, with his advance guard, his picked troops known as "the Battalion of Death", spurred forward, and would have taken the city by surprise, if he had not mistaken the high tower at the south-east corner of the wall for the city gates. The garrison had just sufficient time to close them, and there now began a siege of eighty-one days.

During these months of siege there was time to organise and instruct the new recruits, levy taxes and commandeer stores throughout the countryside. Proclamations were issued in which were incorporated Christian tenets, and the T'ien Wang had to make certain regulations regarding his women.

While Hung was having trouble with his harem his enemy, the Emperor Hsien Feng, was for the first time enjoying true bliss with a woman who suited him. Yehonala had just been chosen from the parade of girls offered by the families of the Imperial clansmen to the Manchu Emperor, and had become his favourite concubine. After each night of love, Hsien Feng lay abed half the day with her, and would have forgotten to read the memorials of his despairing generals had not she, being full of ambition and already desirous to rule China, urged him to it. The thousands of eunuchs who served in, organised, and in fact ruled the Forbidden City were already beginning to take note of the favourite's power over the Emperor, and to win themselves into the good graces of the future Empress.

Hung's trouble appears to have been that he would have no eunuchs. Whether he had an inordinate dislike of stemming the life force and robbing another man of the right to beget children, or whether his distaste for the practice was due to the desire for general reform and the spirit of a modern age, or whether he had found in the scriptures some authority for his disapproval of this custom, in fact he appears to have rejected it. His harem was therefore waited upon by maidservants only, which meant that many such female workers had to be recruited, and his enemies were quick to believe that they were all his concubines. Without the aid of eunuchs, it was difficult to preserve propriety when the harem was on the march. "No subject is ever to look upon the face of any of the inmates of the harem," ran his proclamation of November 15th 1852. "They are to glance to the ground. What is said in the harem must never be reported outside." Evidently gossip had been rife, for henceforth not even a minister was allowed so much as to mention the name or rank of any lady of the royal harem on penalty of death.

He was enjoying now the company of his heir, who at three years old caused him both pride and entertainment. The "Young Lord", for such was the title recently accorded to him, was almost exactly the same age as Hung's nephew, the son of the Western Prince, Hsiao, and to see the two little boys dressed from head to foot in Imperial Yellow, and tumbling over each other in their childish games, was a source of delight to both fathers. Already the T'ien Wang had three other sons by his concubines, and now he granted the infants their titles as princes, and ordained that his daughters should be addressed as "Pieces of Gold". The etiquette of his future court was taking shape.

By the month of November it was time to raise the siege of Chang-sha and move on, for the army was now swollen with recruits and rich with silver, but oil and salt were giving out, and new sources of food must be found. Moreover, the prestige they would have acquired by taking the capital city of a province might have been offset by the difficulty of getting out again. They had not forgotten the lesson of Yung-nan. It was important, however, before marching on in safety, to give the Imperial troops a good drubbing, and also to boost morale by some ceremony which would increase the dignity of the sovereign. The T'ien Wang therefore held a grand levée in public, and with all the due and prescribed rites assumed the Imperial seal and the usual Imperial title of "Immortal One"—Wansui. Its literal meaning was "Live for Ten Thousand Years!", and it was more an expression of hope, well-wishing and benediction than an assured promise of paradise, so that it did not encroach upon the title of the Divinity.

When the troops were deployed to challenge the Imperial army one wing, numbering 3,000 men, was found to be in considerable danger. The whole body of them thereupon knelt in prayer upon the field, and then rose to charge, and drove the enemy back successfully. It was indeed a Holy War, and Shang-ti was on their side, and the source of their courage. Yet despite this victory, the ground round Chang-sha had taken its toll, for Hsiao had been directing the gunners when one of the antiquated Chinese cannons had exploded. He was killed instantly, and the whole army mourned their gallant young general, mouthpiece of the Redeemer, the Western Prince. They buried him there on

the outskirts of Chang-sha, while Hung lamented the loss of his
brother-in-law, and gave to his little nephew the title and rank
of his heroic father. Of the five original princes only three were
left—Yang and Wei, who were already jealous of each other's
power, and Shih Ta-kai, whose preoccupation with his duties as
President of the Board of Civil Administration and general of
one of the armies gave him little time to keep an eye on the doings
of Wei.

On November 30th, the Taiping forces abandoned the siege
of Chang-sha and marched towards the Tung Ting lake, taking
with them thousands of adolescent boys conscripted from the
neighbourhood to act as loaders, runners and bearers, and to be
trained as the nucleus of future armies. Thus the T'ien Wang
left Chang-sha, and all unwitting left behind in its vicinity the
one man who was eventually to defeat him—Tseng Kuo-fan.

The Vice-President of the Board of Rites, who had been so
busy in Peking two years ago drawing up proclamations for the
succession of the Manchu Emperor Hsien Feng, had in the
month of August received news of his mother's death. Following
immemorial custom, Tseng immediately resigned office and
quitted the Forbidden City to retire to his home in Hu-nan
province for the necessary months of mourning. Like the Roman
Cincinnatus, this Chinese patrician—he was of pure Chinese stock
and not a Manchu—was looking forward to a peaceful country
life and the cultivation of his vegetables. But when he approached
his home, which lay thirty miles from Chang-sha, he learnt of the
siege. The countryside was reduced to a chaotic state, and it
became immediately apparent to him that something must be done
if hearth and home were to survive the threat of anarchy. Whenever the Taiping force moved on, local banditry sprang up in
its wake, and every bad character took advantage of the collapse
of law and order. Tseng Kuo-fan had received a very rude shock.
No one in Peking had dreamed that matters were quite as serious
as he now perceived them to be. No one had dared to report
to the Emperor how calamitous were the defeats of the Imperial
troops.

Tseng walked between his rows of cabbages, hoe in hand, and
very deep in thought. He was of low stature, stoutish, dark of
complexion, with a black straggling beard and moustache. He
wore a battered and ancient straw hat with the ease and elegance

with which a country gentleman always enjoys old clothes. The family was not rich, nor did they own vast estates. Tseng's niche in society could perhaps be best compared with that of an English squire or Scottish laird, if that squire or laird could have claimed authentic descent from one of Christ's apostles, and have lived on the same piece of land since the first preaching of the gospel—for Tseng's original ancestor had been the most famous of the disciples of Confucius in the sixth century B.C., and the family had continued to live in Hu-nan ever since.

He was regarded, therefore, by his neighbours with considerable respect, and he was already becoming known in Peking as a superb scholar. In his turn he respected tradition, and, although he was a Chinese, he had no racial hatred for the Tartars. He had a sufficient knowledge of history to be aware that in the medieval era of the great Khan, Kublai, the Tartars had seized the Dragon Throne; but history always repeats itself, and the barbarian invaders were always in the end forced to adopt Chinese customs and civilisation, because they could not rule the Empire without the help of the Chinese literati. It was more than two hundred years ago that the present Manchu dynasty had usurped power, and within a generation the Chinese officials had tamed their conquerors, and now the Manchus were as much the slaves of the old Chinese traditions as anyone. There was, therefore, no point in ousting them. It was better to maintain the *status quo*. Least of all would Tseng ever lend himself to help the Taipings supplant the Tartars, for these long-haired rebels were teaching a new doctrine, which cut at the root of all tradition. Thus Tseng Kuo-fan, champion of Confucius, was to be matched against Hung, the champion of Christ.

Tseng's personal character was above reproach, and it was perhaps a pity that this admirable country gentleman, whose face, with its expression of firm purpose, was to remind Europeans of Oliver Cromwell, lacked the vision to see that the *status quo* could not be maintained, that a new spirit of reform must in any case prevail. The difference between the two future opponents can perhaps be summarised by saying that Tseng, although possibly the more worthy character, lacked vision, while Hung Hsiu-ch'uan had received a vision of the future, but in his own personal character there was a certain flaw of instability through which Yen-lo, that old serpent, was hoping to shatter him.

The situation in Hu-nan grew worse as news came from the north of the almost uninterrupted progress of the Taiping armies. At the present rate they would be in Peking within a few months! Tseng had at least this much vision: he realised that nothing could impede the advance of the long-haired rebels or obviate the anarchy around him, unless a completely different class of men was enrolled to aid the cause of law and order; and they must receive a new morale and a pride in drill and discipline. The long-haired rebels had proved there was nothing wrong with Chinese valour and courage: it was only a question of how to evoke it. Virtuous men from stable and honest homes would not join the Imperial army because of its evil repute, but they must be made to see that, when their homes were in danger, it was the duty of all men to band together and form a home guard.

Tseng, therefore, began to recruit this home guard, to which he gave the name of the Hu-nan Braves. Beginning in a small way, he drilled and disciplined a local militia free of all association with the corrupt old regiments, and gave it a new and excellent morale. With the co-operation of the local officials he equipped it with a fleet of river-boats, because it was by the waterways that the long-haired rebels were now everywhere advancing. Within a short period Tseng found himself the only man who could check anarchy, and the Imperial commanders were sending for his help from every direction. His successes were at first limited by the fact that, since the "Braves" had been raised as a home guard, they were most unwilling to leave their home districts unprotected to fight elsewhere. But Tseng's personality and demand for a long-distance policy eventually persuaded them to accept his orders without question, and his forces began to be a power in the province.

About this time, he was joined by a man of considerable intelligence, one Li Hung-chang, a native of the neighbouring province of An-hui, who had had to flee from the Taiping advance. Li began to train under Tseng and to act as his secretary. All day they worked together, and in the evening in some uncomfortable tent studied, not only the maps of the province, but philosophy and the Classics. "You can study at your own fireside," Tseng would say, "or in the wildernesses, or in busy market places, or whether you are raising vegetables or swine. But if you cannot apply yourself and are not independent, you can never study, whether at home, or in a quiet country place, or in the haunts of gods and fairies."

On this particular evening, however, they were not studying philosophy but a rough and somewhat inaccurate map of the central provinces of China, and the progress of the long-haired rebels was causing them something near despair.

When the insurgents had left Chang-sha, they had marched to Yi-yang on the great inland sea of Tung Ting, taken that city, and requisitioned thousands of boats. They had crossed the lake, and on December 13th had taken Yo-chou at the north-east end of the water, and with it the Imperial arsenal of the whole district and a further 5,000 boats. From there a huge waterway communicated direct with the Yang-tze, and at the point where the great river and this waterway were joined three cities, one on each furthest bank and one on the tongue of land dividing them, so that in fact the three cities, Han-yang, Han-kow and Wu-chang, were for all practical purposes one city, and could have been joined by bridges. Of them Han-kow was the most important, because it was the great commercial centre to which trade came down from all the upper reaches of the Yang-tze and its tributaries, and from there was shipped to the coast.

This Triple City, for so it might be termed, housed more than a million people and had fallen to the long-haired rebels. On December 23rd they had taken Han-yang and then Han-kow, commandeering another 10,000 junks and firing that city, before they took Wu-chang on January 12th, 1853. Not only did they know how to throw fire torches, but they had with them competent engineers, sappers, miners and workers in wood and metal, and one of them, as Tseng realised, knew how to organise a river fleet, for the whole mass of insurgents had taken to the water and was sailing triumphantly down the Yang-tze. They had even had time to turn back and wreck his own precious flotilla, and now there was no money left in the provincial treasury to purchase and equip another. Nevertheless he had one or two victories on land to his credit, and that was more than any other Imperial commander could claim.

He was waiting now for approval of his actions from Peking, and an answer to a suggestion he had made about patents. For Tseng had realised that half the trouble of the Imperial commanders lay in the fact that the Board of Revenue in Peking had no power or resources to grant financial aid, and therefore, despite his dislike of bribery and corruption, he had *in extremis* recommended the sale of 4,000 patents to official rank.

In Peking the news of Tseng's victories caused at first a reaction surprising to anyone unacquainted with the problems of the dynasty—how the Tartars were to maintain themselves as rulers of an alien land. On receipt of the good tidings Hsien Feng immediately expressed to the courtiers gathered round him his joy and relief. "What a miracle!" he is reported to have said. "To think that Tseng Kuo-fan, a scholar, without training in arms, could achieve such a wonderful conquest!"

Whereupon a Grand Counsellor was quick to remind the sovereign, "Tseng, a Vice-Minister on leave, is nothing more than a private subject. It is not a blessing for the dynasty to have private subjects who could, if they were so minded, gather together thousands of men at a single call."

The Manchu Emperor fell immediately silent, filled with dismay at the thought that Tseng, who against all regulations was becoming a power in his native province, whence he could gather adherents the more easily, might in his turn become a threat to the Dragon Throne. Should he, or should he not, confirm Tseng's appointment to the position of Commander-in-Chief in Hu-nan, which Tseng had in fact made for himself? The answer came from his favourite concubine, and it was Yehonala's first exhibition of the statecraft for which she was to be famous. Someone must be trusted, therefore why not trust the only man who had so far been able to cause some check to the rebels' advance? Once she had staked her reputation for judgment upon Tseng, he was from then on her protégé, and was to prove in the end that her judgment was sound. His appointment was not only confirmed, but his request about the patents was granted.

He went back with a more cheerful mind to study on the maps the progress of the long-haired rebels. The Taipings had by now swept on down the Yang-tze, and on February 24th had taken An-king. If the Yang-tze was regarded as a serpent, Tseng pointed out to his secretary, Li Hung-chang, then the Triple City was its head, and Nanking was its tail; but, and he placed a finger on the map, the way to kill a serpent was to break its back, and An-king was the vital spot on that back where it must be broken, if it was ever to be destroyed at all.

There were others who were studying the progress of the rebels
—the Catholic priests. As soon as the insurgents had debouched
from the Kwang-si mountains, the priests had been on the alert.
They alone of all the Europeans had access to the interior, but
they were not much better informed than the British in Canton,
for a very simple reason. While the British had only so far come in
contact with the non-Christian Triads, the Catholic priests had
not dared to make overt contact with the Christian Taipings, for
fear of compromising their little flocks of converts dotted in secret
all over the interior. In nearly fifty years the Protestants could
claim only a few hundred converts at the open ports; in nearly
three hundred years the Catholics could claim only a few hundred
thousand out of a race of more than 300 million; and yet ironically
enough, now when a whole people was on the move, claiming to
be Christians and in need of guidance, the hands of both Protestant and Catholic missionaries were for the moment tied, the
Protestants because they had as yet no contact with or knowledge of the interior, and the Catholics because they feared to
bring disaster upon those Chinese who were already converted.

Father Clavelin of the Society of Jesus, writing from the Jesuit
College of Zi-ka-wei a few miles outside Shanghai on August 28th
1852, had given the first picture of events from the missionary
point of view. "These rebel chiefs are men of valour and skill,
giving themselves out to be the avengers of their nation. The
Kwang-si revolt has had the effect that Christians in neighbouring
provinces have been persecuted. They are accused of being the
instigators. In Hou-kuan a Chinese priest and several Christians
have been seized and thrown into prison. . . . Monseigneur
Baldus, Vicar Apostolic of Hu-nan, has just written to tell us that
he has to be much on his guard, because he is regarded as one of
the rebel chiefs."

At last the news was breaking everywhere amongst the
Europeans that the rebels, who had seized Central China and
were at any minute about to take Nanking and the mouth of the
Yang-tze and debouch on to the coast into the midst of the
European open treaty ports, were their co-religionists. The news
confirming previous rumours broke, when it did break, in a star-
tling fashion, and came from the lips of none other than Jen-kan,
whose mysterious disappearance had caused such anxiety to his
cousin, the T'ien Wang.

Now at this minute Jen-kan was sitting in Hong Kong in the small Victorian plush-upholstered study of the Reverend Mr. Theodore Hamberg, who was taking down from his dictation not only the account of Jen-kan's own adventures, but the whole history of Hung Hsiu-ch'uan's life.

Mr. Hamberg was a Swede, sent to China by the Evangelical Missionary Society of Basle. A fellow missionary was to describe him as "a person of intellect, one of nature's noblemen". He was the first European to learn the Hak-ka dialect, and gave his labours to that people and a dictionary of their dialect to the world. To doubt that he made a true transcription, therefore, as some sceptics, biased against the Taiping form of Christianity, were to do, would be unfair both to his character and to his capabilities.

The account that Jen-kan now gave of his own adventures was this. He had obeyed the very first summons of Hung Hsiu-ch'uan when the Taiping army issued forth from Thistle Mount, and had promptly set out with forty of his fellow Christians and kinsfolk; but, meeting too thick a fence of Imperial military lines, had sent his flock back to safety, and had himself penetrated further with only three companions. He had changed his name and attempted disguise, but had eventually fallen into the hands of his enemies. He had been bound, ready for transport to the nearest execution yard, but in the dark he had managed to free his hands, and in the blinding rain had escaped to some hills. To such straits had he been reduced that at one time he had contemplated strangling himself with his own girdle. For weeks he had lived in a cave without food. Then he had found shelter with a good Samaritan, who had turned out to be a Christian convert, and had conducted him to Hong Kong and to safety and asylum with the British.

Now here he was in Mr. Hamberg's study, and he was telling the honourable missionary teacher how it had all begun, from the day of his cousin's birth, and even the history of the ancestors before that event; about the visions, the reading of the tracts and the first spreading of the gospel in Kwang-si, right down to the present time. And with his trained Chinese memory he could quote not only his cousin's odes and hymns, but the very words he had spoken on solemn occasions.

As for the future, Jen-kan was content for the moment to make no more attempts to join his cousin, but to take the opportunity, so long denied him by circumstances, of receiving full instruction in the Christian faith. That he might have the means of supporting himself and those of his family who had been able to join him, Mr. Hamberg was proposing to publish the account he had just given of the origins of the rebellion, and to devote the proceeds to Jen-kan. It was so published in the following November of 1853 under the title *The Visions of Hung Siu-Tshuen and Origin of the Kwangsi Insurrection*, and caused a tremendous stir amongst the Europeans, but already the substance of it had by that time reached the newspapers.

The Viceroy and Governors of An-king had fled. On March the 4th the Taipings had taken Wu-hu, and on the 7th yet another prefectural city on the Yang-tze. They were within a few days' march of Nanking, the capital of Central China, distant only a few more days' march from the European Treaty port of Shanghai. And not till this last moment had the Europeans become fully aware that the rebels, with whom they would very shortly have to have dealings, claimed to be their co-religionists.

15

THE CITY OF NANKING was as large as Paris and was built, like Rotterdam, in the water, surrounded by small creeks and canals which connected with the Great River. Its red sandstone walls were fifty feet thick, and the many gateways were like long, dark tunnels through the thickness. The area within was not all built up. There were vast parks and green pleasure grounds. And crowning all was the inner citadel of the Tartar stronghold, walled again, within which the Banner garrison was quartered with all their wives and children. Not only was the city the capital of Kiang-su, one of the most fruitful of the eighteen provinces and larger than Holland and Belgium put together, but, as its name indicated it was the southern capital of all China, and from here the Mings had made their last stand against the Manchus.

Surely, thought the inhabitants, Nanking with its huge fortifications would hold against the long-haired rebels? From all the surrounding neighbourhood refugees poured into the city for safety, including most of the Chinese Catholics from the vicinity. The Manchu Emperor Hsien Feng announced that he would on March 21st memorialise Heaven. "I, the Emperor, shall pass the night at the Altar of Heaven, and shall pray with fervour for the peace of my subjects." His prayers were to come too late.

The rebels were advancing so rapidly that on March 6th the mandarins closed the gates against further refugees. The Taipings had sent notices throughout the countryside demanding surrender and the delivery of seals of office from all officials in the nearby towns and villages. The people were notified in advance to paste up a paper with the word "Shun"—"Obedient!"—over their doors. So once again the history of the Exodus was repeated, and the angel of death passed over those who had marked their door-posts.

By the time the Taipings came in sight of the great red sandstone walls, the Viceroy and Lieutenant-Governor had fled. Nanking lay before them, like a jewel amongst the peach trees for which it was famous; and outside its walls rose the Porcelain Pagoda, that wonder of the Chinese world. Two hundred and fifty feet high and built in nine stories, its entire surface was covered with white and gold tiles, and on each floor were golden images of the Buddha. Because of its idols it was, to the Taipings, an abomination in the sight of the Lord, and was destroyed on the very first day of their arrival on March 8th. The rebels now investing the city numbered 80,000. They had plenty of cannon and equipment, were well fed, clothed and armed, and were in high spirits and sure of success.

Within the city were 6,000 Chinese soldiers, and to defend the inner citadel there were 7,000 Tartar Bannermen with between 20,000 and 30,000 of their wives and children.

On March 19th 1853 the Taipings sprang a mine under the north-east angle of the wall, stormed the breach and took the city. It was to be exactly eleven years and two months to the very day before the Imperial forces retook it by springing a monster mine in the same place.

The Taipings now poured in and began their attack upon the inner citadel. The Bannermen, vitiated, idle and lacking all morale, made no resistance. They sank to their knees, crying,

"Spare my life, prince!" Only one hundred escaped. For the rest, the Taipings boasted, "We killed them all to the infants in arms. We left not a root to sprout from." On March 23rd the Tartar women were locked in an empty building, prayers were said, and then it was fired. The men were marched to the execution ground, and the roots of their pigtails were examined. If the occiput was flat and Hun-shaped, the man was executed. If it was sharp, he was thought to be a Chinese and spared.

More than 20,000 human beings perished, and their bodies were thrown into the Yang-tze. Some of the corpses impeded the progress of the huge sacred Dragon Boat, a processional barge with an enormous gold figure-head of a dragon, which was bringing the T'ien Wang in state to what was henceforth to be his capital. As he stepped out on the landing stage and received the obeisances of his princes and officers, he cast a glance at the swollen human carcasses in the water. In his vision, Hung had been bidden to spare his brothers and sisters. Perhaps the demons he had been ordered to slay were those within himself. On the other hand, in fairness to him, he did no more than did the children of Israel when they slew the Amalekites and when Moses swore perpetual war against them in the name of the Lord.

Now that Nanking was in their hands, the Taipings were for the first time in contact with Christians, the one hundred and forty Catholics who were gathered in their chapel with the door, according to rebel regulations, wide open for inspection. For the first two days the rebels came in and out, doing no harm, except that one ignorant fellow, not yet understanding what were and what were not legitimate images, overturned the crucifix. On the third day an officer and platoon arrived, and demanded an explanation of the Catholic prayers. His comment was that the Catholic religion was good, but not entirely the same as that taught by the Commander-in-Chief, Yang. The officer promised to return. Meanwhile other bands of rebels came to have a look round. Some of them, probably the recently recruited Triads whose Christianity was still very superficial, were menacing, and one Taiping soldier broke the figure of Christ on the crucifix, which had been replaced on the altar. He threw it down, accused the cowering Chinese Catholics of being idolaters, and threatened to massacre them. The Catholics managed to send a message to a Taiping officer, who came by night with a lantern, and straightway promised to protect them. On his orders, placards were next day posted up to give the chapel full protection.

Meanwhile all over the city families were firing their houses over their own heads, as an honourable means of suicide, rather than submit to the family being broken up. For now the usual Taiping regulations were being enforced. Able-bodied men were being conscripted, adolescent boys taken away for training, and the women segregated into houses for females only. On March 25th, which was Good Friday, the two houses flanking the chapel were fired by their owners, and, as it was forbidden to issue into the street, the Christians nearly perished between the two blazing buildings. In the nick of time Taiping officers arrived to save them, but the Catholics were then accused of being the incendiaries, for which the penalty was death. The decapitation of a confessor was about to take place, when another officer arrived to intervene. The Christians were then trailed around from prison to prison all day, and one old man was brutally speared to death. They had been exhorted to recite the Taiping prayers, but had declared themselves ready to die as martyrs. Now, however, it was explained that the desired words, pai-siam, signified submission to the new government only, so they replied that as it was not a question of their faith they would submit. They were unbound, fêted and honoured, and taken back to the chapel. Because of the placard on the door, the Christian families of women and children were not split up, but the men were forcibly enrolled. On the whole, considering the barbarities going on around and the dangers of misunderstanding, this first meeting between Taipings and Catholics gave promise of future possibilities.

By shutting the females into the city, thus at once protecting their morals and making them hostages for their husbands, the Taipings were able to impress a further 100,000 soldiers and workers. The walls were repaired, and now an entirely new policy and strategy was adopted by the T'ien Wang. It proved disastrous, but it is doubtful whether Hung could have made any other decision.

Until then the objective had been Peking. As far as a punitive expedition was concerned, it was still the objective, but the T'ien Wang now decided that it was not to be his capital. The last Ming Emperors had ruled from Nanking. Perhaps he did not wish to choose a capital so near the frontier of Manchuria. For a

Manchu Emperor or for Kublai Khan it was a question of policy to be near the Tartar lands. But for a true Chinese Hung could argue that the greatest city of Central China was more suited. If so much was sound sense, it would nevertheless have been wiser to keep his armies together, and first possess himself of Peking before making a choice of capitals. His difficulty was that the veteran troops with which he had left Thistle Mount had in the space of twenty-seven months covered 1,400 miles, the distance from Paris to Moscow. Not only was there a need for consolidation of previous conquests—he had already taken the capital cities of four of the eighteen provinces—but psychologically the troops must be able now to feel that there was a stabilised centre, a home from which they could sally and to which they could return. He was henceforth the nominal ruler of 30,000,000 subjects, more than the entire population of the United States of America in that year. He had picked the richest and most populated provinces, but unless he consolidated his conquests, he would lose what he had gained, for in fact he held only the several keys of the main waterways.

Perhaps there was another reason which induced him to remain in Nanking, now renamed the Heavenly Capital. Perhaps his desire to identify himself with Ming traditions was urging him to wrap himself in the cocoon of a Ming emperor, as strong as silk itself, within the Imperial cell of a palace, isolated and waited upon by drones, the slave of ceremony, but still withal the master of the mystique which rules insect life.

His decision made, he divided his armies and sent them forth. Detailed to march on Peking were 75,000 men under the command of a certain Lin. On May 12th the Taipings landed on the north bank of the Yang-tze and defeated the Tartar regiments sent from the Forbidden City, and on June 19th they appeared before the capital of Ho-nan province, Kai-feng, which numbered a million inhabitants.

In Kai-feng existed the only Chinese community of Jews, who had arrived from Persia in the second century. They had failed to preserve any prophecies regarding an expected Messiah, but they kept the Sabbath, and at the autumn festival they carried the scrolls of the Law in procession round their twelfth-century synagogue. Perhaps in this hour of need they carried it in special procession, for they were praying that the long-haired rebels would not take the city. They knew nothing of the new dispensation of Christ, least of all how the Taipings were interpreting the Messiah's teaching.

Their prayers were answered, for the Taiping army abandoned the siege, and continued its march north. City after city fell, and in October they moved on to Tsing-hai. This last town lay only twenty miles south of the city of Tientsin, and Tientsin was both the inland port and the strategic key to Peking itself, which lay no more than a hundred miles further north. Panic spread in the Manchu capital. The Imperial generals either feigned sick, or rushed from the threatened areas on the excuse of recruiting, or reported false victories, or committed suicide. Disgusted and terrified, the Emperor gave orders that those remaining should "behead the offender with one hand, and write the report with the other".

A Censor exercised his privilege to memorialise the throne and criticise the administration, and by mistake his criticism was published in the Imperial Gazette, causing both scandal and despair. He described the state of Peking at that time. The Tartar garrison troops were not able-bodied. The sentries were shivering and ill-clothed, and their weapons useless. Taiping spies were already hiring houses in the capital. It was well known that the usual rebel tactics were for spies to take up positions near the gates both inside the city walls and on the side of the suburbs. Then a confusion was caused, a riot ensued, and before the authorities knew where they were the gates had been seized by an advance guard of rebels. The Peking court officials were inventing excuses to get away from the capital. Already 30,000 families of the rich had left. Nine-tenths of the houses were empty. There was no more employment for the poor. The destitute, issued with free cotton wadded garments, were selling them to pay their rents. If the poor were further neglected, the Censor warned, they would side with the rebels. Rice was scarce. Money was wanting. What even the Censor did not dare to say was that the Imperial family had packed their treasures and were ready to fly to the Emperor's hunting lodge in Tartary.

In his despair, Hsien Feng had called in 4,500 Mongols from beyond the great wall, a dangerous measure, as he knew, for thus had the Ming dynasty fallen by calling in the Tartars. Barbarians were more easily called in from Siberia than they could be expelled. But he trusted the man to whom he gave command of them, Senkolintsin, the son of a Mongol chief, who had been educated in Peking to be a lama priest. The Emperor had noted and advanced him, and had given him to wife a princess of the Imperial family.

Curiously enough, there was a prophecy amongst the Taipings that their empire would be endangered by a Buddhist priest. Anything less like a priest than the terrible Senkolintsin would have been hard to conceive. He swept down with his Mongol cavalry and his unwashed, raw-flesh-eating people, and behold! there were rank upon rank of them drawn up in squadrons, their eyes oblique beneath conical fur-edged hats, their loose coats belted over baggy trousers which disappeared at the knee into high boots, and they carried swords and lances, as well as bows and arrows slung across their backs, and rode their sturdy Siberian ponies like centaurs.

The Taipings had no cavalry, and now, caught between the Mongol squadrons and the Imperial troops which had been pursuing them from the south, they were repulsed. From Thistle Mount to Nanking had been a march as long as from Paris to Moscow, from Nanking north to Peking was equivalent to a further march from Moscow to the Urals, and they had very nearly accomplished it. Winter was coming on, and the Taipings now found themselves without sufficient clothing in the far north, and they were 950 miles from their base. Also the food was strange, and they missed their usual rice. In February 1854 they began a rearguard action, and though guerrilla warfare was carried on for another year until the death of the expedition's commander, Lin, the great chance of taking Peking in October 1853 had been lost by reason of the Mongol cavalry and the weather.

Hsien Feng breathed again. So did the Jews of Kai-feng, and while they repeated the Shema, "Hear oh Israel: the Lord our God is one Lord", the Heavenly King, the T'ien Wang, in his new palace at Nanking was reading in the Gospel of Mark, "And there came a voice from heaven saying, thou art my beloved Son, in whom I am well pleased". Hung had leisure again to make his own examinations into theology. Now neatly with his brush he wrote a marginal comment.

"It is God. He descended upon my Elder Brother, and led him away. How can it be that the Holy Spirit became my Brother's body? Christ plainly said, there is only one very God. How then did his disciples fall into the mistake of saying that Christ is God? If theirs is the correct explanation, why, there must be two Gods. It may be wrongfully explained by saying that Christ is God, and that on his ascent he was united with God. How is it that before the time of David my Elder Brother saw God, and that God spoke to him; how is it that when I went to heaven I saw that there were in heaven God the Father, and the Mother of Heaven, his wife, and Brother Christ? There was also my heavenly sister-in-law, who is now descended."

Who was this Bride of the Lamb? Hung continued with his careful calligraphy. "The kingdom of God the Father and the New Jerusalem which came down from heaven is fulfilled in the present celestial capital." For the moment Hung was satisfied to accept the Christian symbolism. "The New Jerusalem," he wrote, "is the present Nanking. God and Christ have descended to make us Lords, and open the lower celestial hall, so the heavenly hall of God is among men. The wife of the Lamb of God is my heavenly sister-in-law. Now this heavenly sister has also descended, and called me husband's brother."

No wonder that the Imperialists thought that the Taipings, with their acknowledgement of a Mother in Heaven, were a sect of Catholics. Meanwhile the Heavenly King set himself to bedeck the Bride of the Lamb and to make Nanking worthy to be the City of God. He was building a palace, whose roofs of green and yellow, between two minarets, were visible above an enclosing wall forty feet high. On this wall were hung, for the people to see, his religious proclamations written on yellow satin and signed with the Vermilion Brush. Within the palace, wooden columns with ornately carved capitals bore up rafters painted blue and red and gold. In the courtyards dwarf trees vied in beauty with flowering shrubs and flowers. In the outer courtyard were two vast gongs on which officers desiring audience must beat, and between them at the entrance door was a table, whereon petitions and memorials could be placed. From time to time women servants would come to fetch these, for there were no eunuchs to pass freely between palace and people.

When the T'ien Wang gave audience, he came to his throne not in a sedan, as did Hsien Feng, but in a sacred Dragon car pulled on wheels by his women servants. He wore a crown of gold on such occasions, a high Ming structure, surmounted by a fabulous bird in the true metal, and hung with pendant jewels. His necklace of heavy golden bosses was already spoken of by those who believed that there was much treasure hoarded in the city.

He did not build a temple, for of the New Jerusalem St. John had said, "And I saw no temple therein; for the Lord God Almighty and the Lamb are the temple of it". Liang Fa had said that a clean audience hall was all that was necessary. The gongs of the T'ien Wang's palace woke the people to prayer, and were repeated from house to house and from gong to gong, thrumming and humming throughout the city as the people knelt to pray in their own houses.

Only the princes and officers had homes, for most of the population was segregated, the men from the women, and lived in barracks or hostels. No shops or markets were allowed within the city walls for fear of spies entering. The keys of the city gates and of the T'ien Wang's palace were given into the charge of Kwangtung men only. The old janitor, who had nursed and dandled the sovereign as a child, sat now in the entrance way to the palace, for he was trustworthy. Hung had need of trusty men, for already faction was growing in the army: jealousy between Kwang-si men, led by Yang, and Hung's own Kwang-tung men. Hung had begun to be afraid of Yang's growing desire for power. Yet he was the most able of the generals. Hung had sent him not with the northern expedition to Peking, but west, back up the Yang-tze to consolidate previous conquests on the long route they had all travelled.

A long route indeed, and not only in leagues but in experience, thought Hung. He himself had come a very long way. Whence had he come? It was, he knew, the initiatory question of the Triads: "From where do you come?" And the answer was, "From the east, from the dawn, from the source of light." It was inconceivable that he had not existed before his birth at Hua. "Everyone born," he now wrote, "first receives the soul, and afterwards the body of flesh. The Lord of souls creates a soul, and then sends it into the mother to get a body put to it. The body is begotten of the mother, but the soul is of the Lord of souls."

Hung had been so much absorbed in the history of Israel that now he fell into the trap of those who study the past: the longing of the historian to help, to warn, even to share the burdens and certainly the glory of those in whose history he has steeped himself. Hung was seized with a desire to share in both the glory and the sufferings of the chosen people, the Jews, and in his writings now claimed to be the re-incarnation of Melchizedek. Christ's words, "Before Abraham was I am", were used to prove the pre-existence of souls, and Hung continued, "When I was in heaven at the time of Abraham, I have some recollection of knowing that the Father was about to send the Elder Brother to be born of the seed of Abraham. I therefore went down and blessed and saved Abraham." From St. John's revelation he went on to quote passages about the woman clothed with the sun and the great red dragon who sought to devour her son, and Hung took this to refer to his own present incarnation, for Shang-ti had especially sent him into the world to exterminate the demon Yen-lo. "Lo! The serpents and beasts are slain, and the empire enjoys Great Peace. It is fulfilled."

But Yen-lo was very far from being slain, and the Taiping empire was not at peace. The Prince of Darkness was on the contrary congratulating his black host that the T'ien Wang had been induced to shut himself in a palace like some ancient Taoist Emperor, isolated from his people and from the modern world, in an atmosphere where poetry and imagination could easily degenerate into fantasy. It was a pity, from Yen-lo's point of view, that Hung so often used his hours of loneliness to pray on his knees to Shang-ti. While that went on, anything might yet happen. As for the war, men were dying in their millions, but that did not necessarily give them into Satan's power.

In the same month that Lin had been detailed to march on Peking, Yang and Shih Ta-kai had gone west down the Yang-tze to retake all the cities and important strategic points which had been abandoned on the original march through. They retook An-king, capital of An-hui province, the spot on the serpentine waterway which Tseng Kuo-fan regarded as so vital. Then Tseng himself was defeated, and in a moment of despair he attempted suicide by throwing himself into the water, but his aides-de-camp held him back. He retreated to hold Chang-sha, and to learn to hold his own impatience. Henceforth his bull-dog qualities would rule him. He would never let go. In later years he was to write to his youngest brother, who had been rather a wild lad, but who was already serving under him, and would presently become his best general, about the need for patience and determination.

"The two great defeats you have sustained may be Heaven polishing its hero in preparation for a great advance. The proverb says, 'By each humiliation you endure, your knowledge is that much enlarged.' My greatest progress has been in the periods when I suffered defeat and shame. Under such circumstances one should grit his teeth, discipline his will, collect his spirit and stretch his wisdom—by no means must he faint and indulge himself."

Certainly Tseng was being "polished" by adversity. On June 26th 1853, the Taipings retook the Triple City (Han-kow). Yang, the Eastern Prince, was wounded in the neck and fell headlong, but he recovered, and it was the Imperial Governor's neck which suffered decapitation. The whole of the south bank of the Yang-tze was now in Taiping hands again. For the next decade battle was to be waged along these same arterial waterways and each town was to be taken and retaken a dozen times. Tseng, however, had conceived a general policy and strategy to which he was to stick like a limpet; and that was to retake and consolidate the west and drive the Taipings slowly eastward. The tactics of this ten year campaign are no longer of interest, but the situation in the vicinity of the coast vis-à-vis the Europeans can only be appreciated if it is remembered that, whatever new provinces the Taipings acquired in the east, Tseng was always slowly and steadily containing them from the west, rolling them up from the interior towards the sea.

In October of 1854 Tseng retook the Triple City, and the immediate effect of his temporary ascendant was that further Imperial troops were liberated to join in the so far half-hearted siege of Nanking, which had been going on in an ineffective manner ever since the T'ien Wang had established himself in his Heavenly Capital. On and off for ten years Nanking never ceased to be beleaguered, but for most of the time the Taipings could afford to laugh at the incompetence of the little force camped within sight of the walls, and their regiments could issue both in and out as they chose. Now, however, the investment of the city became temporarily more effective.

From the moment when the Taipings had first taken Nanking

their advance east had continued. The mouth of the Yang-tze was vital to trade, and on April 1st 1853, only twelve days after taking the Heavenly Capital, the Taiping fleet under Lo Ta-kang had captured the city of Chin-kiang on the south bank of the Yang-tze at its mouth; they held it for the next four years.

Refugees began to stream towards Shanghai, round the bend of the coast southwards. Something else was also streaming in that direction. Five hundred men were almost immediately employed by the T'ien Wang in Nanking to print Bibles from Gützlaff's translation, and if the printing was done on poor paper it was because they were being turned out in thousands. A proclamation was issued that henceforth in the Taiping empire the Bible would replace the Classics as a text-book for the civil service examination. This would mean that the entire literati of China would eventually be forced to be conversant with its teaching. Meanwhile the scriptures were put on rafts and were floated down to the Imperial camps in an effort to convert the enemy. The Tartar troops called them "goblin books".

Refugees carried rumours about these "goblin books" to Shanghai, for which they were making in the hope of finding asylum in the British and French concessions. The Foreign Devils would protect them! Anything foreign would protect them. The people even posted European newspapers on their doorposts in the hope of keeping out the brutal and licentious, whether Taiping or Imperialist soldiery (and of the two the Imperialists were thought to be the worst). There was panic in Shanghai.

The Imperial administration had done its best to conceal from the foreigners that the rebels claimed to be their co-religionists, but without success, thanks to Jen-kan and the "goblin books". The officials had jumped to the conclusion that the British and French might go to war to aid their fellow Christians, but it was a wrong conclusion. European powers of the nineteenth century did not go to war on such grounds. Moreover it was a civil war, and neither Britain nor France had the slightest desire to be embroiled. They hoped the upheaval in China's domestic household would quickly be put to rights one way or the other, so that trade might not suffer. It was a different matter, however, when the Imperialists swung round and jumped to yet another wrong conclusion, that the British might be inveigled into assisting them against the Taipings.

In the hopes of retaking the mouth of the Yang-tze, the Tao-t'ai at Shanghai had hired and fitted out a pirate fleet of lorchas, sailing vessels built to European designs by Portuguese or Chinese shipbuilders, as opposed to native junks. He had fitted them with foreign guns and manned them with Cantonese and Portuguese seamen, but the fleet had been defeated and wrecked by Lo Ta-kang. The Tao-t'ai now approached Consul Alcock and asked to hire Her Majesty's sloop *Lily* and British war steamers from Hong Kong. To help Imperial morale, his propaganda announced prematurely that the British Navy was coming to the rescue of the hard pressed Imperial forces.

All these last years Thomas Meadows, who had lately been transferred from the Canton to the Shanghai Consulate as interpreter, had been sending reports not of the religious characteristics of the insurgents, for of them he as yet knew nothing, but of the political situation caused by the rebellion. Britain was not taken off her guard, and had long ago decided to maintain strict neutrality in China's civil war. It became, therefore, urgent to counter the Imperialist propaganda, and not only to refute openly any suggestion of lending British ships, but to send a representative to the Taiping capital and make perfectly plain that Britain would remain neutral so long as she was not attacked.

Sir George Bonham, Governor of Hong Kong and British Plenipotentiary in China, had arrived at Shanghai in H.M.S. *Hermes* on March 21st, only two days after the fall of Nanking, ready to cope with the situation. News of the city's fall broke in Shanghai on April 5th, and on the 22nd H.M.S. *Hermes* left Shanghai with Sir George Bonham on board and with Thomas Meadows to act as his interpreter.

Since British Governors and Plenipotentiaries had to rely largely on their interpreters, it was a pity that there were not more men of the character of Meadows. He had first arrived at the Canton Consulate in 1842, having studied Chinese at Munich University, as well as having acquired a cosmopolitan education and outlook. Of Viking stock from Northumbria, over six feet tall and bearded, he was a giant of a man not only physically, but also mentally and spiritually. He alone of all his contemporaries was to have a clear vision of the future, not by virtue of any mystic powers, but because as a humanitarian he could appreciate the greatness of the Chinese people, and foresee an issue for them from their afflictions. Conversant with their Classics, able to appreciate a civilisation which went back four thousand years, he had a respect for this nation which the European merchants and missionaries of that era were often too ignorant to share. Moreover he kept touch not only with the literati but with the common folk, and his passion for duck-shooting and the possession of a boat led him many miles into the interior, whence he had been sending secret reports to Bonham concerning the advance of the Taipings.

Twelve miles below Chin-kiang, now held by the rebels, H.M.S. *Hermes* passed the new fleet of Portuguese-built lorchas which the Imperialists had hired. They had red flags almost indistinguishable from the British red ensign. Lo Ta-kang's batteries promptly opened fire on the lorchas, and included the *Hermes* amongst the targets. Captain Fishbourne, in command, refrained from returning the fire, and an explanatory note was sent ashore warning the Taipings of the British intention to proceed up river for purposes of friendly negotiation, and demanding that the Nanking batteries should not attack.

At Nanking, Meadows went ashore with letters giving notice of the British Plenipotentiary's arrival. He had with him a young naval lieutenant. They were conducted to a house outside the walls where a guard of honour flanked the entrance, and within were bidden to kneel before two dignitaries, clad in yellow silk and seated amongst many secretaries and retainers, who were standing. Tom bowed and uncovered, but refused to kneel. At first he was not offered a chair. On enquiry he was informed that he was in the presence of Wei, the Northern Prince, and of Shih Ta-kai, the Assistant Prince.

Wei cut short Meadows' preamble by enquiring whether he worshipped God the Father. Tom replied that the English had done so for eight or nine hundred years. The two princes nodded to each other in satisfaction, and Tom was then offered a chair. He began to explain that the British wished to remain neutral, and that the Imperial fleet of lorchas was not entitled to fly the red ensign. But the Taiping princes appeared far more anxious to discuss religion than military affairs. Were not both the Chinese and the British children of God, and therefore brothers? Had Meadows heard of the Heavenly Rules? Tom asked if there were ten in number, and then repeated the Commandments to Shih

Ta-kai's delight. God had helped the Taipings and therefore it would be wrong for the British to help the Manchus, and, what was more, it would be no use, for no one could fight against the Heavenly Father, affirmed the Prince.

Meadows then got around to explaining that Her Majesty's Plenipotentiary could not proceed to any meeting unless it were previously settled where, by whom, and how he was to be received.

"However high his rank may be," Wei calmly and proudly announced, "he cannot be so high as the persons in whose presence you are now sitting."

Tom was already forseeing that the Taipings were going to be just as difficult to deal with as the Manchus, who for three hundred years had kept up the pretence that China *was* the world. His enquiry as to who exactly Hung Hsiu-ch'uan was, and what position he occupied, confirmed his fears.

"He is the true Lord and sovereign," answered Wei. "The Lord of China is the Lord of the whole world. He is the second Son of God, and all people in the whole world must obey and follow him. He is your Lord also."

Fortunately Wei did not insist that Meadows should acquiesce in this statement. It was provisionally arranged that the Plenipotentiaries of Britain and Taipingdom should meet next day in an official yamen, and Meadows withdrew.

There was shortly sent aboard a document from the Taiping authorities, which had the immediate effect of postponing the meeting. It was headed "A Mandate", and began, "Commands are hereby issued to the brethren from afar that they may all understand the rules of ceremony. Whereas God, the Heavenly Father, has sent our Sovereign down on earth, as the true sovereign of all nations in the world, all people who wish to appear at his court must yield obedience to the rules of ceremony."

When Meadows submitted the full translation to his chief, Bonham frowned in irritation. Oh dear! Were they going to ask him to kow-tow? His frustration, and the grunts with which he now voiced his annoyance, were amply justified. For more than a hundred years Britain had been asking the Manchu Emperor to receive an ambassador, in the hopes that direct communication with the highest authority in the Forbidden City might circumvent the intrigues of the mandarins and bring about amicable

relations between the two nations. Court etiquette demanded that
a foreign envoy should kow-tow. This the British could not do.
Their refusal was not based on any foolish pride. They were
perfectly ready to kneel and put their heads three times to the
ground, if that was considered the courteous thing to do. But the
trouble was that the kow-tow was not just a courtesy: it had a
tremendous political significance. It was the acknowledgement
that the envoy so prostrating himself was the subject or vassal of
the Emperor of China, and that he was merely the representative
of a subject race bringing tribute. As the whole purpose of approaching the Emperor was to make him comprehend that
Britain, France and America were independent powers and of
equal importance in the world with China, the situation remained
at an impasse, for from the Emperor's point of view ceremony and
tradition forbade him to admit that he was not the sovereign of
the whole earth. As the British had refused to kow-tow to the
Manchu Emperor, they very certainly could not do so to any
rebel princelings.

Meadows was therefore instructed to return the "Mandate"
with a written message explaining Bonham's views on the full
national equality of the British with any and every State, together with a copy of the Treaty of Nanking, and an assurance
of British neutrality provided British property was not attacked.
He explained that he was unable to prevent the sale of vessels by
private owners to the Imperialists, but that British subjects had no
right to continue on board and would not be protected, and the
vessels would have no right to the national colours.

Meanwhile the Taipings were paying unofficial visits to
H.M.S. *Hermes*, and Captain Fishbourne was most impressed
with their bearing and behaviour. "In a manner quite unlike any
Chinese we had ever met," he wrote, "they at once met us on
the most friendly terms. The appearance and bearing of all these
men gave me the idea that they were clever, decided and determined; and from the constant solemn appeal to heaven to witness
their assertion, or in reference to their belief, they showed themselves to be under a settled conviction that their mission was from
thence." The ratings also took a liking for the Taipings, and
allowed them to swarm over the ship, and were astonished that
nothing was stolen, as would have been the case in Canton or
Shanghai.

On May 3rd there was received on board an answer from the
Taiping authorities inscribed on yellow silk. It caused consterna-
tion, and was apparently written at the direction of Yang, the
Eastern Prince, just before he left for his campaign in the interior, but it had no doubt been approved by the T'ien Wang,
himself. Long ago Hung, when first reading the tracts of Liang
Fa, had picked on those verses of the forty-fifth chapter of Isaiah,
"He shall build my city," and concerning the barbarians, "In
chains shall they come over, and they shall fall down unto thee".
Hung had taken them as referring to himself. And now he was
rebuilding Nanking, and here were the barbarians coming to
kow-tow all according to prophecy! In justice to Hung, his attitude was no different from that of the Manchu Emperor, who
equally hoped for submission from the Foreign Devils; but if
Hung had been able to free himself both from Imperial tradition
and from the misunderstanding of the scriptures, and to show a
new spirit and appreciation of international problems, the British
might have been so astounded and impressed that the course of
history might have been changed.

The document was headed "Of the Heavenly Kingdom of
Taiping—by true Divine Commission", and began—

"We hereby issue a decree to the English from afar, who have hitherto revered Heaven and have come to give in their allegiance to our
Sovereign. . . . The Great God, the Heavenly Father, the Supreme
Lord, in the beginning created, in six days, heaven and earth, land and
sea, men and things. . . . But from the time that evil spirits entered into
the hearts of men, they have not acknowledged the great grace of God,
the Heavenly Father, in giving and sustaining life, neither have they
acknowledged the great merit of Jesus, the Heavenly Elder Brother, in
the work of redemption; and they have caused lumps of clay, wood
and stone to do strange things in the world. Hence it was that the Tartars, the demon Huns, succeeded in thievishly possessing themselves of
our Heavenly country.

"But happily the Heavenly Father and Heavenly Brother have from
early times displayed divine manifestations among you English; and
you have long revered and worshipped God, the Heavenly Father, and
Jesus, the Heavenly Brother, so that the true doctrine has been preserved, and the gospel has had its guardians.

"Happily now again, the great God, the Heavenly Father, the Supreme Lord, has manifested his great grace. He sent angels to take the

Heavenly King, our Sovereign, up into heaven; and there personally gave him power to sweep away from the thirty-three heavens the evil spirits, whom he expelled from thence to below."

An account of the "descents" of Shang-ti and the Saviour followed, and of how God had aided "our Heavenly King in assuming the sovereignty of the world".

"Now since you English," the document went on, "have not held vast distances too far, but have come to acknowledge allegiance here, not only are the armies of our Heavenly Dynasty in great delight and joy, but in the high heavens even, the Heavenly Father and Heavenly Brother will also regard with pleasure this evidence of your loyalty and sincerity. We therefore issue this special decree, permitting you the English Chief, with the brethren under your superintendence, constant ingress and egress in full accordance with your own inclination and wish, whether to aid us in the extermination of the demons or to pursue as usual your commercial avocations. And it is our earnest hope that you will, with us, achieve the merit of diligently serving our Sovereign, and, with us, repay the goodness of the Father of souls.

"We now bestow upon you English the new Books of Declarations of the Taiping Dynasty, in order that the whole world may learn to serve and worship the Heavenly Father and Heavenly Brother, and also to know where the Heavenly King exists, so that all may offer their congratulations where the true commission to rule has fallen."

The Books of Declarations turned out to be most of Hung's compositions up to date: his essay on the original worship of Shang-ti in China; prayers of the Taiping liturgy; the Ten Commandments with Hung's comments and hymns; the new Three Character Classic; the Ode for Youth; the accounts of the "descents" of God the Father and Son; various proclamations; regulations for court etiquette; and the new calendar.

All these would take time to translate and analyse. The immediate task of Bonham was to disabuse the T'ien Wang of his idea that the British had come to pay allegiance, and then, having made plain the position, waste no more time but proceed down river and be ready if necessary to protect the foreign Concessions at Shanghai. Meadows therefore handed the answer to Lai-shi's cousin, Lai Wen-kuang, who was not next in rank to the highest princes. He had been coming aboard often to see Meadows, who found him a polite and courteous individual, and had bestowed on him a telescope, much to Lai's delight.

Bonham's answer was direct and uncompromising, as it had to be.

"I have received your communication, part of which I am unable to understand, and especially that portion which implies that the English are subordinate to your Sovereign. Owing to its contents, I am now compelled to remind you that my nation, by Treaty entered into with the Chinese government, has obtained the right of trading at the five ports of Canton, Fu-chou, Amoy, Ning-po, and Shanghai; and that if you or any other people presume to injure, in any manner, the persons or property of British subjects, immediate steps will be taken to . . ."

And here Bonham threatened to do to the Taipings what Pottinger had done to the Imperialists ten years ago, take Nanking with British guns.

On the way down the river, the Imperial lorchas used the *Hermes* as cover from behind which to fire at Lo Ta-kang's batteries, and she was slightly hit by the Taiping return fire. This time Captain Fishbourne replied in kind. There were letters of apology, and Meadows went ashore and met and spoke with Lo Ta-kang, who was wearing full dress of yellow and red uniform, and was then a man of about fifty, middle-sized and square, with a business-like and cheerful manner.

"The Tartars," the ex-pirate told him, "wish to set our two nations at variance, in order to avail themselves of any advantage arising therefrom. This, we presume, is already seen through by you."

A shrivelled elderly figure in a yellow and red hood then piped up. Meadows did not ascertain his name. "The Imperialists," this man said, "spread all kinds of lies about us. They say we employ magical arts. The only kind of magic we use is prayer to God." He recounted how the whole host had prayed at the time of the breakout from Yung-nan. "If it be the will of God," he went on, "that our Taiping King shall be the sovereign of China, he will be the sovereign of China. If not, then we will die here."

On the whole Meadows was very favourably impressed by the Taipings, and the only slight annoyance had been that medieval-minded document which presumed that the British were vassals of the T'ien Wang. But as the Manchu Emperor had equally fantastic ideas about being supreme, there was nothing in the Taiping attitude which time and experience might not cure.

16

ALMOST THE FIRST ACT of the T'ien Wang, when he had established himself in his Heavenly Capital, was to write and invite Mr. Issachar Roberts, for whom he had continued to hold the highest regard, to come to Nanking, and help the Heavenly King instruct his subjects.

"Though it is a long time since we parted," he wrote in May of 1853, "yet I constantly cherish a remembrance of you. Now that the grateful breezes of spring salute men, I, while distant, have thought of you, my venerated elder brother. . . . I have written you several times, but have yet received no answer to my letters."

Hung then went on to explain that so far, in the midst of war, he had had insufficient leisure to give the people full religious instruction, but had promulgated the Ten Commandments.

"Those who understand are not many. Therefore I deem it right to send," he went on, "and request you, my elder brother, if you are not disposed to abandon me, to come and bring with you many brethren. . . . So shall be obtained the true doctrine . . . wishing you happiness, your ignorant younger brother, Hung Hsiu-ch'uan, salutes you."

Roberts, writing to the local European newspapers, confessed that he could hardly call to mind the identity of the rebel chief. It was embarrassing to have to admit that he had so little memory of a man who was now become the subject of main concern to all the missionaries. Issachar immediately wrote to the American Commissioner for China, Mr. Humphrey Marshall, and asked permission to go to Nanking, "to assist that the gospel may be made plain". Marshall refused permission on the grounds that "such activity at this juncture would constitute the most powerful sort of un-neutral act", as he informed his government in June of that year. Marshall, a servant of the State, might have been able to justify his attitude, but why Issachar, a missionary, should have preferred to obey the Commissioner rather than his God was less understandable.

The great chance and the right moment were missed, for it was to be more than seven years before Roberts at last reached Nanking. In the interval the T'ien Wang proceeded to promulgate his own weird theological doctrines, and was in the end to prove too proud to retract his *ex cathedra* pronouncements. But Hung was not proud in this year of 1853 when he wrote an appeal to his "venerated elder brother" for help.

On the return of H.M.S. *Hermes*, the Taiping Declarations were handed to the Reverend Dr. Medhurst for translation and analysis of the religious views contained therein.

On May 23rd the Bishop of Victoria in Hong Kong wrote to the Archbishop of Canterbury, "In the event of ultimate success, they may, if more perfectly instructed, become the pioneers of the pure gospel of Christ, or, if neglected, they may degenerate into the most ignorant of mere fanatics and iconoclasts."

On May 6th the Reverend W. Milne of the London Missionary Society had written to his brother, "The Imperialists may ultimately overwhelm the insurgents by multitude, but at present the skill and courage of the latter form a striking contrast to the want of discipline of the former." Then he proceeded to analyse the Taiping Declarations, and went on, "Yet it must not be concealed that, with all the elements of good they seem to have extant among their institutions, there are certainly exceedingly obnoxious and pernicious features. The Emperor gives out (in the Three Character Classic above named) that he himself is a son of God, and a brother of Jesus." Milne was shocked that the Taiping Emperor "professes to receive continuous revelations from God". And the polygamy indulged in by the princes—"the people make no concealment that the Emperor has thirty-six wives"—made the missionary warn his brother and the Missionary Board not to be carried away by semblance of good "mixed up with much that is presumptuous and criminal".

Sir George Bonham himself was very sceptical, and thought that the Taiping religion had only one purpose, "to sway the minds of those whom they are anxious to attach to their cause".

In his despatch to Lord Clarendon at the Foreign Office he wrote, "Few will be prepared for so extraordinary a sect, and for tenets so absurd, intermingled as they are with Christian principles". Bonham's view that the Taipings' profession of the Faith was only a means to wheedle guns from the British proved to be false, for the T'ien Wang was losing far more important allies than he could ever hope to gain: the entire class of Chinese literati and many of the Triads. In 1854 alone, a body of 2,000 Triads coming up from Kwang-si to join the Taipings went over to the side of the Imperialists rather than be compelled to accept Christianity. Many of the Chinese literati set their faces against Christianity because it was imported along with opium, and thought to be equally pernicious. The great and wealthy British opium merchants in Shanghai, for their part, would hear no good of the Taipings, for the T'ien Wang had forbidden the smoking of opium on pain of death. These merchant princes in Shanghai and Canton could bring heavy pressure to bear on the British administration in the Concessions.

After reading Medhurst's translations of the Taiping Declarations, the Bishop of Victoria wrote to Sir George Bonham, "Do the elements of truth preponderate over error? Are the defects the work of Satanic power, or the natural shortcomings of men without instructors and guides, having their minds distracted amid the arduous toil of campaign? We do not hesitate to assert that ours is the latter and more favourable view."

The translator, Dr. Medhurst, reported that, "The first extravagant idea which seems to have occurred to the mind of the chief is to imagine himself in a peculiar sense the Son of God. His visions were the product of a diseased brain." To his brother, however, he wrote in a more hopeful vein, regarding the T'ien Wang's promise to make the Bible the text book for all future Chinese examinations. "If this project be carried through, we may anticipate that Christ will supplant Confucius."

As yet the missionaries had no documents from which to deduce that the T'ien Wang was what is technically known as an Arian heretic, that is to say, one who believes that Christ is only the firstborn of God's creatures and not co-equal, co-eternal, uncreated; a heresy long ago rejected by the Roman, Greek, English and indeed all established churches. Hung's verses on the Atonement, and his references to his Heavenly Elder Brother, gave no

indication of this, and were both beautiful and theologically un-
assailable. The missionaries therefore had good cause for hope, and
there was no reason to fear that their governments would hinder
the spread of the Taiping dominions, for the Western Powers
were determined to remain neutral, or so it seemed.

This determination was to be somewhat weakened in the next
eighteen months by the behaviour of the Triad rebels acting in-
dependently of the Taiping Emperor. Three out of the five
European treaty ports were seized or threatened by the Triads.
On May 18th 1853 they captured Amoy and held it for five
months, and on September 7th of the same year they seized
Shanghai and held it for eighteen months. Such seizures concerned the walled Chinese city only, which a neutral power had
no right to defend. The foreign Concessions always lay outside
the walls of the Chinese city, and these could be legitimately
defended by the neutral powers owning them. But in the case of
Shanghai, and nearly all the other open ports, the Concessions lay
immediately next to the city walls, and it was a problem in
practical tactics how to defend the one without the other. The
effect of allowing the Triads to take the walled city of Shanghai
was to make the Europeans feel "jumpy" about all rebels, for the
Triads were not Christian and not disciplined, and the Europeans
had to live in close proximity to them for a considerable period,
so that afterwards they felt less inclined to be sympathetic to the
Taiping rebels. The leader of the Shanghai Triads called himself
a "Generalissimo under the great Ming dynasty" and sent in his
allegiance to the T'ien Wang, but, because the Shanghai Triads
would not conform to his discipline or to Christianity, the Taiping
Emperor refused to accept their allegiance or to send them help.

All the missionaries were by now aware of the difference between the Taipings and the Triads, but the latter did no harm to
the teachers of Christianity. They set guards to protect foreign
property, and generally behaved fairly well. Then the Imperialists
arrived to invest the city, and the situation grew more dangerous
for those living near the walls. In December 1854 the French
Admiral Laguerre ordered a Triad battery to be dismantled, as the
crossfire was endangering French houses. The Triads refused, a
rumpus started, and the French joined the Imperialists in assault-
ing the city. The Triads cut their way out, and the Imperialists
sacked Shanghai. The wretched populace complained that "the

rebels were bad, but these are worse". The atrocities committed
and the executions carried out by the Imperial troops were beyond
belief. The effect of the Triad revolt in Shanghai was therefore
threefold: first, the Europeans had been made to feel nervous
about the close proximity to "rebels" in general; secondly, the
revolting executions to which they were daily witness made them
long for the civil war to be ended, no matter who was the winner;
and thirdly, the French got a name for having acted in a non-
neutral manner, and for being generally anti-rebel and pro-
Imperialist. This last effect was to make the task of the French
Jesuits more difficult in years to come when they had to do with
the Taipings.

As for Canton, the third of the five European Treaty ports
affected, the Triad rebellion had been going on ever since the
first rising in favour of Celestial Virtue. The Triads had never
actually managed to seize the walled city, but it was now closely
invested by land and blockaded by Triad pirates from the sea,
and the whole province of Kwang-tung was in rebel hands. In
1854 Yeh, the Viceroy, appealed to the British authorities to raise
the blockade, and the new Governor of Hong Kong, Sir John
Bowring, was unwise enough to acquiesce and lend British ships,
ostensibly against pirates, thus covering himself from breaking
the declared policy of neutrality in the civil war.

With new supplies Yeh was able to turn against the Triad rebels,
and presently made open boast that in the space of six months
he had decapitated 70,000 insurgents, men and women. There
were not enough baskets in which to send the heads to Yeh's
yamen to be counted, so he gave orders that only right ears need
be sent. Innocent men and women were executed to make up the
required number, and high pavilions were erected to allow those
who preferred to confess guilt, and thus save their families, to
commit suicide by jumping from them. Altogether, before Yeh's
career came to an end, one million people perished in Kwang-tung
province alone at his hands.

The Europeans came quickly to realise that there was no cohesive factor among the Triads, and that their rebellions were
sporadic and would have little bearing on the future history of
China. From the first it was apparent that the Taiping empire
established at Nanking was on the contrary a very different matter, and that the T'ien Wang might well possess himself of the

Dragon Throne and found a new dynasty. Not only were his troops disciplined, but he had proved himself a brilliant strategist, and was continuing so to prove himself, because, although he had adopted the usual Imperial custom of immuring himself in a palace, he was personally directing his armies from it with considerable skill. Moreover, his own person provided the cohesive factor. The mystique of the Elect of Heaven was as effective as ever, perhaps even more so now that it issued from behind mysterious palace walls, wherein he dwelt remote.

To find out more about these Taipings, while remaining neutral, became therefore an urgent necessity; and in November 1853, only a few months after the return of H.M.S. *Hermes*, and while Shanghai city was still in possession of the Triads, it was the turn of the French Minister to take a ship, the *Cassini*, up to Nanking.

France's trade interests in China were small compared with Britain's, but her prestige vis-à-vis the Taipings was more at stake, for the Jesuit mission and nearly all the Catholic missions in China were being heavily financed by French money, and the new French Empire of the latest Napoleon was looking forward to the honour and glory of converting the whole Chinese people.

Until the fall of Nanking, the Catholic priests had kept away from the rebels, fearing to be implicated and accused by the Imperialists of having instigated the rebellion, in which case Chinese Catholics would have been sought out and persecuted by the Manchu officials. As soon as it was known, however, that more than a hundred Chinese Catholics were inside the fallen city, the Jesuits—the Society of Jesus was responsible in the provinces affected—tried to get through the Imperial lines to succour their flock. On August 15th 1853 Father Brueyre and Father Nicholas Massa, dressed as Chinese and carrying recommendations from the French Minister for their safety, got as far as Chin-kiang, where Lo Ta-kang was commanding the mouth of the Yang-tze, but were held up by the Imperial troops besieging the city. Courteously, with much drinking of tea, and endless prevarication, and the usual Chinese delaying tactics, the Imperial officials firmly ordered them back to Shanghai, and indeed provided "escorts", a polite euphemism for armed guards, to take them there.

On August 28th Father Languillat wrote from the Jesuit college outside Shanghai to Father Broullion, sending him a copy of Hung's Three Character Classic, in which he found everything

orthodox à peu près as far as the history of the Creation, the giving
of the Law, and the Redemption were concerned. As for the
visions of Hung himself and his mission, he left Father Broullion
to make what he could of it, and suggested that the only means of
knowing more was to go and find out.

Eventually it was Father Clavelin who was chosen to accompany the French Minister, Monsieur de Bourboulon, on the
voyage of the Cassini to Nanking, and he duly sent his report to
Father Languillat on January 6th 1854, when he returned.

As had happened to the Hermes, the Cassini was fired on once
as it approached the Nanking batteries, since it was taken for an
Imperial vessel, but an officer in a small boat soon came alongside
with an apology. Father Clavelin was impressed by his polite and
honest bearing. On December 7th the priest went ashore with the
Legation Secretary, who was to make arrangements for the Min
ister to meet a high Taiping authority. They went on horseback
as far as the city walls, and there was considerable delay at the gate
by which they had chosen to enter, so that Father Clavelin had
time to look about him. The people passing to and fro were well-
dressed, and silk and satin were quite common. The crowd was
curious but not hostile. Amongst them the priest noticed a young
man who was trying to catch his attention, and the man now
surreptitiously displayed a rosary and a medal. While the French
Secretary negotiated for passports and escorts, the priest held a
hurried and whispered conversation with the owner of the rosary,
and ascertained that the Catholic Christians were all safe, and had
not been persecuted.

The conversation had to be broken off, as now the Legation
Secretary was ready to pass within the tunnel of the gateway. As
they rode through the city, the priest remarked the fact that there
were no beggars, nor any shops. The women were richly dressed
and all had unbound feet, and the streets were full of the adolescent boys which it was the usual Taiping custom to impress into
the army as squires, loaders and runners.

The French Secretary's request for an interview between his
chief and the highest Taiping authorities was immediately
granted, and on December 10th Monsieur de Bourboulon was
received in audience by one of the highest ministers of state, by
name Tchen, who wore blue satin with a red surcoat and a diadem
of gilded lacquer, and was seated under a rich parasol.

Father Clavelin's comment was that the French Minister could there and then have been received in audience by the Taiping Emperor himself, if de Bourboulon had been willing to recognise the T'ien Wang as the legitimate sovereign of China, and to sign a treaty with him. In the hopes of effecting such a treaty, the Taipings pressed the party to stay the night in the city, but only Father Clavelin and his catechist accepted, and it was to be an uncomfortable evening. The supper and the furnishings were both excellent, but de Bourboulon had been firm in stating France's declared policy of neutrality, and now the priest had to bear the brunt of the Taipings' disappointment, wrath and suspicion. He was sent for by Houan, one of the ministers he had already met. Why was France allied by treaty with the demon Tartars, he was asked? Why had the French come to Nanking, if they were not willing to aid the T'ien Wang? Were they spies come to spy out the land and report to the Imperialists? Houan threatened to cut off Father Clavelin's head in his determination to find the truth.

The Taiping Minister's enquiries were justified, for the very day before an Imperial spy had come aboard *Cassini* in Taiping uniform. He had then unwound his turban to disclose his Tartar pigtail, and handed to the French Secretary the visiting card of the Imperial general, with a message soliciting the aid of the French against the Taipings. He had been informed that the French were not come either to attack or to defend Nanking, but only to find out if the Christians were being persecuted. It was difficult to get any of the Chinese to understand the Europeans' desire for neutrality, since the Taipings were expecting aid from their co-religionists, and the Imperial officials expected the Foreign Devils to uphold the authority under which they had been granted concessions at the open ports.

Father Clavelin was fairly sure that the threats to his head were mere bluff to elicit the truth of France's intentions. He suggested with the utmost calmness that de Bourboulon must be sent for to answer such questions, since politics did not concern a priest. His bluff having been called, the Taiping chief invited the Jesuit to share a collation with him, and the evening finished amicably.

On the next day Clavelin was able to have a long talk with the secretary of the Minister Tchen on matters of religion. "Be on your guard," this member of the literati told the priest, "and do

not take for granted as true everything you may hear from the
ordinary men in the street. They are no doubt of honest intentions,
but are ignorant, and have been serving under the Taiping banner
for less than a year. Moreover, as they are always campaigning it
is not astonishing that they are not *au fait* with their religion. They
know the principle dogmas of the Law. They believe in one God
in three persons, in the Creation, the Incarnation, and the Redemption; in heaven and in hell; and they know that they must pray to
Shang-ti. But do not ask more of them for the moment."

"And Hung Hsiu-ch'uan?" the priest asked. "Do you really believe, as is printed in your books, that he is the Son of God, the
younger brother of Jesus?"

"No," replied the Taiping scribe. "God being a pure spirit could
have neither wife nor children after the fashion of men. Only we
believe that just as God himself sent Jesus Christ, his Son, down
to earth to save mankind, so also he has commissioned Hung Hsiu-
ch'uan to extirpate idolatry from the earth. The simple people,
even some of the chiefs, do, I know, attribute to Hung's mission a
more extraordinary and exalted character than this, but, as such a
belief strengthens their confidence in the cause, Hung Hsiu-
ch'uan has not yet thought it necessary to explain the matter more
clearly."

Father Clavelin here reflected that the words father and son
had a much more variable significance in Chinese than in the
French language, and that the Taiping Emperor's claim to be a
son of God might not be so presumptuous as it had first sounded.
"And the revelations of which your books speak," he asked next,
"what are they? Is one to believe that the Heavenly Father showed
himself so unreservedly to Hung Hsiu-ch'uan?"

"Hung is a very religious man," the Taiping secretary replied,
"who loves to meditate, and to consult Heaven, especially when
he finds himself in difficulties. Then he retires to be entirely alone
and to meditate what he ought to do. After he has prayed by
himself, he says always, 'This is what Heaven inspires', or else,
'Behold, this is what the Heavenly Father and Jesus have come to
tell me'. And as in fact the action thus proposed has invariably
been successful, it is not astonishing that the ignorant masses believe that he holds actual interviews with the Heavenly Father."

Father Clavelin next asked if the Taipings honoured the Holy
Mother, as Chinese Catholics were accustomed to call the Blessed

Virgin. He was not immediately understood. "The mother of Jesus," he repeated.

"Yes," the secretary answered, nodding to show that he had understood, "we call her the Venerable Matron." But he did not know that her name was Mary. Time was needed, he said, before doctrine and printing could be clarified and perfected, and he pleaded for patience and understanding. On being questioned about certain references to a heavenly sister as well as a heavenly mother, he explained that the real sense was not that the Heavenly Father and Heavenly Elder Brother both had wives, but that in heaven all would be brothers and sisters.

The evening was drawing in, and the secretary now bade the priest good night, and took with him to bed for further study the Catholic books of instruction with which the Father had presented him. The next morning he enquired who and what was a Pope, and, on being informed, he said Hung Hsiu-ch'uan planned to destroy idolatry first in China and then in the neighbouring kingdoms. Afterwards he intended to go to Europe to visit his brother Christians, worshippers like himself of one God. Then only would he explain himself fully and categorically, and would settle all these points.

From the same informant Father Clavelin learnt the story of how Feng had found the Catholic manuscripts promised to Hung in vision.

"One cannot deny," ran Father Clavelin's report, "that there is something in their relationships with each other which justifies these long-haired rebels calling each other brothers. They give the impression of being of one family." He was favourably impressed also by their community life and common treasury, which supplied clothing and food, and made shops within the city unnecessary. "As for us, we were fed on simple food, it is true, but plentifully, and as guests to be honoured. Several times the secretaries and scribes had meals with us. Before and after each meal they said a prayer to the Heavenly Father, while we said our benediction and graces. Twice a day they make their prayers to Shang-ti either in a hall or big chamber. The firing of ten cannon shots gives notice when the Heavenly King is at prayer. For our part we were allowed to pursue our spiritual exercises in the midst of them with complete liberty."

Clavelin next interrogated another member of the literati on how the Taipings treated those who would not pray with them. The scribe answered, "Those who will neither pray nor renounce their idols are put to death. Those who believe in nothing and pray to no one we leave alone, except for an occasional bambooing. If any such massed together in a real anti-religious movement, they would be put to death."

Father Clavelin was then acute enough to tackle the man on the really burning question. Would it not be better, the priest suggested, since the Taipings spoke so much of brotherhood, to exhort and admonish rather than to kill? To strengthen the bond of family union rather than break it, as he had seen was being done? To spare at least the Tartar women and children?

Denaturalized children of the Heavenly Father could not be treated as brothers, was the answer. As for the camps and hostels for women, they were only a temporary expedient.

Altogether Father Clavelin spent two days and nights as guest of the rebels, and the last night must have been the most difficult and certainly the most consequential of his life, for he had been invited to remain permanently in Nanking, where he would have been able perhaps to convert the entire rebel host to Catholicism. In a bedchamber where the lamplight flickered on the red and blue and gilded rafters and on the satin hangings of a chief's bed vacated in his honour, the Jesuit priest rose from saying his office to pace sadly up and down. The northern army of the Taipings was almost at the gates of Peking, and he believed the Manchu dynasty might fall. He was impressed by the confidence of Hung in his mission, the firm and regular administration and the good discipline of the rebels. If the Taiping army failed to take Peking, it would return south, and then he foresaw (quite correctly) that civil war would continue "eternally". If the Taipings did win, what would be the function of the Catholic priests? Hung with his mission and his harem was not unlike Mahomet, but then, as the Jesuit Father reminded himself, Mahommedanism did have certain resemblances to Christianity. The field was open to the Catholics. There were no Protestant missionaries in Nanking.

From time to time he sank to his knees, and gave himself once again to prayer in this moment of difficult decision. If the present dynasty of Manchu Emperors prevailed, and the *status quo* was maintained, then the Imperialists would in future mistrust Christianity as identical with the religion of their mortal enemies.

Next day Father Clavelin was aboard the *Cassini* writing his report to his superior to explain why he had left Nanking. "Would it not be possible to give the rebels a certain direction, in a word to Catholicise them? That is no doubt the dream of more than one missionary. You will say I have a splendid opportunity, why let it escape? Why not stay at Nanking? Reverend Father, when a sword is suspended over one's head like another sword of Damocles, I mean the fear of ruining everything by taking such a decision, how would you have me resolve to take it? In the opinion of the best informed people I have consulted, to stay among the long-haired rebels is to make myself party to the rebellion, and to break openly with the Imperialists. In the hope of a success which is still very uncertain, I should expose to certain danger nine-tenths of our Christians. It would be to sacrifice all our other missions who would blame their miseries on our imprudence and temerity."

In the next ten years there would be no good opportunity for Catholic priests to return to Nanking, because the future politics of the French compromised their position. Had Father Clavelin been able to foresee this, he might have stayed. Had he been able to foresee that the Manchu dynasty, tottering as it was, was bound in any case to fall, that it was not a choice between Manchus and Taipings but between Taipings and Communism, he almost certainly would have reversed his decision. For the Catholic Christians—and there were not more than 300,000 in Clavelin's day—would in any case suffer, and the chance that Hung might have fulfilled his appointed destiny, and become not only the acknowledged Emperor but a Catholic, was extremely good at the time. Mercifully the Jesuit priest was not aware of the full import of his decision, and God does not, it is to be trusted, expect men to have prophetic powers. Clavelin felt that his first duty was to protect the flock of existing converts, and his decision was perhaps justifiable.

The Protestants, however, had no flock in the interior, and therefore had a free hand to act with no hostages to fortune. As to why they remained inactive for the next six years, the answer lies in the fact that now a series of palace intrigues began in Nanking, and terminated in a typical "Kremlin purge" in 1856, leaving the Europeans gasping at the scandals, unable to ascertain exactly what was taking place behind the Taiping "satin curtain", and dubious as to whether the rebels' profession of Christianity was not just a blasphemous piece of nonsense.

Scandals began almost as soon as the *Cassini* left Nanking. To begin with, the French officers, true to form, had collected any news they could about life in the harems. The T'ien Wang had far more than thirty-six wives! At least, there were hundreds of women in his palace, and they were presumably his wives. And Yang, the Eastern Prince, was also a terrible Turk with the females, and had almost as many concubines as Hung. Young virgins, of course, wrested from their families, and sobbing. The French enjoyed themselves a lot discussing it all, and even Father Clavelin was led to believe in the stories of Christian virgins facing worse than death. But the Imperial clansmen could have told them that often their own Tartar daughters had been known to commit suicide rather than be forced to enter the harem of the Manchu Emperor, not because they feared a fate worse than death, but on the contrary because they could not face a life of perpetually disappointed virginity. Grandeur demanded that Eastern potentates should keep a large harem of marriageable and well-born females, and domestic comfort demanded a vast army of housemaids, but rarely did an Emperor or Turkish Sultan distribute his favours to more than a few women. Hung's actual number of wives at the time of his death proved to be eighty-eight, which, compared with Solomon or the Grand Turk, was a modest number.

The American Commissioner, Mr. Robert McLane, aboard the U.S. frigate *Susquehanna*, visited Nanking in May of 1854 to explain America's position of neutrality, and took with him the Reverend Dr. Bridgeman to observe Taiping religious customs. McLane was irritated, as Bonham had been, to find that America was classed as a "tribute-bearing nation", and like Bonham was sceptical about the genuineness of the Taipings' profession of Christianity, though Bridgeman found some of them very reverent and devout, while others were quite the reverse. Dr. Bridgeman was correct in this observation. Had the missionaries not understood that if Shang-ti had indeed commissioned Hung, then Yen-lo would be hard at work?

The Prince of Darkness had certainly been very busy, and some of his earnest endeavours at corruption were at last bearing beautifully worm-eaten fruit. First he had got rid of Clavelin by confusing the priest's sense of duty, and now he was about to scare away the Protestant missionaries by outraging their Victorian ideas of what was proper. They were brave and ready to suffer martyrdom, so to frighten them Yen-lo needed something very unsavoury: sex, blasphemy and mass murder, a combination nicely calculated to make them draw in their surplices from contamination.

17

ALL THAT IS KNOWN of the palace scandals which so shocked the missionaries is contained in a certain document printed by the appropriate officials in Nanking. As far as the Europeans could make out from this source, the drama had opened with Wei, the Northern Prince, conducting the person of Yang to the sovereign's palace. Yang, in a state of trance and speaking as God the Father, had thereupon reproved Hung Hsiu-ch'uan for kicking a pregnant concubine, and particularly for wearing his boots when administering the kick. Far from resenting Yang's part in the proceedings, the sovereign had replied by according him the title of the Comforter, and he was also apparently to be acclaimed as the Holy Spirit—though in fact this title was never granted to him. The whole unsavoury episode was then made public in this printed proclamation, ostensibly to advertise the miracle of the Heavenly Father's descent.

No wonder the missionaries turned cold and shuddered! In the name of all that was depraved, they asked, just what Satanic powers were involved? Nevertheless some Europeans did wonder why, if the sovereign had suffered such humiliation, he should choose to publish it to the world. The inner history of a Kremlin purge is never easy to disentangle, and the Victorians had little experience to guide their attempt.

The Taipings were becoming divided by dissension and factions. There had always been a slight jealousy between Hung's Kwang-tung men and the Kwang-si men of Yang. There was also great rivalry for honours and power between Yang and Wei. There was yet a further division—the difference between the veterans, the original God-worshippers, who had a genuine belief in Shang-ti and the Heavenly Elder Brother, and the newly conscripted recruits, who had had no time and possibly no inclination to study the gospel teaching. If the Taiping sovereign could establish himself on the Dragon Throne within the next year or two, all might be well; but if the civil war dragged on, then gradually the veterans would be killed off, and each new band of conscripts would further corrupt both the discipline and the religion of the rebels.

Yang was not only Commander-in-Chief: he was by far the best general in the army. He was probably loyal to Hung, his own brother-in-law, and therefore would stand in the way of the Northern Prince's conspiracy to seize sole power. Wei must therefore lead Hung to believe that it was Yang who threatened his throne, and then the enraged sovereign would liquidate the Eastern Prince, thereby leaving himself defenceless against his real enemy, Wei.

Only by supposing that Wei used hypnotic powers to direct the Eastern Prince is it possible to reconstruct the character of Yang as a feasible whole—volatile and vulnerable, but orginally the recipient of the gift of tongues. On the assumption that Wei did have some such hold over the psyche of the Eastern Prince, then what actually seems to have happened was this. According to the published account, on December 25th 1853, a Sabbath, Wei visited the Eastern Prince and spent the evening with him, and it can be presumed that he used his hypnotic powers during their hours alone together. Wei then withdrew, but was almost immediately recalled to Yang's palace by a message which informed him that the Eastern Prince was speaking in trance as the Heavenly Father, and commanded Wei to conduct him to the sovereign's palace. This Wei promptly did.

Hung was warned that the mouthpiece of Shang-ti was on his way, and he came out to meet Yang's sedan at the palace gate, receiving the representative of Heaven upon his knees. When the Eastern Prince began to speak, it was clear that he had no knowledge of the words he was uttering, and was in deepest trance. This was where Wei had made one bad miscalculation in his plotting: far from resenting reproof and punishing Yang for the ac-

cusation which now came from his mouth, Hung welcomed the
advent of the miraculous even at the cost of his dignity, for there
had been no such manifestation since the occasion at Yung-nan. He
was not, therefore, angered by Yang's opening words.

"You are very much at fault. Are you aware of it?"

Hung's conscience was probably clear of any particular crime,
but he was willing to admit that all men were sinners, and so he
replied, "Your unworthy son knows that he is at fault, and begs
the Heavenly Father graciously to forgive him."

No specific crime was mentioned by the mouthpiece of Shang-
ti, but Hung was ordered to receive forty blows. The T'ien Wang
must have been utterly taken aback. It was the cunning Wei who
now pleaded for a remission of sentence, but Hung, gathering his
wits, had decided that humility can never threaten a man's position so dangerously as pride can threaten his soul. He was willing
to submit himself. "Your unworthy son will comply with your
requisition," was what he said. The mouthpiece of Shang-ti acceded, however, to Wei's request for mercy. His last solemn words
to Hung were an exhortation to be henceforward counselled by
Yang, because, said Shang-ti, "I shall now go back to heaven".

Wei then took the Eastern Prince home. On the way he informed the bewildered automaton, now restored to himself, that
his lips had been used by Shang-ti, who had descended. "Has he
indeed!" was Yang's recorded comment. "Truly he gives himself
a great deal of trouble on our account."

It seems fairly certain that Wei now gave Yang exact instructions on how he was to counsel the sovereign. While the Eastern
Prince returned to the palace for this purpose, Wei went off to see
to the printing of the official account of the affair—which, as has
been said, was published ostensibly to advertise the miraculous
descent of God, but really to lower the prestige of the T'ien Wang.

Meanwhile Yang was repeating to Hung the reproaches with
which he had been primed by Wei, who had no doubt carefully
chosen them as calculated to rile Hung beyond all bearing. These
reproaches—which Yang believed to be the same as those he had
already uttered in trance—were the accusations of brutality in the
harem which were subsequently made public in the official document.

What was the truth of the affair? Had Hung merely lost his
temper with a housemaid over some minor misdemeanour? He

was known to be irritable with stupid and slow-witted persons. Or had he indeed assaulted one of his pregnant concubines in a loathsome fashion—kicking her with his boots on? The picture published by his enemies does not at all fit with that given to Father Clavelin of the man who constantly withdrew to pray alone to the Heavenly Father. Amidst the intrigues and the obvious plotting to seize his throne, which was presently to become manifest, it seems fair to give Hung the benefit of the doubt. That there was not a shred of truth in the slander is, moreover, suggested by the fact that Hung immediately raised Yang in rank and accorded him fresh titles of honour. Thus it seems that he must have realised that Wei was plotting against him, and was endeavouring to secure Yang's loyalty. The publication of the account under the borrowing of his own seal may have opened his eyes to where the real danger lay. It is possible that he was being held powerless and a prisoner in his own palace. The mystery remains unsolved, but the titles he accorded Yang gave the Devil cause for joy.

The missionaries, following Dr. Morrison's translation of the New Testament, added *shen* (spirit) to *sheng* (holy), and with *feng* (wind) produced a compound *Sheng-shen-feng* for the Holy Ghost. The titles now granted to Yang appeared blasphemous only because the missionaries had not yet understood that Hung was an Arian heretic. His comment to the third chapter of St. John's Gospel, "God alone is most high. Christ is God's first born", was unknown to them. Since God alone was most high, and Christ was his firstborn son, a mere prophet, then it followed that the Comforter, whom Christ promised that he would pray the Father to send, would also be a man, a man who "shall testify of me. And ye also shall bear witness, because ye have been with me from the beginning." These words of Christ from St. John's Gospel were taken by Hung to mean that all men had existed from the beginning with Christ, but particularly were the words addressed to Hung Hsiu-ch'uan. There were to be three persons, therefore, specially involved in the setting up of the Celestial Kingdom of China—Christ, Hung himself, and this promised Comforter. He had no conception of the triune nature of the Godhead, only of three men associated as brothers-in-arms. "Christ plainly said," wrote Hung, "that there is only one very God. How then did his disciples fall into the mistake of saying that Christ is God?"

In Hung's mind there was therefore nothing blasphemous in supposing that the third man, the promised Comforter, who was to complete this trinity of brothers, was that very man who had helped him to set up the Kingdom of Great Peace—the Commander-in-Chief of the armies, Yang.

"The Eastern Prince is the beloved son of God," he began to write, as he sat at his Imperial writing desk in the palace. He paused, stroking the beard which he had lately grown, and which was now black and bushy. Then he gripped his brush for a finer calligraphy, and began again. "The Elder Brother, myself, and the Eastern Prince, before the heavens and earth, were, by the favour of the Heavenly Father, born from the womb of his original wife, the Heavenly Mother." Not in earthly fashion, of course. Father Clavelin had been told that there was no physical generation in heaven. As usual Hung was allowing poetry and alchemical symbolism to run away with him. "The Father knew that in the New Testament there were mistakes. Therefore he descended to the Eastern Prince, and proclaimed that the Holy Spirit was God, and the wind was the Eastern Prince." Hung used two different characters for the different functions of God and Yang, of Spirit and wind, but alas, gone were the days when he had refused to allow any errors in Liang's tracts to be corrected. So far as the missionaries were concerned, to suggest that there were mistakes in Holy Scripture was to tread on very dangerous ground.

North of the Yellow River, whence Hung's first army had just fought its way back from Peking, there were many Chinese Mohammedans, left there in the medieval era of the great Khans, and after Hung's death they in their turn would rise in rebellion against the Manchus. Had he been able to meet them now, he might have accepted Islam, for as an Arian heretic he would have had much in common with them. His belief in the one God, a personal deity and the Father of all men; his hatred of images; his belief in the judgment, paradise and hell; his harem; and his Holy War were all allowable in Islam. But Hung had never heard of Mahomet. Nevertheless, for him Christ exactly fulfilled the position that Mahomet holds for a musselman. And Mahomet had married, and produced many descendants. Hung had finally persuaded himself that, in the paradise wherein souls pre-exist before incarnation on earth, Christ's feminine principle, the Yin, must also have existed as His wife. He now described the face which had haunted his dreams. "The Heavenly Elder Brother's wife, virtuous and very thoughtful, constantly urging the Elder Brother to be deliberate and cautious." No longer was she the symbolic city of the New Jerusalem. Had not Christ often referred to himself as the bridegroom, Hung reflected? Nevertheless, in his vision of the mother of Christ, he remained true to whatever Catholic doctrine he had picked up. She was not the Queen of the Western Paradise of the Buddhists, for Liang's tracts had particularly condemned the Western Paradise with all its fanciful gods and goddesses. She was the T'ien Mu, the Heavenly Mother, who had borne Christ, and by virtue of her son's universal brotherhood she was the mother of all men. She was "kind, very gracious and affectionate, delicate in her attentions, and noble in conduct, and in everything incomparable."

If Hung's eyebrows met in concentration as he wrote, it was nothing to what happened to the eyebrows of the missionaries when they read his latest proclamations. Their eyebrows shot up to the roots of their hair. Failing to understand that Hung did not raise Christ to the throne of divinity, his pronouncements seemed to drag God down to the level of a mere family man, who had a wife and daughter-in-law. And that pock-marked, swarthy scoundrel Yang was apparently conceived to be part of the nature of God. Their failure to understand Hung was pardonable, for, in all the literature handed to Sir George Bonham, Christ was acknowledged as the Redeemer, whose atonement for all mankind had been fully efficacious. Whatever else Hung was, he was no logician, and had altogether ignored that verse in the psalms, "None of them can by any means redeem his brother, nor give to God a ransom for him". As for what Hung meant when he declared that Yang was the wind and the Comforter, it was simply a poetic title, purely honorific, and so the ordinary folk regarded it.

After the first act of the drama in 1854 there was to be an interlude before the blood-bath of 1856, but the events in those intervening years came swiftly one upon another. Britain, France and America declared themselves neutral in China's civil strife, for at all costs the first two Powers must avoid being involved in the Far East, because on January 4th 1854 the Crimean War had broken out. It was fought to control Russia's desire for expansion in Asia, but the Allies could not afford to fight it on two fronts.

Britain's ordinance of neutrality was therefore very strict. It became a misdemeanour punishable by not more than two years' imprisonment to take sides with either the Imperialists or the rebels, either by enlistment in their service or by procuring warlike stores.

Altogether the last half of 1855 was a time of jubilation for the Taipings. They held all the strategic points along the middle reaches of the Yang-tze. Fifty thousand more rebels from the secret societies had just joined the T'ien Wang's forces, and Yang had retaken the Triple City. The defeat of the Taiping northern army in its attempt to take Peking was well-balanced by Yang's victories in the west. Tseng Kuo-fan was in despair. Once again he contemplated suicide by riding into the enemy's cavalry, but was held back. Suicide was considered the only honourable answer to defeat. General after general in the Imperial forces took his own life.

While Hsien Feng hesitated, wondering whether to risk once again calling the Mongols, the voice of Yehonala, now raised to the rank of Empress, was recognisable in his edict to Tseng. "We conceive that it would not be difficult with one roll of the drum to take these wretched vagabonds and sweep them from the face of the earth." The clatter of her mirror upon the dressing table is almost audible, and the flash in her beautiful eyes can almost be seen. As a woman Yehonala was impatient of the difficulties involved in strategy and tactics, but she was wise in statecraft and clever at choosing men. For all his present disgrace, Tseng was her chosen instrument, and though, through the mouth of the Emperor, she might censure him, she would not recall or degrade him. If he could not achieve victory, she thought, then nobody could. But in the coming year of 1856 it was not Tseng who conquered, but Yen-lo, the Prince of Darkness, who came to Yehonala's rescue and checked the Taipings.

Wei had been working for a long time upon the T'ien Wang's fears. Ever since Yang's trance he had been insidiously suggesting that Yang was bidding for supreme power. Perhaps he even dared to suggest that the trance had not been genuine, and that the Eastern Prince had merely sought an occasion to humiliate the sovereign. Hung was growing more and more suspicious of the Commander-in-Chief. At the same time Wei was implanting in Yang's mind the idea that to him alone their past victories had

been due, and that the sovereign had not sufficiently acknowledged and rewarded him. Yang had already been accorded the
title of "Live for Nine Thousand Years". Now Wei chose a
moment when he had his own adherents in the city, and Hung's
Kwang-tung men were on campaign. Then he put Yang up to
demanding the title of Wan-sui, "Live for Ten Thousand Years"
or "Live as an Immortal". It was the ancient prerogative of the
Emperor alone to be thus acclaimed.

Hung was thunderstruck. This was a demand for co-sover-
eignty. He saw now that his enemies were seeking to betray him.
He sent for Wei, but Wei counselled him to submit first and strike
later. He pointed out that Hung had insufficient loyal troops for
the moment, and promised to strengthen the sovereign's hand
later, if for the moment he would give way. Virtually a prisoner
in his own city, Hung was forced to submit, to swallow his rage,
and allow himself to be borne by his sixty-four sedan porters in
state procession to the palace of Yang, there to grant to his
brother-in-law the coveted title. The man who had once been the
mouthpiece, if not of Shang-ti at least of some virtuous and
benevolent influence, was now a creature corrupted by the alien
spirits he had in his foolish pride invited into himself. He came
out to receive the title, and his swarthy, pock-marked face was
swollen with vain glory. His triumph was short-lived.

Wei now produced the men for Hung's revenge, and Shih
Ta-kai was taken into Hung's confidence. Orders were that Yang
alone should suffer for his treasonable ambitions. Treason was
one of the Ten Crimes for which even an Emperor could not
remit sentence.

On the night of September 2nd 1856 Wei struck. He inveigled
Yang to his own palace, and from behind screens and curtains his
assassins leapt upon the Eastern Prince and sliced his head from
his shoulders. Then at last Wei showed his hand. Not content with
carrying out the T'ien Wang's orders for Yang's death, his
soldiers fell upon the city, and carried out an organised massacre.
The condemned were Yang's wives and children, together with
20,000 of his adherents.

Hung was appalled. Even his own sister had perished. Helpless
and a prisoner in his own palace, he was unable to prevent the
slaughter, which continued for six weeks.

On the night of Yang's murder Shih Ta-kai had been absent

from Nanking. His main army was at An-king, with orders to hold it at all costs against the Imperialists, but he himself had been sent for urgently by Faithful—the young Li Siu-cheng, who had joined the army on its march on Yung-nan. Now a general, he had appealed to Shih Ta-kai to come to the rescue of Lo Ta-kang at Chin-kiang, which was being heavily attacked by the Imperial forces. Eventually Lo Ta-kang was killed and the city fell, but the Taiping garrison broke out and was rescued. In the midst of this action came news of Wei's coup d'état. Shih Ta-kai rode back post-haste to Nanking, only to find Hung virtually a prisoner, and Wei in power.

At a banquet given by Hung the two generals broke into open quarrel. Shih Ta-kai had been the devoted friend of Yang. Some even said that they had sworn a brotherhood oath. Shih, who had retained his good character and the idealism of his God-worshipping days, had consented to Yang's death only because he believed Yang threatened the throne, but, like Hung himself, he now saw how he had been deceived. Before hands could fly to swords, Hung reconciled the two generals, thus giving Shih Ta-kai a chance to escape, to get out of Nanking and summon the army to his sovereign's aid. Shih left the palace knowing that he had only a bare half-hour's grace before Wei's assassins would follow him. He made haste to warn his own family, and then laid his clothes by the river to simulate suicide. He scaled the wall near the south gate with the aid of a rope, for he knew that Wei's police had charge of the gates. Then he climbed aboard a fishing boat and pulled for An-king, which his own army was holding.

When Wei learnt that Shih had made good his escape, he stamped in his fury. "Those who allow a mountain tiger to escape," he raged, "are guilty, and it is my fault. If I had seized him at the table it would have been as easy as roping a pig." He sent a hundred guards at once to invite all Shih's family to dinner. They politely refused, but were urged at the sword's point to obey. Shih's old mother, aged seventy-two, was bundled on to a horse, his son was bound, and altogether eighteen of his family were taken to Wei's palace and slaughtered, including his six sons, two daughters and three pretty concubines.

Meanwhile Hung Hsiu-ch'uan, in the isolation of his palace, sat with his head in his hands groaning. He had had ample time to appreciate how he had been deceived. How could he have been so stupid as to be caught by that same old trick, which the assistants of Issachar Roberts had played upon him so many years ago? Putting a man up to make undue demands in order to destroy him was a stratagem that he of all people should have recognised. He saw now that Yang, for all his vainglory and his love of titles and honours, would never have threatened his sovereign's supremacy. He saw now that Yang, foolish, stupid, volatile and easily influenced, had been as clay in the hands of the real villain. Hung's repentance was terrible, but, before he could make amends to the soul of his murdered brother-in-law, he must first outwit his long-hidden enemy.

As soon as he had gathered sufficient of his own Kwang-tung men into the city, he fell upon Wei, aided by the mob, who had been outraged by the late purges. There were no mass killings this time, however. Only two hundred perished, and Hung sent the head of Wei to Shih Ta-kai in token that his family was revenged. He sent also a desperate appeal to Shih to return, and strengthen the centre and the dynasty, for now he had no veteran generals left save Shih Ta-kai, and his faith in the rising genera-tion of army commanders was small. Shih came at his summons, but stayed only for a while. His heart was broken, and he was outraged. He went back to his own troops, determined from henceforth to carry on his career as an independent war lord: perhaps, if he could win for himself a territory in the far west, he would re-establish the Kingdom of Great Peace in ideal fashion, far away from the corrupting influence of Nanking. He might then admit the suzerainty of the T'ien Wang, for he bore him no malice, and was to continue for the next seven years to fight on Hung's side; but he would remain independent as far as the direction of his own troops was concerned.

Meanwhile Hung was safely back upon his throne, and the blood-bath and the liquidations were things of the past. He had time to give himself to repentance for Yang's death, and to make amends, for it was the firm belief of the Chinese since time immemorial that honours conferred on the dead by an emperor raised their rank in paradise, in much the same way as a pope could declare that the departed were numbered amongst the saints.

Thenceforth September 2nd was to be always a memorial day of Yang's ascension to heaven. To obviate the danger of having

Taoist priests to close the coffin of the dead, thus continuing
heathen practices and superstitions, Hung had lately decreed that
those who died were to be buried in silk only, coffinless, in order
that the body might more quickly return to dust, and the
thoughts of men be turned to the soul in heaven. If Yang's body
was buried without a coffin, at least he was accorded full honours
in Hung's proclamations.

"The Prince of the East in ransoming the sick suffered equally with
    the Elder Brother,
And when he fell with the pestilence, he returned to the place of
    spirits to thank the Father for his goodness."

The pestilence was a euphemism for the sword of Wei. Nobody
was deceived. All the literati took pride in finding gentle adum-
brations for stark passions. If a love affair had to be called "a
meeting of swallows", how much more must a "death affair", a
murder, be called a pestilence. "The Eastern Prince," wrote
Hung, "having attained merit deep as the azure heaven, has
suffered for the sins of the world, and gone to the skies." The
T'ien Wang was genuinely repentant, and as the murder of Yang
weighed heavily on him, the fate of Wei perhaps brought him
now, all too late, to consider Christ's words, "All they that take
the sword shall perish with the sword", for what he next wrote
had within it the beginnings of a new spirit, the spirit of the
gospel message at last, which both Jesus and Confucius had
proclaimed. "From of old those who have killed others have afterwards killed themselves. Who will say that the eyes of Heaven
are not opened wide? From of old those who have saved others
have thereby saved themselves, and their souls have been taken
up to the heavenly courts. Do as you would be done by and you
will always be right."

Despite the fact that Tseng Kuo-fan took advantage of the
dissension in Nanking to recapture the Triple City, at the beginning of 1857 Taiping territory included 70,000 square miles,
or rather more than the land of England and Wales, and numbered
a population of 25 millions.

There was now a big chance that the Taipings might defeat
the Imperialists totally and finally, because international politics
were bringing the Western Powers into conflict with the Manchu

administration, and Imperialist forces were being diverted to fight against the Foreign Devils. The chance was missed, and for the rest of 1857 the Taiping armies made no headway, for the reason that the T'ien Wang had lost all his ablest generals. Of the five original princes, only Shih Ta-kai remained alive, and he had become an independent war lord.

Hung, mindful of how he had been betrayed, dared nowadays trust no one with extensive powers, save only those of his own blood. For this reason he appointed his two stupid elder half-brothers as his chief ministers. Faithful and Cockeye (who had also joined up on the march to Yung-nan) rallied magnificently to the support of the dynasty and became the two leading generals. Hung gave them each the title of prince, but he treated them to none of his confidence and friendship, and, to lessen the importance of any one general, he now gave away the title of prince to every least commander. For their part, Faithful and Cockeye could make nothing of the stupid Hung brothers, whose orders they must henceforth accept. There was no united command at the one moment when fate presented military opportunity.

As for Hung Hsiu-ch'uan, disillusionment had brought on melancholy. Somehow a copy of *Pilgrim's Progress* had fallen into his hands, a Chinese translation, and it had become his favourite reading. From the accidie from which his spirit was suffering, he sought greedily to be delivered by another vision, just one more glimpse of the celestial spheres. It was so long now since he had seen the heavenly halls! In *Pilgrim's Progress* he found some assuagement for his thirst, but his very greed for the comfort of revelation perhaps now led him astray. Unwilling to remain thirsting in the desert, his soul began to follow the mirage which his all too poetic imagination easily produced in his unconscious.

He fell into a coma or trance for two whole days, and once again he was escorted by musicians playing upon harps, reeds and drums. Thunder went before his face like the herald cock. A celestial host conveyed his chariot by the great road in the east up to heaven, where beautiful damsels met him at the gates. Once again he was given the seal, "that very seal wherewith the Lord made heaven and earth". Once again the Heavenly Elder Brother came to his aid to chase away the demons. In his coma he stirred, and his family heard him cry out, "O my brother, help me", and they knew that he spoke to Jesus. When at last he came to himself, he declared that he had seen the souls of his two half-brothers in heaven. Yen-fa and Yen-ta were much gratified, and, to bolster their difficult official positions, published a proclamation to the effect that they had accompanied their sovereign to heaven, though they had unfortunately no memory of their experience. "We have written as commanded by our true sacred Lord," they announced, "but as the T'ien Wang speaks heavenly language, we can only comprehend two or three sentences out of every ten."

Their reputations needed some reflected glory, for, as a result of their incompetence, the Taipings had just lost two important cities. Things would have gone hard for them if the Imperialists had not been fully occupied in keeping the Western Barbarians at bay.

18

DESPITE THEIR DECLARED policy of neutrality, Thomas Meadows feared that, as soon as the Crimean War was over, Britain and France might be tempted to intervene in China's civil strife, and he had been writing a book, giving his views on the rebellion, and warning the public against the evils that would follow on any interference by the Western Powers.

On religious grounds he pleaded that the Taiping movement was a chance to Christianise China, a chance that would not occur again in a million years, and that Britain should not quench the flame, however feeble its present light.

On political grounds he argued even more strongly for a policy of non-intervention. China must be allowed to work out her own destiny, for only thus could she evolve healthily, and become a world power. And it was a necessity that she should become a strong self-governing modern nation in order to counter-balance

Russian ambitions to dominate the world. China alone could fulfil this rôle. To interfere with her spontaneous evolution would be to sap her strength, and the setting up of puppet governments or the propping up of the Manchu dynasty by foreigners would only delay her renaissance. Russia alone had territorial ambitions in China, and if Russia should ever succeed in conquering China, then woe betide the rest of the world. Nothing would be so distasteful to the Russian aggressors as the "establishment in their contiguity of 360 millions of Bible-studying Christians, who would oppose to fanaticism another fanaticism".

Thus Meadows foresaw the course of history for the next hundred years, and what he feared most was any attempt "to urge, or entrap, or *endrift* (for there is always someone who slips the cable, and *that* danger is the greatest) the maritime powers of the occident into a coarse repression of the Taiping Rebellion."

It was Harry Parkes who "slipped the cable", and justified all Meadows' fears. Harry had come out to China at the age of four-teen, a blue-eyed, typically Anglo-Saxon boy, and an orphan. He was the son of a Staffordshire clergyman who sprang from a family of ironmasters, and he had been sent to the care of his cousin Mary, who happened to be Mrs. Gützlaff, the wife of the missionary and famous sinologue. With Gützlaff as his tutor it was hoped that Harry, by studying the Chinese language, would be able to make a career in the consular service. Now at the age of only twenty-eight he had achieved the rank of Consul at Canton, and he was to sway British policy in China for the next ten years. His friends admired his manly open countenance. His enemies described him as having a stereotyped hollow smile and oblique design. Of middle-class origin, he had won to distinction very young, ranked as a diplomat and judge, and on occasions could wear his blue uniform with silver lace and gold buttons with an air. In fact he had *arrived*. And he was longing to teach the "Chinks" a lesson.

In fairness to Parkes, the Chinese had twisted the lion's tail well-nigh past endurance. For nearly a hundred years the British had suffered taunts and insults from the mandarins. If China did not want to trade with the British, such behaviour would have been comprehensible, but China did want the trade. It was most lucrative, and the profits were the perquisite of the Emperor. China wanted the trade, but wanted it on her own impossible

terms; wished to profit, while openly calling the Europeans
Barbarians and Foreign Devils; desired them to bring goods to
Canton, while confining them to the desolate strip of land outside
the walls, the Factories; would not admit a foreigner into the
city; would not permit a meeting between the Viceroy and the
British Governor at Hong Kong. Finally, the Emperor would not
receive an Ambassador in audience.

"Entrance to Canton is the key to the whole difficulty,"
Parkes had written to Lord Palmerston a few years previously.
If the Chinese could be forced to eat humble pie over this one
small but crucial point of contention, then the mandarins would
have to realise that Britain was a world power who would only
agree to trade on the usual international civilised terms. Now
the Crimean War was over, and Britain no longer had her hands
tied, she was prepared to force the issue, and therefore the situation was such that a match was bound sooner or later to be put
to the gunpowder.

The occasion was presented on October 8th 1856 when the
lorcha *Arrow*, a small sailing vessel which was to give its name to
the Arrow War, put into Canton. She was thought to be an opium
smuggler, and certainly her crew were notorious Chinese pirates,
but under a recently passed British ordinance she had a licence
to fly the British flag. The Viceroy imprisoned her crew and
hauled down the flag. Parkes lodged a complaint, and was struck
in the face by one of the Chinese petty officials. Matters went
from bad to worse. The rights and wrongs of the case were later
fully discussed in Parliament, but the history of the Arrow War
is a story apart, except in so far as it affected Hung Hsiu-ch'uan.

Very briefly, what happened was that Parkes, riled beyond
bearing by the treatment he had received, decided to make the
quarrel an excuse for the armed action which he had long desired
to employ. When he discovered that the lorcha's licence to fly
the British flag had in fact expired, and that the Viceroy had
been within his rights in seizing the Chinese pirates, he kept the
matter secret, and shifted his original demands for the return of
the crew to a demand for entry into the city of Canton. Backed by
Sir John Bowring, the Governor of Hong Kong, and the British
naval forces at his disposal, he sent an ultimatum to the Viceroy,
claiming free access to the city and the right of the Governor to
confer in person with the Viceroy.

Unfortunately for Parkes the Viceroy was none other than the infamous Yeh, who had boasted of executing 70,000 rebels in the space of six months, and who had collected the right ears only of close on a million decapitated heads. The son of a village apothecary, whose silver had started him on the road to office, Yeh not only had a monstrously corpulent body and the features of an ape, but was as obstinate of mind as he was cruel. He refused the ultimatum, and the British naval force promptly bombarded his yamen, in reply to which he offered thirty silver dollars for the head of any Englishman, and attempted to murder Sir John Bowring and his entourage by poison introduced into the bread at Hong Kong.

By January 14th 1857 it was plain that Britain was in fact once again at war with China, Imperial China; and Admiral Seymour applied to the Governor-General of India for troops. To be more exact, the British were at war with the Viceroy of Kwang-tung province, for it was a curiously disconnected world in those days. The Emperor had determined that Yeh must fight his own battles, and that the foreign trade must not be interfered with elsewhere in China, lest the Imperial revenues be effected. The desire to have an audience with the Emperor and to have a permanent representative at Peking, both of which measures the British believed would circumvent the machinations and "squeeze" of the mandarins, might have been worth struggling for if the Imperial Court had really had executive power in the provinces. But in fact the only thing which united the provinces, each as large as a European country, was the mystique of the Dragon Throne—a mystique which could straightway evaporate and vanish if the Son of Heaven met with representatives of the Western Powers on equal terms.

When news reached Nanking of the bombardment of Canton, Hung was greatly elated. To think that the Viceroy of that Tartar Demon, Hsien Feng, had been shelled in his own yamen! The bombardment must have damaged the neighbouring examination hall, the place where he had once sat sweating and toiling. Now, surely, the English would come to his aid. They would join with him, and together they would defeat the odious Tartars. Then, after the completion of victory, he would visit Europe; and he would bring back with him the Pope and Queen Victoria as honoured guests to his Heavenly Capital, and the three of them would be able to discuss together the interpretation of the scriptures, and all the brethren in the West would join with him to do reverence to the Heavenly Elder Brother, and to worship their one Heavenly Father.

Hung's face, as he sat enthroned to receive his new young generals, was unusually benign. They were astonished, for in his determination to keep the rising generation in order, and not to lay himself open a second time to treachery and betrayal, he could simulate great rage, and even threaten the disobedient with death. But now, under the golden crown of the Mings, above which towered the fabulous jewelled bird, his face was smiling, for he was confident that the English would certainly henceforth be his allies.

Unfortunately for him, Hung had entirely failed to understand, as so many foreigners did fail to understand, that Britannia was rigidly bound within the pattern of her own racial psychology. If, as she intended, she succeeded in giving the Manchus a sound thrashing, it would follow that to the beaten dog she must give a bone. If, as Meadows was acute enough to note, she knocked a man down, she could invariably be counted upon to pick him up again, as soon as conscience and chivalry were allowed free play. So invariable was this pattern of racial psychology that Britannia might have done well once in a way to consider carefully which of two antagonists she really wanted to see on his feet before she started hitting out, because it was a good bet that whichever she struck first was going to end up in the more favourable position. And the bewildered foreigners might have done well to study the classic tale of how the Black Prince waited at table upon his defeated enemy, the King of France.

Already Britannia's conscience was at work. A debate in the House of Commons in February led to the fall of the Whig government. Gladstone, Lord John Russell and Disraeli all joined with Cobden in condemning first the issue of licences to fly the British flag to vessels which were merely nominally British-owned, and secondly the high-handed action of Parkes which had resulted in the bombardment of a peaceful city. The incident of the *Arrow* had been used as an excuse, they declared, and all along the government's intention had been to force entry into Canton. The government spokesmen denied that such had been the intention, and argued that respect for the flag was vital to trading conditions, which would deteriorate if traders had no confidence in the safety of life and limb. Lord Palmerston's government was defeated by sixteen votes, and a general election followed.

Although Britannia's conscience was now awake in the minds of certain politicians, nevertheless to ordinary folk China was still as far removed as the planet Mars, and her inhabitants could hardly be considered human beings. "Old Pam" had led the country well for many years. The electors sent him back with an increased majority, and Cobden and several of his colleagues lost their seats.

Meanwhile there had been an enforced delay before dissolution, and to bridge the intervening months Lord Clarendon, the Foreign Secretary, had sent out Lord Elgin as special High Commissioner and accredited as Ambassador to the Court of Peking. With him were sent sufficient troops to prosecute the war which was *ipso facto* being waged.

Lord Elgin got as far as India, when on May 10th the Indian Mutiny broke out. He saved the situation there by acting on his own initiative and diverting the troops intended for China to India, but it meant a long delay before he could prosecute the punitive expedition to China, and meanwhile Yeh was laughing at the embarrassment of the British, and with every hour's delay Britain was losing face.

At last, on September 20th 1857, Elgin, in advance of his troops, reached Hong Kong. With him he brought his brother Mr. (afterwards Sir Frederick) Bruce, who was later to succeed him as British representative in China, and his attaché, Mr. (afterwards Lord) Loch, together with Mr. Lawrence Oliphant, who was to write the account of the special mission.

Elgin had been chosen for his broad knowledge of affairs. He had been Governor of Jamaica and Governor-General of Canada. His wide intellectual forehead and the bald dome of his head gave him an appearance venerable beyond his years. He preserved a placidity of aspect and demeanour, but he had a very keen eye for what was going on around him. Harry Parkes immediately distrusted his mildness and desire for conciliation. A Whitehall statesman, thought Harry, who could know nothing of the trials of men on the spot. Parkes might have been surprised to know what Elgin thought of him and his actions, but such thoughts were committed to Elgin's private journal only.

The French were now ready to join in the project to take the city of Canton, for France had her own reasons for wanting to bring China to book. Some months earlier l'Abbé Auguste Chapdelaine had been put to death after cruel torture in Kwangsi, that is to say in the vicinity of the southernmost borders of the Taiping territory. No doubt the mandarin responsible had, quite wrongly, suspected him of inciting Christians to join the rebels. Christianity, just as Father Clavelin had feared, had become more than ever suspect to the Imperial administration.

The Americans were so anxious to hold back Britain from too aggressive action, which they feared would injure trade, that they were believed to have double-crossed the British in giving secret information to Yeh's spies. Nevertheless, despite peaceful pretensions, both America and Russia sent out Plenipotentiaries to improve the shining hour, for they hoped to take the opportunity of reaping trade concessions from the Manchu government, once it had been brought to see reason by British and French arms. Elgin would have felt happier if his arms had been more fitted to the task laid on him. In return for diverting the British regiments to India, he had received in exchange only quasi-mutinous Bengal troops. But the real cause of his unhappiness was his conscience.

On Saturday, December 12th, the troops and arms now being assembled, Elgin sent his ultimatum to Yeh, and wrote in his journal, "He is to have ten days to think it over, and if at the end of that time he does not give in, the city will be taken. We are in for it now. I have hardly alluded in my ultimatum to that wretched question of the *Arrow*, which is a scandal to us, and is so considered, I have reason to know, by all except the few who are personally compromised. I have made as strong a case as I can on general grounds against Yeh, and my demands are most moderate."

Yeh refused the terms, and Harry Parkes posted notices warning the people to leave the city, while on December 22nd Elgin confided to his journal, "We actually steamed past the city of Canton, along the whole front, within pistol shot of the town. A line of English men-of-war are now anchored there in front of the town. I never felt so ashamed of myself in my life, and Elliot remarked that the trip seemed to have made me sad. There we were, accumulating the means of destruction under the very eyes, and within reach, of a population of about 1,000,000 people, against whom these means of destruction were to be employed! 'Yes,' I said to Elliot, 'I am sad, because when I look at that town, I feel I am earning for myself a place in the Litany immediately after "plague, pestilence and famine".' I believe, however, that as far as I am concerned, it was impossible for me to do otherwise than as I have done. I could not have abandoned the demand to enter the city after what happened last winter, without compromising our position in China altogether, and opening the way to calamities even greater than those now before us. I shall," he went on, "do whatever I possibly can to secure the adoption of plans of attack which will lead to the least destruction of life and property. Now I hear that the Commanders will not be ready till Monday, which the Calendar tells me is the 'Massacre of the Innocents'! If we can take the city without much massacre, I shall think the job a good one, because no doubt the relations of the Cantonese with the foreign population were very unsatisfactory, and a settlement was sooner or later inevitable. But nothing could be more contemptible than the origin of our existing quarrel. A great city," he concluded, "doomed, I fear, to destruction, from the folly of its own rulers and the vanity and levity of ours."

On December 27th the bombardment began and lasted twenty-seven hours. The population of one and a half million stampeded, and many more people perished in the stampede than by the shells. The Allied troops scaled the walls and entered, Yeh was taken prisoner and sent to India for safe keeping, and the British and French Forces now took over military occupation of the city. The first object of Elgin's expedition had been accomplished. The second and more important purpose of his mission could now be pursued.

His instructions were to sail north to the Gulf of Chih-li and then up the river leading to Tientsin. Tientsin was the gateway to Peking, and the object of going there was to make pacific overtures to the Emperor, and to insist, by force of arms if necessary, that the Emperor should appoint a special Commissioner with full powers to treat. An agreement was needed for which the Emperor could not afterwards disclaim responsibility, and it was thought that this could only be achieved in the vicinity of the capital.

The Manchu officials did everything in their power, short of employing real force, to prevent the British and French from reaching their destination. There were a few skirmishes, but for the most part the expedition was held up by delaying tactics and parleys, for the Imperialists dared not try their strength against British guns. With an army of scarcely 2,500 men and the naval forces on the station, Elgin sailed up the river to Tientsin, and on June 5th he confided to his journal, "I went to have my first official interview with the Chinese Plenipotentiaries. I made up my mind, disgusting as the part is to me, to act the rôle of the 'uncontrollably fierce barbarian', as we are designated in some of the confidential reports to the Chinese Government which have come into our hands."

It was bluff, but it worked. On July 3rd 1858 the Treaty of Tientsin was ready for signature, and there was a formal procession a mile long of guards, British military bands, and sedan chairs to the Temple of the Oceanic Influences to sign it. Ships were dressed, and crews manned the yards as the procession went by. The American and Russian Plenipotentiaries were full of good humour, for they were sharing in the benefits of the trade concessions which French and British arms had won.

Thus Elgin signed what was tantamount to the death warrant of Hung Hsiu-ch'uan, the Heavenly King, the Taiping Emperor. If the victory had not been so easy, if Elgin had met with armed resistance, instead of being able to cut through Chinese territory like a knife through lentil curd, Britain in desperate straits might have found herself allied to the Taipings. But now she was bound by treaty to the Manchus, and clauses 9 and 10 of the Treaty provided that "British Merchant ships shall have the authority to trade upon the Great River [the Yang-tze]. The upper and lower valley of the river being, however, disturbed by outlaws, no port shall for the moment be opened to trade. . . . So soon as peace shall have been restored, British vessels shall be admitted to trade at such ports as far as Han-kow [the Triple City]." Furthermore, "To Nanking and other cities disturbed by persons in arms against the Government, no pass shall be given, until they shall have been recaptured."

Thus at one stroke of the pen the British made peace with the Imperial government, and were henceforth under obligation to support the Imperial régime. Because Britannia's conscience was far from easy after the bombardment of Canton, she would hereafter be prone to show her former enemies special favour, and to abide loyally by the terms of the Treaty. At the same time the temptation to regard the Taipings with disfavour was held out, for she was promised an enormous new field for trading, access to which was only denied her for just so long as a curious sect of religious fanatics, rebels against the established powers of law and order, continued in existence. In another clause of the Treaty, missionaries were now and for the future entitled to travel in the interior with passports from the authorities. No longer would the Roman Catholic priests have to wear Chinese dress, and go in fear of their lives. Passports could be obtained to anywhere in China—*except* to the territories of those who claimed to be fellow Christians. There were to be no permits to the missionaries to visit the rebels. Officially Britain and France were to remain neutral in China's civil war for another five years or more, but the "drift", which Meadows had feared, had begun. The temptation to the Western powers to avail themselves of the new trading areas would be great, and somehow guns would easily reach the Imperial forces, while those who smuggled them to the Taipings would do so at considerable danger.

The Imperial forces which had retired from Nanking in August 1856, because of their preoccupation with the Foreign Devils at Canton, now re-established their great camp outside Hung's Heavenly City. The investing army numbered 30,000 and would be increased to 100,000 within a year. Inside the city there were only about 15,000 Taiping troops, for the rest of the T'ien Wang's forces were defending or attacking other strong points. The Taiping capital was in danger, and when the rebels learned that the Imperial Commander of the beleaguring force was their old comrade in arms, a certain Chang, who had gone over to the enemy, they brought out his wife and children, and put them to torture and death before the walls and within the traitor's sight.

Could such men be Christians? Their criminal law and their penal code were medieval, and even stricter than the Mosaic, but they were living in a medieval age. The Christian princes of medieval Europe, and particularly the Crusaders, had not behaved very differently, and all contemporary Europeans were agreed that the Taipings were no whit worse than the Imperialists, in fact rather better.

It was noted by Western nationals that, notwithstanding the barbarous customs common to both antagonists, the Taiping régime had within it the germ of reform. Throughout their territories the people were divided into units of twenty-five families, each with a common treasury and a place of worship. Landlords were recognised, and a land tax exacted, but it was a moderate one. The redistribution of land remained a promise only, for in the midst of civil war such a huge re-organisation had proved impossible to put into practical effect. Slavery was totally abolished on pain of death. Marriage might no longer be arranged in terms of money, and foot-binding was frowned upon. Old folk's homes had been set up, a necessity when sons and daughters were conscripted. One or two examinations had been held with the Bible as the new text-book, and the Heavenly King was attempting to abolish in the literate circles of officialdom the use of frivolous expressions of courtesy, and the tedious reiteration of classical idioms and allusions. He was hoping to encourage the use of effective words. A military and naval school had been suggested, as well as a banking system and the standardisation of weights and measures.

If such ideas were inclined to be on paper only, it was because the Taipings were fighting desperately for their very existence; but the leisured court at Peking had not even begun to harbour such revolutionary conceptions. Nevertheless, ideas on paper only cannot be counted as a harvest, and the real fruits by which the Taiping régime might be known and judged were the personal characters of the younger generation, those who had been reared in Hung's school of thought. Of them all the Faithful Prince was the shining example. He had at last been accorded some of the confidence and trust of the Heavenly King, and he was presently to acquire the respect of Europeans and the admiration of Gordon.

Within the city of Nanking he had come now to seek audience of the T'ien Wang. Dismounting from his war-horse, he beat the huge gong at the sovereign's gate, and from the eunuchless palace issued the women whose duty it was to lead him to the Heavenly King. "I beat the gong," he later wrote. "The Chief mounted his throne, and I persuaded him to let me go from Nanking to gather troops."

The Faithful Prince then summoned his forces and took Yang-

chou on the Grand Canal to the north. Here, instead of beheading the prefect, as the Imperialists would certainly have done,
he gave his defeated foe 350 taels of silver for travelling expenses,
and bade him take himself off. The seed had fallen on good ground
as far as the Faithful Prince was concerned.

Meanwhile, Nanking was still closely besieged. "The thought
that my Sovereign and my mother were there shut in at Nanking
caused me bitter tears day and night," wrote Faithful, whose
mother now enjoyed the comforts of the Prince's own palace,
where she lived together with his wife—he had only one—and
family. The days of marching through the wilderness, and life
in a hostel, had been exchanged for comparative luxury, but death
by starvation or the sword might come at any time.

Despite the shortage of food in the city, a modest banquet was
being held beneath the green and yellow curving roofs of the
T'ien Wang's palace to commemorate with proper ceremony an
event of great importance. Since the Golden Age of China it had
never been the custom for the sovereign to appoint the heir
apparent to the dynasty except by death-bed testimony. It had
been found by sad experience that the elevation of the Emperor's
son to such a position invariably led to palace intrigues, murders
and even mass purges, and that it was on the whole better to
postpone any coup d'état until after the death of the sovereign.

Hung had nevertheless decided otherwise, for he was determined to ensure the continuance of the dynasty, and now he had
proclaimed, "We, the Ruler, have given the Young Lord, our
son, to be adopted by Jesus. . . . The Young Ruler, as one-half the
son of Jesus, and one-half our son, is the recipient of the protection
of Heaven. Thus for generations the Young Lord, as the son of
Shang-ti, inherits from the Elder Brother and oneself the whole
Empire." Only from God and Christ could the Heavenly
Mandate be received. Thus had Hung himself received it in vision.
Therefore it could only be passed on to his son if the boy were
adopted by Christ himself.

The ritual of adoption had always led to complications, as the
Caesars of the late Roman Empire found. Hung would presently
discover that he was in a worse theological tangle than ever,
for he was forced at the same time to write, "The Saviour and
the Young Lord are sons of the Heavenly Father". How could
an individual be both the son and the grandson of God? Hung

was treading perilous ground, for to confuse the generations was an unforgivable offence against Chinese sentiment and Confucian principles.

Unconscious of the pitfalls in doctrine that were to open before him, Hung was in happy mood, as he was drawn to the banqueting hall in his Dragon car to celebrate the elevation of his nine-year-old son to his newly exalted rank. To mark the boy's pretended maturity, he had been given four wives, a distinction of purely symbolic significance, and as meaningless as the eighty-eight wives who now added to Hung's prestige, if not to his comfort.

Hung's nephew, the little Western Prince, whose father had been blown to pieces at Chang-sha, was of the same age as the Young Lord, and together they made all the due and proper bows to the Heavenly King. Then the Young Lord glanced shyly at the damsels, his allotted wives, who appeared for a little while to grace the feast, but he was really more interested in the sound of the enemy bombardment, and was anxious to talk to the Western Prince about this latest onslaught from the Tartar batteries.

Together with some few of the highest officials, Hung's brothers, now suffering from the obesity brought on by good living, were just settling down after saying grace to enjoy the well-cooked food, which even in the palace was none too plentiful, when all at once a thunderous noise, and the almost simultaneous tearing sound of timber splitting, momentarily paralysed the company. There at the sovereign's feet lay a smoking cannon ball. The faces of the courtiers had blanched, and now they sprang solicitous and voluble to his aid. The T'ien Wang had not so much as moved. Seeing their white cheeks and shaking hands, he laughed, the laugh which had once come so readily to him, but was now rarely heard. Then he drew himself up in his great chair. "I have received Heaven's command," he reassured them, "and have mounted the throne as Heavenly King. What to me are a million demon soldiers or the falling of cannon balls like rain, or even their generals?"

They admired his calmness and courage, but the army officers were often worried because they said he relied too much on Heaven, and would not always attend to their counsels and demands. Yet amongst what might have been merely heterogeneous bands of brigands, it was in fact his faith and vision which alone provided the cohesive factor. Without the strange mystique which he diffused, the movement would have long ago disintegrated into separate hordes of bandits.

Now once again he proved that this mystique, this faith in the mission entrusted to the Elect of Heaven, was of the utmost practical value, for, as the people in the city grew fearful of the outcome of the siege, he wrote them a battle song, and so greatly did the refrain affect them that the words were presently on every lip. They sang it in strange Chinese quarter tones, and the hymn of faith kept them steady, and gave them new courage until rescue came. It proved so popular that finally it was engraved on the dynastic seal, as the song which had saved the city.

"Our Heavenly Father, God, mightily reigneth;
Therefore, the Celestial dynasty shall stand for ever and ever.
Our Heavenly Elder Brother, Christ, mightily bears our burden,
Therefore the Celestial Hall is full of glory, for ever full of glory!"

As the missionaries and European visitors were later to find, it was a mistake to condemn entirely the Taiping movement on the sole grounds of Hung's tangled theology and any of his personal failings to practise Christ's teachings, for the fruit it had borne in the hearts of the simple people, who sang such songs, and in the character of the Faithful Prince, could not be ignored. Moreover, there was now to be added a further harvest, the harvest of the gospel teaching sown by the missionaries in the heart of the man who was even at that moment striving to penetrate the enemy lines, and bring help and better religious instruction to his cousin Hung.

Jen-kan, future Prime Minister and Foreign Secretary of the Kingdom of Great Peace, was at last on his way to Nanking.

19

AFTER HIS ARRIVAL IN Hong Kong as a refugee seeking political asylum, Jen-kan had been instructed in the Christian faith and baptised by Mr. Hamberg. Then early in 1854 he had embarked for Shanghai in an attempt to join Hung at Nanking, but had failed to get through the enemy lines. He returned to Hong Kong to find that Mr. Hamberg had died. Jen-kan then became employed by the London Missionary Society as a catechist, and for the next few years had ample opportunity not only to receive but to deliver instruction in the Christian faith on orthodox Church of England lines.

It was Dr. Legge of the London Missionary Society, later the first Professor of Chinese at Oxford University and the translator of the Confucian Classics, who found work for Jen-kan as a teacher at the mission. Miss Legge in her reminiscences wrote that Jen-kan was her father's friend, "and not only this, but a friend for whom Dr. Legge felt special affection and a warmth and admiration such as he gave to hardly any other Chinaman". Like his cousin, the Heavenly King, he was outstandingly tall and peculiarly attractive, and was greatly liked by all, both English and Chinese. The Reverend J. Chalmers, who had a part in instructing the new catechist, was told by Dr. Legge on one occasion that a new attendant at the mission services constantly sought Jen-kan's company. "Ah," Chalmers rejoined, "then he is sure to be getting good."

In the missionary magazine at Hong Kong it was reported that "Jen-kan soon established himself in the confidence and esteem of the mission. His literary attainments were respectable; his temper amiable and genial; his mind was characterised by a versatility unusual in a Chinese. His knowledge of Christian doctrine was largely increased, and of the sincerity of his attachment to it there could be no doubt."

This man, excellently grounded in Christian doctrine, and able to disentangle the Heavenly King's mistakes in theology, was about to come to temporal power in the Kingdom of Great Peace, but he came too late. "There is no hope now," wrote Mr. Edkins of the London Missionary Society, "that the Heavenly King would submit to having his opinions criticised and corrected, even if Christian missionaries could obtain the opportunity of conversing with him. He would not now become the humble disciple of foreigners." Nearly seven years had passed since Hung had first invited foreign missionaries to take up residence in Nanking, and none had accepted the invitation, so it was hardly to be wondered at that the T'ien Wang had grown intransigent.

Jen-kan's journey to Nanking began to all intents in 1857, when a young friend of the Hung family (later to be known by the soldiers he commanded as Four-Eyed-Dog), having rescued Jen-kan's womenfolk from prison in Canton, brought them to Hong Kong.

He and Jen-kan, disguised as pedlars of ink and stationery, then set out together for Nanking, leaving Jen-kan's family in the charge of the mission, and his brother Sye-po as chief servant or "Number One Boy" to Dr. Legge. Their travels were to last a long time, and to take them far inland. They were near the Triple City, still attempting to get through enemy lines, when they met with Lord Elgin's ships, which, with the Plenipotentiary aboard, were making an expedition up the Yang-tze.

The expedition had come about in this way. After the signing of the Treaty of Tientsin in July, and before copies of it were sent back to London and Peking for final ratification by both sides, there were dinners in Shanghai to celebrate Britain's peaceful relations with the Manchu Government, and, in the delightful atmosphere of good wine and good food, the mandarins, with Machiavellian cunning, made a suggestion to Elgin. Would the noble lord, the representative of Her Britannic Majesty, not care to prospect the territories in which presently his countrymen would be at liberty to trade? Would not a little trip up the Great River benefit His Excellency's health? The representatives of the Son of Heaven would do all in their power to give him passports and to welcome him, should he elect to make such an expedition to prospect. As for the few rebel strongholds that might exist between Chin-kiang and the Triple City, the bandits would not

dare to interfere with the terrible fire-ships of the British! Such
was the mandarins' invitation, and the noble lord accepted it with
alacrity. With the ships on the station and at his disposal, he would
be able to plot the river course of the almost unknown Yang-tze,
and bring back information to his government on the possibilities
for trade, and he could decide at which points to set up trading
stations—once the rebellion was squashed, of course.

Thus the Manchu officials insidiously tempted him to join with
them in routing the rebels. It had long been a British ambition,
as they knew very well from former applications to that effect,
"to open up the Yang-tze". Let the barbarians think that this
should be their reward, smiled the mandarins to themselves, and
when the rebels were routed, then some excuse would be found
for keeping the Foreign Devils out.

So on November 8th 1858, just a week after the announcement
that the Indian Mutiny was ended, Elgin embarked on H.M.S.
Furious and, with the *Retribution,* the *Cruizer* and two gunboats,
sailed up the Great River. He had become a little sickened by the
Chinese methods of conducting diplomacy, and he had begun to
see the point of view of men on the spot like Parkes, and Mr.
Thomas Wade, Chinese Secretary to the Governor, and Mr. Lay,
who had drawn up the Treaty. Furthermore, the Indian Mutiny
had tended to make the British antipathetic to any sect of people
which bore such a sinister name as "the long-haired rebels". And
finally, only the existence of these same rebels stood between
him and the power to present the British Crown with the rich
jewel of the Yang-tze trade. On government instructions he had
still to observe neutrality in China's civil war, but it is not surprising that he showed no sympathy for the Taipings, such as
he had felt for the populace of Canton, when bombarding that city.

"It must be remembered," he noted in his journal, "that rebels
are parricides by Chinese law, and that, in so far as we can
judge, nothing could have been more brutal or more object-
less than this Chinese rebellion. They systematically murdered
all—men, women and children—of the dominant race, and their
supporters."

Lord Elgin had been well primed by the old Tartar Prince
Kiying, the Emperor's uncle, who had been one of the Com-
missioners to sign the Treaty of Tientsin. Kiying had, no doubt,
glossed over the atrocities committed by the Imperial forces—

Yeh's executions, for instance. Nor did Elgin know that the Emperor was even now presenting poor old Kiying with the silken cord and the order for self-strangulation, because he had for the second time signed a treaty opening the Celestial Empire to these outer barbarians. Elgin was under the illusion that the Manchus were now Britain's friends. He was to be rudely awakened in the following year, but meanwhile he had set his face against being friendly with the Taipings.

The British ships had to proceed at a very low speed, because the native charts were inaccurate and the Chinese pilots inefficient, so that the vessels constantly went aground and had to be hauled off the banks. While the ships' officers took soundings, and prepared more accurate charts for the day when the traders would follow them, Elgin and his suite were able to look about them from the decks.

They passed Chin-kiang at the mouth of the river, a mouth so broad that it was a sea, and they saw the temple which the rebels had wrecked. The city, he was told, had once possessed a population of half a million. Now it was in Imperial hands again after four years of Taiping occupation, and the officials had found there a population of only five hundred. He was not told that it was the invariable custom of the wretched people to escape from the atrocities of the Imperial army, which always followed their retaking of a city. But when it was pointed out that no shops existed Elgin conceded that "the system of public granaries and the community of goods sufficiently account for the entire absence of shops and trade". He had grasped that the Holy Treasury of the Taipings was the first organisation of a communist state, and that it *was* organised.

Letters had been sent to the rebels that the British were not coming to fight them, but that they must not impede British ships, as, ran the message, "We are proceeding up the river in the exercise of our Treaty rights." The ships, however, had to pass through the fleet of Imperial junks which were investing Nanking, and under battery after battery of the Taiping defences. The Imperial fleet of course took advantage of the cover provided by the British ships to sail closer, so it was not surprising that the last Taiping battery opened fire, even though a British gunboat had preceded the British convoy with a flag of truce. The British returned the fire, until they came to anchor out of range above the city. So much might have been excusable from a neutral power in the heat of the moment. But now the two ships' captains proposed to return to Nanking next morning and hammer the Taiping batteries into ruins and their garrisons into submission, and to teach the impertinent rebels a lesson. Elgin's agreement to their proposal was hardly in accordance with his duty as Ambassador of a neutral power. The Taiping batteries were duly silenced, and an ardent young midshipman was heard by Oliphant to say, "They seem determined not to show us any sport!" Thus encouraged, the Imperial fleet plucked up sufficient heart to begin a fierce action, which the British left them to pursue. The Taiping admiral then appealed to Elgin for help, in answer to which the Plenipotentiary sent a curt note to the effect that the Taipings had brought the disaster upon their own heads, for "no interference with Her Majesty's ships would be tolerated".

At the next town up the river the Taipings delivered a written apology for the mistake at Nanking of having fired on the British, together with conciliatory presents and the Taiping Commander's appeal for some ammunition, which was of course refused. The river was here empty, as no Imperial junk dared show itself above Nanking. From now until they arrived at the Triple City, nearly 400 miles away, Elgin and his suite would be in Taiping territory. From the decks they watched an army of 5,000 Taipings march out of one town en route for another, their yellow and red uniforms shining in the sun and their pennants and flags waving.

At Wu-hu Mr. Oliphant and a companion went ashore to ask the Taiping authorities for leave to buy beef and vegetables. They were received in a yamen, which they found dilapidated, and were invited to be seated at a table on which stood large carved silver jars. The walls were hung with rolls of yellow silk, inscribed with texts as much Confucian as Christian. The dignitary who received them wore robes of yellow silk and an orange turban, below which his long hair was collected into a bag. Oliphant wondered if, concealed within it, he kept his pigtail, for it was rumoured that many Taipings did retain the queue, so that in the event of capture, or defection to the enemy, a quick tonsure would make them presentable to their foes, as submissive subjects conforming to the Tartar regulations.

There was apparently no time to talk of religion, for beef and vegetables were more urgent, and the secretary, in a crimson robe and green goggles, took down particulars of the ships' requirements. Oliphant on his return noted that the suburbs were in ruins. He did not wish to face the fact that a deadly and major war was being waged. The suburbs were always in ruins, for they were the weak spot and the real danger to the retention of any city, piled as they were against the walls, and harbouring the spies who sought to take possession of the gates. Both sides were merciless in disposing of the suburbs of all the contested cities.

Oliphant was pleased to hear from the ship's Chinese pilot that the Taipings harried and squeezed the peasants, and retained the best-looking women for themselves. He was not so pleased when the pilot ruefully admitted that the Imperial forces did exactly the same. Such was war! The same man grew far more heated when he began to discuss the atrocious wickedness of the Taipings in calling everyone brother and sister, and thus not distinguishing between the generations. The inquity of this challenge to Confucian principles left Elgin's secretary cold. But Oliphant had to concede that the next rebel town presented a very un-Chinese appearance of whitewash and cleanliness. It had lately been re-built, and he watched a battle in progress on a neighbouring hill.

When the ships reached An-king, the rebels fired on them. "We knew," wrote Oliphant, "it was impossible for them to have had news of the Nanking episode." Notwithstanding which, the fire was returned, "and we drove them from their forts into the arms of the Imperial forces". This was the city which Tseng Kuo-fan regarded as the key to the possession of the Yang-tze, the "back of the serpent" which must be broken here if anywhere. Yet Britain, who had formally declared her neutrality, was prepared to endanger thus the Taiping garrison.

The Triple City (Han-kow), which was as high as the ships were to go, was back in Imperial hands. Oliphant recorded that all the idols were destroyed, and had not yet been restored, and he observed the general devastation caused by war. But Elgin and his suite were too busy discussing trade, and noting the price of native calico as against Manchester cotton, to observe much else. Very grudgingly the Governor-General agreed to receive Elgin at his yamen, and the Imperial guards turned out to make a show. They wore red jackets and carried spears, matchlocks, and bows and arrows. Some of them were even armed with tridents. Amongst the procession were the executioners in conical blood-stained hats, carrying their plaited thongs for castigation. The cavalry, also in red jackets, rode rough ponies and were armed with matchlocks. Attached to each regiment of infantry was a harlequin figure in flesh-coloured tights, decorated with signs which looked to Oliphant like black tadpoles—they were the Yang-Yin symbol—and these *premiers danseurs* bore only straw shields decorated with gorgons' heads, their sole function being to strike terror to the heart of the enemy. Against such primitive arms the Taipings could hold their own. Neither side was equipped to withstand British guns.

It was while Elgin was high up the river, in the vicinity of the Triple City, that a mysterious messenger brought a letter to the ship, with a request that it be delivered to the Reverend J. Chalmers in Hong Kong. The messenger, a Taiping spy, as quickly disappeared again. The letter was from Jen-kan, and it acquainted his former teacher that he had got so far on his journey safely.

The British ships then began their return journey down the Yang-tze, but the river had fallen five feet, and, despite frequent soundings, the ships constantly went aground. This time the channel necessitated passing directly under the batteries at An-king, where the rebels would have them at a disadvantage. The Taipings, for obvious reasons, however, could not afford to quarrel with the nation possessing fire-ships and unlimited guns. An apology was sent for the previous episode, a safe conduct prom-ised, and an invitation extended to visit the city, which Wade refused.

At Wu-hu there was waiting a further apology for the firing at Nanking, together with the famous yellow silk document from the Heavenly King himself.

Hung had been suffering from cruel disappointment. A year ago he had felt assured that his co-religionists would join with him in his war to exterminate the Tartars. Why, he asked himself, should the foreign brethren wage a separate war against a mutual enemy? And why had they now made peace with the Tartars and begun to help them, and to show hostility to the Taipings? Did the foreign brethren not understand that they were merely being used by the Tartars, who would turn and rend them whenever the opportunity presented itself?

Hung had surveyed the map on his palace wall, as he thought over what kind of appeal he could write to the British, who had proclaimed neutrality, and had just reduced his batteries to ruins. The map was entitled "The Entire Territory of the Heavenly Taiping Dynasty to endure for a myriad, myriad years". On it a square block of land, surrounded by seas, represented China. In the centre another smaller square, surrounded by walls, represented the Heavenly City of Nanking. The rest of the world was represented by specks in the ocean, amongst which England and France were two islands in the north-west corner.

It was a very unreal representation of the globe, and when later a European saw that map he gasped, but the maps at Peking were not very different. For two centuries the Europeans had been trying to persuade the Son of Heaven that China was not the entire world. If Hung had at this moment shown any appreciation of the real state of affairs and international problems, Elgin's keen eye might have lit up with a new interest. But the British had just fought a small engagement to prove that, though in one sense they might be barbarians in prosecuting war, yet the British Empire did represent rather more than a speck on the earth's surface, and that its Sovereign's representatives were worthy to be received on equal terms by the Ruler of the Celestial Empire. To have to start the process all over again with a new dynasty, whose ideas on geography were exactly similar to those of the Manchus a decade ago, was really too much to expect of British patience.

Even so, Hung's composition might have won more attention had he followed his own precepts of using effective words only. True, he refrained from classical allusions, but only to give himself more space for the 172 lines of poetry which came bursting from his mind, and in which he wanted to tell the foreign brethren all about his visions and religious views and adventures right from the beginning. Mr. Wade must have groaned as he sat aboard H.M.S. *Furious* translating the verbose epistle for his chief.

It began all about Shang-ti, God, and how Hung was the uterine brother of Jesus, whatever that might mean. Mr. Wade sighed deeply. Next came an account of the so-called "descents" of God in 1848. Mr. Wade had read all about that before in the

pamphlets brought down by H.M.S. *Hermes*. Why couldn't a
Chinese ever get on with what he had to say, he wondered? Then
back again went the poet to an account of his vision in 1837,
rather more interesting, and bearing out the account in Hamberg's booklet; now forward once more to the rescue of Feng
from prison by means of God's intervention. There followed a
eulogy of the late Yang, called the Redeemer from Sickness; of
how he was wounded in battle, and how he eventually succumbed
to pestilence. Mr. Wade clicked his tongue in disgust. It was well
known how Yang had died. Unexpectedly the poet then broke
off into a long exhortation to his own followers to be loyal. Now
what could that have to do with Her Majesty's Ambassador? Or
was the man so proud of his rather feeble powers as a versifier
that he merely wanted to show off his literary talent to someone,
to anyone?

Just when Mr. Wade felt that he could bear it no more, he
came upon a line worthy of greater attention. Yes, here was the
pith of it at last: an invitation to visit the court.

"Foreign younger brethren of the Western Ocean, listen to our words—
Join us in doing service to the Father and Elder Brother, and ex-
   tinguishing the stinking reptiles.
Foreign brethren, come rejoicing to court.
By the memorials of our ministers,
We have been informed of the coming of the brethren to the Heavenly
   Capital.
We have desired our ministers to treat you with courtesy."

Now was the man mad, or was he not? Mr. Wade wiped his
brow. For two centuries the Manchu Emperor had refused to
grant an audience. Did this invitation to come to court constitute
an invitation to an audience? If so, reflected Wade, it would
have to be refused, for as the representatives of a neutral power
Lord Elgin could hardly accept it and risk not only the displeasure of the Manchu Emperor but the possibility of becoming
embroiled by the rebel's appeal for an armed alliance. But the
opportunity could be taken, perhaps, for some of Elgin's suite
to visit the city, more especially as one passage of this long and
turgid literary effort was making Mr. Wylie rather hot under his
clerical collar. Wylie was employed by the London Missionary

Society, and he had accompanied Elgin's expedition up the Yang-tze with a view to reporting how matters fared with the souls of the rebels.

"When travelling in Kwang-tung some time ago," wrote Hung in prose, "in the hall of worship we addressed Lo-han." This, Mr. Wylie recognised, was an allusion to the Reverend Issachar Roberts. "We then told him that we had been up to heaven," Hung went on, "and that the Heavenly Father and Heavenly Elder Brother had committed to us great authority. Is Lo-han now come hither or not? If he be, let him come to court and speak with us." It was nearly six years since the Taiping chief had first appealed to Roberts to come and help him teach the people, and now here he was renewing the appeal. Mr. Wylie felt really rather uncomfortable. The least he could do would be to accompany Wade and Lay and Oliphant into the city, and then at any rate he would be able to make a report to the Missionary Board.

In a snowstorm they crossed the muddy plain, which lay between the river banks and the suburbs. Then Wade, in a very high-handed fashion, commandeered some ponies from a minor official, and they rode the remaining six miles round the city to the gate indicated, for six out of the thirteen gates had been bricked up, and it was a city as large as Paris. On their way they observed the ruins of the Porcelain Pagoda.

They were received by the Faithful Prince. He had just arrived back in Nanking with forces sufficient to make the immediate future of the city safe. He was wearing a high Ming headdress embroidered with dragons, which Oliphant, extremely antipathetic to the Taipings, secretly dubbed "a fool's cap". Wade did the talking, demanding future safe conduct for those ships which had perforce been left grounded up river. The Faithful Prince reassured him on this point, and then began to talk of their common religion. Were they not all brothers of one family? Wade rather tactlessly asked what had become of Yang, and the Prince, somewhat embarrassed, replied that he had gone to heaven. He said that his own army now numbered several hundreds of thousands. There were no new Taiping publications with which to satisfy the visitors' curiosity, nor was there any temple to which he could take them other than the T'ien Wang's palace, and for that a more special invitation was needed.

The guide who conducted the visitors through the city spoke of there being four large Taiping armies outside Nanking. Despite the proscription, a third of the people smoked opium, he said. Food was short, and he himself would like to escape from the Taiping capital. As for religion, he could repeat grace before meals, but grumbled that he did not understand the sermons. Perhaps the same complaint might have been voiced by members of European congregations, but Oliphant seized on it. After a visit of one day only, he wrote, "We found the rebels making war like Jews, living like the worst description of professing Christians, and believing like—Chinamen." That he was biased was shown by his writing within four pages of this comment on the subject of trading conditions up river at the Triple City, and the future need of ships with a light draught. "At the same time this problem [the need for ships drawing little water] cannot be solved until the rebels are dispossessed of their position for 150 miles upon the banks of the Yang-tze-kiang. We cannot expect the Chinese Government to permit us to trade with the insurgents."

Oliphant foresaw that there would be a danger that the now more or less "opened" Yang-tze would be used by privateers to run guns to the rebels, and that this was going to give the British authorities a headache. Had he known it, already there was a ship approaching the orient carrying the man, Mr. Lindley by name, who was to become the most famous of all the gun-runners, and whose written account of the few years which he spent with the Taipings at Nanking was to provide a closer picture of the Faithful Prince and his admirable qualities than Mr. Oliphant had been able to portray after one short interview.

Mr. Wylie had seen very little more of the Taipings than Oliphant, but back in Shanghai on March 3rd he felt the necessity of reporting his views to the London Missionary Society. He noted both the iconoclastic zeal and the respect for ancestral halls and tablets showed by the Taipings. "The monstrous doctrine they have adopted," he went on, "of Hung Hsiu-ch'uan being the second son of God and on a par with Jesus Christ, however it may be excused by reference to historical parallels, is I fear a most serious obstacle to their humble reception of the truth." He then proceeded to discuss the possibility of setting up a mission in Nanking and was very dubious of its being wise to do so. "Not that I think such a mission altogether impractical," he concluded, "but it will require extreme prudence on the part of any who should undertake it."

In the seven years of Hung's rule at Nanking the missionaries, both Catholic and Protestant, had shown such "extreme prudence" that not one of them had spent more than a few hours in the city as sightseers, and Mr. Roberts had been too cautious even to attempt the trip.

In the spring of 1859 Jen-kan, with a price on his head, penetrated enemy lines and at last arrived in Nanking. It was exactly ten years since he had bidden Hung farewell when his cousin had set out on his final journey from his home in Hua to Kwang-si.

Death had claimed four of the five original princes, and Hung had been deserted by the remaining one. He was aware that his elder brothers were of small intelligence, despite their faithfulness, but he dared not trust the army generals after his experience with Wei, and even to the Faithful Prince he was stern. He had just suffered a rebuff from Elgin's refusal to come to his aid. He was alone and desolate, and now he fell upon Jen-kan's neck as affectionately as Imperial and Confucian etiquette would allow. Here at last was a man of his own blood, whom he could trust, and furthermore an able and literate man, and finally a fervent Christian.

Jen-kan was at once made Prime Minister and accorded the title of Shield Prince. He hoped to persuade his cousin to accept the orthodox doctrines with which he himself was now acquainted, but, after ten years of promulgating his own ideas, the Heavenly King would need time and much persuasion. In the midst of a war which was a life and death struggle, it was hardly possible to tackle the intricacies of religious controversy. First, Jen-kan decided, the war must be won. Nevertheless, he did at once attempt to institute some reforms. On the civil side, he promised to introduce railroads, steamboats, fire and life insurance companies, and newspapers. On the religious side, missionaries were to be allowed to travel, to live and to preach everywhere. He set to work to try and counter the ignorance of the citizens, a task which, because of Hung's ever growing tendency to isolate himself in the palace, had been neglected. The Ten Commandments and the Sermon on the Mount were placarded on all the gates of Nanking. And at the entrance to the private palace which the Heavenly King had given him, Jen-kan had the Beatitudes carved on a great stone 11 ft. by 9 ft., bearing his seal and the date, 1860.

How strange it was that here was he living in a palace, while his brother was still "Number One Boy" to Dr. Legge! He sent him a thousand dollars to distribute to old friends, including the missionary, but Dr. Legge wisely refused the gift, fearing lest it was the spoils of banditry, for which nicety of conscience the mandarins hailed him as a "righteous man". He was nevertheless not entirely out of sympathy with the rebels. "They clearly abjure idolatry," he wrote to the Religious Tract Society, "and recognise the duty to serve the true God. They make known Jesus Christ as the only and all sufficient Saviour, and they lead the people to rejoice in the prospect of the future life. If the insurgents held only these principles, we could not refuse them a large measure of our admiration. The starting up on a sudden of hundreds of thousands of men and women professing these views in China, is a phenomenon in which I dare not but magnify the power of God."

Within a few months of Jen-kan's arrival, the Imperial forces investing Nanking grew to 100,000, and the Taipings were desperate. "We had no gunpowder," wrote the Faithful Prince. "The T'ien Wang preserved his air of unconcern for all outward matters, and as usual relied throughout upon Heaven." Tseng Kuofan's Hu-nan armies attacked An-king, but were shattered by Faithful coming up to the rescue of Four-Eyed-Dog. Six thousand Hunanese fell in the battle, and among them was Tseng's third brother. The year 1859 dragged on, and if the T'ien Wang's generals complained that "he relied as usual upon Heaven", he had good cause to do so, for now the Taipings were to be given another big chance.

In April there had been a general election in Britain and the Whigs were returned. For the rest of the duration of the Heavenly Kingdom of Great Peace in China, British policy was directed by Palmerston as Prime Minister, Lord John Russell as Foreign Secretary, and Sir Frederick Bruce, who was now on his way back from Britain with the Treaty. The turning-and-rending process, which the Taipings had foreseen, was about to come into force. The mandarins had hoped to use the British against the rebels. Afterwards they had intended to turn against the Foreign Devils. The first part of the programme had failed, but the second could still be carried out. When Bruce and the French Minister arrived at the Taku forts in order to take the Treaty to Peking for final ratification, the ships were ambushed by the forces of the Mongol Prince Senkolintsin, and heavy fire from the forts destroyed three British gunboats and killed several hundred men. The Allies withdrew.

For the moment there was nothing for the British lion to do but to retire to Shanghai and lick its wounds. But it was plain to all that the Manchu Government must be taught that this was not the way to receive diplomatic Ministers coming to ratify an agreed Treaty. Britain and France would have to go to war again. Lord John straightway appointed Elgin to return to China as Ambassador Extraordinary, while an expeditionary force was prepared. A speedy settlement was necessary, because a rupture with the French was feared. Napoleon had just met Victor Emmanuel at Genoa, and Britain was scared by his annexation of Savoy and Nice.

Palmerston and Russell, while determined to teach the Manchu Emperor a lesson, were most anxious to avoid bringing down the dynasty. No one would squarely face the fact that the Heavenly Mandate to the Manchu dynasty was already outrun, for the Manchus had promised to open up the Yang-tze to trade. So had the Taipings. But it was obvious that the latter, if they were capable at all, would take years to establish themselves. No one except Meadows foresaw that, by interfering with the natural course of history, the period of chaos would be prolonged rather than shortened. The policy was therefore to punish the Manchus, and then afterwards prop up their throne. Already the policy was at work, for at this time the Manchu administration was so weak that the Viceroy of Kwang-tung asked the British and French not to end their military occupation of Canton city, because he could no longer hold it from the rebels if the Allies withdrew.

Meanwhile 10,000 troops could not be assembled immediately. By slow steam and sail it would take just over twelve months for the new expeditionary force to be ready, and, while the preparations proceeded at Hong Kong and Shanghai and the game of war went on, the Heavenly King and his Faithful Prince played a major card.

20

NANKING WAS so closely besieged in the last months of 1859 that there were grounds for believing that Tseng would at last win the fruits of victory after his years of toil. But he had not reckoned with those moments, described by Father Clavelin, when the Heavenly King withdrew into his chamber and prayed to his Heavenly Father. To the Faithful Prince went the credit for the brilliant strategy which saved Nanking, but actually it was Hung who gave the orders, as Faithful admitted in his autobiography.

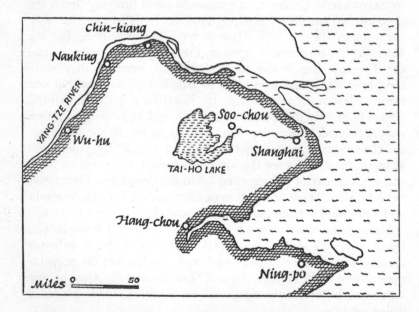

Showing how the land over which the Faithful Prince and Gordon waged war, formed by parts of the provinces of Kiang-su, Che-kiang and An-hui, takes roughly the shape of a tiger's head.

This then was the plan. The land outlined in silhouette by the outflow of the Yang-tze, the open sea, and the next great river to the south, was shaped very roughly in the form of a beast's skull, a tiger perhaps, which gazed forever out to sea to the east. On the flattened ear stood Nanking. At the mouth was Shanghai, on a small river which debouched into the sea like saliva from the fangs. At the lowest point of the throat stood a provincial capital of enormous importance, Hang-chou.

On February 2nd 1860 the Faithful Prince issued out of Wu-hu on the Yang-tze, and, with only 1,250 men as the advance guard of 7,000, cut straight down the line of the tiger's cheek to besiege Hang-chou, thereby threatening to decapitate the entire head of the tiger, and possess himself of the ports through which the Imperialists were buying foreign arms. The Imperial generals were thrown into panic, and raised the siege of Nanking to come to the rescue, only to find that the initial move had been a feint. Faithful had cut back again, and now on May 6th entirely defeated the disorganised Imperial armies, thereby relieving Nanking for the next three years. Tseng, in the far west, refused to come to the aid of the vanquished generals. He had hung on for the last eight years in the west, slowly consolidating his conquest of the interior, and he was not prepared to risk sacrificing his advantage. He did, however, engineer the appointment of his colleague, Li Hung-chang, to cope in the east as Governor of Kiang-su, the province affected.

The defeat of the Imperialists had been frightful. The pirate Chang, an ex-Taiping and now an Imperial general, had 10,000 of his men destroyed in one engagement. The Taipings spread like a flood into the tiger's head. The defeated Imperialists ran for Soo-chou, the capital. It stood in a network of channels at the corner of Tai-ho lake, which took the place of a great eye in the tiger's head. Soo-chou was the Chinese Venice, famous for its beautiful women and its silks. Knowing full well the atrocities committed by the Imperial troops, the citizens closed their gates against the remnants of the defeated army, and in fury and revenge the Imperial soldiers burned its suburbs.

The Faithful Prince with a huge force pursued the flying rabble, taking all the important towns on the way. The Imperial General Chang drowned himself in despair, and was given honourable burial by Faithful. The Imperial General Ho, who was supposed to have held Soo-chou, also committed suicide.

Ho's problems in the last month of his life are a witness to how grotesque was the situation in international politics. He had begged the British and French to come to his aid and help defeat the Taipings before the Allies marched on Peking. He had begged Hsien Feng to make peace with the Europeans, so that he would be free to turn all his forces against the rebels. None of his pleas had met with success. Britain, for all that she meant to punish the Manchu Emperor a little, was determined to keep him on the throne, while remaining officially neutral in the civil war. The French offered to send 15,000 of their troops to protect the priests in the vicinity of Soo-chou, but Bruce persuaded them to refrain. Nevertheless, the possibility was seriously discussed both by Ho and by the British and French, of the Allies simultaneously attacking the Manchu Emperor and his Taiping enemies.

The only coup which Ho was successful in bringing off was to persuade an American filibuster to act as a mercenary and muster some foreign arms. His name was Frederick Townsend Ward, and he came from Salem, Massachusetts. With a hundred foreigners and an unpleasant rowdy called Burgevine as his second-in-command, he was ready for a little adventure. Ho, never dreaming that the little adventure was to end by compromising the British into taking up arms against the Taipings, then strangled himself by way of apology to the Dragon Throne. He left Li Hung-chang, the new Governor of Kiang-su, to cope with the organisation of the mercenaries.

Apart from Ward's small force, soon to be known as the Ever Victorious Army, there was nothing now to prevent the Faithful Prince's advance on Shanghai—nothing, that is, except the British and French defence of the walled city, of which Faithful as yet knew nothing.

"Hung summarily ordered me to take Soo-chou, allowing me a month to do it," wrote the Faithful Prince in his autobiography, and true to his trust Faithful accomplished the task. "We had no sooner reached the Ch'ang Gate", he wrote, "and had thought of investing the city, than we were met by the whole of the people in the Ch'ang Gate Street, who came out to welcome us. The shops were all covered with placards, the tenor of which was that the people were unanimously in favour of the complete extermination

of Chang and Ho's troops, in consequence of these having committed such depredations on the populace after their defeat at
Tan-yang. In the city we found several civil and military officers,
some amongst whom were Manchus. None of them received any
injury, and when they were anxious to return home and were
without travelling expenses, funds were provided them and boats
in which they might take their departure." Faithful had set his
face against any general massacre of Tartars. He was an honourable soldier and a simple Christian, and was admired both for his
benevolence and for his courage. To reassure the people, he went
now barely armed to the surrounding villages to reason with the
ordinary folk and persuade them to return to their usual work in
the city.

Faithful presently moved on until he was within ten miles of
Shanghai. In the previous month, in his despatch of May 30th
1860, Bruce had written to Lord John Russell to say that, in
concert with the French, he had decided to defend the walled
city of Shanghai, "on the ground of its being a port open to trade,
and of the ultimate connection existing between the interests of
the town and of the Foreign settlements, the former of which
cannot be attacked without great danger to the latter."

Bruce's decision was a flagrant breaking of the undertaking to
remain neutral in the civil war. By no possible arguments, however specious, could the defence of the Chinese walled city be
regarded as a neutral act. That Bruce had heavy responsibilities
for the safety of his countrymen was an excuse that might have
justified his action, if he had openly declared to the Taipings that
he had decided to reverse the policy of neutrality, at least in this
one instance; but unfortunately, as it was to turn out, he gave
them no such official intimation. That chaos and misunderstanding should ensue was, therefore, only to be expected.

Meanwhile, with the Taipings established in Soo-chou, which
was a comparatively short distance from Shanghai, the missionaries could for the first time in ten years contact the rebels with
ease. Conscience began to prick, and when Jen-kan, the Shield
Prince, one-time catechist of the London Missionary Society, sent
an invitation to the missionaries to come to Soo-chou, conscience
could no longer be denied.

The Reverend William Muirhead wrote to his brother on June
30th 1860, to tell him how three American missionaries had an-

swered the invitation, and had been agreeably surprised at their reception by the Shield Prince. "Save of course the bloodstained evils of war, these brethren are convinced that elements are in existence and at work, which indicate the movement to be fraught with good, and to be intimately connected with the future Christianisation of China."

The Reverend Joseph Edkins, when an elderly widower, had taken as his second wife a girl of twenty. She came from the Orkneys, and was gentle, pretty, with large dark eyes. Jane's heart was full of faith in God and devotion to her husband, but her health was already in danger from the climate. Her youth, her sweetness, her courage, and alas her delicate health were all to be factors in preventing Edkins from deciding to give his life to instructing the Taiping rebels; and his problem bore witness that, whatever arguments there may be for or against the celibacy of the clergy, certainly missionaries in the midst of a dangerous civil war should not be torn asunder by duties to tender young brides. She, however, was always gallant and smiling in the desire to help her husband spread the word, and she made no demur when she heard that he was to sally forth with the Reverend Griffith John and two other missionaries to Soo-chou. John, like Edkins, was employed by the London Missionary Society. "Nothing can be more erroneous," they reported in the Missionary Magazine of July 16th, "than the supposition that it is purely a political movement."

Bruce was at first unwilling to let the British clergy go to Soo-chou. On that same July 16th, while Shanghai was filled to overflowing with refugees, and the Europeans began frantically to dig trenches to protect the Concessions, he wrote to Lord John Russell to explain his reluctance. "I fear, chiefly, the indiscreet visits of missionaries and others to their headquarters, as it may convey the impression to them of our sympathy with, or fear of, them, and in either case they would be encouraged to present themselves in this neighbourhood."

On the next day, the 17th, Jen-kan wrote a letter to the "Honourable Envoys" informing them that the Taiping Army, under the command of the Faithful Prince, would move towards Shanghai for the purpose of making a treaty, and because the Europeans had invited them thus to do. It seems plain that he was really under the delusion of having been invited. Afterwards there was much speculation about exactly what deep game had been played. Those who were violently anti-Catholic suggested that the French priests had invited the rebels in order to engineer the massacre of the Taiping heretics. It is more likely that certain gun-runners or opium merchants were at work.

The letter from Jen-kan took some time to get through enemy lines. Before it did so John and Edkins, having at last obtained permission from Bruce, had left for Soo-chou. On the morning after they left, Bruce received Jen-kan's letter. At Lord Elgin's special request Harry Parkes, the Shanghai Consul, had been seconded to service with Elgin's suite, and Tom Meadows had therefore been transferred from another open port to act as Consul at Shanghai. Bruce now instructed him to return Jen-kan's letter unopened, and to decline to receive further communications. Within the fatal letter were overtures for peace, notice of how the Faithful Prince would bring an embassy to Shanghai for a parley, and instructions on how foreign and religious buildings were to be marked for safe protection. Meadows, purple with indignation, could do nothing but obey his chief. The letter was returned unopened.

Meanwhile the missionaries were on their way to Soo-chou, travelling by boat along the network of canals through flat rice-land. On the way they chatted to the country folk who were now, by force, subjects of the T'ien Wang. The peasants said that for their part they did not care who was Emperor, so long as they might have peace. The veteran Taiping troops from Kwang-tung and Kwangi-si were good types and humane, they declared. Farmers were left free to get on with their work in the fields, and the Taipings paid honourably for the farm produce.

Presently Edkins and John approached the great moats surrounding the walls of Soo-chou. The waterways were crowded with ferry boats, the local omnibuses, and with cargo boats as heavy as drays. Only the mandarins' junks with their huge umbrellas and gongs were missing, and so were the brothel boats, from which the painted white faces of the prostitutes used to smile.

The missionaries were received by the Shield Prince in full state on August 2nd. Jen-kan was wearing robes and a coronet, but he rose from his princely throne and gave the visitors a hearty handshake. "He said," wrote Griffith John, "that our visit made

him very happy, and that his heart was quite set free. He then
made kind enquiries about his old friends in Shanghai."
"The kingdom of Christ must spread," declared Jen-kan to Mr.
John, "and overcome every opposition. Whatever may become of
the Celestial Dynasty, there can be no doubt concerning the matter."
The clergymen were invited to dine with the Prince. The meal
began with a hymn and a prayer, and then Edkins said grace. The
next day the missionaries found the Shield Prince very agitated,
for he had just learned that his letters to the foreign Powers had
been returned unopened, and that the Chinese walled city of
Shanghai was held by British and French troops. "The first," Mr.
John wrote, "he spoke of as a personal insult to himself, and the
second as a direct violation of the principle of neutrality. In both
points he is decidedly right. We could not but feel a secret sympathy with him. He told us that the chief (the T'ien Wang) is
doubtless a very pious man, notwithstanding all his errors. He
devoutly worships God, and is a constant reader of the Scriptures.
The Bible and *Pilgrim's Progress* seem to be his favourite books."
After spending only three days in the city the missionaries returned to Shanghai. Although Edkins had been shocked to find
that Taiping applicants for baptism were admitted to the font after
not more than one day's instruction, nevertheless none of the
missionaries were prepared at this juncture to leave their flocks
in Shanghai to give the Taipings fuller instruction.
In Shanghai the talk in the Concessions was all of the approaching rebels and the digging of entrenchments. There were some
jokes about the "Coolie Kings", "high life below stairs", and the
fact that the Eastern Prince, the defunct "Comforter", had once
been a tea-porter. That Christ's disciples had been simple fisher-
men of Galilee was conveniently forgotten. There were nevertheless many among the Europeans who disliked the idea of
abandoning neutrality. "The blight of expediency grows like a
parasite about our politicians," wrote John Scarth, the merchant
who had been one of the negotiators of peace with the Triad
rebels six years before. "They have aided in attempting to prove
that error was blasphemy, and instead of fostering the flame have
endeavoured to hide the light. " Foreign trade alone was responsible for Shanghai becoming a great metropolis, and James Forrest
of the Consular Service deemed that its prosperity in the last eight

years had been due to the increase of trade coming from the Taiping territories.

Despite what anyone might say, in fact the British and French were determined to defend the Chinese city, and not to let things get out of hand, for the reason that nearly all their forces had left a month ago for the punitive expedition to Peking, and with the few that remained it was all the more necessary to make a firm stand. Wolseley, later Field Marshal and Viscount, was in command at Shanghai of only one regiment of Sikhs and another of Punjaubies. With so little real power, any vacillation might be fatal, if the rebels chose to attack the Concessions.

The walled Chinese city lay foursquare on the north bank of the river, and to the west of the square were the Foreign Concessions. To get to the Concessions it was necessary to skirt the south wall, and the way between it and the river bank was narrow and confined, closely built with suburbs. Here stood the Roman Catholic Cathedral, which the French were determined to defend, though it would have been in no danger if Tom Meadows had been allowed to open and answer Jen-kan's letter. The French, therefore, burnt the suburbs, so that no cover should be afforded to the enemy, thus proving that European criticism of the Taipings, for having taken similar steps to destroy other city suburbs, was biased.

Refugees were flocking into Shanghai, and within the walls the normal population of 300,000 was swollen to unknown proportions. The people were pasting up the *Illustrated News* over their doorways, in the hope that a foreign document would give them protection.

Bruce's refusal to accept Jen-kan's letter, wherein the Faithful Prince had given exact and particular instructions as to how foreign houses and churches were to hang out yellow flags so that he would be able to distinguish and protect them, was already bearing fruit. The famous Jesuit College for orphans at Zi-ka-wei lay seven miles to the east of the city, in the path of the Taiping Army, and its director, a Neapolitan called Father Louis de Massa, followed the Catholic custom and wore Chinese dress and the pigtail, the mark of subservience to the Manchus. The Faithful Prince was not, therefore, too greatly to blame for the fact that his soldiers, seeing no yellow flag, mistook the priest for a Chinese, broke into the College, attempted to impress de Massa as a bearer,

and, when he protested, slaughtered him together with a number
of his native pupils. The French would not forgive Faithful, despite his apologies, because in the heat of war his ignorant soldiery
had killed de Massa for the reason that they had failed to recognise
that he was a Christian.

Bruce sent the gunboat *Kestrel* with a French steamer up river
to give the Faithful Prince warning that the Chinese city would be
defended by the Allies. His excuse for not having previously made
the position clear was that he had trusted Mr. Edkins to tell Jen-
kan of the Allied decision. Why he should have trusted to a missionary, whose journey to Soo-chou he had tried to prevent, to
deliver such an important message as that Britain was about to
commit an unneutral act is hard to understand. To add to the
confusion, the gunboats now took the wrong route amidst the
network of canals, and the despatch was never delivered.

Thus on August 18th Faithful attacked the Imperial entrenchments one mile from the west gate of Shanghai. The Cantonese,
of whom there were many in the city, would have risen and
delivered it to him, but the British and French were in position on
the walls, and Faithful came on not knowing that foreign guns
were trained on him. He came at the head of only a small force,
his personal guard of 3,000 men, because he was expecting to be
welcomed for the parley, to which he afterwards claimed that the
French had invited him. As he advanced a storm broke, and the
tropical rain made the ground very slippery. Suddenly the foreign
guns opened fire. Before the Taipings could turn themselves
about, 300 of them fell, and Faithful himself was wounded in the
cheek. He gave orders to retreat to Zi-ka-wei, and in the oozing
mud the retreat was not easy.

At Zi-ka-wei he organised a real attack, and for the next three
days he assaulted the city; but the narrow confined way between
the river bank and the south wall was a death-trap. Nevertheless,
despite the havoc to his troops wrought by foreign guns, he posted
a notice of protection on the Roman Catholic Cathedral, and left a
mission house in his path untouched.

Repulsed at last by the foreign guns, he fell back once again to
Zi-ka-wei, and there at last James Forrest was able to deliver the
despatches which the *Kestrel* had failed to present.

Faithful's written reply to Bruce was a protest. He claimed to
have been invited by the French for a parley. His letter regarding

the precaution of yellow flags had been ignored. The foreigners had broken their agreement to remain neutral. He swore that the perfidious French would not in future be permitted to enter Taiping territory for trade. (This meant that for the future the Jesuits would have little chance to Catholicise the Taipings. Father Clavelin had missed the only real opportunity.) "I came to Shanghai to make a treaty in order to see us connected together by trade and commerce," ran Faithful's letter to Bruce. "I did not come with the purpose of fighting you. But," he went on, "if you continue to be directed by the Imperialists, you must not blame me if hereafter you find it difficult to pass along the channels of commerce, and if there is no outlet for native produce to pass to you."

This threat hit the British on the raw. In the view of many merchants, like John Scarth, more trade had reached Shanghai since the Taipings held the Yang-tze than ever before. As the Taipings could strangle it if they chose, it was a short-sighted policy, these merchants thought, to antagonise the rebels.

That Faithful was a Christian, and perhaps a better one than his sovereign, is shown by the records, but he was also a very fine soldier. While he had the right to protest against the fumbling of the diplomats, and though he had at first advanced peacefully with only his small personal guard, it was none the less true that strategically the city was a necessity to him. He would in any case have been bound to try and take it, for in the terrain of the tiger's head Shanghai took the place not only of the tiger's mouth but of its fangs. It was the arsenal through which the Imperialists were receiving British guns. It is equally true that Faithful would have succeeded in taking the city if the British and French had not intervened, and that with Shanghai as his arsenal Hung would probably have won to the Dragon Throne. Now, however, Faithful's threat to renew the attack was empty, for he was aware that his force could not again meet the foreign guns.

Little Mrs. Edkins, who had all the while been confined to bed with a fever, began a letter to her mother on September 1st. Her knees were still very shaky from the fever and dysentery, and sitting at her escritoire she felt the heat. Victorian corsets were stuffy contraptions in tropical weather, and with a finger she tried to loosen her tight collar, ornamented with a cameo brooch. "We have now calm and quiet in Shanghai," she wrote. "Last week it was not so. The thunder of the cannon, and the bursting of the shell, were frequently to be heard." She remembered how she had tossed miserably on her bed throughout the noise, and how her temples had ached. "The rebels arrived, and were received in this manner," she went on. "They behaved in a most respectful way to foreigners, entered some of the houses several miles from this, and when they found the inmates worshipped Shang-ti (God) they were very kind and polite, and had a proclamation put on the door to the effect that, if violence were done to the house, a severe penalty would be inflicted on the perpetrator. They did not return our fire at all."

Bruce, knowing that he would be in for trouble from the Opposition at home for having broken the agreement of neutrality, wrote by the same post to Russell. The more the Taipings could be blackened, the more his action would be justified. "Jen-kan has sent the missionaries a pamphlet," he reported, "which has made a considerable impression on them. I see no guarantee for the soundness of his doctrine or the purity of his life. I rather look upon his pamphlet as a crafty device to conciliate the support and sympathy of the missionary body at a time when the insurgents meditated the seizure of Shanghai."

When the matter came up for debate in Parliament the following spring (March 12th 1861), Lord John Russell was able to quote an American Baptist missionary, a Mr. Holmes, who had by that time grown disillusioned with the Taiping form of Christianity. "Their doctrine is really a blasphemous parody of Christianity. Some among them claim to be the sons and brothers of Christ!" The House of Commons was suitably astonished and horrified. Only Tom Meadows and Dr. Legge openly protested that tangled theology is not a cause for armed intervention.

Shortly after Mrs. Edkins posted her letter, Issachar Roberts at long last felt the call! He arrived from Hong Kong, and, hearing that the Faithful Prince had retired from Shanghai to Soo-chou, there presented himself. He arrived at a time when the people of Soo-chou were suffering famine, due to the disorganisation of the entire province in the civil war, and they were, in a spontaneous gesture of gratitude, erecting an ornamental arch in honour of the Faithful Prince. This they did because of his care and humane treatment of the populace, and because he was paying from his own pocket to feed the destitute.

He had taken several more towns in the terrain of the tiger's head and had enrolled a large number of volunteers in Kiang-si and Ho-peh, and a division of his army was still investing Hang-chou at the tiger's throat. But on September 20th, only a month after his advance on Shanghai, he was at his headquarters in Soo-chou and was enthroned to receive Mr. Roberts. He was surrounded by his Miau bodyguard, whose shock-headed locks were in contrast to his own neatly coiled hair, over which he wore a crown of real gold. He was the only prince to have been accorded such an honour by the T'ien Wang. The other princes, or "Wangs" as they were called, wore coronets of beautiful lacquer, which Europeans referred to scornfully as "pasteboard crowns", but that of Faithful was of the true metal, surmounted by a tiger and a bird, and hung with amber and pearls. Below it, his wounded cheek showed purple, and had resulted in a slight impediment of speech. His spectacles were somewhat incongruous beneath the crown, but, though he was small and spare and wiry, he wore his dragon-embroidered yellow robes with a dignity that was undeniable.

"He received me with all kindness and courtesy," wrote Mr. Roberts to the *China Mail*, "and the probability is will accompany me to Nanking in a few days." The letter went on to speak of how the Faithful Prince desired peaceful relations with the foreigners. "He is greatly at a loss to know how two nations worshipping the same Great God, like the Western Powers and the Heavenly King, can fall out and fight. I have preached once to the Prince and his Counsellors and to about a hundred and fifty of his highest officials by invitation, and received from all every attention and courtesy that I could ask."

Faithful then proceeded to enquire of Roberts why the missionaries did not come and teach as they had been invited to do. It was an embarrassing question. Roberts preferred to dwell on an aspect of the movement which shocked him. After dining with the Prince he attended a religious meeting, where provisions were heaped before an altar in honour of Shang-ti, in much the same way as at Harvest Thanksgiving. There was the usual praying, hymn singing and burning of prayers, but it was the heaping of the provisions which the Baptist could not stomach. He wrote recording his doubts as to the ceremony having any other meaning in the eyes of the mass of worshippers than was attached to the

rites performed by the Emperor at the Altar of Heaven in Peking.
Within a few days Mr. Roberts left Soo-chou en route for
Nanking under the escort of the Faithful Prince. Faithful, much
against his will, was answering the summons of his sovereign to
return at once to the capital. Forty military commanders and some
tens of thousands of men were on the point of coming over from
the Imperial Armies to join him at Soo-chou. He might lose this
valuable advantage if he left the terrain of the tiger's head, yet he
dared not disobey, for the T'ien Wang's summons was imperative.

Once again the master mind, although isolated behind the barriers of Imperial etiquette and immured in a palace, had seen what
was the necessary move. The Allies were advancing on Peking. It
was late September. The Taiping Armies must go north, make
confusion worse confounded, and seize the Forbidden City while
the Imperial forces were in flight from the Allies.

How surprised Lord Elgin would have been if, after battling
his way to Peking, he had found not the Manchu, Hsien Feng,
but the Chinese Hung Hsiu-ch'uan upon the Dragon Throne! But
now Faithful, able tactician that he was, made the fatal mistake of
refusing to obey the orders of the broad strategist. No wonder
that, as Faithful later recorded, "The Heavenly King was exceedingly angry, and his rebuke was such that I could not put up with
it." The Prince was determined that he must first return to Soo-
chou and accept the allegiance of the new contingents.

Hung, as he sat in audience, crowned and seated on his throne,
smiled scornfully. "Are you afraid of death?" he taunted his
Commander-in-Chief. "I, the truly appointed Lord, can, without
the aid of troops, command great peace to spread its sway over
the whole region."

"What," wrote Faithful afterwards, "could I say to this? I was
unable to reply. All I could do was to breathe and sigh."

Hung had unfortunately used the wrong arguments with his
obstinate general. His qualities as a visionary and poet gave Faithful the excuse to discount his qualities as a strategist. The prince
won his way, permission to return to Soo-chou and collect his
new contingents. Seventy thousand Imperialists came over to him.
Then, as a compromise, the T'ien Wang agreed that the four main
Taiping armies should be launched westward against Tseng, first
to relieve An-king, and then to retake the Triple City, where they
were to meet in a pincer movement. They issued forth in October

1860. Had Faithful obeyed his sovereign, they might have been in Peking.

It had taken the Allies just over a year to assemble the punitive force. The British had 12,000 men, and the French 6,000 odd. Elgin had insisted on having Harry Parkes on his staff. Parkes was maturing under the weight of responsibility. He was no longer the brash young man who had initiated the Arrow War, which had led in turn to this war. Elgin for his part had grown less mild towards the mandarins since their treacherous attack upon his brother, Sir Frederick Bruce, as a treaty bearer.

The Allied Expedition sailed at last on July 21st 1860, just as the Taipings were expected to advance on Shanghai. The Taku forts were heavily defended by the Mongol Prince Senkolintsin, but were taken, and the Allies fought their way to Tientsin, which they reached on August 25th. As Elgin's instructions were to avoid at all costs bringing down the Manchu dynasty, it was with much relief that, after inflicting a severe defeat on the Mongol forces, he received offers from Prince Senkolintsin for a truce. If peace could be patched up, he would not have to assault the capital. But, alas, Elgin had not even yet plumbed the depths of mandarin treachery. On September 17th Harry Parkes and Mr. Loch, together with several officers and a small escort of Indian cavalry, rode to the agreed place of meeting within the enemy lines to make arrangements for the conference, bearing the white flag of truce.

Received at first with courtesy, they set about their various jobs, and the party became divided. Parkes and Loch were then seized, bound, and flung at the feet of Senkolintsin. They were fortunate in being transported by waggon, roped like pigs, to Peking, where they were cast into the most terrible of all gaols belonging to the Board of Punishments. The rest of the party was never seen alive again. Most of them died because they were bound so tightly that their limbs developed gangrene.

As soon as Elgin had been advised of what had happened, battle was joined again, and now there was no help for it but to march on Peking, if only to deliver Parkes and Loch from a cruel death. The march began. The Emperor Hsien Feng fled to his hunting lodge at Jehol, taking with him his young Empress, who was now the mother of the heir. On October 6th, at about the time when the T'ien Wang had ordered his Taiping armies to be in the north,

the Allied Army occupied the Summer Palace, and the mandarins
set Parkes and Loch free. The Forbidden City was entered, and
the Allies demanded half a million taels of silver as indemnity for
the war, while the Russians ingratiated themselves by attempting
to make the Allies abate the claim. The bodies of the dead prisoners, who had been confined in the Summer Palace, were now
recovered and buried with full military honours, and Elgin decided that, to punish the Emperor for their death, and for breaking
the truce, he would burn the Summer Palace, which the French
had already looted.

On October 24th Prince Kung, the Emperor's brother, had perforce to sign the treaty, the Convention of Peking. The terms
were roughly identical with the Treaty of Tientsin which Bruce
had sought to have ratified the year before. The French procured
a superb site for a cathedral in Canton, the right to rent sites at all
open ports, and the restitution of old church properties and ceme-
teries. Already passports to the interior were being written out for
the priests by the French Minister. "Given at Peking . . . on
condition that (so-and-so) shall not go under any pretext whatever into the towns and villages occupied by the rebels." The
earlier desire of the Jesuits to Catholicise the Taipings was forgotten in viewing the exciting prospects and possibilities which were
opening up.

Standing amongst the ruins of the Summer Palace, a young
Scottish major, Charles Gordon by name, sighed to see the destruction. Then he hurried off to join his regiment and the army,
which was being speedily evacuated back to Shanghai. Very few
lives had been lost in the north, but in Shanghai the Imperial
execution ground was the usual bloody shambles, and the decapi-
tating often took place in the open streets of the suburbs adjoining
the Foreign Concessions. Ward's little army of mercenaries
brought in the victims. The execution of the Taiping prisoners
was a sight not easily avoided by the Europeans, and it went on
from day to day.

Gordon's mother was a very religious woman, and so was his
sister. They had provided him with a Bible, and now for the first
time the constant shedding of human blood began to make him
reflect upon the meaning of life, and the problem of human suffering. Until now he had not bothered very much to think about such

things. He had served in the Crimea, but the gallantry of men in battle, and the acceptance amongst Christian nations of certain chivalrous standards in the prosecution of war, had so far hidden from his eyes the bestiality of which men were capable. Very different from the heroic charge of the Light Brigade was this calculated butchery, to be witnessed every day in the open streets; the sight of truncated necks in which the vertebrae and oozing blood vessels were visible, the long hair trailing in the mud of the gutter, and the eyes staring upwards, oblivious of the settling flies.

For the first time Gordon turned to the Bible for understanding, a lonely soldier at last finding his soul. In after years he was to win the reputation of never being parted from it. They said he carried the sword in one hand and the Bible in the other. This was not strictly true, for such was his personal courage that he led assaults carrying only a cane in lieu of a sword. The Chinese came to believe that the cane had magic properties. Certainly his thoughts became wrapped in the Bible, and there is a strange irony in the fact that this soldier, a most righteous man and believer, was deputed by fate to destroy not one but two mystics, fanatics, madmen or whatever they truly were. Both claimed to have received a divine mission from Heaven: first Hung Hsiu-ch'uan, the Heavenly King, in China; and afterwards the Mahdi in the Sudan, whose title means "The Expected Guide".

Some people thought that Gordon himself was a visionary and slightly mad.

21

BETWEEN THE SUMMER of 1860, when members of the clergy first visited Jen-kan in Soo-chou, and the spring of 1861, at least five missionaries went to Nanking, but not one except Mr. Roberts remained for more than a few days. Hung had adopted a new and dangerous attitude, as was shown in the verses he had addressed to Lord Elgin: "Which is right amongst the writings of the Father and the Elder Brother, it is impossible to know. He who would choose the true must ascend to High Heaven." He claimed now to have the right to correct whatever he considered to be errors in the scriptures and in any commentaries sent him by the missionaries.

For nearly eight years the missionaries had found reasons which forbade them to approach the T'ien Wang, so that it was not surprising that he had grown intransigent. Nevertheless, even at this late date something might have been accomplished if the clergy had been prepared to show great patience, to establish a permanent mission, as they were invited to do, and to teach by example. Unfortunately they came with the purpose of disputing on theology, and of upbraiding the Heavenly King for his mistaken beliefs. As they were unwilling to kow-tow they were not, with the sole exception of Mr. Roberts, received in audience, and the disputes were conducted by means of written correspondence only.

Mr. Holmes, an American Baptist, was the first to write out a questionnaire. Did the T'ien Wang claim to be God or man? In the Gospel of St. John it was written, "No man hath ascended up to heaven". So how could the Taiping chief boast of such an ascent? The dignitary responsible for lodging Mr. Holmes refused to forward the questionnaire to his sovereign, because of its hectoring tone, and Mr. Holmes promptly departed.

The Reverend Griffith John of the London Missionary Society stayed seven days, and made an earnest attempt to be co-operative. He obtained an edict giving full religious toleration for missionaries of all denominations, including Catholics, to preach in Nanking and the Taiping territories. On December 5th 1860 he wrote to his mother that the Faithful Prince "begged me to inform the foreign brethren that the following are his views: 'You have had the Gospel upwards of eighteen hundred years, we only as it were eight days. Your knowledge of it ought to be correct and extensive, ours must necessarily be limited and imperfect. You must therefore bear with us for the present, and we will gradually improve.' "

Mr. John left Nanking because he wished to wait, before setting up a permanent mission, until such time as the development of the civil war made it possible to have direct and easy communication with the coast, from where he could draw his financial support. He was not willing to depend for his sustenance upon the Heavenly King, and thus be less able to argue with Hung about his heretical beliefs. Although he took his leave of the Taiping capital with high hopes and favourable opinions, he later refused to return. The reasons for his change of opinion seem to have rested on his examination of the reports of his colleagues: in them he took special offence at Hung's apparent assertion "that Christ has three sons and two daughters. What he means by this statement," wrote Mr. John to his brother on March 6th, "I really do not know. He is either an impostor or insane." It is doubtful whether the Welshman had properly understood the correspondence conducted in Chinese, for it seems that Hung used the word son freely, particularly whenever he meant to emphasise that a soul was beloved by the Heavenly Father.

The Reverend Joseph Edkins, also of the London Missionary Society, now came to share a lodging in Nanking with Issachar Roberts, and together they conducted several theological disputes with Hung. For a week or more letters shot backwards and forwards between their quarters and the sovereign's palace. Unfortunately Edkins came to his task with a mind biased against any of Hung's claims to direct revelation. "This foolish story, which describes a sort of trance," was how Edkins referred to the accounts of Hung's vision. "The Taiping enterprise has originated not in imposture, but in fanatic delusion." Notwithstanding his prejudice, he found that "Hung's mode of writing is thoroughly respectful and friendly in its tone. He looks upon the Christians of England and America as good men teaching the true religion."

The Heavenly King was nevertheless not prepared to play the part of the humble pupil. He quoted scripture readily and held his own in the theological arguments, though from a most unorthodox basis.

He first answered Issachar's reproof for having given Yang the title of Saviour. Yang had only saved from sickness, not from sin. As for Christ alone being the head of the Church, that referred to the spiritual Church. But of the Temporal Church he,

Hung, and the Young Lord were, with the Father and Elder
Brother, at the head. In other words he claimed to be a kind
of pope of the Church Militant. One edict to Issachar contained
nine reasons for maintaining that Christ was inferior to the Father,
and Hung quoted Edkins as having stated that Arius was condemned for this view, and went on, "Assuredly the council was
wrong, and Arius right."

At last the missionaries, after all these years, had got at the
truth. "He has no proper conception of the divinity of our
Saviour," wrote Edkins, "only of his humanity. He knows him as
a man, and understands the title, Son of God, to be applicable to
Him (Christ) as a man elected and adopted as the Son of the
Father. So he looks upon himself as similarly elected and adopted
to be the head of the new theocratic kingdom, which the Taiping
revolution is intended to inaugurate. Hence, too, he also calls the
Eastern prince a Son of God. He has written to Mr. Roberts, 'You
also are a son of God.' " Hung had just returned one of Edkins'
comments, and from the phrase referring to Christ as "the only
begotten Son of God" had erased the word "only".

It became evident, therefore, that it was a waste of time to
argue with the T"ien Wang on the subject of the Yin Principle
and the possibility of Christ's having a female helpmate in heaven.
It was more urgent to ascertain what he believed about the Deity.
"In the image of God created he them" (Adam and Eve) seemed
to have been taken by Hung to mean that God also had his female
counterpart. Edkins and Roberts strove to give him the idea that
God was formless.

Hung promptly replied at length in poetical measure. "Not
having seen God, do not say that He has not been seen. The
Elder Brother and I have seen the Father, plainly and certainly
so. In the year 1837 I went to heaven, taken there by the Father.
My eyesight failing, I cannot correct all the papers you have
presented."

Again Edkins remonstrated by letter that God had no visible
form. Hung countered by replying, "The sacred countenance
only the Son of God can see."

"He contradicts in a decided but good-humoured tone," Edkins
had to admit. "He says that when taken to heaven, the Heavenly
Father told him that he was his son. He hopes to persuade
missionaries to recognise him as a sort of Son of God. In this

point there appear to be good grounds to suppose that his reason is affected."

While Edkins and Roberts endeavoured to disabuse Hung of his weird ideas about Christian theology, Hung for his part was doing his best to persuade them to believe in his divine mission. "I have written to you many letters. Do you cordially recognise the fact that I have gone to heaven, or do you not? Do you, with all the Western brethren, perceive my meaning? Do you acknowledge the holy will of God? Think of the risen sun shining in the heavens?" He meant himself. "Will you not awake? Will you not believe?" Mahomet himself had no greater faith in his mission than had Hung.

At last it was arranged that Roberts was to be received in audience without the necessity to kow-tow. Wearing yellow robes, as ordained by the T'ien Wang's court etiquette, he was ushered into the presence, and there for the first time for fourteen years Lo-han and Hung Hsiu-ch'uan came face to face. Hung asked Roberts if he remembered him. Issachar hesitated, and then, being strictly truthful, replied that he scarcely did. He vaguely remembered a young man of talent, clean-shaven and good-looking, about whom he had written to the newspapers soon after the publication of Hamberg's pamphlet; but this crowned monarch nearly fifty years old, large of stature, with a flowing black beard, and robes stiff with golden dragon embroideries, was a person whom he could not recognise. Being unwilling to kow-tow like the other courtiers, or to turn to the adjacent altar of the Heavenly Father and kneel as they did, lest he be misunderstood or be found guilty of bowing down to false gods, Issachar felt somewhat ill at ease, and after a few words of courteous welcome from the T'ien Wang, he was no doubt glad to withdraw. Perhaps Hung was as disappointed at the appearance of Lo-han as Issachar was dumbfounded by the enthronement in state of his one-time pupil, for the invitation to an audience was not repeated, and for the future correspondence was once again confined to letter writing.

Both Edkins and Roberts delivered sermons in the streets of Nanking on the Sabbath, and they listened to the prince-generals preaching to their troops amidst a sea of flags waving in the wind.

Edkins was now offered a house in which to set up a mission, but the contamination of the well-water (because day-labourers were refused access to the city to carry away night-soil in the customary manner) made him fearful for the health of his tender young bride. To bring her to this stronghold of brigands to die of dysentery was more than he could bear. After all, there were many other and easier fields requiring harvesters. "Mr. Edkins feels duty calls to Nanking, while inclination says the north," wrote Jane to her parents. "I am quite contented to go to Nanking." Her husband, however, decided to follow the easier path. They went north to the new mission at Tientsin, where, sadly but ironically enough, Jane died within four months of the dysentery from which her elderly Joseph had tried to protect her.

The Reverend William Muirhead's report was perhaps the fairest and most important. He also was from the London Missionary Society. The task laid upon the clergy did not merely concern the soul of Hung Hsiu-ch'uan, but those of his subjects also, of whom there were twenty-five million. Had the seed fallen on good ground, and, despite the T'ien Wang's personal failings and heresies, could his followers be considered Christians? This was what Muirhead wanted to know.

"Fighting, as they think, under the banners of the Heavenly Father and Heavenly Brother," ran his account, "they contemplate a happy issue as a matter of course. As the Shield Prince's followers were assembling in front of his palace and our rooms, a young man came upstairs. I asked him if he was going to join the army? He said, 'Yes.' 'Was he not afraid of being wounded or killed?' 'Oh, no,' he replied. 'The Heavenly Father will befriend me.' 'Well, but suppose you should be killed, what then?' 'Why, my soul will go to heaven.' 'How can you expect to go to heaven? What merit have you to get there?' 'None, none in myself. It is entirely through the merits of the Heavenly Brother that this is to be done.' 'Who is the Heavenly Brother?' 'I am not very learned,' he said, 'and request instruction.' I then began to tell him that He was the Son of the Heavenly Father, but before I had finished the sentence he replied correctly. 'What great work did Christ do?' I asked. The young man gave an explicit statement of the Saviour's work for sinners, of his coming into the world, suffering and dying in the room of sinful man, in order to redeem us from sin and misery. I enquired if he believed all this. 'Assuredly,' was his reply. 'When did you join the dynasty?' 'Last year.' 'Can you read?' 'No.' 'Who instructed you in these things?' 'The Tsan Prince.' (One of the Ministers of State.) 'What does he in the way of instructing his people?' 'He has daily service in his palace, and often preaches to them alike at home and when engaged in the field.' 'What book does he use?' 'He has a number belonging to the dynasty.' 'Can you repeat the doxology of the Heavenly Father?' He went over it correctly. It contains, in simple language and in rhythmical form, the fundamental tenets of Christianity. 'Are there any special laws or commands connected with the dynasty?' 'There are the ten Commandments.' 'Repeat them.' He went over a number of them, till he came to the sixth."

At this point the missionary and the young soldier agreed to differentiate between murder and killing men in battle in the exercise of a soldier's duty. The Taiping lad had to admit that murder and depredations were committed by the raw recruits, of whom there were, alas, far too many, and he was willing to concede that those who thus broke the Commandments would go to hell when they died, despite serving under the T'ien Wang's banner.

It was becoming more and more apparent that, as Tseng drove the Taipings eastward, and as they daily recruited new contingents, the influx brought opportunists, brigands and vagabonds into the army, who could have no possible claim upon the sympathy of the missionaries. Perhaps it was for this reason that, despite Muirhead's attempt to give a picture of a typical young Taiping soldier, his final report, as incorporated in the Parliamentary Papers presented to the House of Commons, was not favourable to the rebels. He found that the T'ien Wang was the head and soul of the movement, which from the secular point of view was at the moment only destructive. True, the future programme of the Taipings, if carried out, would mean unthought-of progress. Every branch of Western industry and civilisation would be encouraged. But he was doubtful if, given success, the Taipings had the intelligence to carry out their plans.

Muirhead here missed the point emphasised by Chinese history, namely that, given success, a new dynasty could thenceforth command the allegiance and co-operation of the entire Chinese literati to carry out any policy instituted by the Dragon Throne. Even Bruce had to admit that the change would be quietly accepted throughout China once decisive military victory had made it a *fait accompli*. From the religious point of view, Muirhead thought that the movement would only serve to introduce a spurious kind of Christianity. Here he made no allowance for the chance that, given time, Hung, or if not Hung himself at least his son, could have been won over by the Catholic or Protestant missionaries who would have been welcomed to his court. His report showed a resentment of the fact that the Chinese were too proud to be taught by foreigners, and a regret that the missionaries were too divided in their opinions and conduct in relation to each other to make their message effective in the face of such difficulties. Like Griffith John, he felt that it would have been easier to preach to a heathen ruler, rather than to a pseudo-Christian or heretic, and he therefore left Nanking after little more than a week.

Meanwhile Issachar Roberts had been accorded the title of "Heaven's Righteousness", and, when all the other missionaries departed, he stayed on, inhabiting an uncomfortable room above the two offices pompously known as the Boards of Revenue and Rites, in which little but the coal was kept. Perhaps he felt that after seven years of neglect he owed the Taipings a special effort. But alone, and speaking only Cantonese dialect, he could do very little, and his one admirable quality now showed itself—his genuine devotion to his God. He put aside sectarian wrangling and sent an appeal to the Catholic missions to come and help spread the gospel.

Unfortunately his appeal arrived at a time when the Jesuit priests—and there were only fifty in the affected provinces—were killing themselves in an attempt to succour the refugees in and around Shanghai. They were distributing 40,000 cups of rice daily. In the French Concession alone there were 700,000 refugees in the year 1862, and there were three million in the vicinity in the following year. Eleven priests died of overwork, and cholera had broken out. The Jesuit Fathers were all, if not of French nationality, at least under the protection of France, and the French, who had driven the Triads out of Shanghai in 1853 and burned the suburbs, and were accused of having betrayed the Faithful Prince, were no longer received in favour by the Taiping princes. The priests could, therefore, meet only with the rabble, the raw recruits who were becoming every year more of a menace to the innocent population, and who carried out their orders to destroy all idols with an ignorance, and a pleasure in general destruction, that failed to distinguish between the images of Kwan-yin, Chinese goddess of Mercy, and those of the Blessed Virgin.

Nevertheless, as soon as it had become apparent that many Catholic Christians were living under Taiping dominion, some of the Jesuit Fathers had begun to grow their hair long, so that they could pass secretly into rebel territory and succour their flocks. Father Clavelin, writing in September of 1861, thought that the time had come when the Jesuits would have to make a real effort to return to Nanking, particularly in view of Roberts' appeal. But before anything further could be done, the political situation had changed again, and Roberts had executed an astonishing *volte face*.

While the Jesuits were deliberating, the Heavenly Capital was receiving several visits from various Europeans. Admiral Hope had sailed there with an expedition on February 11th 1861, his purpose being to exact from the T'ien Wang a promise not to attack Shanghai in the future. Harry Parkes was his spokesman, and Hung grudgingly agreed through his ministers not to attack that city for a period of twelve months. It was a promise detrimental to his interests, since Shanghai was the arsenal through which the Imperialists were buying arms, but he faithfully kept his word. To Parkes' demand that a British gunboat, the *Centaur*, should be permanently anchored off Nanking, ostensibly to mark the ever-changing flow of the river with beacons to guide trading ships, but more immediately to prevent gun-runners from supplying the rebels, Hung gave a refusal. He had sought counsel of his Heavenly Father, and, as his ministers informed Parkes, had received a vision forbidding his sanctioning such a measure. "Tut, tut, tut! Won't do at all," burst out Harry, his blue eyes flashing. "He must have *another* vision."

British pressure won the battle of wills, and Admiral Hope and Parkes sailed on up the Yang-tze to the Triple City, there to exert further pressure upon the Taiping general, Four-Eyed-Dog, and induce him to refrain from attacking Han-kow. The campaign of the four main rebel armies, due to converge here, had not been progressing well, and Parkes' covert threats of reprisals if the Taiping general should defy his warning not to attack, further disrupted the union of Faithful's troops with those of Four-Eyed-Dog.

Consul James Forrest, who was also paying a visit to Nanking, earnestly desired, like Meadows, to preserve neutrality. He thought that, as regards trade, there was no indication that the Taipings would not make as good traders as the Manchus, given peaceful conditions. Even Bruce, writing to Lord John Russell, had to admit that "raw silk comes down as usual from the interior". The rebels allowed trade to go down, but officially the British would not allow guns to go up. Nevertheless, the gun-runners were beginning to prove too many for the British authorities, for the temptation to make a private fortune was great. Ward's band of mercenaries was activated by no other motive than personal gain, but, since they were on the side of the Imperialists, Bruce's policy favoured them, whereas those who supplied arms to the Taipings were written off as rowdies. Mr. Lindley, who was to prove the most famous of the gun-runners, was accused of being such a rowdy, a mere adventurer, but viewed dispassionately he was more of the type of an Elizabethan pirate.

Lindley had turned up in Hong Kong as second officer of a merchant steamer in the summer of 1859. There he explored sing-song houses, gazed with distaste at the girls with floured faces and bulging ankles over hoof-like bound feet; did a little drinking, theatre-going and duck-shooting, and chaffed the boat-women who laundered the linen of the foreign sailors. Then, on shore at Whampoa near Canton, he fell into a romantic adventure. One of the bum boats brought, instead of his laundry, a deliciously pretty Portuguese lady-in-distress, against whose sixteen summers, peach-like skin, and huge, dark, tearful eyes he had no defence. Her father, a Portuguese from Macao, had forcibly betrothed her to a wealthy Eurasian, whom she detested, and with her servant girl she was seeking to run away. Would he give her a passage to Hong Kong? Her name was Marie. He could not say "no". He smuggled her aboard and hid her in the sailroom, while he put the British Consul's search party off the scent. Lindley became promptly engaged to the young beauty, and duly delivered her to her friends in Hong Kong. Within six months they in their turn took the girl to Shanghai to live with her relatives there. To follow her, Lindley took a job as chief mate in a small steamer. In order to get a register, this boat was nominally British, but she was owned by a Chinese, and was carrying dollars to the Taipings. "If outsiders can be made to believe the Taipings bad," explained the skipper, "they will not trust themselves or their money amongst them. So those who know better are able to monopolise the silk trade."

The ship was carrying £13,000 sterling for the purchase of silk, and Lindley went with her up the Yang-tze. She had a 9-lb. pivot gun and a 4-lb. swivel gun in the bow, and her crew consisted of eight Europeans and six Chinese. They were fired on by the Imperialists and returned the fire, but the Imperial gunboats retreated on finding that the crew was European. Since the British arsenals had been thrown open to the Manchu government, these Imperial gunboats were formidable. The river was also swarming with pirates, and no one knew who was who.

On the way back Lindley left his ship, and with his servant and interpreter came to Soo-chou, which was by then in Taiping hands. Here he gained an audience with the Faithful Prince, who for the next four years was to be his host in Nanking. In the Heavenly Hall of the yamen Faithful sat enthroned, wearing the long yellow robes of his rank, stiff with gold, and the golden crown surmounted by the tiger. He carried a jade sceptre, and round him stood his Miau bodyguard. On the walls of the yamen were hung the Catholic Stations of the Cross. "I no sooner found myself before the Faithful Prince than I respected him," wrote Lindley. "He appeared so unmistakably a master spirit, with the innate nobleness of presence of one born to command." Gordon shared Lindley's respect for Faithful. The Prince was about thirty-five, light, active, wiry and small. He had a dark complexion, but his features were almost European. His eyes flashed and twinkled, and he had ceaseless nervous movements, though he was perfectly cool in battle.

Lindley, seeing a chance to make sufficient money to set up house with his intended bride, accepted a commission from the Prince, and became captain of a schooner to run arms and victuals up the Yang-tze. But, alas, in the spring of 1861, on one of his periodic returns to Shanghai, he found the house of his beloved empty and pillaged, and the fair one missing. The Eurasian to whom she was betrothed had abducted her. In the misery of a man deprived by violence of his female, Lindley sought word high and low of her whereabouts, and at last heard that she was confined as a prisoner in a lorcha at Chin-kiang. He straightway hired a junk, the better to disguise his purpose and identity, trailed the lorcha up river, boarded her in a stirring rescue scene twelve miles below Nanking, and, hotly pursued by his piratical rival, made all sail for the cover of the Taiping batteries. Under them he hoisted the flag given him by Faithful, and thus brought his sweetheart to live within the walls of the Heavenly Capital.

The runaway couple were welcomed by the Commander of the forts and batteries, a literate gentleman who had been a high mandarin at the Triple City, and had gone over to the Taipings. After dinner the women appeared, and the officer's four-year-old son sat on Lindley's lap and prattled the Lord's Prayer. At 10 P.M. prayers, hymns and Bible-reading closed the day.

The next morning the couple were escorted into the city to Faithful's palace, where the womenfolk took charge of Marie. Every day Lindley watched the women of the palace teaching their children the Lord's Prayer with black characters on a white board. He married his Marie according to the Taiping rites, their hands joined in solemn ceremony before all the family of the Faithful Prince, and a benediction was pronounced in the name of the Father, Son and Holy Spirit. Then he went to war.

There were many Europeans already serving privately as mercenaries with the Taipings, just as Ward's force was employed by the Imperialists. Lindley became an artillery instructor and fought in several battles, but presently he was more urgently needed to continue his original task, the supply of guns and victuals. According to his account, the British had taken to transporting the Imperialists up river from Shanghai, safely past Nanking under cover of the British flag, to reinforce the investment of An-king. In fact, everyone was using everyone else's flags in order to run commodities and arms to whichever side they favoured. The Consul at Chin-kiang, where British permits were checked, wrote to Bruce the following year to say that an American boatmaster had confessed to bringing 500 muskets and 500 lb. of powder from Shanghai. He flew foreign colours while passing the native custom houses (thus avoiding the Manchu officials), but on getting near Chin-kiang hauled them down, and passed up as a native boat (thus avoiding the British authorities).

The Imperial war junks were useless, wrote the Consul. Useless, according to Lindley, except to extract "squeeze" money. On one occasion, in order to avoid the Imperial customs boat, he wore

British naval uniform and a sword, and produced a newspaper, *The North China Herald,* in an attempt to pass it off to the Mandarin as his commission in Her Majesty's forces. For once the mandarin was not taken in, and threatened to execute him, unless of course he was prepared to pay a ransom to line the mandarin's pockets. Luckily, since he had not sufficient silver on him, Lindley was rescued by an American river boat flying the Imperial flag, which towed him into Nanking for the moderate price of 300 dollars. The officers of H.M.S. *Centaur,* at anchorage opposite Nanking, must have had their hands full checking permits, and endeavouring to carry out a policy of neutrality which was becoming more and more of a farce.

From the reports of Forrest and Parkes, both of whom visited Nanking in 1861, it is possible to reconstruct a picture of the Heavenly Capital as last seen by Europeans before its fall. Above the gates hung Christian edicts, together with the decapitated heads of those who had broken the Commandments. Outside was a village of lepers, which received no charity. There were forced labour gangs, each man tattooed with the characters of the Kingdom of Great Peace; the crowds within the gates importuned the foreign brethren to sell them opium and ammunition. The moustached officers, mounted for the most part, rode through the streets, their wide black trousers straddling the high Chinese saddles. Their yellow sashes were stuck with swords and pistols below their tight red jackets, braided according to their regiments. They were always attended by dashing, rollicking boys, the "squires", who carried their rifles. The women were good-looking and well-dressed in silks looted from Soo-chou, and there was a preference for garish colors amongst both sexes. At every reception guests were greeted with music and the firing of guns. Despite the proscription of alcohol, the chiefs kept secret supplies of gin in their cupboards. They fed off exquisite porcelain and drank from vessels of silver and gold, but Forrest shuddered at the spittal on the floor, while no doubt his Chinese hosts were horrified by the use of handkerchiefs put back dirty into a pocket. On Friday night a large flag was set up in the street, on which characters proclaimed, "Tomorrow is the Sabbath. Each should be reverent and worship". At midnight cakes and fruit were made ready, and then to the noise of deafening cymbals, firecrackers and gongs the people began to chant, "Praise God, the holy and

Heavenly Father . . . the Supreme Ruler pitied mankind, and sent his firstborn . . . upon a cross they nailed his body. He shed his precious blood to save all men."

Forrest chatted to the old janitor, who had dandled the infant Hung, and he dined with the Shield Prince, the most enlightened Chinese he had ever met. Jen-kan had grown fat, but was of pleasing countenance. He had a passion for modern sciences, and his private sanctum was littered with telescopes, revolvers, windsor soap, a barometer, an alarm clock and mixed pickles from Fortnum & Mason, together with priceless specimens of carved jade, of which he was a connoisseur.

Parkes had a less entertaining time sitting outside the T'ien Wang's palace, while he waited for the answer to the demands which he was making on behalf of Admiral Hope. The crowd in the outer court was mostly of ill-dressed boys, the "squires". The paintwork of the entrance was dilapidated. He watched the charcoal, wood and hot water placed before the gilded gates for the women servants to fetch. On either side of the gate stood two American brass howitzers, rows of halberds, and two immense gongs. The sleepy gate-wardens woke to cane the boys who were teasing them, and from within the palace he could hear the clamour of women and of gongs being beaten. Presently a yellow satin edict was brought out and placed by the women on a table for the guards to uplift, yet another of Hung's poetic efforts.

22

WITHIN THE PALACE the Heavenly King was becoming more and more of a recluse. When he realised that his powers as a strategist had been overruled by Faithful, the tactician; that the chance to march on Peking at the same time as the Allies had been lost; and that the foreign brethren had set their faces against him; then Yen-lo, the Prince of Darkness, whispered that all was lost. To combat his melancholy and fear of predestined catastrophe, he sought desperately for signs from Heaven, and began to record and attach importance to any and every dream.

In January 1861 he published an edict bidding all his prince-generals take more wives, the number to be in accordance with their rank. His probable motive was to ensure that from his literate Christian leaders a new generation should be bred to support the dynasty, but the edict did not endear him to the missionaries. Worse was to follow. He attempted now to extricate himself from the muddle which had been caused by his earlier declaration that the Young Lord, his son, had been adopted by Jesus. He had been anxious to ensure that the mandate to rule China should come to the youth direct from Heaven, but he had found himself forced to use such a clumsy phrase as, "Father, Son and Royal Grandson are together Lord of the new heaven and earth". He was faced with an even greater difficulty because he had at the same time confused the generations—an inexcusable sin in the eyes of those who followed Confucian principles. Each generation owed reverence to its elders, and should not therefore address those elders as brother and sister.

Hung now sought to explain that, though generation proceeded from generation of men, none ever proceeded further than being sons of God. Seated at his writing desk and deep in thought, his brush had idly drawn the character for "Wang". It was the character which was used both for his own title of "King" and for the title of "Prince", which he now gave to all his commanders, of whom there were close on two thousand at this date.

He drew the character again, thus, 王 , and decided that it would serve for an illustration of the lesson he sought to teach. He put a dot above it, to represent the Supreme Lord, the indefinable God, the source of the perpendicular line of Life. The three horizontal bars could then represent, first Christ the highest, Saviour of the world; second and smallest, the Young Lord, watched over by both Christ and his earthly father; and, bottommost, himself. Each was thus distinct in person and generation, yet each was equally close to the descending lifeline of God. He published the result in an edict, and at about the same time wrote, "The Father and the Elder Brother, together with me, three persons constitute one". This seemed an inexcusable blasphemy, but he was probably working from the twenty-first verse of the seventeenth chapter of St. John: "That they all may be one; as thou, Father, art in me, and I in thee, that they also may be one in us."

While the T'ien Wang was concerning himself with matters of religion, the Faithful Prince was struggling with the campaign of the four armies due to converge on the Triple City. The campaign was not working out according to plan. This had been partly due to Parkes' diplomacy, but chiefly to the courage and persistence of Tseng.

At one time Tseng had faced almost certain capture and death, but he had clung on, and would not move out of the area. He had just refused an offer of help from Russia. He wanted no foreigners in the interior, least of all the Russians, but nevertheless he had begun to see that the British might be used. If he stuck to his original plan to mop up the west, the interior, he could so exert pressure and roll the rebels eastward that they in their turn would be bound to break out towards the eastern sea ports. British patience would then crack under the strain of trying to preserve both neutrality and the valuable property in the Concessions, and the rebels would be caught between the upper and nether millstones, while Chinese prestige would not suffer by having to call for aid.

The year 1861 was fraught with major events both in China and in the world, and the international situation left Britain to cope by herself in China, for Napoleon was busy in Mexico, and on April 12th the American Civil War broke out. The blockade of the Southern States of America had the immediate result of causing an acute cotton famine and untold suffering in Lancashire. The need to find other sources of cotton, even the short staple variety of the Yang-tze valley, became imperative, and it was essential for the British to secure the peaceful conditions necessary for trade.

In August of the same year the Emperor Hsien Feng, debauched, drunken, degenerate and unable to recover his spirit from the shock he had received when the Allies had entered Peking, died at his hunting lodge at Jehol in Tartary, from which he had never returned since his flight there. The party which plotted to murder the Empress, and to seize her five-year-old son, the heir apparent, and rule through him, was outwitted by the Emperor's brother, Prince Kung. By a coup d'état in November, he placed the Empress in power to "administer the government with suspended curtain". Henceforth she, who had been the favourite concubine, would by right of her own personality and intelligence continue to be the absolute ruler of China until her death, albeit from behind the curtain in front of which successive children, puppets, were seated by her on the Dragon Throne.

Her first act of state as regent was to give Tseng entire control of all the armies, and she appointed him to be a cabinet minister and Junior Guardian of the Heir Apparent. This she did in recognition of his great victory. He had just taken An-king, the strategic point which he had long ago described as the spot on the serpent's back where alone the back could be broken. Under the command of Cockeye, An-king had endured siege for so long that by the end of the summer human flesh was being sold in the open streets at fourpence per pound. On September 5th 1861 the Imperialists broke in, Cockeye escaped, and the Imperial troops then fell upon the people and put to death 20,000 men, women and children. The Europeans on the coast groaned when they heard of the slaughter. There was nothing to choose between Taipings and Imperialists when it came to wholesale massacre of enemies, except only in the case of the Faithful Prince. Where he was in command, quarter was given.

Henceforth An-king became Tseng's headquarters. The Taipings, beaten back from the Triple City, and with An-king now lost, broke eastward, as Tseng had foreseen they would do. The Faithful Prince doubled back to lead a vast army into the province of Che-kiang, which lay like a paw supporting the terrain of the tiger's head. The city of strategic importance in this paw was the open treaty port of Ning-po. Its capture by the Taipings was now to prove the test case as to whether Britain would continue to remain neutral. Whereas there had been a reasonable excuse for defending the Chinese walled city of Shanghai in the previous year, because the Foreign Concessions were literally piled against those same walls, there was no such excuse to be found in the case of Ning-po, for a river's mouth divided the Chinese city from the foreign property. As the rebels approached Ning-po, the British government's instructions were clear. The British were not to enter into the quarrel. Let the Taipings take the city, and prove their ability to govern it. The city fell on December 9th

to an army of 75,000 under one of Faithful's generals, by name
Hwang, and Parkes was able to report that the rebels had behaved in an exemplary fashion.

Unfortunately neither Bruce nor Lord John Russell was in a
position to control the adventurous spirits of the men on the
spot, and Admiral Hope's reports show that, despite all declarations of neutrality, real desire existed amongst the men at the
top to bolster up the tottering Manchu dynasty. When, therefore,
the adventurous spirits compromised Britain's position, Bruce was
always ready to recognise a *fait accompli*, and to alter his policy
accordingly. Captain Dew of H.M.S. *Encounter* was the man on
the spot at Ning-po. He first seized and withheld the customs
duties from the Taipings, so that they were short of money to
administer the city, and then after a few months used their failure
to administer as an excuse to help the Imperialists retake it. His
action was condoned until he joined forces with Ward and his
mercenaries, and carried British arms more than thirty miles
beyond the area of the city. He was then sent home from the
China station in disgrace, but the harm, as far as the Taipings
were concerned, had been done. They had lost a major strategic
point.

To return, however, to December 1861, the defeat of the
Taipings in the west by Tseng was for the moment more than
counter-balanced in the east, first by the taking of Ning-po, and
then by the capture of Hang-chou. This latter, a provincial
capital, had been besieged since the spring of 1860, when Faithful had first cut down the angle of the jaw of the tiger's head
to where it lay at the beast's throat. For twenty months now
it had been closely invested, and it was the turn of the Imperialists to turn cannibal and sell human flesh in the streets for
a few pence per pound. Faithful, with an army of 500,000,
having doubled back from the interior, took the outer walls of
the city on December 29th 1861, but the inner citadel, in which
the Tartar garrison lived, held out for another twenty days.
Faithful, in whose heart the true spirit of Christianity had, according to Lindley, who knew him well, taken firm hold, used
those days to memorialise the T'ien Wang on the need for mercy.
Hung, more aware than usual, since the massacre at An-king,
that vengeance is a two-edged weapon, granted Faithful his desire.
The Prince thereupon offered safe conduct to all the Tartars.

The Manchu Governor first defended the citadel, and then committed suicide, after which Faithful entered and allowed all the
officials to go free. When they came to take their leave of him,
"In this world," they said, "we cannot be friends with you, but
in the world to come you shall not be forgotten. You are a man
of eminence, and it is only to be regretted that you have not a
good sovereign."

Although Tseng had defeated the Taipings in the west, nevertheless the Heavenly Kingdom of Great Peace, in the closing
month of 1861, was still the size of England, with a population
of twenty-six million. The T'ien Wang held possession of the
richest soil in China, producing more cotton, tea, rice, barley
and silk than any other part of the Celestial Empire. But once the
Taipings had been driven eastward towards the coast, it became
vital that Faithful should consolidate his position there. The
terrain of the tiger's head was now his, with the fatal exception of
Shanghai—the very fangs of the tiger, the port through which the
Imperialists were buying arms. The promise not to attack it for
twelve months had been kept, and the time had now expired.
"We must take it to complete our dominions," wrote the Prince,
and he went to Soo-chou to prepare the attack.

When his intention was known, Shanghai reached its peak
period of panic in early January of 1862. Thousands of refugees
flocked both in and out, uncertain where to seek safety. The
country folk sought the shelter of the walls, prepared to risk
siege and starvation, for they hoped the Europeans would defend
the city. The citizens flocked out to the country, fearful of being
pinned inside the walls and slaughtered by one or other of the
belligerents. The British watched the streams of hopeless, destitute
people, trundling their wheelbarrows, loaded with their few
wretched possessions, blocking the approaches and the canal
bridges to the city. Many threw themselves into the water to
seek peace in death. It was the moment when the Jesuits were
most hard-pressed to succour the thousands of suffering human
beings, and were none the less contemplating setting up a mission
in Nanking. Their hopes of converting the Taipings, and the
confidence of the Europeans in general, were badly shaken when
Issachar Roberts chose this moment to execute his *volte face*.
He suddenly quit Nanking, and published a retraction of his faith
in the genuine character of the Taipings' profession of Christian-

ity, together with an exposé of the personal depravity of Jen-kan.
Three months later he had to retract his accusations.

To reconstruct what probably did in fact take place, it is
necessary to remember that Jen-kan had proved himself, in the
course of six years' service to the missionaries, to be an exemplary
character, for whom Dr. Legge had the highest regard, and that
James Forrest considered him the most enlightened Chinese he
had ever had the pleasure of knowing. At the same time the
consensus of European opinion was that the Taiping penal code
governing the impressment of young boys into the army was
cruelly strict, the penalty for deserting and trying to rejoin their
families being death. But as that was in fact the Taiping law,
Roberts was tilting at windmills in trying to circumvent it because of any personal feeling for a particular youth.

He took such a fugitive from justice under his protection, and
employed him as his Number One Boy. Jen-kan and his brother
then arrived to demand the surrender of the culprit. A quarrel
broke out between Issachar and the Taiping princes, and Roberts
presumably was reduced to hysterics and tears, for he must have
hidden his face, and hence was unable to bear true witness of
the scene. Taking refuge on a British gunboat, he then wrote
to the newspapers giving an account of the quarrel and stating
that Jen-kan did "come into my house in which I was living,
and with malice aforethought did murder one of my servants with
a large sword in his own hand, in my presence, without a
moment's warning, or any just cause. And after having slain my
poor, harmless, helpless boy, he jumped on his head most fiend
like." Unfortunately for Roberts, three months later his protegé
turned up in Shanghai very much alive, having suffered only a
stiff bambooing. Issachar, much embarrassed, had to admit that
he had supposed the youth had been beaten to death: mention of
any sword was now omitted.

The missionary's behaviour was throughout puzzling and
slightly hysterical. By temperament he may have been afraid of
violence—it had taken him seven years to pluck up sufficient
courage to penetrate Taiping territory—or his emotions concerning the youth may have been more involved than was normal.
Father Clavelin's letter of this date says that Roberts' prestige,
"if it be true that he ever had any, is very much fallen". The
Reverend William Dean, fellow-Baptist, ignored him in his

biographical sketches of all the well-known missionaries in China
at the period. Lindley wrote that he was generally regarded as
ignorant and uneducated. Thus he passes from the story in which
he might have played such a different rôle. But his published
accusation did damage to the Taiping cause in the interval before
he was forced to retract it.

On this occasion, with the Faithful Prince preparing to march
on Shanghai, there could be no misunderstanding between the
Taipings and the British authorities. It had been most clearly
stated to the Taipings that, while remaining neutral in the contest as regards the rest of China, British forces would defend
any place within a thirty mile radius of Shanghai. At the end of
January 1862 the Taipings crossed this line and advanced to within
fourteen miles of the city.

The initial defence of the perimeter was carried out by the
mercenary force in Manchu pay, the Ever Victorious Army,
as it was called, under the command of Frederick Ward, but by
February 21st the British and French Allied forces, numbering
just over 2,000, went into action. For the next five months warfare
was carried on, and the Faithful Prince, although only a third of
his men were armed with muskets, continued to have the best of
it. The situation was a very involved one, because the natural
lie of the land took no account of any political proviso about not
advancing beyond the thirty mile radius, so that practical tactics
forced the British to advance further, thereby breaking the agreement to remain neutral outside the agreed limit. In an effort to
abide by the letter if not the spirit of the law, Bruce arranged
that the mercenaries of Imperialists should take over, hold and
garrison whatever towns the British forces took by assault beyond the thirty mile perimeter.

The fact that the Allies were now providing Taiping prisoners
as fodder for the Imperial executioners in the yards and streets of
Shanghai was an unpleasant one which Europeans had to face
daily, as one of the unavoidable sights of the suburbs where they
lived. Legge, Forrest, Meadows and many others protested against
any further action. Equally distasteful to men of conscience was
the fact that British and French troops looted the fallen towns
as freely as did the Imperialists. Their officers had openly to
organise a fair distribution of the loot in order to avoid jealousies
and friction. Both Taipings and Imperialists were slaughtering

freely wherever their regiments passed, and young Major Gordon, serving under General Stavely with the British forces, grew daily more revolted by the scenes of carnage among the civil population. These frightful and hideous barbarities had been going on for *more than ten years*. Was the civil war never to end?

Gordon's attitude was typical of all that is best in the British. He had no interests in trade or politics, and he hated the sectarian wranglings of the missionaries. He could not be bought, but, once he was convinced of the right course to take, he was prepared to die for his convictions. The terrible human suffering that he was now witnessing not only strengthened his new-found belief in the existence of God, but brought home to him his duty as a faithful servant of God to end human suffering however and whenever he could. At the same time he became convinced that the Taipings were incapable of founding a dynasty and government which could give China peace.

As to whether Gordon's opinion was justified, it did indeed seem as if all that the Devil had plotted had come to pass: the veteran God-worshippers had been swamped by raw, brutal-minded recruits; the T'ien Wang's pride had prevented a rapprochement with the missionaries; Hung was becoming more and more of a dreamer and recluse; and now he was beginning to despair. Divided as they were now into either dreamers or bandits, the Taipings were perhaps no longer suited to organise a civil administration. Nevertheless, while Yen-lo had reason to congratulate his minions from hell, the Allies, had they only known it, had no cause for self-congratulation that the days of Hung Hsiu-ch'uan were numbered; for the time factor had been largely responsible for the corruption of his character and the failure of his mission, and the Allies were largely responsible for the time of his endurance having been so prolonged. If they had really abided, as Meadows had counselled, by the spirit of neutrality and not merely by the letter, and if Roberts and the missionaries had answered Hung's appeal in 1853, the course of history might have been very different. As the Allies had unwittingly aided Yen-lo, they would have to pay the price—the postponement of China's rebirth for a hundred years, the collapse of all mission work in China, and the loss of a Christian dynasty to represent a world power. Interference in other people's affairs is always to play Yen-lo's game, whereas to recognise China's man-of-the-moment, whether he be heretic, or atheist and communist, is at least a recognition of truth, and truth is not so easily turned to the Devil's purpose as delusion.

Despite all the efforts of the Western nations, the Faithful Prince had been victorious until the month of May, when Ning-po was retaken by Captain Dew. Ward and the mercenaries were defeated at T'ai-tsang on May 21st, and shortly afterwards Ward fell in battle in the vicinity of Ning-po. The intervention of the foreigners and the strength of their arms had been an unpleasant surprise to Faithful in the past five months of fighting. "The onslaught of the Foreign Devils upon a city was very fierce," he wrote, "and they usually accomplished their work in ten or twelve hours. Their guns were exceedingly powerful, and every one of their shots took effect." Nevertheless, he held his own, and with Lindley's help was obtaining more foreign rifles every day. But now in May he was recalled by the T'ien Wang to Nanking, because of the desperate situation there. Tseng had at last mopped up the west and all the course of the Yang-tze as far as Nanking, and his brother General Tseng had finally arrived to encamp under the walls of the Heavenly City.

Faithful was investing Sung-kiang, a town in the tiger's head, and, "I was on the point of gaining the desired success," he wrote, "when news was received that General Tseng had taken Wu-hu, Ch'ao-sien, Wu-wei, Yun-tsao and the East and West Pillars. As the bamboo, when once split, splits easily all the way down, T'ai-p'ing and Ho-chou had likewise fallen. These successes had been followed up, and General Tseng was now investing the capital. The Heavenly King sent three messengers in one day to urge me to return." Faithful had hesitated, "knowing that Tseng's strength rested mainly in his gunboats, against which I could bring no naval force to bear, and knowing, moreover, that his troops had always been victorious, and that their strength was somewhat formidable, I had hence no inclination to engage them. My idea was to pour supplies into Nanking, as well as all the ammunition and wealth procurable from surrounding cities, and wait for two years, when I could then come to its rescue; as I felt confident that the beleaguering force would in time lose their fighting spirit, and I should be able to cope with them."

Far away in Nanking the Heavenly King was torn with doubts as to why his generalissimo failed to obey his most urgent summons. Wei had betrayed him, Yang had failed him, Shih Ta-kai had deserted him. Would the Faithful Prince now follow suit? If so, then truly all was lost. If Faithful had obeyed his orders in the autumn of 1860, he, Hung, might by now have been sitting upon the Dragon Throne in Peking. One of his generals, General Ching, had not only deserted but had gone over to the Imperial side, and was become Second-in-Command to Li Hung-chang in the terrain of the tiger's head. Was the Faithful Prince contemplating the same treachery? Hung had never dared to accord him the intimacy which Yang had so abused. He could not therefore see into the mind of his generalissimo, and he wrote now a threatening letter, for he held the family of the Faithful Prince as hostages in Nanking. "Three decrees have called upon you to hasten and save the capital. Why do you not send troops, what are your intentions and designs? You have been honoured with a high position, and do you not know my laws? If you do not obey this decree, the law must inevitably take effect upon you."

Faithful was also stricken with a sense of impending doom. "I lost all care for worldly matters. My only desire was to see my mother, who was over sixty years of age, and who had nourished me from childhood upward." Against his judgment, and for her sake, Faithful now obeyed his sovereign. He handed over Hang-chou and Soo-chou to his officers, together with sufficient troops to hold the strong points in the tiger's head, and with more than 100,000 men marched to the relief of Nanking in June 1862.

On his arrival in the vicinity there followed fifty-six terrible days, terrible for the Imperialists as well as for the Taipings, terrible for the Tseng brothers as well as for Faithful. Back and forth the strife raged, and pestilence broke out in both camps, followed by a fearful spell of cold. Try as he would, Faithful could not dislodge Tseng's forces, and at last, in a desperate attempt at diversion and on the orders of the T'ien Wang, he crossed the Yang-tze and made a dash northward towards Peking. But the move, which might have been decisive the year before, came too late.

It was plain now that the issue would be decided in the terrain of the tiger's head and below the walls of Nanking itself, at the tiger's ear. With Faithful now north of the Yang-tze, and his troops starving and caught by the cold weather; with Shih Ta-

kai at last cornered in the far west (he was executed on January
31st 1863); and with Four-Eyed-Dog decapitated by the end of
1862, Tseng felt that the time was drawing nearer when at last
he might rest from his labours. Yet while the Taipings held most
of the terrain of the tiger's head, they still had a good chance to
recover, and had they not often recovered from a low ebb?
Tseng knew only too well that they had. Anything still might
happen, some sudden break-out, some new resurgence; anything
if it were not for the fact that his colleague, Le Hung-chang,
had got the British behind him.

23

IT WOULD BE UNFAIR to Tseng Kuo-fan to suggest that
Gordon won the war. Tseng, although he was a reactionary, was
a great man, an admirable character, and it was his courage and
determination and persistence in the face of adversity which defeated Hung Hsiu-ch'uan. Gordon was the first to admit that
his small force alone could have done next to nothing against the
Taipings. But it is equally true that, when fate hangs in the
balance, a mere feather can decide the issue, and British guns
weighed more than a feather. To Tseng, therefore, belonged the
credit and the glory—if such it can be called—and certainly the rewards of his twelve long years of pertinacious struggle. But the
cities in the terrain of the tiger's head fell to Gordon because, as
Faithful said, the Foreign Devils' arms could take a city in twelve
hours of bombardment, whereas the Imperialists needed months
to beleaguer a town and starve out the inhabitants. Nor is it certain that Tseng could have concluded victory if the time factor
had not been speeded up.

The year 1863, therefore, is the story of Gordon and the Ever
Victorious Army. Li Hung-chang, the Imperial Governor of the
province affected, had in the past year suffered many a headache

in his attempts to keep the mercenary force of Foreign Devils
under control; or rather to control their officers, for the men were
a force of drilled Chinese, trained by the Europeans. Of their
officers, the majority were American, but some among them were
British, German, French and Spanish, mostly of a seafaring type,
very touchy as to precedence, and nearly every one of them out for
personal gain. The force, originally established to keep the
Faithful Prince from Shanghai on the occasion of his first visit,
had been organised and most ably commanded by Frederick
Townsend Ward, an American who had won the respect of all
parties as a man of honour and a generally good type. Unfortunately, when he fell in battle on the outskirts of Ning-po in
September of 1862, the command of the mercenaries devolved
on his second-in-command, Burgevine, whose reputation, both
as a loose fish capable of being bought by the highest bidder at any
time, and as a brute and a drunkard, was universally known.

On October 24th 1862 he took his Taiping prisoners and blew
them from the guns to celebrate his recapture of a town. The
Times of India rang with the scandal, and pointed out the
atrocities to which Europeans were lending themselves. On the
other hand a contemporary, Andrew Wilson, editor of the *China
Mail*, was able to write a few years later, in his retrospective
account of the Ever Victorious Army, "What might be exquisite
torture to the nervous vascular European is something much less
to the obtuse nerved Turanian. Every doctor who has had to
perform operations on Chinamen knows how little they suffer in
comparison with more sensitive races." There was nevertheless
much public feeling that the Western nations had no right to
criticise the Taipings for atrocities, when they were providing
arms and men for the Imperialists, who were on the whole considered to be the more brutal of the two. Gordon, later taxed with
the cruelties of his Chinese troops, declared they were only cruel
in the heat of battle, and soon chummed up with the prisoners
afterwards. So much was probably true of the rank and file,
private soldiers not being very different the world over, but nothing could be said in defence of the cold-blooded reprisals ordered
by the Imperial commanders. And Burgevine, a Frenchman by
race and an American by nationality, had become as brutalised as
his Manchu paymasters. Moreover, he was quite unreliable, and

Li Hung-chang knew that he was selling munitions in secret to the Taipings.

At about this time Li Hung-chang received an offer from the Russians to lend him 10,000 men, but Li had been well trained by Tseng. He mistrusted Russia, and did not want to have so large a force of foreigners loose in China. He had come to the conclusion that, of all the Western powers, the British, despite their rapacity for trade, were the most suitable for his purpose. They had more arms to sell than France, and he was now convinced that they had no desire for territorial acquisitions, whereas Russia daily extended her territory in the direction of Manchuria. He must get rid of Burgevine, and then, if he could engineer the appointment of a British officer of decent repute to command the mercenaries, there was hope that the British would become sufficiently involved in support of that officer to give just enough help to make Tseng's victory certain without robbing him of the glory of it. The way had been prepared by Her Majesty's Order in Council of August 1862. It was now permissible for an officer in H.M.'s forces to take up an appointment under the Imperial government of China.

Li Hung-chang went to work in subtle mandarin fashion. First he ordered Burgevine and his force to Nanking, knowing full well that the American would not dare to remove himself so far from European support and protection. Burgevine refused. Then for months the Chinese banker whose business it was to pay the mercenaries held back payment, until Burgevine was forced to take action; and, as had been calculated, he took it in the wrong way. He arrived with his rowdies at the bank, quarrelled furiously with the banker, struck him on the face, and seized the silver. He was straightway dismissed from the service of the Chinese government and, though Bruce spoke up for him, Li Hung-chang was adamant. Bruce did not want the mercenaries to be commanded by any national of the big powers, for he foresaw that the power would thereafter be involved. Yet to such a length had the rowdiness, irresponsibility and roving power of the mercenaries grown, that Bruce gave way, because, unless a reputable officer were soon put in control, "We should," he wrote, "be constituting a force which would be as dangerous to us as the insurgents themselves".

Charles Gordon, therefore, on March 26th 1863, received the

command of the Ever Victorious Army. His first campaign, which lasted until December, is no longer of interest in detail but only in terms of general character. He had first to reorganise his force of about 4,000 Chinese, including his Chinese N.C.O.s and, most difficult of all, his heterogeneous assortment of foreign officers. The men had poked fun at themselves as being clothed as "imitation Foreign Devils". But under Gordon they very soon learned to be extremely proud of the uniform of an army that was at last becoming in truth ever victorious. Gordon himself, leading them to the assault of town after town, and first into the breach with only his officer's cane by way of arms, became their hero, and even the Taiping princes treasured photographs of their gallant enemy.

The territory over which they were fighting was a completely flat alluvial plain, intersected by canals and waterways at every turn. There were no roads, merely narrow footpaths at the edge of the rice fields, up which the troops could only march in single file. Gordon therefore collected a flotilla of steamers and gunboats. In such a country an armed steamer, a "fire-ship", was worth 3,000 men.

The tactics employed were for Gordon to provide the spearhead of the attack, and assault and take a town, and then for British regulars to move up under command of General Brown, and garrison and hold whatever Gordon had captured. But Bruce soon condemned this practice when it took place outside the precious thirty mile radius. Li Hung-chang and the ex-Taiping General Ching were, however, very ready to take over the task, more especially because the investment of Nanking was proceeding so well, under Tseng's younger brother the general, that in March 1863 the Commander-in-Chief, Tseng himself, was able on his visit from his headquarters at An-king to ride close up to the walls on his tour of inspection.

Gordon also undertook some inspections, but of a different kind, and they were forced upon him. He could not shut his eyes to the horrors going on around him. On the road to Chan-zu he passed near a joss house where thirty-five Imperial soldiers had been strung up to the wooden triangles, on which it was the custom to stretch prisoners before the torture of "cutting into a thousand pieces". They hung there dead, in the position of crucifixion, their flesh partly burned away. It was as though the scene at Golgotha had been monstrously multiplied by some action of a spectroscope. In the ditches and along the footpaths and in every village lay women with their breasts cut off. In fact Gordon was witnessing all the atrocities and horrors of a barbarous war, and he clutched his Bible ever more tightly in his hand. Although he believed the Taipings to be incapable of government, there was no gainsaying that the Imperial soldiers were equally barbarous in their treatment of the civil population.

He was sickened, and had decided to relinquish the command which was involving him in such atrocities, when news reached him which altered his decision. It had been suspected that Burgevine, with his nose out of joint, would be tempted to accept the Taiping bribes to go over to their side. Gordon, incredulous of this, had given his personal pledge to Li Hung-chang that Burgevine would take no such action. Now the news came that Burgevine had in fact joined the rebels at Soo-chou. En route for that city in a gunboat, he had managed to blow himself up with his own pivot gun, and there he was in Soo-chou, drinking more heavily than ever to forget the pain of his wound, while in his lucid moments he helped the Taipings to organise the defence of the city. He had taken quite a number of the mercenary officers with him, together with some three hundred more European adventurers. Thus Gordon lost face with Li Hung-chang, and felt that he must make good the defection of his officers by continuing meantime to accept service under the Chinese government.

Now the Faithful Prince came back to the scene. He had gone 400 miles on his road to Peking, and had defeated the Mongol general, Senkolintsin, when an urgent message from Hung recalled him to Nanking, which was by now in a desperate position. Not only were the rebel entrenchments round the city taken by General Tseng on July 13th 1863, bringing the Imperial forces pretty well up to the walls; but the city also appeared to be threatened by a flotilla of warships and gunboats which the Imperial government had bought from the British.

Caught by the cold in the north during the previous winter, and now short of rations, Faithful and the remnants of his army struggled back, only to find that the forts protecting the river-crossing at Nanking were in Imperial hands. Under the fire of the enemy batteries, the Taipings were ferried by any and every available boat in an attempt to win to the other side of the Yang-tze, and to the safety and shelter of the city. First from starvation, and now from enemy fire, Faithful lost an army of 100,000 men. Only 15,000 gained entry to Nanking, and, while the Imperial cannons bombarded the city, on that same day one of the cannon balls struck and killed Lindley's little Portuguese sweetheart-wife, for which loss Lindley was to take vengeance.

Faithful had lost his troops because there was no longer room to encamp or deploy, let alone feed them, on the outskirts of the closely beleaguered city. Before his expedition to the north, he had besought the Heavenly King to change his policy. He had warned him that the capital could not be held. General Tseng had so besieged it that the city was deficient of all needs, and from outside there was no prospect of rescue. Passionately he had urged his sovereign to abandon the city while there was yet time, and make a dash for the west, where, even at the eleventh hour, it might have been possible to refound the Kingdom of Great Peace in some remote corner of the mountains of Szechuan, even as Shih Ta-kai had tried to do. But the T'ien Wang had refused to abandon his capital, and had wrathfully reproved his Generalissimo.

Faithful now made a second attempt to persuade his sovereign to cut his way out before it was too late. Forth he rode to the celestial palace with his attendants, and from his warhorse he dismounted at the gates of the great wall, within which the roofs of green and yellow curved this way and that, between minarets hung with bells. Humbly and on foot he entered the forecourt, and bade his squire strike the great gong, the official appeal for an audience. He knew that his sovereign had felt the shadow of doom. He knew also that the Heavenly King, since assuming his reigning title, considered it beneath the dignity of the throne to show any signs of apprehension, any doubts of success, any of the numbness of despair which was slowly creeping upon him. How then could he present the case to his sovereign as desperate? Yet he must try, and, while he was ushered into the robing room which led off from the hall of audience, there to don his gold-encrusted yellow robes, he strove to find the arguments he might best use.

In the private Imperial quarters Hung Hsiu-ch'uan gave himself quietly into the hands of his female attendants, but his head was sunk upon his breast, and his mind abstracted, as they sought to array him in the Dragon robes, the collar of gold bosses, the high Ming crown. Beneath it his long hair was greying fast, but it was coiled and hidden beneath the silken turban. Only his beard showed the weight of the years, for it was silvered, and he would not look in the mirror which his women held up, for he knew that age would soon come upon him, and his mission remained incomplete. If he allowed himself to think of failure, of all the millions of lives given in vain, then indeed he would no longer be able to carry his head as an Emperor should. Yet there was nothing, nothing, on which he could pin his hopes. At least, there was no hope of material aid which he could bring forward to meet the arguments of his Generalissimo, waiting now to be received.

Nevertheless he, Hung, would not, could not fail. Had not the Heavenly Father himself issued the mandate by which he should rule the Celestial Kingdom of China? Desperately he sought for renewal of confidence in the divine promise, and at last the words of Holy Scripture came into his mind to comfort him. "Thinkest thou that I cannot now pray to my Father, and he shall presently give me more than twelve legions of angels?" Yes, that was the answer. To live and die together was the covenant of blood-brotherhood. It might be that his Father would not send the angels. It might be that twenty million men had died, and that he also would die, but not in vain. Nothing would be in vain while he trusted in the truth of his vision. Never, never, would he be persuaded to run away, or to mistrust the purpose of his Heavenly Father.

Thus he went to face the arguments of his Generalissimo un-perturbed, sitting upright and regal in the Dragon car which his women drew, like the chariot of some great golden idol, towards the hall of audience.

The Faithful Prince waited there upon his knees, head to the ground, as the Heavenly King took his place upon the throne. At either side of the sovereign stood his brothers, together with the Young Lord and the Western Prince, all of them incapable counsellors, for the brothers were slow of wit, and the two princes were not yet sixteen years old. For some reason Jen-kan was not present, though he was in the city.

Then Faithful made his ritual kow-tow, the three abject obei-sances, and remaining on his knees began his plea, eyes to the ground, for it was considered disrespectful to gaze directly at the face of an Emperor, be he the Manchu Son of Heaven or the T'ien Wang. And while he spoke, Hung kept his gaze above the Generalissimo's head. The sunlight was reflecting the red and blue and gold of the painted ceiling in pools of light upon the tessellated floor, and between the shadows of the ornately carved pillars it caught the flecks of dust and the spiralling of the incense upon the altar of the Heavenly Father which faced the throne.

General Tseng, ran Faithful's report, had made himself master of the road outside the South Gate. By capture of the bridge he had stopped all ingress and egress by the West Gate. And by the capture of yet another bridge he held the approach to the East Gate. Of the Taiping army which had marched north, only 15,000 men now remained. The capital could not be defended. The one hope was to break out, and strike west. And so—

Here the Heavenly King cut him short, and there was indignation in the sovereign's voice at what he persuaded himself was the pusillanimous attitude of the only proficient general remaining to him. "I have received the commands of Shang-ti and Jesus to come down upon the earth and rule the Empire. I am the sole lord of ten thousand nations." He waved his hand, indicating the square world of which China was the chosen centre, and the islands of the barbarians, his humble tributary states. "What should I fear?" he went on, but there was a catch in his voice, and the Faithful prince took the opportunity to remind him that the army was decimated, the capital untenable for any lengthy period.

"You are not asked for your opinion in anything," Hung rejoined, angry at the interruption of the pronouncement of Imperial orders. "And the government does not require your supervision. You can please yourself whether you leave the capital, or whether you remain. The Empire, hills and streams, I hold with an iron grasp, and if you do not support me, there are those that will." He raised his voice, remembering the words of scripture which had given him comfort, seeking anew the faith with which to inspire his followers, fixing his gaze above the head of the Generalissimo where the sticks of incense sent a spiral of prayer up to Shang-ti. "You say there are no soldiers. My heavenly troops are more numerous than the firmament. What fear have I of the demon Tseng? If you are afraid of death, then you *will* die."

For a moment Hung closed his eyes, thinking of all those who had betrayed or deserted him. Had he any reason to hope that here at last in the Faithful Prince he had found a man who would really prefer death to treachery, who would really prove that his name was justly bestowed? Past experience had made him bitter and sceptical. He dared not open his heart to the general and simply trust him. So once again he resorted to threats. "The affairs of state do not concern you, but are in the hands of the Valiant Prince, my second brother." Here Yen-ta bowed his acknowledgement. "And if, when the young Western Prince issues any orders, anyone disobeys, such a one is sure to be executed." The lad's hand went dutifully to his little ornamental sword, while on his knees the great Generalissimo, who had led army after army to victory, bowed his head.

"Let me pray the Heavenly King to kill me now," Faithful humbly prayed, "in order that I may escape injury at some future day. Not half a moment's leisure have I enjoyed during my period of service." His voice broke, as he thought how little personal happiness had ever come to him, and how long and heavy the years had been, since he had first been wrenched from his quiet village home. "And now," he went on, "because I bring to your notice the real state of affairs, you revile me in this way. I am ready to yield up my life in your presence, as a free tribute to you, and as an earnest of my zeal and loyalty in your cause."

Then, scarcely restraining his tears, the Faithful Prince quitted the palace, after he had been given leave to withdraw. "During the whole time that I was a commander," he wrote, "I never enjoyed a moment's comfort, but was beset with worry and continual vexation. The Heavenly King was more averse than ever to answering memorials. He did not want to listen to anyone."

Nevertheless, there was something about Hung which drew the Faithful Prince, and made him acknowledge the cause, and feel even yet the zeal to serve it. Faithful's own moment of choice was long past. He had become too important now to have any hopes that, if he defected to the enemy, the Imperial government might pardon him, as it had pardoned General Ching. If the T'ien Wang could not see that, Faithful could. There was no choice open to him now but to endure. Had there ever been a moment when he could have chosen otherwise? Truly from the moment when, as a lad, he had been impressed into the Taiping army, there had been none. To have gone back then to his burning village would have meant death at the hands of the Tartars. If the Imperial government had held out hopes of pardon in the intervening years, many would have defected, but not Faithful, for his mother and his loved ones were from thenceforth hostages of his loyalty. And above all reasons was the sincere and simple devotion of soldier to his God—the God whom Gordon was also struggling to serve.

For all these reasons Hung had no cause to fear that the Faithful Prince would betray him, but he could not have foreseen the lengths to which the prince's personal loyalty and integrity of character would go. On the following day Hung, regretting his harshness, and now convinced that the Generalissimo's patent emotion had been genuine, sent the prince an embroidered robe by way of compliment, and to quieten his mind. Faithful thereupon wrote memorial after memorial, requesting permission to go and take charge of affairs at Soo-chou. What was the point of staying pinned up in a death-trap? Better to die on the field. Gordon and Li Hung-chang were at last moving upon Soo-chou. If they could be made to suffer a great reverse, there was just a chance that Tseng would divert troops from the siege, and the capital might be relieved and revictualled.

Hung, more and more aware that in the valour of the Faithful Prince lay his only hope, chewed his moustached lip and vacillated, loath to let him go, and yet appreciating that such a sortie might be the only chance to save the dynasty. At last, on condition that the Generalissimo pledged a private fortune of 100,000 taels of silver with the commissariat fund, and left his mother and family in the capital, he granted the exeat for forty days only. "But if the amount required is not forthcoming," he threatened, "or if you fail to return within the prescribed period, the law must take its due course." He was still fearful that his only proficient general might abandon him.

Faithful sold the trinkets and jewellery of his wife and daughters to meet the required demand, and taking every soldier he could gather, a mere 7,000, sped to the relief of Soo-chou, not yet closely invested, but threatened by the fall of the key-towns round about it. With him went Lindley, intent on his own particular coup, whereby he hoped to wreak vengeance on the slayers of his Marie.

Thus in November 1863 the Faithful Prince, the Chung Wang

to give him for once his Chinese title, after more than seventeen months' absence, rejoined those Taiping armies which were still fighting in the terrain of the tiger's head, and gave them once again a chance of victory. True, he brought only 7,000 men with him, but Gordon declared that the renown of his name and the confidence which it inspired was alone worth 5,000 men, wherever and whenever he chose to appear on the scene.

Faithful's first action was to hold a council of war in Soo-chou with all the princes or "Wangs" who were in charge of the city. For himself there was no longer any possible choice between loyalty and defection, but the cause was in such grave danger that he felt that those who still had any hope of pardon from the Imperial government could not be greatly blamed for seeking it. Those who were considering defection, however, must speak now or forever hold their peace, for he must know on whom he could rely, and thus avoid the loyal contingent being ensnared by the treachery of any would-be deserters.

The Moh Wang, in charge of the defence of the city, was one of his most trusted officers. The second-in-command, the Na Wang, had entered the army as a lad, and had received all his training and instruction from Faithful himself, but it was rumoured that he and his followers had designs of surrendering. Faithful now told them all plainly that the Heavenly King was being blinded by those around him as to the real danger, and that they could each suit themselves, surrender or not, but that there was no occasion to have any disputes or treachery amongst old companions in arms.

They sat in closest council as the Generalissimo in his red padded battle jacket, his manner unpretentious, spoke to them freely and invited equally free comment. "The present time," he was saying, "is one that will not admit of my detaining you, if you have conceived any plans of your own. I am the chief of our nation, of notoriety, and no one can secure me against harm if I surrender." He glanced enquiringly at the Na Wang, and the Na Wang spoke up without hesitating.

"The Faithful Prince can make his mind easy on this point. We would not think of abusing his confidence. We have accompanied him from youth to this time, how is it possible that we should have any bad intention?"

The Sing Wang now leaned across the table to echo the Na

Wang's sentiments. "Had we any other plans in view we should not have shared such privations with you these last few years."

In the same manner the rest of the Wangs spoke up, and the Moh Wang smiled and nodded at Faithful, as if to say, "You see we can trust them all, despite rumour". He fingered the bronze hilt of his sword, as though longing to be immediately engaged with the enemy.

Faithful felt reassured. "The officers mentioned," he afterwards wrote, "and under my charge, had seen a good deal of service, and it was entirely owing to their strength and courage that I obtained my renown. They were therefore very dear to me. I had no idea that they had entertained feelings of enmity against the Moh Wang for some time past." Nor did Faithful seem to realise that his own loyalty and determination to defend Soo-chou automatically lessened the chance of any would-be defectors of receiving pardon from the Imperialists, for the surrender of Soo-chou was the only action with which they could bargain for their lives. Fortunately for him, it was the Faithful Prince's long-established rule never to sleep in a walled city. Each night he retired to his camp outside the walls, where his personal guards were well trained to be ready at the instant for movement in any direction.

Meanwhile Burgevine and his 300 European rowdies had become very well aware that they had backed what looked like being a lost cause. Lindley found him squatting upon an empty powder barrel, and as usual a little drunk. Burgevine's "nasty side look", which Gordon had once remarked on, was much in evidence. He had sent a secret appeal, as from one occidental to another, asking Gordon to get him and his men out of the mess. Gordon had thereupon brought the steamer *Hyson*, his best fire-ship, within easy distance of the Taiping outposts, and, by mutually arranged plan, the European adventurers had pretended to storm the vessel, had boarded her, and had laid down their arms, grateful to be carried back to safety by Gordon. Burgevine, whether from drink or incompetence, had failed to make the rendezvous.

Now, after Lindley had left for Shanghai on his own secret business, Burgevine, well primed with rum, used his position as a Taiping officer to come up to the outposts, and shot two innocent and unsuspecting Taiping sentries dead in order to get across to

Gordon's lines. There he proposed that he and Gordon should join forces, and make themselves independent of both Taipings and Imperialists by setting up their own kingdom, marching to Peking and seizing the Dragon Throne. That such a suggestion could have been made shows how weak was the Manchu régime which Britain was endeavouring to prop up. Gordon very properly sent the unprincipled rascal to Shanghai under armed escort, where the authorities of the Western Powers decided to overlook his actions on condition that he would leave the country.

Shanghai was just then in an uproar. The European partisans of the Taipings were jubilant because of Lindley's recent feat, whereas those who favoured the Imperial cause vowed that he was as great a rogue and rowdy as Burgevine. He had just pulled off his coup with the aplomb of a Francis Drake.

Gordon's power lay in his fire-ships, which could steal up the canals under cover of the bamboo groves, and suddenly belch fire upon the Taiping infantry. Of them all, the steamer *Hyson* carried the most fire-power, and the Faithful Prince had commissioned Lindley to obtain at all costs a ship which could challenge the *Hyson*. He was ready to pay Lindley £20,000 for such a vessel.

Lindley had no hope of being able to buy such a ship on behalf of the Taipings. It was against British regulations to sell arms to the rebels, and, while rifles could be bought on the side and smuggled through the lines, it was patent that a large steamer could not be so concealed. Sheer piracy was the only hope of acquiring such a vessel.

At dusk on a certain evening a small junk could have been seen paddling its way across the harbour at Shanghai. In it Lindley and his accomplice, a man called White, had their caps well pulled down, and scarves wrapped about their faces, for they had no desire to be recognised while they made their first reconnaissance of the coveted prize. The steamer *Firefly* had been sold to the Imperialists, and had been operating against the Taipings. Her Captain Ludlam had just brought her in full of Taiping prisoners, who were being marched away even now towards the execution ground. Captain Ludlam had also gone ashore to make his report at General Brown's headquarters. The steamer was expected to weigh anchor again at 1 A.M. Meanwhile the darkness was coming down, and heavy rain was beginning to fall. It promised to be a night as murky as any conspirator could desire.

The General's after-dinner port was good, and Ludlam stayed on to drink it, in the hope that the weather would have cleared before he need betake himself to his ship. He knew that Captain Dolly had taken temporary charge, so there was really no reason why he should not enjoy a pleasant evening for once.

Lindley's spies had kept him well-informed. When he came up the ship's side with White, it was too dark for the Cantonese servant to be immediately aware that the man with the commanding manner in the uniform of the mercantile marine was not Captain Ludlam, and by the time he did realise it, he was covered by Lindley's revolver, while White jumped to batten down the hatches, thus imprisoning Captain Dolly, together with the mate, the gunner, and the engineer. The quartermaster had managed to jump overboard and was on his way to raise the alarm, but by the time he could do so the *Firefly* had weighed, and was going full steam ahead for Soo-chou by way of the canals.

Lindley came too late, however, to help his Taiping friends in Soo-chou; and he was greatly condemned by the British partisans of the Manchus because, after the crew of the *Firefly* had surrendered to him on the promise of a safe conduct to the Imperial lines, they were done to death. Lindley tried to keep his promise. He claimed that he saw Dolly and his crew on their way to safety, and that the Imperialists must have slaughtered them without distinction of persons, as they often did; but it is probable that they were in fact murdered by the Taipings, wreaking vengeance for a fearful piece of treachery which had just taken place at Soo-chou. Lindley, now wanted for piracy by the British authorities, had to slip out of the country. As soon as he arrived back in England, he did all that he could do for his friend the Faithful Prince, which was to write a two-volume book under the name of Lin-le in defence of the Taiping cause, pleading with the British public to cease arming and supporting the Manchu rulers.

Gordon should have been the first one to sympathise with Lindley for any evil conscience he might feel for failing to secure the lives of those prisoners to whom he had promised safe conduct, for it was an exactly similar failure on the part of Gordon which made it impossible for Lindley in turn to keep faith. When the news broke of what had happened at Soo-chou Gordon's personal honour was found to be tarnished. The British escutcheon, even, was felt to be blotted, and public opinion was outraged. To a man of Gordon's temperament the wound to his personal honour went deeper and was probably more painful than was the case with Lindley, but they had both been playing with pitch, and it was not surprising that some of it had stuck.

While Lindley was still in Shanghai on his *Firefly* exploit, Gordon began his attack on the stockades round Soo-chou. General Ching, the ex-Taiping, had a force co-operating with the Ever Victorious Army, and Li Hung-chang, as Governor of the province, was keeping a certain direction of military affairs.

Now there began exactly the kind of treachery against which Faithful had tried to ensure. The Na Wang sent word to General Ching that he and all the princes, with the exception of the Moh Wang, were ready to surrender and come over, together with the garrison of 30,000 men. They proposed that Gordon should attack, and that they should pretend to make a sortie, a feint, the object of which would be to shut the Moh Wang out of the city. The plan had to be temporarily abandoned, however, because at the crucial moment the Faithful Prince arrived to counter-attack Gordon. Though he came with only 400 men from his main camp, the appalling width of the moat round the walls of this Chinese Venice forced Gordon to fall back, and he began to realise that, although he had over 4,000 men, Soo-chou might yet hold out for a long time.

The Na Wang and his fellow princes now despatched further secret messages to General Ching, and the Moh Wang's suspicions became aroused. He sent for his fellow officers, and after they had dined with him, and had offered up prayers, the usual grace and thanksgiving, they donned their robes and lacquer coronets, and adjourned to the council chamber. There, seated round a table, the Moh Wang, by suggesting that only Kwang-si and Kwang-tung men were trustworthy, gave them a subtle intimation that he knew of their plotting. The immediate answer he got was a small two-edged dagger in the back, and, as he fell forward over the table, all the other Wangs drew their swords, and his head was soon rolling on the floor.

Gordon and his European officers condemned the cowardly assassination of a brave and intelligent man, who had never despaired in the midst of his difficulties, and had always been good to foreigners. There was now, however, nothing to prevent the surrender of the city, and the princelings were prepared to surrender it in return for their lives. It was on Gordon's promise that they relied, for he was known and admired by all as a man of honour, a "righteous" person.

Unfortunately there was no real cohesion and clear communication between Gordon, General Ching and the Governor, Li Hung-chang; and the last had lately lost his brother by Taiping treachery, and bore a grudge.

On December 5th, when Gordon entered the city to treat with the Wangs, General Ching informed him that the Governor had extended mercy to them all. On the 6th Gordon went into Soochou again. The Wangs were all ready to ride out at noon and surrender the city, and the Na Wang was in very good spirits. They were all unarmed, and rode off together laughing. Gordon then proceeded to the East Gate, where to his consternation he saw a large force of Imperial soldiers firing their muskets crazily and yelling, the sure prelude to barbarous behaviour. Gordon called them to order, forbade them to fire, and reminded them of the terms of surrender. Just then General Ching rode through the gate, his wide blue coat caught up and pinned to his belt behind, through which his pigtail was thrust, and his hands fidgeting nervously on the hump of his high Chinese saddle. He appeared so agitated at his unexpected meeting with Gordon, and, on being questioned about the manner of taking over the city, equivocated so much, that Gordon became suspicious, and straightway determined to go to the Na Wang's palace to protect it.

He found it gutted, and was immediately importuned by the prince's elderly uncle to protect the cowering females. Gordon was unarmed, and was accompanied by an interpreter only, so he hesitated. But after another glance at the tearful women, he agreed to conduct them to the uncle's own house. When he got there he was promptly surrounded by 500 armed Taipings, who declared their intention to hold him as a hostage for their own safety, for already the screams of those being slaughtered and the yells of their assassins were ringing out in the streets.

Meanwhile Li Hung-chang had executed every princeling who had come out to surrender, trusting in Gordon's promise that their lives would be spared. The city was being given up to plunder. Word of the Moh Wang's death had already reached the camp of the Faithful Prince, and he had clapped spurs to his horse and led his army of 10,000 men to safety long ago. Nothing, therefore, could save the Taipings in Soo-chou except the ægis of Gordon— and he, while rapine and murder broke out all over the city, was held powerless as a hostage, stunned and horrified, from the after- noon of December 6th until the morning of the 7th. All through the night he heard the screams of the dying in the streets outside the courtyard where he was imprisoned, and the Taiping women huddled sobbing round his feet, murmuring their strange Christian prayers whenever they heard the yells of the assassins draw closer.

At last Gordon, who still had no idea that the Wangs had been executed was allowed to go himself under the escort of a Taiping guard to the South Gate, where he was promptly taken prisoner by the Imperialists for being in the company of the long-haired rebels.

Finally he escaped and rejoined the Ever Victorious Army. He refused to speak to General Ching, who was seeking a reconcilia- tion. He went instead, with the son of the Na Wang, to the edge of the moat to see for himself the eight headless bodies of those whose safety he had guaranteed. Speechless with rage, he next sought an interview with the Governor, but Li Hung-chang made excuses to avoid the meeting. Gordon thereupon took the Na Wang's son and the decapitated head of the late prince, his father, and departed on his steamer for his headquarters, whence he im- mediately sent in his resignation.

Feeling flared amongst the Europeans in Shanghai. Some con- demned Gordon for ever having lent himself to be employed by such fiends. Others turned their hatred toward the Imperialists. Li Hung-chang had to think up an excuse to the British, from whom he was buying arms. It was a poor one. He claimed that the Wangs had issued from the city with heads unshaved (this is to say, not having made the acknowledged sign of submission), and that they had been armed; furthermore, that they had demanded to retain the governance of the city on behalf of the Imperial army. No one for a moment believed the Governor. In his attempt to placate Gordon he persuaded the Empress to offer the British officer both titles and money, but no apology was sent. Gordon returned the money and gifts and refused the titles with a dignified reply.

The Ever Victorious Army therefore remained at its headquarters for the next four months, and, while the officers fretted in idleness, the British Achilles sat in his tent refusing to be reconciled with China's Agamemnon, or to attack the Trojans, the Taipings.

24

THE FAITHFUL PRINCE had left Soo-chou with his army of 10,000 on November 30th, in order to hold on to the town of Tan-yang and the remainder of the Taiping possesions in the terrain of the tiger's head. His brother was holding a nearby town, and in late December they met to confer. Faithful was determined to make a lightning visit by night to Nanking. He wanted to know how his mother fared there. She represented in his Chinese mentality the whole idea of family, and in his thoughts of her was included love for his wife and children. His brother advised him strongly against the visit, foreseeing that the T'ien Wang would never again let him depart from the capital, but Faithful bore in mind that his exeat had only been granted for forty days. They were nearly up, and his womenfolk might suffer if he extended the time.

Riding by night with only a few followers, the Faithful Prince came back for the last time to Nanking in late December of 1863, and at once the bells and gongs were rung throughout the city to notify the Heavenly King of his arrival. Faithful's desire to return to the terrain of the tiger's head had no chance of being granted, for now the whole population of the city presented a petition to the sovereign, asking that he should remain to protect them. In him alone they had confidence, both as a commander and as a man. He was just and merciful and benevolent, and was accustomed to feed the hungry from his private purse. The previous year Faithful had had 80,000 people on his relief list, nourished by his private charity. Now, however, he could do nothing for them, for supplies had been cut off.

In the narrow streets thieves and robbers multiplied. In desperate need of food, a hand would reach out from the shadows of an alley to clutch at the means of life, or a dagger strike quickly on a dark night. Spies were everywhere, ready to work for the Imperialists in an attempt to ensure their own pardon, against the moment when Tseng's forces would break in. To guard against betrayal by such traitors, the Heavenly King resorted to the strictest measures. The penalty for receiving any communication from the enemy, without immediately passing it to the Taiping authorities, was instant death, not only for the offender but for all his family, and the traitor himself was flayed or pounded alive.

The Imperialists had a large flotilla on the Yang-tze, armed of course with British guns; and double and treble entrenchments ran above Nanking to the Porcelain Pagoda Hill, which commanded the city, and thence north along the line of a creek to the hills, where lay the Ming tombs. Here the rebels held a strong position, but the forts below the capital were in Imperial hands. Tseng's younger brother, the General, was in command of the Imperial forces, while Kuo-fan himself remained at his headquarters at An-king, giving overall direction. General Tseng's men had very few muskets, not because they could not purchase them from the Europeans, but because few knew how to use them. The Imperialists were relying on famine to reduce the city, and it was to be a prolonged siege. Nevertheless, as Tseng Kuo-fan inspected the lines of investment early in 1864, he felt full of hope that his task was nearing completion, and he wrote home concerning the peculiarly dark, ashy-looking clouds hanging over the city, and wondered if it indicated that Heaven was about to bring the Taiping rebellion to an end.

If doom hung over Nanking, it hung also over the terrain of the tiger's head, for now in March 1864 Gordon once more took up arms, and Achilles agreed to be reconciled with Agamemnon. For nearly four months the Ever Victorious Army of mercenaries had stood idle at its headquarters in the town of Quin-san, while the officers quarrelled as to who should succeed Gordon. There was a real danger that they would one and all go over to the side of the Taipings, and to circumvent this possibility Li Hung-chang proposed to reconstitute the force under some other European officer. Gordon now pointed out to Bruce that, if Li were allowed to take this course, the British government would have lost con-

trol, and *therefore* he was prepared to resume command. Bruce
wrote to him, "We have supported this government (the Manchus) from motives of interest, not from sentiment." He went
on to infer that Gordon was perfectly right to continue to ignore
sentiment, since that was the attitude adopted by British policy.

Gordon was incapable of such an unsentimental approach to
the problem. He persuaded himself that, since the Taipings were
unable to produce a peaceful administration, the sooner the
rebels were routed the better, and that, with regard to the slur on
his personal honour, he must grasp the nettle which had stung
him, and vindicate himself by giving peace to China. It was
curious that, while holding this belief, he yet chose for his personal bodyguard the Taiping prisoners who had surrendered and
gone over to him, as though he found in them some rock on
which to build, lacking in the other Chinese troops. There were
those both in Shanghai and in England who criticised him with
scorn for lending himself yet once again to a cause which had so
besmirched his honour, but he ignored the abuse; and, with
Bruce to back him, he swept through the terrain of the tiger's
head, mopping up towns and taking the important point of Chan-
chu. Cockeye was caught and executed by the Imperialists, who
had just lost their General Ching. On March 31st a Franco-
Imperialist force recaptured Hang-chou at the tiger's throat, and
Tseng in the same week wrote home regarding Nanking, "The
melon is almost ready to cut".

The poor in Nanking were now facing real starvation. Since
December no one had enjoyed more than one small meal a day,
but henceforth only the wealthy could get even as much as this.
Faced with the horror of the reports on the condition of the
people, which the Faithful Prince had brought him, Hung's mind
began to lose touch with earthly reality. Yet even in his madness
he kept touch with a greater reality.

He wandered in his palace garden, distraught at the responsibility, fearful of showing fear, alone, unhappy, his faith shaken
and almost dead. Almost, but not quite. Faith in his mission might
die, but not faith in his Heavenly Father. His thoughts turned
this way and that. . . . "Give us this day our daily bread" . . .
Christ had fed the five thousand with only a few loaves and
two fishes. Was there here a mystery capable of being understood?
Had the disciples perhaps spoken in the esoteric language of

alchemy? How could a substance be made to multiply itself? He remembered how the Elixir of Immortal Life could turn all things to gold by the merest touch of its precious tincture. Not to "vulgar" gold, but to the true metal of spirituality. "As above, so below"; earth, its elements, and finally bread were only the counterparts of what existed in heaven. How, then, could he bring down bread from heaven? "I am the bread of life," his Heavenly Elder Brother had declared. "Moses gave you not that bread from heaven, but my Father giveth you the true bread from heaven." Manna! Hung was praying now for the secret. Manna! What was it? How could he obtain it?

His gaze roved over the exquisitely laid out garden, with its lily pools and ornamental arches, its dwarf trees and flowering shrubs and fruit trees already heavy with blossom. Abstracted in thought, his hand plucked idly at some of the taller flowers and herbs, which spring had made palely green and beautiful. Without considering what he did, he plucked a piece of tall grass and began to chew it, and then all at once it came to him, the answer to his problem.

It was the answer of a madman. It came to him in the intricate language of alchemy, and yet his growing insanity was held steady, his mind for the moment held safe within the sanity of Christ, who had spoken of removing mountains by faith. Faith, then, was the philosopher's stone, the Elixir, the true tincture which could change the nature of the elements.

He went back to the palace with a bunch of young leaves and grasses from his garden, and there, doffing his wide-sleeved robe, he called for a brazier. Before the eyes of his astonished female attendants, he then gave himself to the art of cooking, as he had not done since he had been a peasant boy in his mother's cottage. He rolled the leaves into balls, and steamed them. Eaten with faith, they must, they must nourish.

Thus when the Faithful Prince came next for audience to tell him that the people were starving, the Heavenly King showed him the concoction on which he himself now solely subsisted, and, calling it "sweet dew" from heaven, or manna, he bade the people go out and gather ten loads each.

There was plenty of grass in the city. From neglect, it grew four feet high in some of the empty streets, but men cannot eat grass, and the people did not understand Hung's act of faith.

They did not comply with the order, and Faithful shrugged his shoulders. He believed in the Heavenly Father and in Jesus, but he was a simple and practical soldier, and he knew now that his sovereign was mad, and that they were all doomed. He guessed, moreover, that the T'ien Wang himself knew that they were all doomed, but, with his mind elevated, would not review the past or speculate upon the future. Nevertheless, because madness and elevation of mind can meet up somewhere in realms beyond earth, he still retained a simple man's respect for Hung's aspirations. But there was another thing he knew, and that was that General Tseng had established a relief fund for the destitute beyond the Imperial lines. So on April 1st Faithful, on his own initiative and against the orders of his mad sovereign, mustered 4,000 women, opened the gates, and sent them to safety. General Tseng lodged them in a stockade, and allowed the country folk to take any of the females as wives who were willing to go.

So weak was the garrison by the end of May that the ramparts were almost empty. A death-like stillness hung over the city. No longer were flags seen waving above the walls, but sometimes, at the risk of life, a party of Taipings would lower themselves by ropes over the wall to gather the small crop of lentils which grew between the city and the Imperial stockades. These stockades were now up to within a hundred yards of the walls. Miles and miles of stockades, mud forts and ditches stretched round a city as large as Paris, and the troops lining them were provisioned by small shops, canteens, and sutlers who cried their wares within earshot of the starving.

The plight of the Taipings was known to their European sympathisers, and on May 31st, in Parliament, Cobden, Bright, Lord Naas and the Hon. Mr. Liddell supported Colonel Sykes in a protest against the government's policy of supplying arms to the Imperialists and of allowing Her Majesty's officers to serve under the Manchu command. The outcry against Gordon, for having once again taken up his appointment after the betrayal of his honour at Soo-chou, had not been without effect, and on June 1st the Order in Council, which permitted British officers to take up employment under the Chinese, was recalled. The cancellation came too late to have any effect, however, for Gordon had already completed his task. He had resigned before the new regulation could reach him, for the simple reason that he had already mopped up all the towns in the terrain of the tiger's head, and his Manchu paymasters wanted no Europeans to share in the glory of the final storming of Nanking.

Indeed, General Tseng was not very anxious to share the fruits of his labours even with Li Hung-chang, and, although the long-protracted resistance of Nanking at length forced Tseng Kuo-fan on June 15th to order Li Hung-chang and his troops to proceed there, lest it be thought that the Tseng brothers were jealous of their personal glory, yet it was a relief when Li Hung-chang, with much oriental delicacy of feeling, begged off. Thus he acknowledged to the world that the defeat of the Taipings was due to the courage and persistence of the Tseng family alone.

Caution was still needed, however. In the previous month Tseng had written to his brother the General, "Since the capture of Soo-chou and Hang-chou, there has been a keen desire for the capture of Nanking. I myself am not so concerned about its early capture, as about its safe capture. Therefore I have written you several tens of letters enjoining caution." He could never quite remember that his younger brother, the wild lad of those long ago days in Peking, was now a veteran warrior with grey hair. "Hung and Nanking," Kuo-fan went on, "are entirely different from other persons and places. I am worried for fear that, in your over-haste, you may wear yourself out, and your soldiers may be too exhausted to seize the opportunity when the mine is sprung."

There were 80,000 Imperial troops encamped round a city wherein the garrison was starving, but "Hung and Nanking are entirely different". Thus in six words Tseng acknowledged that the mystique of the Heavenly King's person, and his strange and sudden moments of lucidity as a strategist, were still feared by his enemies. He was still the cohesive factor round which the Taiping princes and people rallied. But, alas, Hung's physical powers were failing. Even his great faith was not sufficient to transmute the grass of the highways and byways into sustenance for his body, and he would eat nothing else. From June 1st no further supplies of food could reach the city, and the mining of the walls began.

"Gordon came today, and he believes your fortifications are good and your discipline strict," wrote Tseng Kuo-fan from Anking to his brother on June 15th. Gordon had visited Nanking as a freelance to give advice, and had himself chosen the north-east angle of the walls for the digging of the great mine.

The smaller mines had had insufficient effect upon the great walls, 40 feet high by 50 feet thick. But the thunder of the ex-plosions had rung in the ears of the Heavenly King, as so many knells to tell him that the Heavenly Mandate had at last expired. What Heaven can bestow, Heaven can also withdraw. Such had always been the accepted belief of the Chinese with regard to the throne. Of how and in what manner Hung Hsiu-ch'uan ac-knowledged the recall of his mandate to rule China it is too early to speak, but it must be remembered that, according to Chinese tradition, the action that he took was not regarded as cowardly; it was the only honourable means whereby disgrace and failure might be wiped out, and whereby a man might memorialise Heaven of his sorrow in not having been better able to obey its commands.

One last deed he had to do, before he went to account to his Heavenly Father for the failure of the mission with which he had been entrusted. The gongs and the bells rang out, as his female attendants advanced from the inner courts to place upon the usual table a yellow satin document. Upon it the Heavenly King had written with his sacred Vermilion Brush his last edict, and his officers, not dreaming it was his last, for none but the closest of his ministers knew what was afoot, bowed, and carried it with the usual reverence for display upon the surrounding walls of the palace. And there it hung for more than nineteen days, spar-kling in the hot July sun—the Shema of Israel, begotten spontane-ously in the mind of a Chinese. At once it both refuted and supported the creed of Athanasius and both supported and re-futed the heresy of Arius. It was the last challenge to fate of a mystic who knew that there are no perfectly adequate words in Chinese, Latin, or any other language in which to express that the Son and the Father, and at last all sons and the Father, are and shall be at One.

"Now I hereby declare to heaven, earth and men, that God the Heavenly Father is alone most excellent, who was from the spreading out of the heavens until now the exceeding great creator of all things."

For sixteen days Hung's brothers and the Faithful Prince kept secret the death of the Heavenly King. When the news did begin to leak out, the populace was reduced to the depths of despair.

Meanwhile Tseng Kuo-fan, knowing nothing of the event, wrote a very wonderful letter to his brother, showing that though, as a strict Confucian, he avoided attributing any personality to that First Principle which he termed "Heaven", yet in the hearts of all good and courageous men—and such he was—it cannot but be acknowledged that "Heaven" has a will and purpose of its own.

"Those who conduct great enterprises," he wrote, "regard wisdom as first in importance and ability as secondary. The accomplishment of a great task rests half on human planning and half on Heaven's will. Some years ago when you were attacking An-king, I told you that you need not try to act for Heaven. The strength of walls or trenches, the valour of the army's spirit, the energetic suppression of communications, resolute struggling against relieving enemy forces—these are matters where human planning can take the lead. The early or late capture of a city, the number of the enemy slain, the health or illness of our troops, whether good generals are wounded or not, the accession of relieving forces to the besieging armies or their reduction by having some sent off to relieve other places, whether the walls are completely razed or victory is reported without great effort—these are matters accomplished by Heaven's will. For instance, if you are in the examination hall being examined, human thought determines whether the essays are written according to rule and the poetry is without mistakes in the even and slanting tones. But whether the officer selects them or you secure the degree early or late, are matters governed by the will of Heaven. If you fear that Heaven's will cannot be relied on, and try to go beyond the desire of the gods; or that human wisdom is not safe, and try various expedients, these arise from a lack of wisdom. In your impatience to capture the city, you show a desire to usurp Heaven's management. I hope that you will always cherish thoughts of fear for Heaven, and seriously and calmly let things take their natural course, and they will turn out for the best."

On July 3rd General Tseng captured Dragon Shoulder Hill, thus giving him power to dig the great mine at the place chosen by Gordon. On the 8th the Faithful Prince made a sortie to try and prevent the work, but he was driven back. He had proved the position to be hopeless, and now that the Heavenly King no longer breathed, he was tempted to try and surrender. But he could not elude the spies of the Hung brothers, and in the end he decided that he could not desert the Young Lord.

The lad of sixteen, on whom had devolved the sovereignty of the Kingdom of Great Peace, was utterly unprepared for life, let alone for kingship. He had never since childhood been outside the palace walls. Now, as though resigned to some fantastic scene from Götterdämmerung, he commanded a great circle of brushwood to be made ready, a funeral pyre to encircle him, and he proposed to take refuge within it and fire the pile, whenever the city should fall. But he waited for the day, because life is dear at sixteen, and there was some hope in the fact that the Imperial troops were in danger of losing their fighting spirit. Thirty or more of their tunnels had failed to explode the wall.

They had spent a fortnight in preparing the great mine, and now, just as they were about to charge it with powder, the Faithful Prince made another sortie. He and his cavalry troops, disguised in Imperial uniform, swept down, and, with fireballs in their hands, wrought havoc among the engineers. He was driven back, however, for nothing could now break the iron band round Nanking.

As soon as he had once again retired behind the gates, the Imperial storming party moved into position, and sitting upon the mother earth, their hands touching the soil of China, General Tseng and his officers took a voluntary oath that they would die if need be that day to restore their native land.

Forty thousand pounds of gunpowder was now in the mine, and the fuse was touched off. There was noise like thunder, and for a moment the smoke, the dust, and the flying bricks made it impossible to distinguish what had happened. Then, as the air cleared, the breach, 60 yards wide in the 50 feet thick wall, became visible. The Imperial troops rushed the gap. The rebels promptly fired a powder magazine, which closely adjoined that part of the wall, and in the explosion many of Tseng's men fell; but nevertheless the Imperial army was at last well and truly into Nanking, and the carnage began.

Street by street the city was defended, until night drew on, and the flames from the T'ien Wang's palace lit the sky. Who had fired the palace? Where was the Heavenly King? And where, above all, was the Heavenly Treasury? It was reputed that Hung's wealth was as vast as the sea. The rebel chief and his so-called princes must not be allowed to escape. The treasure must be delivered to the Imperial Board of Revenue. The responsibility for all this fell heavily upon General Tseng. But to his astonishment and consternation, the people would not surrender, and each step of the way had to be fought, while Heaven alone knew where Hung Hsiu-ch'uan might be. General Tseng had no idea that the rebel chief had died on the last day of June. He was amazed and confounded that of 20,000 Taipings in the city not *one* surrendered to him. He put 7,000 prisoners to death, and many more thousands committed suicide. Of the princes and captains alone, 1,500 burned their houses over their heads or drowned themselves. The creek was piled to its banks and solid with the bodies of the dead. The streets were blocked with bonfires, and behind them the people had locked their doors, put torches to their houses, and knelt to pray and sing their strange hymns. Above the noise of the crackling flames, and the sporadic firing of muskets, and the shrieks of those being executed by the sword, could be heard the weird chanting.

> "God is the superintending Lord,
> Do not be agitated by alarms.
> Rely on him with a true heart,
> And then you will go to heaven."

> "We praise God, our holy and Heavenly Father.
> We praise Jesus, the only Lord and Saviour of the world,
> Who redeems men from sin
> By the endurance of extreme misery.
> Upon the cross they nailed his body,
> Where he shed his precious blood
> To save all mankind."

For three days the palace fire raged, casting a lurid light on the dangling corpses of Hung's wives, who had hanged themselves on the trees in the garden. Amongst them swung the limp form of the once beautiful Lai-shi. At last not a tile of the palace remained, but there was no treasure. There had never been any treasure, other than the revenue necessary for buying rice and arms. And the Heavenly King was dead, though where he was buried General Tseng could not yet learn. He had identified the bodies of many of the Wangs, including those of the young Western Prince and the fat Hung brothers, caught escaping with their gold and jade seals of office. They had babbled pitifully of God, as they bent their necks to the executioner's sword. But within the first few hours it was known that the Faithful Prince had made good his escape, shepherding the Young Lord to safety.

Returning wounded from his last sortie, Faithful had ridden first to take leave of his family, and then on to the sovereign's palace to protect his young Prince. It was Faithful who had fired the palace, and under cover of the confusion had tried first one gate and then another to gain an exit from the city. He had with him a thousand of his picked troops, and to the Young Lord, a novice to the saddle, he had given up his war-horse, the sturdy Tartar pony trained for battle, and himself rode a weak and useless animal. "Though the Heavenly King's days had been fulfilled," he wrote afterwards, "the nation injured through others baffling and deceiving him, and the state lost, still, as I had received his favours, I could not do otherwise than evince my faithfulness by endeavouring to save his son."

At last Faithful's troops managed to force one of the gates, and then they all clapped heels to their horses. Guns were fired, and shouting broke out from the walls. The alarm had been given, and soon General Tseng's cavalry was thundering after them. "I was parted from the Young Lord," wrote Faithful. "As he had never ridden before, and had never been subject to alarm and fright, it is more than probable that he was cut up. My pony was unable to go, for in addition to its not being a war-horse, it had already been used during a whole day's battle, and was weary. Had I retained my war-horse, I should undoubtedly have got away."

Without food and with their steeds spent, the troop separated at daylight to seek shelter and hiding in field or ditch. Faithful found refuge alone in a ruined temple by the wayside. Unfortunately, the small pouch of jewels which he carried with him was examined by inquisitive villagers, and it betrayed the identity of a prince. They gathered round and with menaces demanded the loot, but when they found that it was indeed their much-loved Faithful Prince who had come among them, they besought him to shave his head, and offered to help hide him. He demurred, however.

"I am a great minister of a nation now extinct," he answered them, "and of a sovereign now no more. Had I not escaped, I should not have been alive, and even if I now live, it will not be fair to any men who have fallen. I cannot have my head shaved." Thus for a while he was ready to face death, for he was exhausted and famished, and it seemed useless to go on. But presently they managed to persuade him, and he was about to submit to the shears, when, a rumour having got about of a prince and his jewels being in the neighbourhood, Tseng's cavalry caught up with him.

The Faithful Prince heard the clatter of hooves and the jingle of harness as the troopers dismounted, and without more ado he came out from the doorway of the ruined temple to face his enemies. Amongst them, tightly bound and mounted upon a led pony, was the Shield Prince, Jen-kan, one-time catechist of the London Missionary Society. The eyes of the two Taiping princes met in a glance of understanding. One of the villagers drew his sword and slew an Imperial soldier, but Faithful bade the peasants put up their swords. His hour was come, and he knew it.

He was taken to Nanking and there confined in a large cage, until it should be known what manner of death he was to die, and Tseng Kuo-fan, who had arrived by steamer from An-king, commanded that he be given writing materials wherewith to write the usual "confession" to the Dragon Throne. It was not expected to be a confession of repentance, but rather an historical document for the records of the Han-lin College library. In fact it was an autobiography, and Faithful wrote 7,000 characters in the eight days of his confinement. While he did so, a number of the Taiping Wangs, who had been likewise caught escaping, passed every day before him on their way to execution, saluting him with a deep bow of respect, and giving him what news they might of how matters fared with the brethren. The Young Lord had escaped to the city of Kwang-teh in An-hui, and had been given a great welcome there; but Faithful did not live long enough to learn how that city too was taken by the Imperialists, and how the Young Lord fled to the hills, only to be reduced there to starvation, so that, when he was at last captured, he was wishful for death, and went to his execution on October 25th glad at the age of sixteen to be rid of a life which had lasted too long.

As to deciding on the manner of Faithful's death, the matter was causing Tseng Kuo-fan some concern. Immediately after the fall of Nanking he had sent an express courier to Peking, travelling 200 miles a day, and bearing the red banner of "Decisive Victory". The news broke far and wide. "You can have but a faint idea," Gordon wrote to his brother, "of the relief the fall of Nanking is to me. As long as it held out, my late officers held themselves ready to join the rebels if there was a chance of success." The heterogeneous group of Europeans he referred to may have been, like Burgevine, out for personal gain only, but there was no doubt that there existed both in China and in Britain men like Tom Meadows, who mourned the now irrevocable loss of that one chance, albeit a slender one, which could only occur in the course of a million years, the chance that China would elect to become part of Christendom.

Peking was jubilant. Back by express courier came the edicts from the Empress, creating Tseng a marquis and Senior Guardian of the Throne, entitled to wear the double-eyed peacock feather, and giving to his brother and to Li Hung-chang the rank of earl. Even the barbarian, Gordon was not forgotten. He was endowed with the high honour of "The Yellow Jacket". Back also came the Empress's decree with regard to the Faithful Prince, and her demand for the head of Hung Hsiu-ch'uan. Faithful was to be sent to Peking there to suffer "death by a slow and ignominious process", before his head also was displayed as a warning and example.

Tseng, taking his customary post-prandial three thousand paces as an aid to digestion, paused before the bars of the cage where the Faithful Prince sat writing the last page of his autobiography. Tseng, exactly like Hung, was merciless in the execution of his enemies while the outcome of the war still hung in the balance. In the spirit of a Spanish inquisitor he had allowed the massacres at An-king and Soo-chou and Nanking. But, now that he was victorious, he could afford to put away that spirit, and he was remembering how his revered ancestor had sat at the feet of Confucius, and had heard the great sage deliver his famous dictum, "What you do not desire, do not inflict on others".

This man, Li Siu-cheng, whom the long-haired rebels called

the Faithful Prince, had proved himself a worthy and honourable foe. Tseng privately determined that, though he must die, it should not be by any lingering process to please a woman's spite. He should meet a soldier's death by the executioner's sword, and he must meet it now, quickly, while he, Tseng, still had time to pretend that he had not yet received the Imperial orders.

That very day, therefore, on August 7th 1864, the Faithful Prince was executed together with Jen-kan, and Tseng wrote to make his excuses to the Empress. "It seems to me that the high prestige of our Sacred Dynasty needs no such sending of petty rebels to Peking as trophies. There would be some danger of his starving himself to death on the journey, or a rescue might even be attempted, for this Li was extraordinarily popular with the common people. I therefore decided to behead him, and the sentence was duly carried out." With the letter he forwarded the autobiography, after perusing it and censoring anything that might offend the Imperial glance. "His idle and nonsensical words have been expunged," wrote Tseng. That is to say, all references to that offensive religion known as Christianity had been deleted from the only copy to be preserved for posterity, so that the precise character of this Taiping prince's faith was attested only by such men as had known him personally.

With regard to the Empress's demand for the head of Hung Hsiu-ch'uan, Tseng carried out her orders to the letter, for it was both urgent and politic to prove that the man was dead. After the fall of Nanking, eleven days went by before Tseng could be certain. Out of 20,000 people only a very few remained alive to be examined. They swore that the Heavenly King had died by his own hand, but the Imperial government must have proof. At last Tseng's officers brought in a woman to his temporary headquarters in the city. Young and good-looking and desolate, she faced her examiners, and broke down under their questioning. Yes, she, his concubine, had herself helped to prepare the body of the Heavenly King for burial.

Between Tseng's guards she was marched to the corner of the palace garden, where, under a pile of brushwood, it was apparent that the earth had lately been disturbed. While they began to dig, the woman, Huang, crouched upon the ground at Tseng's feet and, weeping, told him how the Heavenly King had died.

On June 30th he had called for gold leaf, and had mixed it

with his wine. Then, raising the cup, he had cried out in the
utmost distress, "It is not the Heavenly Father who has failed me,
but it is I who have failed the Heavenly Father." Several times
he had cried out in a voice made terrible by his agony of spirit
this same self-accusation. Then he had drunk the cup even to the
bottom. By midnight the effect of the poison had caused him to
writhe in torment, and shortly after he had died.

The exhumation party had by now completed its task. There
before them lay the body of Hung Hsiu-ch'uan, and Tseng examined it that he might report to the Empress. It was the body
of a powerfully built man, the head bald, and the beard and
moustache streaked with grey. He was buried in his yellow
Dragon robes, and even the feet were wrapped in Dragon
embroideries, stained now with earth, for he had been buried
coffinless, according to his own religious decrees. Tseng gave
orders to decapitate the corpse, and to burn the body. The head,
set upon a spike, was straightway sent to Peking, that the Empress
might gaze upon it before it was set over the gateway of the city
as a warning to rebels.

Thus Hung Hsiu-ch'uan ended his long long journey from the
peasant's cottage to the Dragon Throne. His head was placed at
the foot of that throne. No record remains to explain more fully
those terrible cries of self-accusation and repentance before he
took his own life, but that his faith in the existence of the Heavenly
Father persisted is clear.

For weeks the decomposing head hung above the gateway,
while the people of Peking, used to such sights, passed in and out
upon their business with hardly a glance at it, for they could
not see the invisible form of Yen-lo, that old serpent, wreathing
himself triumphantly round all that remained of the Elect of
Shang-ti, all, rather, that remained on earth. Of the blackening
head Yen-lo certainly had possession, but what of Hung's soul?
He had failed in his mission. He had himself admitted his culpa-
bility in his last hours of tortured self-searching. Would he never
again be admitted to those heavenly halls of his vision?

Once again he had failed the test, the examination. Only those
who gained the highest degree dined with the Emperor. Only
those who survived the judgment drank the fruit of the vine anew
in the Father's kingdom. Could he ever again be admitted to the

Presence? What plea could he bring before the Recording Angel at the Celestial Board of Rites?

Perhaps the plea was spoken for him, for the Celestial Elder Brother had promised to be with him always and to accompany him to the uttermost regions, and despite all his sins, his crimes, his failings, Hung had never ceased to trust in that promise. He could not enter the heavenly halls by virtue of any degree nor in the celestial hierarchy could he be considered "Talented"; least of all was he a Qualified Student, for no man ever qualifies for heaven by his own merits. There was only one way by which he might enter—as a Presented Student, presented by his Heavenly Elder Brother to the Supreme Lord and Father of all men, by virtue of the one perfect and all-sufficient sacrifice upon the Cross.

HISTORICAL NOTES

AFTER THE FALL of Nanking, the Imperial government destroyed nearly all the records and literature of the Taiping dynasty, as such documents were considered subversive and dangerous. It was the Europeans who preserved whatever could be collected and translated. The present account is merely a synthesis of already existing literature, which has never before been grouped round the central character of Hung Hsiu-ch'uan or put into chronological order to give a picture of his life.

The account of the visions is taken almost verbatim from Hamberg's pamphlet, the only change being from Victorian to present day language.

To tell Hung's story in flowing form for popular reading has presented certain technical difficulties, for the only picture of his personal character is given by Jen-kan, whose account stops short at the moment when the rebel standard was raised. Thereafter all the material, and it is scanty, is provided by Hung's political enemies, with the exception of the Faithful Prince's autobiography, which was written in the hope of obtaining pardon, and so does not tend to dwell on Hung's good characteristics. I have therefore given considerable space to Hung's youth, and have attempted a reconstruction which only departs from Jen-kan's account in one or two very minor points.

Although Yang, Hung's brother-in-law, was known to have been a tea-porter, there is no historical evidence that Hung met with him or with his other brother-in-law, Hsiao, before the coming together of the God-worshippers; but calculating the ages of Hung's two sisters from Hamberg's account, they would have been beyond marriageable age if they first met their husbands in Kwang-si in 1850, and I have therefore presumed that the marriages were contracted earlier. I have thus been able to introduce the characters of Yang and Hsiao at moments when the reader has time to distinguish and remember their names, peculiarities and physical appearance, which are all historical; whereas if the five princes, with their Chinese names and titles of Eastern and Western, etc., had all been introduced at one period on one page, the ordinary reader, to whom Chinese names are in any case difficult, would not have been able to take them in. In the belief that the spirit is more important than the letter, I have deliberately reconstructed these passages, though I believe they may come very near the truth.

There is no record of Hung ever having visited the theatre, but contemporary opinion suggested that his visions may have been influenced thereby, and the play I have chosen to describe is one that was seen in Canton by Mr. G. T. Lay in 1841.

I have also attempted to show that some of Hung's pronouncements which contemporary Europeans thought particularly fantastic are explicable only in the language of alchemy.

As regards Celestial Virtue, his execution and confession are historical facts, but his identity has remained a mystery and my reconstruction is only an attempt at a solution. All contemporaries were, however, agreed that he was of no importance to the movement. Only Professor W. J. Hail in his book *Tseng Kuo-fan and the Taiping Rebellion*, published in 1927, strove to show that Celestial Virtue was the real founder of a movement later taken over by Hung and Yang. He based his argument on the assumption that Hung and Yang, with their "grotesque insistence on their superstition", could not have led such well-organised armies. The fact that Celestial Virtue confessed to having contracted a brotherhood relation with Hung, and the implications to be deduced from this, have so far been ignored; but, for those specialists who are interested, my interpretation of the known facts is borne out by the account of page *153 et seq* of *The History of the Insurrection in China* by MM. Callery & Yvan, where the description of the rites of blood-brotherhood entered into by a certain rebel chief, Hung, gives occasion to believe that the interpreter at the French Consulate, although confused by unfamiliar names, was nevertheless providing the clue. That the rite was part of the initiation of the Triad Society is known, and is described in *The Hung Society* by J. S. M. Ward & W. G. Stirling.

As has been stated on another page, no dialogue has been used in this historical reconstruction, except what was authentically recorded by contemporaries.

CHRONOLOGICAL TABLE

1814 (January 1st) Birth of Hung Hsiu-ch'uan at Hua in Kwang-tung.

1834 (August) Hung's first examination at Canton. He is given the Protestant tracts.

1837 (April) He receives his first visions while in a trance which lasts for forty days.

1839 (November) The Opium War breaks out.

1842 (August 29th) The Treaty of Nanking is signed.

1843 (Autumn) Hung first reads the tracts.

1844 (June) Hung first arrives in Kwang-si.

1845 (January) Hung arrives back in Hua.

1847 (February) Hung seeks instruction from the Rev. Issachar Roberts.

(July) He takes refuge again in Kwang-si, and finds the congregation of the God-worshippers.

1849 (August) The gift of tongues is manifested amongst the congregation.

1850 (February) The Emperor Tao-kuang dies, and Hsien Feng succeeds to the Dragon Throne.

(July) The Triads of Canton rise in rebellion.

(September 28th-October 3rd) The first clash of the God-worshippers with the Imperial forces.

1851 (February 1st) The raising of the Taiping standard.

(September 28th) The capture of Yung-nan.

1853 (March 19th) The Taipings capture Nanking.

(April 19th) H.M.S. *Hermes* sails to visit the Rebel Capital.

(December) The French ship *Cassini* visits Nanking.

1854 (January 4th) The Crimean War breaks out.

(February) The Taiping army, sent north to Peking, begins a rear-guard action.

(May) The U.S. Frigate *Susquehanna* visits Nanking.

1856 (September 2nd) The murder of Yang, the Eastern Prince.

(October 8th) The *Arrow* sails into Canton Harbour.

1857 (May 10th) The Indian Mutiny breaks out.

1858 (May 20th) The Allies take the Taku forts and advance to Tientsin.

(July 3rd) The Treaty of Tientsin is signed.

(November 8th) Lord Elgin sets sail up the Yang-tze.

1859 (June 26th) Sir Frederick Bruce's embassy is ambushed at the Taku forts. The Taipings are closely besieged in Nanking.

1860 (February 2nd) The Taipings break out of Nanking. They take Soo-chou, and occupy the country towards Shanghai.

(June) Ward originates the Ever Victorious Army and the missionaires begin to visit Soo-chou.

(August 18th) The Taipings attack Shanghai, but are repulsed by the Allies.

(August to October) The Taku forts are taken by the Allies. They advance on Peking and burn the Summer Palace, and the Convention of Peking is concluded on October 24th.

1861 (February 11th) Admiral Hope's expedition sails for Nanking to tell the T'ien Wang not to attack Shanghai, and Hung agrees to leave it unmolested for a year.

(April) The American Civil War breaks out.

(August) The Emperor Hsien Feng dies.

(September) Prince Kung's coup d'état places the Empress in power, and she raises Tseng Kuo-fan to be Commander-in-Chief of all the Imperial forces.

(November) The Taipings' attempts to seize the area of the Triple City are frustrated.

(December) The Taipings break eastward and take Ning-po on the 9th and Hang-chou on the 29th.

1862 (January) The Taipings attack Shanghai and are repulsed by the Allies.

(May 10th) Captain Dew, R.N., retakes Ning-po from the Taipings.

(September 18th) Ward is killed.

1863 (January) Burgevine is dismissed from his command of the Ever Victorious Army and Colonel Gordon takes command (in March).

(September) Gordon invests Soo-chou.

(December) The Fall of Soo-chou, and the execution of the Wangs. Gordon resigns.

1864 (March) Gordon resumes command of the Ever Victorious Army. Hang-chou is retaken by a Franco-Imperial force.

(June 30th) Hung Hsiu-ch'uan commits suicide.

(July 19th) The Fall of Nanking.

(August 7th) The execution of the Chung Wang or Faithful Prince.

BIBLIOGRAPHY

ASHLEY (Hon. Anthony Evelyn Melbourne): *The Life and Correspondence of H. F. Temple, Viscount Palmerston.* 2 vols. London. 1879.

BLAND (John Otway Percy) *and* BACKHOUSE (Sir Edmund Trelawny): *China under the Empress Dowager:* London. 1912.

BLAKISTON (Thomas Wright): *Five Months on the Yang-tsze.* London. 1862.

BOARDMAN (Eugene Powers): *Christian Influence upon the Ideology of the Taiping Rebellion 1851–1864.* Univ. of Wisconsin Press. 1952.

BRINE (Lindesay, Commander R.N.): *The Taeping Rebellion in China* (with maps and plans). London. 1862.

BROULLION (le R. Pere, S.J.): *Missions de Chine. Mêmoire sur l'état actuel de la Mission du Kiang-nan 1842–1855,* par le R. P. Broullion de La Compagnie de Jesus, suivi de lettres relative à l'Insurrection 1851–55. Paris. 1855.

BRUCE (James, 8th Earl of Elgin and 12th Earl of Kincardine): *Letters & Journals.* Edited by Theodore Walrond. London. 1872.

CALLERY (J. M.) *and* YVAN (Melchior): *History of the Insurrection in China.* Translated, with a supplementary chapter narrating the most recent events, by John Oxenford. London. 1853.

CANTON (William): *A History of the British and Foreign Bible Society.* Vol. II (p. 405. re the stone carved with the Beatitudes). London. 1904.

CHIANG (Yee): *A Chinese Childhood.* London. 1940.

CLOWES (Sir William Laird): *The Royal Navy.* Vol. 7. London. 1897–1903.

COLLIS (Maurice): *Foreign Mud: A history of the Opium War.* London. 1946.

—— *The Great Within.* London. 1941.

CORDIER (Henri): *Histoire des relations de la Chine avec les puissances occidentales.* 3 Vols. Paris. 1901–1902.

DEAN (William): *The China Mission.* New York. 1859.

EDKINS (Jane Rowbotham): *Chinese Scenes and People, with Narrative of Visit to Nanking by J. Edkins.* London, Edinburgh. 1863.

EDKINS (Joseph): *The Religious Condition of the Chinese.* London. 1859.
—— *Religion in China.* 2nd Edition. London. 1878.
FORREST (Robert James, H.B.M.'s Acting Consul at Ning-po): *A review of Taiping Books.* Article IX in Series No. IV of the Journal of the North China Branch of the Royal Asiatic Society. December. 1867.
GIFFARD (Admiral Sir George, K.C.B.): *Reminiscences of a Naval Officer.* Published privately. 1892.
GORDON (Sir Henry William): *Events in the Life of Charles George Gordon, from its beginning to its End.* London. 1886.
GRANT (Sir James Hope): *Life with selections from his correspondence.* Edited by Henry Knollys. Vol. 2. Edinburgh. 1894.
HAMBERG (The Rev. Theodore): *The Visions of Hung-Siu-Tshuen and the Origin of the Kwangsi Insurrection.* Hong Kong. Printed at the *China Mail* office. 1854.
HSIEH (Pao Chao): *Government of China (1644–1911).* Johns Hopkins Univ. studies in historical and political science. Johns Hopkins Univ. Baltimore. 1925.
LATOURETTE (Kenneth Scott): *History of the Expansion of Christianity.* Vol. 6. London. 1943–1947.
LAY (G. Tradescant): *The Chinese as They Are.* London. 1841.
LAY (W. T.): Translation of the autobiography of the Chung Wang, the Faithful King, written during his confinement after the capture of Nanking. Shanghai. 1865.
LEGGE (Helen Edith): *James Legge, Missionary and Scholar.* Religious Tract Society. London. 1905.
LI (Choen): Translation of "*Le journal de Cheta-kai.*" (Collection de la politique de Pekin) Episodes de la guerre Tai Ping. Pekin. 1927.
LINDLEY (Augustus F.): *Ti-ping Tien-kwoh; the History of the Ti-ping Revolution.* By Lin-le (i.e. A.F.L.) formerly honorary officer, Chung Wang's Guards, etc. 2 Vols. London. 1866.
LIN (Yutang): *My Country and My People.* London. 1936.
LOCH (Henry Brougham, 1st Baron Loch): *Personal Narrative of Occurrences during Lord Elgin's second Embassy to China in 1860.* 3rd Edition. London. 1900.
LONDON MISSIONARY SOCIETY. Letters from the archives.
MAXWELL (Sir Herbert Eustace Bart., of Monreith): *The Life and Letters of George William Frederick, fourth Earl of Clarendon.* 2 Vols. London. 1913.
MEADOWS (Thomas Taylor, Chinese Interpreter in H.M.'s Civil Service): *The Chinese and their Rebellions.* London. 1856.

MEDHURST (W. H., Sr.): Pamphlets issued by the Chinese Insurgents at Nanking, concluding with a critical review. Printed at the office of the *North China Herald*. Shanghai. 1853.

MEDHURST (Sir Walter Henry *the younger*. H.B.M.'s Consul, Shanghai): *The Foreigner in Far Cathay*. London. 1872.

MEDHURST (Walter Henry): *China, its State and Prospects*. London. 1840.

MILNE (William C.): *Life in China*. London. 1857.

MOULE (A. E. The Venerable Archdeacon): *Personal Recollections of the T'ai-P'ing Rebellion*. 1861–1863. Shanghai. 1898.

OLIPHANT (Laurence): *Narrative of the Earl of Elgin's mission to China and Japan in the years 1857, 1858, 1859*. 2 Vols. Edinburgh and London. 1859.

OMAN (Charles William Chadwick): *A History of England in Seven Volumes*. Edited by Charles Oman. Vol. 7. England since Waterloo, by J. A. R. Marriott. London. 1913.

PARLIAMENTARY DEBATES: House of Lords. February 24th 1857.
House of Commons. February 26th 1857.
House of Commons. March 12th 1861.
House of Commons. May 20th 1864.
House of Commons. May 31st 1864.

PARLIAMENTARY PAPERS: Respecting the Civil War in China presented to the House of Commons by command of H.M. August 5th 1853. (1852–1853. (13) LXIX.)
Relating to the Rebellion in China and Trade in the Yangtze Kiang presented to the House of Commons April 8th 1862 (LXIII). Also relating to Gordon's position in China (LXVI).

POOLE (Stanley Lane): *The Life of Sir Harry Parkes, sometime Her Majesty's Minister to China and Japan*. Vol. 1. Consul in China. London. 1894.

SCARTH (John): *Twelve Years in China; the People, the Rebels and the Mandarins*. Edinburgh. 1860.

SICA (Luigi Maria): *Une famille Napolitaine*. Notice historique sur les cinq frères Massa de la Compagnie de Jesus, missionaires en Chine, et leur famille. Traduite de l'Italien par Henri Chauff de Kerguenec.

SPENCE (G. M.): *A Forgotten Flotilla*. Admiralty Archives.

SOCIETY OF JESUS. Letters from the archives at Les Fontaines, Chantilly, Oise, France.

TENG (Ssŭ-yü): *New Light on the History of the Taiping Rebellion*. Harvard University Press. 1950.

TRUMBULL (H. Clay, D.D.): *The Blood Covenant, a Primitive Rite and its Bearing on Scripture*. London. 1887.

WALPOLE (Sir Spencer, K.C.B.): *The Life of Lord John Russell.* 2 Vols. London. 1889.

WARD (John Sebastian Marlow) *and* STIRLING (William George): *The Hung Society, or the Society of Heaven and Earth.* 3 Vols. Baskerville Press. 1926.

WERNER (E. T. C.): *Myths and legends of China.* London. 1922.

WILSON (Andrew): *The "Ever Victorious Army". A History of the Chinese Campaign under Lt.-Col. C. G. Gordon . . . and of the Suppression of the Tai-Ping Rebellion.* Edinburgh. London. 1868.

WOLFERSTAN (Bertram): *The Catholic Church in China from 1860–1907.* London. 1909.

WOLSELEY (Garnet Joseph, Viscount Wolseley): *The Story of a Soldier's Life.* Vol. 2. London. 1903.

INDEX